Reinventing the Americas

Reinventing the Americas

Comparative Studies of Literature of the
United States and Spanish America

Edited by
BELL GALE CHEVIGNY
GARI LAGUARDIA
State University of New York, Purchase

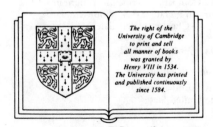

The right of the
University of Cambridge
to print and sell
all manner of books
was granted by
Henry VIII in 1534.
The University has printed
and published continuously
since 1584.

CAMBRIDGE UNIVERSITY PRESS
Cambridge
London   New York   New Rochelle
Melbourne   Sydney

Published by the Press Syndicate of the University of Cambridge
The Pitt Building, Trumpington Street, Cambridge CB2 1RP
32 East 57th Street, New York, NY 10022, USA
10 Stamford Road, Oakleigh, Melbourne 3166, Australia

© Cambridge University Press 1986

First published 1986

Printed in the United States of America

Library of Congress Cataloging-in-Publication Data

Reinventing the Americas.

Includes bibliographies and index.
1. Literature, Comparative–American and Spanish
American.   2. Literature, Comparative–Spanish American
and American.   3. History in literature.   4. Women and
literature.   5. Criticism.   I. Chevigny, Bell Gale.
II. Laguardia, Gari.
PS159.S7R45   1986   809'.891812   86–9652

British Library Cataloging-in-Publication Data

Reinventing the Americas : comparative
studies of literature of the United States
and Spanish America.

1. American literature–History and
criticism   2. Spanish American literature
–History and criticism
I. Chevigny, Bell Gale   II. Laguardia, Gari
810.9   PS 88

ISBN 0 521 30196 3

Contents

v

Preface

Although our title announces a relatively new field of inquiry, the work of inventing America is older than Columbus. What came to be called the New World was a European invention, arguably an inevitable exfoliation of Renaissance science, philosophy, and poetry. Writing is the natural habitat of such invention, and revision was its innermost condition. Conceived in the Old World, the New World may be said to have been written in advance, and then rewritten in the chronicles of discovery, conquest, and settlement. As nations, regions, or peoples came to need and be able to cast their special identity in language, the New World was sought, invented or "discovered," and rewritten again. In the critical study of American literature, another construction is produced, another layer of invention is added. When we set about reinventing the Americas by bringing into contact works of different "Americas" for purposes of comparing them, we are not simply *adding* another dimension of invention. We are doing something more akin to *division*. A comparison is a form of mutual interrogation; when the comparison is of works in different languages, with all the assumptions of divergent inventions buried in them, each divides, or interrogates, the other in such a way that its own assumptions – the inner workings of its constitutive invention – are thrown into relief.

The notion of reinventing the Americas, once entertained, seems to us to have an attractive, even a compelling logic. It draws attention to the common landmass that antedates the invention of America and may even in some manner survive the name. It makes us inquire what Europe has made (in every sense of the word) of America, what America has made of itself, and what might be made if we look at it again, twice, or double, that is, comparatively. Then, regardless of our attention to it, the Americas are reinventing their relationship to one another. There is, on the one hand, the U.S. backyard specter, the possibility that the United States will be called uncle by the whole hemisphere. And there is, on the other hand, the subversive irony of Gabriel García Márquez, who remarks, "Every time I hear my leftist friends complain about North American penetration in Latin America I laugh into my coat lapels because the real cultural penetration is that of Latin America into the United States."[1] Other possibilities – a mutually informed, deliberate, and welcomed political and cultural coexistence, for example – often seem as improbable as a third hand, though comparative research might foment their growth.

Reinvention of the Americas must begin with exposure of the rhetorical incoherence we commit each time we designate the United States by the sign "America," a name that belongs by rights to the hemisphere. To name a part by the whole is to stand a synecdoche on its head. As long as we perpetuate the rhetorical malpractice, we lend linguistic support to imperialist enterprises, and, more to our point here, we confuse our thinking. The task of comparison sends us on epistemological errands. We suggest that, by dismantling the U.S. appropriation of the name "America," we will better see what the United States is and what it is not and at the same time permit Latin America to come into sharper focus. Then the setting of cultural inventions side by side will be facilitated and their distinctive edges the better discerned. (To those who would point to the poverty of "United States"-ish adjectives, we offer the economic clarity of "U.S." as adjective. If "U.S." sounds less grand than "American," that effect is not irrelevant; comparison has a relativizing influence.) Though all the labels are problematic, we generally adopt the term "Spanish America" as best designating the other region we mean to discuss.

A brief account of the history of the project resulting in this volume should illuminate its orientation, its range, and its limitations. The project grew out of the interests of two specialists – one in the literature of the United States, the other in that of Spanish America – in each other's fields and in the relation between them. We rapidly learned that, however natural and important this comparison seemed to us, it had rarely been undertaken. With the help of a grant we organized a conference on comparative modern literature of the United States and Spanish America. We discovered both that many people thought this field of comparison a natural and important one and that very few people were prepared to undertake it. This provocative puzzle came to be an aspect of our inquiry itself. When we observed that comparative studies have usually focused on links between American and European cultures, we were made to reflect on the degree to which our fields were still colonized. We began to wonder whether U.S. scholars shunned an identification that would attenuate the ties with Europe and whether for Latin Americans too close an identity with the United States was perceived as doing the same. The horizontal connection – of cultural traffic across the Atlantic – seemed to retain its original potency. Moreover, working in the United States, which controls much of Latin America economically and politically, we speculated that neglect of attention here to the vertical connection – of cultural traffic north and south along the hemispheric landmass – betrayed a discomfort with confronting the implications of that control. Whatever has in fact inhibited vertical comparison, in undertaking it we have experienced the aptness of this book's title, for comparison has forced us to reexamine many of our assumptions about our fields of specialization and to reinvent "each" America by bearing in mind the other.

We are aware of the dangers of parochialism in comparative studies. Our formation in the United States and its universities will surely affect our reading of Latin America, regardless of our efforts to correct for it. We know too that these "two" areas are not commensurate: Fifty states cannot be weighed against more than twenty republics, and generalizations about either the United States or Spanish America are equally pernicious. In this disparity, however, lies our justification. As Ezekiel Martínez Estrada observed about Latin America, "There is an American unity in what really is not American; the differences, however, those belong to us."[2] That is to say that, insofar as it is a Latin American entity, it is divided; its differences are what are shared. The same may be said of the United States. We believe that the making and remaking of identity out of manifold difference is the constitutive factor of "both" Americas.

We realize that our decision to concentrate on literatures of the United States and Spanish America sets an artificial limit on our inquiry, especially in our omission of Brazil, a rich source of comparison. We also regret our failure to discuss Canada (Anglo and French) and the French or British Caribbean. Moreover, except for William Carlos Williams, we do not deal with the increasing number of writers of Hispanic background who write in English and publish in the United States. More generally, we do not deal with the extraordinary Hispanicization of U.S. culture to which García Márquez alludes. Nor, except for the essay by Jean Franco, do we deal with mass culture and popular culture, although we are well aware that the distinction between these and "high" culture, always exaggerated, can now be sustained less than ever. There are also important and influential figures who are not taken into account or are barely mentioned. Most of these omissions were not intentional but were due to space limitations, to the availability or unavailability of contributors, or to the difficulty of trying to achieve some measure of conceptual coherence in a vast and complex field. We hope that these limitations are taken up as a challenge to stimulate further work and that our pioneering effort is taken for what it is: a beginning.

In the course of our inquiry we have identified issues in the sociology of literature that call for research, issues concerning the comparative production and reception of literature in the United States and Latin America. How writers construe their role and how they are remunerated for their work are questions that bear on literary production. The writer in Latin America has traditionally been less a "professional" than a vatic sage who took an active role in the formation and functioning of society. It is difficult to find counterparts for Bello, Sarmiento, and Martí, who played central roles as legislators, presidents, and revolutionaries, in the United States. On the other hand, the possibility of earning a living by writing was not a real one for most Latin Americans in the nineteenth century. Whereas a politician like Ulysses S. Grant could recoup part of his lost fortune and ensure financial stability for his heirs by writing his memoirs, Domingo Faustino Sarmiento could not expect comparable financial restitution through writing.

A related issue meriting further study concerns the institutions through which the production and consumption of literature take place. Publishers, distributors, booksellers, libraries, universities, and the printed media are vastly more developed in the United States than in Latin America. It is not that these instrumentalities do not exist in Latin America; they have been in place since the late nineteenth century, as Angel Rama in particular has documented.[3] However, the scale of these in the United States is much larger and their access and distribution to the public at large so much wider that the professionalization of the writer as a writer in the United States is more thoroughly accomplished. A series of questions then arise concerning the effect of these differences on what the writer produces. Does this greater professional self-sufficiency in the United States ironically place U.S. writers under the constraints of writing for a perceived public? Conversely, does the freedom from a potential mass market provide a situation of greater creative autonomy for Latin American writers, or does it simply render them financially poorer than their U.S. counterparts?

Another topic that should be more fully explored is the history of literary contacts throughout the Americas. Such a study might begin with the Puritans' anxious interest in the reported opulence of Mexico City, Samuel Sewall's urging "the bombing of Santa Domingo, the Havana, Porto Rico, and Mexico itself" with a Spanish Bible, and Cotton Mather's decision in 1699 to study Spanish in order to prepare such a

text to aid the evangelization of Latin America and the creation of a
Puritan continent.[4] The end of such a study might include Manuel Puig's
sly and creative acts of retribution in turning his attendance at Holly-
wood movies in provincial Argentina into the stuff of innovative fiction.
Our collection of essays touches on some of these interfaces, but in no
systematic way. Our inquiries were not limited to actual contact. Because we are interested in the *problems* of comparison as well as its history, we consider comparisons in which influence may not occur.

Of the many legitimate areas of comparative inquiry, we have marked
out three: literature and the historical imagination, the voice and vision
of women, and perspectives on literary criticism. The introductions to
each, particularly the first two, have been designed not only to introduce
and comment on the essays that follow but also to provide the framework within which readers who lack knowledge of either U.S. literature
or Spanish American literature can most profitably read them. In Part I
we examine how history influences literature and is articulated in it. In
our introduction (Chapter 1) we inquire into the common origin of both
Americas in Europe and the religious and political differences the English
and the Spanish brought with them; the various interracial and intercultural encounters between European, African, and indigenous peoples;
the divergent social, economic, and political evolutions of the Americas;
and the unequal relations between the United States and Spanish America. Against this background, we sketch the evolution of modern literature, attending especially to the comparative development in the Americas of the novel and, to some extent, of poetry; this development is
asymmetrical, often in surprising ways. In Part II we look at many of
these American questions as they have been comparatively experienced,
seen, and articulated by women of the two Americas, with special attention to the obstacles – and strategies for overcoming them – that they in
particular have known. Finally, in Part III we consider the ways in which
literary criticism has participated in the comparative construction of the
Americas, as often obscuring its ground as illuminating it.

The decision to provide a separate section on women should not be
taken to signify that the remainder of the book is concerned only with the
cultural products of men. Nor does it mean that we consider "women's
issues" chiefly as a discrete entity. On the contrary, the kinds of issues that
have been raised by questions about women and literature are not only at
the center of our volume but also at the heart of our inquiry. This book is
the product of the sort of revolutionary thinking about literary canons that
flows from the conscious self-identification of any oppressed group and
that the contemporary women's movement has most recently delineated
and perhaps most successfully promoted.[5] Questioning of the canon by

those who are excluded from it or whose oppression is institutionalized in it results in the exposure of hierarchies – hierarchies of precedence or power. All the issues that concern us in this volume participate in one manner or another in the question of the relation of the "original," "primary," or "dominant" to the "secondary." Thus did Europe stand to America; thus did the United States come to stand to Latin America; thus have men stood to women, and literature to criticism. All of these relationships have been challenged, at present more than ever. We consider our work to be part of this process of interrogation.

Unless otherwise indicated, all Spanish passages have been translated by the editors. The English translation of the title of a Spanish work is provided parenthetically; added italics or quotation marks indicate a Spanish work that has been *published* in English translation.

We are indebted to the SUNY Research Foundation for the grant from their Conversations in the Disciplines program, which we used to mount our conference. At Purchase, the Humanities Division Deans Carl Resek and Frank Wadsworth and Dee Molinari, assistant to the president, also gave us significant support. We are indebted to our colleague Antonio Frasconi for our conference logo, which now graces the cover of this volume. Early in our project Rosario Santos, Gregory Rabassa, and Gregory Kolovakos, and later Saúl Sosnowski, provided useful assistance and advice. For invaluable help in preparing the manuscript we thank Sydney Gura, Dawn Lalli, Belén Laguardia, Joan Mazzari, Mary Lou Snyder, and especially Rosalie Reutershan, who typed much of our final copy. For help in translating, we thank our students Chris Kearin and Cyndi Kolbowski. We are grateful to the Purchase reference librarians, particularly Paula Hane, for expert bibliographical assistance. We consulted our colleagues Lee Schlesinger, Ronnie Scharfman, Maria Gagliardo, and Gregorio Rosenblum for help and advice of various kinds. We are deeply indebted to Jean Franco for a wealth of editorial suggestions. Finally, we thank Electa Arenal, Doris Sommer, and Gene Bell-Villada (who suggested our book's title), three contributors whose continual interest and advice were always encouraging.

NOTES

1 Interview with García Márquez by Enrique Fernández, *Village Voice*, July 3, 1984.
2 Ezekiel Martínez Estrada, *Sarmiento* (Buenos Aires: Sudamericana, 1969), p. 75.
3 See Angel Rama, *Transculturación narrativa en América Latina* (Mexico City: Siglo ventiuno, 1982); *La ciudad letrada* (Hanover, N.H.: Ediciones del Norte, 1984).

4 Stanley T. Williams, *The Spanish Background of American Literature* (New Haven, Conn.: Yale University Press, 1955), pp. 17–18. This book provides a useful starting point for the history of U.S. contacts with the south; a complementary study of Latin American contacts with the north might begin with "Focus: U.S.," the Spring 1976 issue of *Review*, published by the Center for Inter-American Relations and edited by Ronald Christ.

5 Critics including Robert Scholes, Wayne Booth, Jonathan Culler, and Terry Eagleton testified in the early 1980s to the usefulness of feminist criticism and of its potential for invigorating or offering new edge to the general critical enterprise.

Contributors

Electa Arenal (USA) is of Mexican extraction and teaches Spanish and Women's Studies at the College of Staten Island. As a Bunting Fellow at the Radcliffe Institute, she prepared her forthcoming book, coauthored with Stacey Schlau, *Untold Sisters: Hispanic Nuns in Their Own Works*. She is writing a book on the essential feminism of Sor Juana Inés de la Cruz.

Gene H. Bell-Villada (USA) was born in Haiti and grew up in Puerto Rico, Cuba, and Venezuela. He teaches Spanish, Spanish American, and comparative literature at Williams College. His essays on both U.S. and Latin American literature and politics have appeared in many journals. He is the author of *Borges and His Fiction: A Guide to His Mind and Art* and is preparing a book on Gabriel García Márquez.

Bell Gale Chevigny (USA), coeditor of this volume, teaches women's literature and North and Latin American literature at SUNY-Purchase. Her books include *The Woman and the Myth: Margaret Fuller's Life and Writings* and *Twentieth Century Interpretations of* Endgame. Her essays on literature, culture, and politics have appeared in popular and scholarly journals.

Edmundo Desnoes (Cuba) is the author of *Memorias del subdesarollo* (*Inconsolable Memories*) and coscriptwriter with Tomás Gutiérrez Alea of the motion picture based on that novel. His books include *Para verte mejor, América Latina* and an anthology of postrevolutionary Cuban literature, *Los dispositivos en la flor*. He has been living in the United States since 1979.

Lisa Davis (USA) works at the Center for Puerto Rican Studies, Hunter College-CUNY. She is a contributing editor for Central American prose to *The Handbook for Latin American Studies* published by the Library of Congress. Her essays on Spanish American literature and film have appeared in Spanish American and Spanish journals.

Pablo Armando Fernández (Cuba) lived for fifteen years in the United States before returning to Cuba in 1960. He was subdirector of the literary supplement *Lunes de Revolución* in the early 1960s and cultural counsellor at the Cuban Embassy in London from 1962 to 1965. He works in the publications department of The Cuban Academy of Science. His novel *Los niños se despiden* (The Children Say Goodbye) won the Casa de las Américas for the novel in 1968; he has also published several volumes of poetry.

Jean Franco (Great Britain) is director of the Institute of Latin American and Iberian Studies and teaches Spanish American and comparative literature at Columbia University. Her books include *An Introduction to Spanish-American Literature* and *Cesar Vallejo: Dialectics of Poetry and Silence,* both published by Cambridge University Press, and she is writing a book called *Plotting Women* on women and culture in Latin America to be published by Columbia University.

Gari Laguardia (Puerto Rico), coeditor of this volume, teaches Spanish, Spanish American, and comparative literature at SUNY-Purchase. He has published studies on modern and Renaissance literature and on literary theory. He has completed a manuscript on psychoanalysis and historical consciousness in literature and is doing research for a comparative study of modernism in the Americas.

Julio Marzán (Puerto Rico) teaches Spanish American literature at Bard College. He was editor and chief consultant for National Public Radio's recent series on Latin American writers, and also edited *Inventing a Word,* an anthology of Puerto Rican poetry. A volume of his poetry, *Authorized Translations,* is forthcoming. His poems, critical essays, and reviews have appeared in a variety of journals.

Doris Sommer (USA) teaches Spanish, Spanish American, and comparative literature at Amherst College. She is the author of *Populism as Patriarchal Rhetoric in Dominican Novels.* She is currently writing about women's literature and such North American writers as Whitman and Cooper from a point of view provided by the Spanish American writers they have influenced.

Cynthia Steele (USA) teaches Spanish at Columbia University. Her book, *Narrativa indigenista en Estados Unidos y México,* was published by the Insituto Nacional Indigenista in Mexico City. She is writing a second book on the post-1968 Mexican novel.

Luisa Valenzuela (Argentina) has been living in the United States since 1979. She is the author of several books of fiction, including *Clara, Strange Things Happen Here, The Lizard's Tail,* and *Other Weapons.* She has been a Guggenheim Fellow and is currently a fellow at the New York Institute for the Humanities.

Susan Willis (USA) teaches courses on pan-African and pan-American literature and culture through the International Studies Program at Duke University. Her study, *Specifying: Black Women Writing the American Experience,* is forthcoming.

Michael Wood (Great Britain) teaches English and comparative literature at the University of Exeter. He is author of *Stendhal* and *America at the Movies.* He has published many articles and reviews on U.S. and Latin American fiction. He is presently working on a study of Luis Buñuel.

I

History and the literary imagination

1

Introduction

GARI LAGUARDIA AND BELL GALE
CHEVIGNY

Does history allow the view that the Americas share, in a broad
sense, a common or complementary culture? Can we speak of American
literature as projecting – obvious differences notwithstanding – a shared
cultural experience similar to the one literary historians commonly at-
tribute to European literatures? Although we are accustomed to stressing
the differences between the Americas, it is possible to argue that they
share fundamental historical experiences, experiences articulated and
imaginatively transformed in their literatures, that underwrite the integrity of a comparative exploration.

All present-day nations of the Americas arose from European settlement and colonization. This settlement commonly involved the conquest and displacement of indigenous populations, which were subsequently exploited, contained, or accommodated to various degrees. All
the European colonizers of America shared the experience of appropriat-
ing and "domesticating" large expanses of underdeveloped territory, to
wit, the "frontier." Moreover, much of the settlement and development
of the Americas was done with the assistance of black slaves. Thus one of
the distinctive facts about the Americas is that they are a stage where
three races produce, in various proportions, a hybrid culture. Furthermore, all of the Americas at some point experienced a revolutionary
rupture with the colonizing power, and in the formation of new nations,
all of them were obliged to reconstitute themselves self-consciously as
something new.

These central commonalities, however, often developed in vastly different ways. One reason is that the respective conquest and colonization
of the thirteen colonies and Spanish America were, from the outset,
different projects. The United States was first settled by individuals – the
Mayflower is emblematic – who were escaping from religious or political

conditions they found unacceptable. The colonization of Spanish America, in contrast, was carried out by people who, on the whole, had no fundamental quarrel with their society and sought to extend it while enriching themselves.

The religious and sociopolitical differences between the English and Spanish settlers deepened the distinctions between their American projects. The sense of an independent identity that the first U.S. settlers brought with them from England was underwritten not only by their brand of Protestantism but also by the related fact that they represented a specific "liberal bourgeois fragment" – to use Louis Hartz's terminology – of the larger society they had left behind. The Spanish American settlers, in contrast, were Catholic and brought along a corporative semi-feudal mentality to the New World.[1] These differences had a profound effect on the manner in which each of these American societies dealt with the indigenous population, black slavery, revolution, economic development, and national formation.

The treatment of the Amerindians by the Europeans in Spanish America and the United States was influenced not only by the above factors but by the fact that each group of settlers came upon different kinds of Amerindian cultures. In Mexico, Peru, and Central America the Spaniards encountered large and imposing civilizations, whereas in the thirteen colonies the English encountered smaller, less advanced groups of Amerindians. In both cases the Indians were displaced – rapidly or gradually – often with extreme brutality. The viciousness, both real and apocryphal, of the Spanish conquest, however, obscures the fact that, once the Amerindians were subjugated and their humanity certified, the feudal and corporative mentality of the Spaniards demanded that they be incorporated in some way into the social hierarchy. Although in the great majority of cases they were absorbed at the lowest rungs of society to meet the insatiable need for manual labor, the Spaniards also made efforts (often traduced) to place the Amerindian nobility and upper classes in levels appropriate for them.

The U.S. settlers, on the other hand, had no interest in incorporating the Amerindians into their society. As long as the Amerindian lands were not coveted and the Amerindians themselves were not considered threatening, they were left to themselves. But such an ideal situation could not be permanent. When it changed, the U.S. solution was simple: removal or extermination. Thus an anomaly frequently informed U.S. politics: Egalitarian political positions for white Europeans were backed by unusually aggressive anti-Indian policies. Jefferson, for instance, once wrote to Baron von Humboldt that the Indians "will oblige us now to pursue them to extermination or drive them to new seats beyond our reach."[2] Similarly, Andrew Jackson, who represented the interests of the common people against Whig aristocracy, inaugurated the most violent policy of Indian removal the United States had yet seen. To be sure, Spanish America is not without similar examples. Most notable is Argentina – itself peripheral to the Spanish Empire in colonial days – where in the nineteenth century it was the representatives of the "liberal" bourgeoisie (as opposed to the reactionary landowners) who pressed for the final extermination of the pampas Indians.

The subjugation or incorporation of the Amerindian was tied to the progressive acquisition of new territories by the English and Spanish settlers of the New World. Once the initial beachheads had been established, the colonizers faced the temptation or need to penetrate and settle vast expanses of undeveloped territory. Here again the national origin of the respective settlers had a decisive effect on the way the frontiers were developed and on the way that experience was articulated in the national consciousness.

Whether spurred by the prospect of mining precious metals or by the acquisition of land for agrarian purposes, the Spanish settlement was informed by traces of feudalism. The desired end of "pioneer" activity was "latifundiary": the acquisition of large plots of land worked by indigenous labor under conditions that resembled serfdom. The haciendas that eventually emerged were akin to feudal fiefdoms furnished with a hierarchical complement of retainers, serfs, and slaves.

In the United States, in contrast, the penetration of the frontier after the original incursions by trappers and hunters was accomplished on a large scale by individuals who sought to establish relatively small farms that would provide the base for an economically independent existence and eventual prosperity. The bourgeois economy and way of life in the towns and cities of the settled frontier were built around the independent farmer. It was this example of a successful agrarian America that inspired Domingo Faustino Sarmiento in Argentina and spurred his desire to exterminate the Indian and Gaucho "riff raff" of the pampas in order to replace them with Europeans whom he hoped would duplicate the U.S. example and guarantee the stability of a constitutional bourgeois republic.

The slave economy of the southern United States is anomalous in the broad context of U.S. development and by the same token overlaps some styles of Spanish American settlement. As concerns the quasi-manorial institutions and seigneurial attitudes of the antebellum southern planters, the comparison is appropriate; but as regards the institution of slavery itself and the broader conception of race that informs it, the comparison does not hold up.

Paradoxically, it is the intrusion of the Protestant-bourgeois ideology of the nonslaveholding North into the South that gives U.S. slavery an intractable quality that the institution lacks in Spanish America. Given the fact that, in the United States, the notion of individual rights and worth was inextricably bound to notions of property rights, any concession to the slave's humanity tended to diminish the white southerner's perceived right to self-determination. Even in the North such a scale of values was not incomprehensible. It was not an antebellum southern planter who declared, "Negroes . . . must of necessity be slaves. *Theoretical* notions of humanity and religion cannot shake the commercial *fact* that their labor is of great *value* and cannot be dispensed with."[3] The speaker was in fact a member of an old New England family transplanted to Ohio who would later be a scourge of the South: General William T. Sherman.

In Spanish America slaves had a legal personality they did not have in the U.S. South. The Spanish codes made allowances for slaves to purchase their manumission and guaranteed the inviolability of the slave family. In Spanish America slaves had access to the courts, where they could file suit and bear testimony that carried full legal weight against white or black. These legal traditions did not, of course, guarantee observance or humane treatment of slaves. In many cases slaves received better treatment in the U.S. South than in Spanish America. The maltreatment of slaves in Cuba in the nineteenth century is notorious. However, the Spanish American slave codes are evidence that an institutionalized framework existed that allowed and even encouraged the possibility of black freedom, albeit on a very humble level. That no insurmountable ideological convictions blocked the absorption of blacks into the free community in Spanish America is attested by the widespread presence of free blacks from the earliest colonial days, by relatively large-scale miscegenation in all regions of colonial and postcolonial Spanish America, and by the fact that the abolition of slavery in Spanish America came at or shortly after independence and was in no case as traumatic and problematic as it was in the United States.[4]

The achievement of independence by the British and Spanish colonies reveals differences in keeping with the ones discussed above. In the thirteen colonies independence was a confirmation of what in fact had occurred many years before with the initial settlement. The perception of an interruption of a more or less de facto autonomy sparked the break that formalized it. For the thirteen colonies the Revolution did not imply an intrinsic shift of authority. By 1776 in the minds of most colonists fundamental authority resided with them, not the British crown. The Revolution simply confirmed this fact.

This was not the case in Spanish America. Although distant and often ineffectual, the authority of the Spanish crown had acquired legitimacy. Challenges to this legitimacy occasionally arose over the course of the centuries, but as in the case of the Tupac Amaru revolt (1782) in Peru, they were inevitably directed toward the interests of other potentially disaffected elements of the corporative hierarchy (in this case the Creole elites), who then joined forces with the crown to stave off the challenge. Other Spanish American revolutionists, like Francisco de Miranda in Venezuela and Bartolomé Hidalgo in Mexico, met with similar fates. If the Spanish Americans themselves, in spite of the many separate grievances of various sectors of their society, were unable to deprive the crown of legitimacy, Napoleon did it for them when he invaded Spain and placed his own brother on the throne. The continuous legitimacy of the Spanish crown was thus broken on the peninsula and transferred to those Spanish American institutions, such as the *cabildos*, that derived their authority from the pre-Napoleonic crown. The autonomy this rupture provided allowed long-held grievances to focus on what would eventually be a successful revolutionary struggle. Once independence from Spain was achieved, however, the major problem remained: How were the newly independent territories to govern and constitute themselves?

The United States did not face problems of similar magnitude. The thirteen colonies had been accustomed to autonomous government, which had provided them with the conceptual and executive resources to devise a system that, until the Civil War, was able to mediate and resolve by political means the conflicts of competing interests. It was also the good fortune of the United States to have at its back a sparsely populated western frontier to absorb those disaffected by their inability to carve out a piece of inalienable bourgeois prosperity in the East.

Spanish America's historical experience did not provide, after independence, such easy access to a social contract that was at the same time consonant with the declared principles of its revolutionary leaders. In Argentina, José de San Martín's leanings toward some form of constitutional monarchy was probably a more realistic option than the more progressive systems dreamed up by others. San Martín, however, ceded to Venezuelan Simón Bolívar, who chose to emulate George Washington. But whereas Washington's careful observation of the limits of constitutional authority confirmed the nature of the historical forces that had placed him in office and thus ensured stability and continuity, Bolívar's emulation of Washington flew in the face of the historical forces that had brought him to his fleeting moment of triumph. His constitutional restraint only cleared the field for a succession of competing *caudillos,* spearheads of particular interests, who reconstituted the corporate state of the colony often in debased form and destroyed the dream of pan-American unity.

The formation of the U.S. nation followed with remarkable consistency what, in retrospect, seems to have been the logical outcome of its initial self-conception. Its original political institutions were sufficiently resilient to maintain an extraordinary stability even as the nation rapidly expanded geographically and economically. From a predominantly agrarian nation restricted to portions of the eastern seaboard of North America, the United States expanded inexorably westward. By purchase, war, and expropriation it reached the Pacific, all the while transforming itself into an industrial juggernaut. The particular amalgam of self, property, egalitarianism, and democracy that fueled a unifying national myth in the face of multiple sectarianisms and contentions was able to summon enough power to transcend the most formidable crisis in the nation's history: the Civil War. The defeat of the South was followed by the consolidation of economic power in the business and industrial sectors without affecting the productive capacity of the agrarian sector.

Early in the century the Monroe Doctrine and the emerging idea of Manifest Destiny had hinted that the United States intended to be the principal arbiter of the hemisphere. After the Civil War it became clear that the United States would become a world power as well. Massive waves of immigration, which from the late nineteenth century through the 1920s resulted in a repopulation of the United States by ethnic groups very different from those of the founding fathers, did not until the 1960s substantially affect the cohesion of a national identity. The war against Spain in 1898 provided the opportunity for the first U.S. sallies in imperialism. Its successful participation in two world wars confirmed that the United States had become the major Western power. An economy that, in the long run, demonstrated an aptitude for continuing expansion propped up the steadily wider scope of the nation's projection of political power internally and externally.

Spanish America's nations hardly followed the comparatively smooth and inexorable development of the United States after independence. Indeed, for most of them, the first forty years after independence were chaotic. Until about 1860 or 1870 most Spanish American nations experienced a succession of constitutional experiments and failures, civil wars, conflicts with the Indians, and interference from Europe and the United States.

In economic terms, Spanish America was not able to lay the groundwork for a network of economic institutions to transcend the inadequacies of pervasive and inefficient monoproduction. Prohibited or discouraged during the colonial era from producing finished goods that would have competed with those that Spain itself produced inefficiently and obliged its colonies to buy, Spanish America did not have an adequate institutional base for industrialization.

Barred from free trade by a strictly mercantilist colonial policy, Spanish America instead had been structured to provide raw materials for the use of the mother country and had been discouraged from producing, except for internal consumption, agricultural products that would have competed with those of Spain. Thus Spanish America was, at independence, ill equipped to compete in a world dominated by the capitalist-industrial nations.

Instead, the economic mainstay of the respective economies of the Latin American nations remained the production of raw materials, which was subject, then as now, to the vagaries of the commodities markets. Thus the economic history of Spanish America consists largely of a succession of booms and busts connected to the ever fluctuating prices of commodities. Prosperity has come and gone with beef, rubber, guano, copper, and sugar.

These economic patterns had consequences for the development of class structure and political institutions. Unlike the United States, Spanish America never developed a large and dominant middle class. Nor was its middle class deployed in the countryside as well as in the large urban centers. Moreover, much of this small middle class was debilitated by two factors: The virtual institution of absentee ownership separated it from the source of production, and it was dependent, with rare exceptions, on neocolonial powers or international finance.

The absence of reliable and strong native economic and social institutions precluded the development of stable constitutional political life. The vulnerability of the bourgeoisie and the boom-and-bust economic cycles gave dictators of the twentieth century the opportunity to continue the traditions of *caudillismo* established in the nineteenth century during the first chaotic years of independence. There have been periods of generalized, if relative, prosperity, such as 1870–1920 and 1945–65, that have coincided in some cases with periods of deceptive political stability and optimism. On the whole, however, Spanish America has not emerged fully from its initial colonial dependence and its continuing dependence on the economically advanced countries.

The culmination of three revolutions – in Mexico (1920), Cuba (1959), and Nicaragua (1979) – has challenged these historical impasses. In suggesting the possibilities of material independence, these revolutions have had an enormous intellectual and cultural impact on the other countries of Spanish America. The Mexican Revolution has not lived up to many of its initial hopes but has provided Mexico with sixty years of political stability. It has not succeeded in giving Mexico a prosperity comparable to that of the industrialized nations but has presided over the expansion of a viable bourgeoisie that may well constitute the most formidable challenge to the political institutions it has created. The Cuban Revolution has effected profound, if controversial, changes in the structure of Cuban society. If it has not provided Cuba with the prosperity that defines a bourgeois consumer economy, it has leveled the social and economic inequality endemic to most Spanish American countries and improved the material lives of the bulk of its citizens in such areas as public health and education. In addition, to a degree unparalleled by any Spanish American country, it has projected itself on the international stage. The recent Nicaraguan Revolution, though unique in some respects, mirrors these effects.

The literatures of the Americas arise out of these historical matrices. They not only reflect them but also both mythify and criticize them. Even so, a comparison of the literatures of the United States and Spanish America does not always expose differences as stark as the ones sketched above. The differences exist, but they are blurred and sometimes subject to reversal. This is so because the writer not only is the mouthpiece for the reigning ideology of his or her culture but is often an alienated critic of it.

Through their characteristic portrayal of nature, geography, and landscape, nineteenth-century Spanish American and U.S. writers symbolize their respective attitudes toward their environment. Nature is a canvas on which they paint the dreams and anxieties relevant to their identity as Americans and to the formation of their nations. Although U.S. and Spanish American writers, particularly in the nineteenth century, often begin their contemplation of nature from comparable ideological positions, they often end up in different conceptual spaces.

The U.S. writer confronts nature – however wild – as a space destined to fuse with the American self as it inevitably actualizes its predestined dreams. Thus Ralph Waldo Emerson, in a way typical of U.S. writers, does not evoke distance but announces a fusion. For him nature, wild or cultivated, is a presence that is actualized by, even as it actualizes, the self that contemplates it.

The Spanish American writer, in contrast, shies away from an unmediated encounter. American nature, whether hated or loved, dominant or dominating, is almost always constituted at a distance from the self. Moreover, nature is a potentially friendly and fecund "other" that provides the sustaining ground for the civilization that is the true unmediated self. Thus, Emerson's contemporary, Andrés Bello (1781–1865), writing from London in the mid 1820s, evokes an idealized American landscape in his "Oda a la agricultura en la zona torrida." In the flash of excitement provoked by a recently achieved independence, he describes a bountiful and cultivated nature that can serve as the sustaining ground for a moral and collective order. Yet this cultivated nature is advanced not as the product of an unmediated contemplation of it, but rather as the product of memory mediated by classical texts. Moreover, the boundary between self and nature is not blurred but implicitly underlined by the poem's didactic intention of encouraging settlement outside of the towns.

Domingo Faustino Sarmiento, writing twenty years after Bello, is the more typical Spanish American writer. Argentine nature in *Facundo: civilización y barbarie* (1845, Facundo: Civilization and Barbarism) is described as vast, empty, and often majestic; yet Sarmiento does not like it. For him the land as such is an alien place that breeds barbarism and mayhem, where those few who traverse it must be constantly on guard for "the sinister visages of the savage horde, which, at any moment, approaching unperceived, may surprise them."[5] Myra Jehlen has compared passages of Sarmiento's portrayal of Argentine nature to passages from Thomas Jefferson's *Notes on the State of Virginia*.[6] If the landscape is similar to Sarmiento's, the eye of this beholder perceives different patterns. Jehlen shows that, regardless of the vastness of the landscape, it is never impenetrable to Jefferson as it is to Sarmiento. Jefferson is always at the proper angle of vision, and as he surveys the wildness, he sees in it, ready made, the road that leads to American civilization. Jehlen rightly observes that the major difference between the two men – a difference made the more remarkable by the fact that both were nation builders, both became presidents of their native republics, and both held similar liberal ideologies – is that Jefferson achieves a fusion with the national landscape, whereas Sarmiento simply cannot even if he wants to. The list of Spanish American novels of both the nineteenth and twentieth centuries whose theme is a land fundamentally alien to the self is very long. One thinks, for instance, of *La vorágine* (1924, The Vortex) by the Colombian José Eustacio Rivera, where the jungle is absolutely refractory to human effort and where individuals, indeed, simply disappear, as in the last sentence of the book: "The jungle swallowed them up."

This alienation from American nature is rare in U.S. literature. It matters not whether the writer portrays it accurately. Whether the writer depicts a nature that is bountiful or niggardly, exploited or husbanded, it is nearly always an extension of the American self. Such a fusion is itself rare in Spanish America. José Martí is a striking exception in the nineteenth century. It is both perplexing and significant that those Spanish American writers in the twentieth century who seek to effect a rapprochement with nature often identify with those groups who occupied the land before Columbus's discovery. We think, for instance, of Miguel Angel Asturias's *Hombres de maiz* (1949, Men of corn) or, more particularly, of the Neruda of *Canto general* (1938–50). For Neruda and others the simple and confident teleology of Robert Frost's formula, "The land was ours before we were the land's," is neither possible nor productive. Before the self can be fused with place, recognition must be given to history and process. It is true, paradoxically, that there is a Whitmanian egotism in Neruda's projection of a composite self; but the positive recognition of what Sarmiento saw negatively and rejected, the denizens of America who antedated the Europeans, produces perhaps, in the long run, a telos more hospitable to the existence of other peoples than the one, so successful until now, articulated by the U.S. imagination. The Spanish American sense of America as a world occupied by diverse peoples and changing through time is in radical contrast to Emerson's unmediated America. This is a difference that permeates the literatures we are examining.

The encounter between Indians and whites on the American landscape is a potent theme in American literatures. A fundamental difference underscores the way in which the encounter is staged in Spanish America, on the one hand, and in the United States, on the other. Spanish American writers – Argentines are a glaring exception – start with the premise, set during the colonial centuries and reinforced during the independence struggles, that the Indian has a place in society. For U.S. writers, however, removal or elimination is the inevitable if not always the preferred option.

At the onset of the nineteenth century it was clear to anyone who wished to see that in the United States the days of the freely roaming Indian were numbered. Although there was considerable sympathy for the Indian's plight, it had become a virtually irrevocable axiom that the Indian's way of life was incompatible with the needs of an expanding agrarian republic.

Throughout the colonial period and well into the early days of the republic, captivity narratives were among the favorite reading matter of the American public. These works typically converted the experience of captive whites into an allegory that traced their trajectory from capture by the forces of trial, tribulation, and evil through redemption and salvation spiced up with scenes of sadistic violence and muted contemplation of the sexual fate of the female captives.

James Fenimore Cooper, the first important U.S. novelist, draws on the tradition of captivity narratives as well as on informed and sympathetic portrayals of the Indian that coexisted with them. In the Leatherstocking novels he projects the enduring tension that arose out of admiration for the virtues of the Indian's free life in nature, on the one hand, and a commitment to a civilized social order, on the other. Although nostalgia for the disappearing symbiosis between Indian, tracker, and nature wafts through many of Cooper's novels, he never leaves any doubt that "civilization" will, and must, triumph, as Cynthia Steele points out in Chapter 3 of this volume. Moreover, such a triumph inevitably entails the passing of the Indians, no matter if they are noble or savage, regardless of whether their disappearance is justified or regretted. In this way, with considerable resonance, Cooper both confirms and deplores the Jacksonian expansionism of white America. What Cooper does salvage is an enduring and persistent archetype for U.S. literature: the white man and his nonwhite partner – unattached and without issue – who act out a regressive fantasy, which also serves as social critique, on a fading frontier.

Eurocentric U.S. writers like Henry Wadsworth Longfellow adopt a more fanciful approach to the Indians but still posit their inevitable disappearance. The Indian portrayed by Longfellow in the *Song of Hiawatha* (1855) is a "noble savage" in the European tradition. In the "forest primeval" Hiawatha, the ideal Indian, stoically advocates the superior ways of European civilization, redeeming himself even as he ensures his own disappearance.

An approach to the Indian like Longfellow's is adopted by Spanish American writers in whose countries the Indian has, in fact, already disappeared. Both the Dominican Republic's Manuel Galván in his novel *Enriquillo* (1882) and Uruguay's José Zorilla de San Martín in his narrative poem *Tabaré* (1886) present certain Indians as paragons of nobility even as they justify, by virtue of its Christianizing mission, the Spanish conquest that destroyed them. Although "fate" has destroyed the Indians, through myth and recollection they achieve an honored place in the subsoil of the nation.

More prevalent in Spanish American literature is the virtually endless stream of novels, essays, and poems that examine Indians as a "problem" and attempt to locate them properly in national life. Although the approaches are informed by a wide range of ideological positions, most of these writers do not project the Indians' disappearance but rather wrestle with the realization that the Indians are an integral sector of the nation. Juan León Mera of Ecuador writes *Cumandá* (1879) from a conservative perspective. In his view the Indian, though prone to savagery, is also, under proper tutelage, capable of a Christianity more simple and genuine than is the corrupt European. The old colonial conception of the Indian as a ward of the church is thus revived. Most of the literature that deals with the Indian, however, has a more progressive reformist intention and shares the view of the Peruvian poet and essayist Manuel González Prada, who urges freeing the Indian from the "tyranny of the justice of the peace, the governor and the priest, the trinity of the Indian's debasement."[7] Novels of this type include the Peruvian Clorinda Matto de Turner's *Aves sin nido* (1889, Birds without a Nest) and the Bolivian Alcides Argüedas's *Raza de bronce* (1919, Race of Bronze). Later novels add to this tradition by suggesting a radical political role for the Indian in reforming the society. The Ecuadorian Jorge Icaza's *Huasipungo* (1934) and the Peruvian Ciro Alegría's *El mundo es ancho y ajeno* (1941, *Broad and Alien Is the World*) exemplify this tendency.

All of these novels have been criticized for failing to penetrate the individual perspective of their Indian characters and for failing, in spite of their intention, to portray the Indian as anything more than an alien other. More recent writers like Miguel Angel Asturias of Guatemala, José Maria Argüedas of Peru, and Augusto Roa Bastos of Paraguay have succeeded in characterizing the Indian from inside, as it were, with greater verisimilitude and richness and in the process produced indisputably major fiction in such works as *Hombres de Maiz* (1949), *Los rios profundos* (1958, *Deep Rivers*), and *Hijo de Hombre* (1959, Son of Man).[8]

Argentina presents a special case in Spanish America because the Indian is portrayed in terms that suggest similarities with the United States. If U.S. writers evoked the western frontiers as "the great battlefields between barbarism and civilization,"[9] Argentine writers used identical language to describe the battle for the pampas. In Argentina, both the justification for removing the Indian and the crusade that prompted it were acted out more vehemently – even genocidally – than in the United States. Perhaps the vehemence of the Argentines was due to the fact that, like Sarmiento, they were not as confident of successfully settling the wilderness as were the people of the United States. Esteban Echeverría's *La cautiva* (1837, The Captive) presents an implacably cruel Indian horde doing away with a weak, fainting hero and breaking the heart of the strong-willed heroine by killing her children. Thus the final elimination of the Argentine Indian in the 1870s is still regarded as a heroic achievement of "civilization." Leopoldo Lugones, an early twentieth-century modernist, stated, "If the extermination of the Indian is advantageous to the white race, then so be it."[10]

Black slavery and its aftermath left profound traces on the literary history of the Americas; yet there is a marked contrast between the respective degree and style of presence of the black voice in the literatures of the United States and Spanish America. Hispano-Catholic universalism and Anglo-Protestant sectarianism account for some of the difference. Also, in Spanish America (Cuba is the exception) the early and relatively unproblematic disappearance of slavery after independence did not allow for the development of a black literary presence that coalesced around an intense and fundamental focus on the institution of slavery characteristic of the United States.

During the nineteenth century slave narratives became the characteristic genre of the black voice in the United States. Numbering in the hundreds these narratives had certain common characteristics. They polemically stressed the brutality of slavery, the hypocritical religiosity of the slaveholders, and the sexual exploitation of slaves by their masters. Repeatedly accentuating the dignity and courage of the slave, the writers and narrators of these documents undertook the project of constituting themselves through the act of writing or telling.

Such narratives were the foundation on which Harriet Beecher Stowe built her monumental *Uncle Tom's Cabin,* without doubt the most persuasive antislavery polemic in the Americas. Stowe depicts three kinds of slave holders, from the benignly paternalistic Shelby to the obsessively sadistic Legree, demonstrating that they are united in the single violence of ownership of human flesh. She proves that slavery is a national problem: Legree hails from Vermont; an abolitionist discovers her own aversive racism; and the North is complicitous in obeying the Fugitive Slave Law. Although the need to end slavery is never in doubt, Stowe's position on the future of the freed blacks in the United States is that they have none. Her opening premise is that of an unbridgeable but essential difference between the African and the Anglo-Saxon. When he might save a soul by remaining a slave or by dying for others, Uncle Tom refuses to rebel or even to take his freedom. His Christ-like traits are attributed to his race. Only those with a strong admixture of white blood rebel, and even they plan to join an ideal "Christianized community . . . on the shores of Africa."[11] In the last analysis, Stowe's attitude toward blacks may be read as a variation of the national position on the Indian: Be a slave no more, but die for our good or remove.

Only in Cuba is there a comparable body of abolitionist literature, including slave narratives. For most of the nineteenth century, slavery played a uniquely central role in Cuba's economy, and the slave was so integral to Cuban life that Félix Tanco, author of the abolitionist novel *Petrona y Rosalía* (1838), thought that no novel "will ever be perfect or complete if it does not include the slaves who have such a principal part in it." Neither of the two best-known Cuban antislavery novels is as focused on an antislavery polemic as is Stowe's. Gertrudis Gómez de

Avellaneda's *Sab* is less an attack on slavery than a polemic on the exploitation of wage labor under capitalism, and the thematics of blackness and slavery are used chiefly to develop romantic paradoxes. The characterization of the slave Sab is absolutely false and conventional, according to Pedro Barreda. "A white soul enclosed in a mulatto body," he grows to represent a free spirit caged in an enslaved body.[12]

The Cuban Cirilio Villaverde's *Cecilia Valdés* was not published until 1882, but was begun in the 1830s. The novel's plot combines miscegenation and incest and gives a portrayal of slave society so densely detailed that it almost eclipses the antislavery issue. Since Cuba had not yet won its independence, it is not surprising that Villaverde's critique of slavery is imbedded in an attack on colonialism, of which slavery is considered merely an aspect. The real cost of slavery, in his view, is not so much the admittedly terrible injustice it wreaks on the slaves as the corruption the institution brings to the entire society, both black and white.

In this respect *Cecilia Valdés* signals a fundamental difference between Cuba and the United States in their apprehension of race relations. Because whites and blacks share colonial domination, no separation of the races is foreseen in a free Cuba. In this spirit, José Martí declared that, as a result of their shared historical struggle for liberty, "blacks and whites became equal. After this embrace they have not become strangers again."[13] Though Martí was rather sanguine, it is not possible to conceive of Cuban literature without the presence of black culture, regardless of the race of the writer.

Cecilia Valdés not only registered black culture but also celebrated it, presenting its vitality in marked contrast to the decadence of white culture. Thus Villaverde anticipates the Afro-Antillean poetry of the 1920s, which embraced the Dominican Republic and Puerto Rico as well. This movement was sparked largely by the contemporary interest in "primitive" cultures evidenced by the popularity of Leo Froebinius's *Black Decameron* and the cubist and surrealist investigation into the forms of African art but was also encouraged by the work of native scholars like the Cuban anthropologist Fernando Ortiz. What is striking is that of its three major poets, Nicolás Guillén (Cuba), Emilio Ballagas (Dominican Republic), and Luis Palés Matos (Puerto Rico), the latter two were "white." For Guillén and Palés at least, the representation of a black voice served a critical function with regard to society as well as aesthetics. In Chapter 5 of this volume, Susan Willis examines how the non-European perspective allowed Guillén and other black Caribbean writers to infuse standard images with new meanings and configurations.

In the United States, by contrast, the separation between the races figured by Stowe resulted in the development of two very distinct literatures. Being freed into conditions of racism and segregation provided a rich seedbed for writers of the first rank. The tradition of Afro-American literature is continuous; its most intense moments have been associated with broad-based movements for freedom, rights, and dignity, eminently during the struggle for abolition, the "Harlem Renaissance" of the 1920s onward. The shadow of the black on the consciousness of the white writer in the United States is, of course, one of the major features of its literature.

Any comparative discussion of modernity in the Americas is problematic because in both historical and literary terms modernity is characterized by "uneven" development. As we shall show, the several salient characteristics of modern experience – industrialization, a consolidated bourgeoisie, modern capitalism, scientific and technological development, and a mass consumer society – arrived in the Americas at different paces. So with literature, there were few symmetrical developments of any genre across the hemisphere. Nor did poetry and prose develop simultaneously within a single culture. We shall sketch here the complex counterpoint of historical and literary features of modernity as they unfolded.

Some would argue, with justice, that in the United States many of the features of modernity were embryonically in place by the 1830s, thus facilitating the literary explosion that has been called the American Renaissance. The neat fit of the ideology of the individual self with the social institutions and resources of the nation produced an unusually coherent cluster of "American" ideas. The work of Emerson, Thoreau, Hawthorne, Melville, and Whitman, for all its variety, was inspired by these ideas and furthered them. These writers invented or revised existing literary forms that at once embodied the ideas and to various degrees criticized them. They deployed a foundational literature that was also modern in its self-conscious treatment of American literature as problematic.

Such a comprehensive, if often critical, account of the American character was unavailable to the Spanish American writer even in 1870, when the modern period is conventionally said to have begun. Even the incipient modernity of the American Renaissance was accomplished only in bits and pieces by Spanish American writers over a much longer period of time.

The source of this disparity was the vast difference between the ways that the middle class came to inhabit the two regions. In Spanish America the middle class was virtually absent from the countryside and even in the cities was relatively small. The United States, in contrast, was by definition a bourgeois nation and, since its inception, had had a bourgeoisie with strong agrarian roots. Thus in the United States the city and countryside were linked in a way not imaginable in Spanish America. There, the city, in the eyes of the bourgeoisie, was an embattled oasis besieged an an alien countryside whose values and ways of life seemed virtually unassimilable.[14]

The respective focal points of modernity in Spanish America and the United States were asymmetrical. The U.S. writer faced the need to encompass into literary consciousness the growing cosmopolitan cities and the new social dynamics they entailed. The Spanish American writer, however, had to find a way to articulate a problematic countryside in the national discourse.

The novel has been frequently described as the representative genre of an insurgent national bourgeoisie. In the nineteenth century, as we have seen, the Spanish American bourgeoisie was small and doubly weakened by its separation from its own national interior and its subordination to European economic domination. This dual debility was reflected in two limitations of the leading canonical prose genre, the romance: its failure to depict the native landscape and to advance beyond European models. The endeavor of the major practitioners of the genre – Juan León Mera (Ecuador), Manuel Galván (Dominican Republic), Jorge Isaacs (Colombia), and others – was to establish a national identity in its uniqueness. The plot, often through symbolic means, articulated an overriding myth: an enlightened, frequently urban, male protagonist coming into fruitful possession of his national territory.

Significantly, none of these novels directs the myth toward a positive resolution. Failure is signaled on several levels. The myth of national formation miscarries on the literal level of plot: The protagonists of the romantic love stories are invariably foiled. In Mera's *Cumandá,* the Indian heroine, thwarted in her desire to marry the son of a Spanish landowner, flees from the jungle and dies, proof that barbarism and civilization cannot be married. In Isaacs's *María* (1867) the idyllic child of nature dies and her lover retreats to study and mature in England. In Galván's *Enriquillo* the protagonist's love for Mencia leads to a revolt in which he dies.

The goal of establishing a national literature is also undermined because, in attempting to situate the action in an American landscape, the authors, more often than not, depend on French romantic images of American nature derived from Chateubriand or Bernardin de Saint Pierre, and in the case of *Enriquillo,* the story, derived from historical documents, is articulated with conventions borrowed from Scott and Dumas.

Both of these miscarriages contribute to traducing the symbolic plot, which is the rescue of the land from barbaric forces by seeding it, marrying the heroine, or entering into a mutually redemptive relationship with its indigenous inhabitants.[15] Thus the project for a national literature ends in stasis. None of these romances portrays the possibility of a dynamic future on the grounds of autochthonous present reality. Solutions to contemporary problems are found either in the colonial past or in Europe itself. This indicates that the contemporary reality of American settings did not provide these authors with comfortable materials with which to fashion a national myth.

Such regressive fantasy and dependency on European models were not unknown in the United States in this period. One need only recall Thomas Nelson Page, whose fables of antebellum gallantry and racial harmony secured by slavery in *In Ole Virginia* pleased readers facing the complex world of 1887. Even a writer in ideological opposition to Page like the carpetbagger Albion Tourgée relied on the armature of the romantic plot of Scott to support his detailed accounts of Reconstruction in books like *A Fool's Errand* (1881).

But romanticism of right and left could not be sustained under the pressures of modernity. It was swept away by the rigorous realism, for example, of Mark Twain in his caricature of the Grangerford–Shepherdson duel in *Huckleberry Finn* (1884). Henry James created *The Bostonians* (1886), a comic-tragic meditation on the real barriers to national reunion. The belated chivalry of the unreconstructed southerner Ransom is treated with sympathetic irony, and his rescue of the equivocal feminist Verena promises a tearful marriage.

The realistic revision of romance effected by Twain and James was emblematic of the great novels in the period between the Civil War and World War I. Realism in the United States proved capacious enough to document new interest in the diverse regions of the States. What Hamlin Garland did for the Midwest, Sarah Orne Jewett and Mary Wilkins Freeman did for New England, and George Washington Cable and Kate Chopin for the South. At the same time the cities were seen at once as magnets for those stifled in small towns and as sinks of iniquity and violence by Theodore Dreiser, Stephen Crane, and others.

The shocks of the modern that jarred consciousness, the crises that rapid urbanization and industrialization precipitated – these are usually said to have given rise to the realistic novel of the United States and to characterize it. Yet in contrast to the contemporaneous Spanish American romancer, the realistic novelist seems oddly comfortable even with crisis, and far more equal to the tasks of registering contemporary experience. This difference may be attributed to the longer history of the middle class and its broader distribution in the nation as well as to the greater maturity of fiction in the United States than in Spanish America. Not only did both the metropolis and the countryside produce artists, but realists like William Dean Howells often set up a dialogue between farm and town (*The Rise of Silas Lapham*, 1885) or between Boston and New York (*A Hazard of New Fortunes*, 1890). Writers like James extended such fictional itineraries to the Grand Tour and illuminated the national character by scrutinizing its behavior in Europe.

Conversely, writers like Frank Norris registered the shocking effect of monopoly industry on the life of the farm. *The Octopus* (1901) is at once an epic of wheat and an epic of the railroad, and if it is less than coherent, it deploys the extraordinary range of positions that were taken on the critical clash between industry and the farm in his time.

The Octopus suggests a point of contrast between novels of the Americas in the late nineteenth century that is as crucial as the contrast centering on the relation of metropolis to countryside. The difference in response to naturalism reflects and illuminates the growing difference between the U.S. and Spanish American nations as writers came to experience them. As practiced in the United States by Norris, Dreiser, and Jack London, naturalism was notoriously contradictory. The critical analysis and social determinism adopted from French models almost disappeared in its marriage to the passionate optimism or mysticism and, above all, the energy of American naturalists. As ideologically incoherent as Progressivism, naturalism was an appropriate choice for writers of the Progressive period. The spirit of criticism was made to mate with Roosevelt's gusto, and as Alfred Kazin has observed, "the generation dominated by the dream of reform was a generation fascinated by imperialism."[16] Thus Frank Norris, reflecting on the fall of Santiago (Cuba) during the U.S. war with Spain in 1898, declared, "Santiago was ours . . . by the sword we had acquired, we Americans . . . whose blood instinct is the acquiring of land."[17]

The Spanish American novelists who experimented with naturalism were unable to achieve a similar identification with force. They could not very well identify with forces of natural selection that on a broad scale may have implied the disappearance of their national cultures. Thus some writers stop short of articulating the logical ends of the determinism that provides naturalism with its matrix. Instead of relying on natural selection to resolve everything, they appeal to the countervailing power of traditional morality. Writers such as the Mexican Federico Gamboa, who wrote during Porfirio Díaz's reign – a period when the official national ideology of positivism supported notions of social Darwinism that certified the bourgeoisie's right of control – turn a sharply honed naturalist eye on decadent fringes of the Mexican bourgeoisie, suggesting at the same time that moral suasion can correct its faults. The Uruguayan Javier de Viana turns the force of natural selection on the gauchos – an easy alien target – whom he portrays as a degenerate race irreparably fated to disappear. Less sanguine, if more obsessed, Eugenio Cambaceres of Argentina develops bourgeois characters in his novels *Sin rumbo* (1885, Aimless) and *En la sangre* (1887, In the Blood) who are fatally predisposed to corruption and perversion and whose lives are eventually reduced to aimless survival or death. If there exists a vital force that can overcome such entropy, it stems from the alien and "dark recesses of 'revolutionary' Argentina that threaten not just the decadent but the whole bourgeois system."[18] Clearly, modernity did not provide Spanish America with the bases for a naturalism infused with the muscular exhilaration or even optimism of U.S. writers like Frank Norris or Jack London any more than it allowed the earlier romancers the options for positive myth making.

Although the absence of many elements of modernity affected the Spanish American production of fiction, some of its writers found some means of producing a poetry so forceful that it not only attracted world attention but leaped ahead of the production of modern poetry in the United States. Turning the vice of dependence into a virtue, Spanish American poets assimilated a range of European and U.S. literature – the French Parnassians and symbolists and Poe and Whitman were particularly influential – and effected a major revolution in Spanish-language poetry. Among the major poets of this movement were Rubén Darío (Nicaragua, 1867–1916), Julián Del Casal (Cuba, 1863–93), José Asunción Silva (Colombia, 1865–96), Julio Herrera y Reissig (Uruguay, 1875–1910), and Leopoldo Lugones (Argentina, 1874–1938). This revolution had lasting effects not only on Spanish America but on Spain itself. These poets, calling themselves *modernistas,*[19] stripped away the bombast of Spanish romanticism, added a large repertory of metrical innovations to Spanish prosody, enriched poetic vocabulary both by resurrecting archaic words and by introducing neologisms, and experimented with unusual syntactical forms. As Spanish Americans, these poets were unable to draw on the modernity provided by technology, industry, or advancing capitalism as a spur for literary production. Instead, they constituted themselves as a literary aesthetic vanguard.

As a corollary to their aesthetic vanguardism the *modernista* poets explicitly disdained what they took to be bourgeois materialism and overtly challenged bourgeois taboos. Yet many of these poets are shot through with a tense ambivalence that often allows the expression of bourgeois aspirations. These aspirations are frequently betrayed by the poets' fascination with the luxury commodities frequently enumerated in their poems. Such tensions emerge most trenchantly in Rubén Darío, who declares, "No one knows like the artist how to value and love beautiful spectacles, exquisite interiors, marble, silk, gold; all the luxury which common souls are at a loss to appreciate."[20]

A similar renovation of poetic language and practice did not come until a generation later in the United States. It was not until after 1914 that the generation of Pound, Eliot, Stevens, and Williams accomplished for the United States what the *modernistas* had accomplished for Spanish America. The U.S. modernists drew in large part on the same sources – French symbolist poetry – to effect their own break with their poetic past. In making this break they made little use of their own poetic antecedents, Poe and Whitman, whom the Spanish American *modernistas* deeply admired.

The Gilded Age in the United States did not provide its own or succeeding generations with sustenance for the production of significant poetry. However, when we turn to the period beginning after 1914, we find U.S. poets responding to the aesthetic possibilities bequeathed by the Gilded Age in much the same manner as the *modernistas* had earlier responded to their own aesthetic inheritance. Like Henry James before them, but without his attachment to an American innocence, many U.S. modernists looked to Europe and forged their style, if not from an immersion in the ways and mores of European society, then by virtue of an assimilation of the European literary tradition. Like the *modernistas,* they derived from this tradition the tools for an aesthetic critique of their society.

This critique could cut both ways on the political spectrum. Eliot and Pound's drift to political reaction had no direct consequences. Younger modernists like the Fugitive/Agrarians Ransom, Tate, Brooks, and Penn Warren had more influential effects. They articulated a coherent political program that derived its authority from adherence to Tory agrarian values and an attachment to the preromantic European tradition. Their forays into politics and poetry eventually shifted to the study of literature itself. Drawing also from Eliot's critical pronouncements, these men developed the "New Criticism," which, although itself apolitical, "stripped the work of art from its social and philosophic backgrounds and [gave] it an independent quasi-religious status."[21]

Although U.S. modernist poets were generally conservative or reactionary in politics, their assimilation of avant-garde internationalism contributed to the diffusion of models of radical social critique that were usable by critics and writers who admired modernist aesthetics but considered their politics jejeune. Thus, for example, independent marxist critics associated with *Partisan Review* during the period of its greatest influence could hew to the modernist aesthetic while attacking the social and critical values most of those poets advocated.

The fruits of *modernismo* were similarly various and unexpected. José Enrique Rodó built on the foundation laid by *modernismo* a program for Spanish American cultural identity that mixed aestheticism, idealism, moral virtue, and a deep regard for Mediterranean European values. In *Ariel* (1900) he set up a contrast between Spanish America and the United States that attributed idealism to the one and utilitarian materialism to the other. This idea – at its base conservative and drawing ironically from the same philosophical animus that later fueled the critiques of Eliot and the Fugitives – had a long and varied life in Spanish America, inspiring conservatives and radicals alike (one of the founders of the Cuban Communist party in the 1920s was a convinced "Arielist").

Reacting against *modernismo*'s hyperaestheticism while at the same time carrying on its tradition of artistic vanguardism and innovation, the generation of Spanish American poets that began producing around the 1920s, roughly contemporaneous with the first U.S. modernists – César Vallejo, Vicente Huidobro, Pablo Neruda, and others – forged a poetry that combined formal experimentation with radical, mostly marxist politics. The apparent dichotomy between their politics and those of their U.S. contemporaries is not as fundamental as it might appear to be. On the one hand, both positions revolve around the poet's reaction against styles and structures of life determined by advanced capitalism, regardless of whether it was experienced directly as in the U.S. or indirectly as in Spanish America. For such U.S. poets as Eliot and Pound, however different their specific politics, Europe retained a measure of the stable, hierarchical, "vital," and "organic" social relations that preceded the advent of what they viewed as the rootless materialism and disorder of modern life. World War I, which deeply affected both men (see "The Waste Land" and "Hugh Selwyn Mauberly") and which drove home the idea that a culture such as they yearned for was in danger of disappearing, was perhaps a fundamental catalyst in propelling them into the past. Similarly, the Fugitives, in reaction to the same modernity, constructed an image of an ideal culture based on an imaginary antebellum South that combined the ordered rationality of the Enlightenment and the organic rootedness of an agrarian gentry. Pound, like the Fugitives but from a different perspective, located the ideal but traduced promise in the pre-Civil War – indeed, pre-Jacksonian – era.

For the Spanish American modernists, marxism for all its novelty also echoed the past. The move from pre-Columbian communalism and colonial corporativism to a marxist collectivism seemed more in keeping with ingrained tradition than following the path of advanced capitalism. The Spanish Civil War, which played a role in the careers of Neruda and Vallejo comparable to that of World War I in the careers of Pound and Eliot, highlights this point. The defense of the Spanish Republic by American poets releases the possibility of embracing a Spanish heritage redeemed, if briefly, by socialism. Thus Vallejo, moved by the agony of the republic, could declare: "In the Spanish people, America regards its own extraordinary destiny within human history, a destiny whose continuity consists in the fact that it has been given to Spain to be the creator of continents; today she is saving the entire world from nothingness."[22]

Returning to the novel, during the period between the world wars we see in Spanish America several recapitulations of previously essayed themes and forms that point the way to new directions. The Mexican Revolution (1910–20) spawned many novels. The extreme situation of armed social upheaval combined with the perception that Mexico was undergoing a major historical redefinition and reorientation provided materials that, in the hands of writers like Mariano Azuela in *Los de abajo* (1915, *The Underdogs*) and Martín Luis Guzmán in *El águila y la serpiente* (1928, *The Eagle and the Serpent*) could be transformed into outstanding realist-naturalist fiction. The Mexican Revolution became a focal point for many Mexican writers well into the 1960s, providing a benchmark from which they reflected on the nature of Mexican identity and its historical possibilities. Juan Rulfo's *Pedro Páramo* (1955) and Carlos Fuentes's *La muerte de Artemio Cruz* (1962, *The Death of Artemio Cruz*) constitute the apotheosis of the genre even as they transcend it.

The mix of political and fictional energy released by the Mexican Revolution was paralleled by the turn taken by other Spanish American writers as they updated the old Indianist novels. Jorge Icaza's *Huasipungo* (1934), for instance, differs from its predecessors not only in avoiding the articulation of reformist solutions or eschewing romance sentimentalism but in implying that the roots of the Indian's problems are political and economic and that revolution is perhaps an inevitable consequence.

The old conflict between civilization and barbarism is also recapitulated between the wars, crystallizing in two classic novels, the Venezuelan Rómulo Gallegos's *Doña Bárbara* (1928) and the Colombian José Eustacio Rivera's *The Vortex* (1924). The first is a powerful, if obvious, allegory that builds around the encounter, on the Venezuelan *llanos,* between the violent backwoods landowner Doña Bárbara, who differs from the old romance heroine by virtue of her aggressivity, and the enlightened Santos Luzardo. Although the symbolic resolution is the obvious one – the need for the civilized man to nurture and seed the land

and the woman in order to produce a culture in his own image – the novel was a powerful reworking of an enduring Spanish American mythography. *The Vortex* also, if less optimistically, portrays the problems of the backlands, where people live without any law other than that of the jungle, as it were. The depiction of life among the harvesters of rubber in the Colombian jungle is sustained by a prose whose tense violence aptly images the implacable ferocity of the landscape and its fauna. There is, however, another protagonist: the force of international capital that provides the incentive for the extraction of rubber. A more generous and gentle summation of the conflict between town and countryside was provided by Ricardo Güiraldes's *Don Segundo Sombra* (1926). This story, a *Bildungsroman* of a youth in an Argentine town who is taken under the wing of the gaucho Don Segundo Sombra, allows that the way of life on the pampas had its own honorable order and mores. These are transmitted by the older man to the youth, who as he acquires them becomes a man. Although if in the end the gaucho rides off in the vastness of the pampa and the youth remains in "civilization," there is no conflict between the two.

Between the world wars, the novel in the United States sustained the prominence it had achieved in the late nineteenth century. Moreover, with the canonical novels of the 1920s, by Ernest Hemingway, William Faulkner, and John Dos Passos, U.S. fiction began to exert an international influence. The experience of the war and of Europe had had a mutative effect on writers of this generation not unlike the effect the Spanish Civil War would have on Neruda and Vallejo. Like those great poets, these novelists came to think differently about their native land and to express themselves with formal techniques assimilated in Europe from modernists like James Joyce and Gertrude Stein, for example. In particular they adopted the stream-of-consciousness technique, introduced multiple points of view, and violated chronology.

In works of writers like Hemingway and F. Scott Fitzgerald, we see a national tendency dating from Emerson to attend to the inner life of the individual as if it were relatively autonomous. But in Faulkner's work, even his idiosyncratic individuals are deeply marked by social conditions, and in Dos Passos's trilogy *USA,* history itself virtually becomes the protagonist. Novels from other constituencies began to gain recognition in this period. Immigrant and proletarian novels began to appear, both epitomized by Mike Gold's *Jews without Money* (1930), and a fiction of social consciousness and leftist politics emerged, best known in John Steinbeck's novels of migrant workers and Richard Wright's naturalist classic *Native Son* (1940). Wright's work itself followed the explosion of black creativity produced in the "Harlem Renaissance," the best-known writers of which include Jean Toomer, Langston Hughes, Countee Cullen, Claude McKay, Jessie Fausset, and Zora Neale Hurston. The writings of white women as well came at last to be widely accepted, especially through the achievement of such figures as Willa Cather and Katherine Anne Porter.

If the 1920s and 1930s were largely a period of consolidation of previous forms and thematics for the Spanish American novel, in the 1940s novelists began to explore new directions. These narratives mirrored culturally the relative economic self-reliance that resulted when World War II interrupted the flow of imported commodities, obliging many Spanish American countries to produce their own substitutes. During this decade Borges published *Ficciones* (1944) and *El Aleph* (1949), the fantastic self-referential short fiction that exerted such a wide influence and account for his fame as a writer. José María Argüedas of Peru drew on the Quechua language and his intimate knowledge of Indian culture to rewrite the Indianist novel from a perspective near the Indian's own consciousness in his first novel *Yawar fiesta* (1940). Juan Carlos Onetti of Uruguay and Leopoldo Marechal of Argentina essayed avant-garde techniques similar to those used by some U.S. novelists of the 1920s and 1930s in *Terra de nadie* (1941, No Man's Land) and *Adán Buenosayres* (1948). Miguel Angel Asturias of Guatemala published perhaps his best novel, *El señor presidente* (1946), giving rise to a fruitful subgenre of novels about dictators. Alejo Carpentier emerged after a long silence with his first essay on "marvelous realism" and its embodiment in *El reino de este mundo* (1949, *The Kingdom of This World*). This list suggests the expanding range and depth of Spanish American narrative. Retrospectively the 1940s can be viewed as a time when Spanish American prose combined in an assured way its own historical and linguistic resources with the repertoire of techniques provided by international modernism. This coalescence of relative independence as well as a growing self-consciousness about "American" realities made this period comparable to the beginning of the "American Renaissance" in the United States a century earlier.

The triumphant emergence of the United States from World War II as the principal and hegemonic force in Western culture – aided by the enormous exportation of its social and cultural artifacts through the media and the "consciousness industry" – complicates any comparative study of the Americas in subsequent years. Although the United States had shown intense economic and political interest in areas of Spanish America and had backed that interest with many military incursions since 1898, a new and pervasive cultural pressure now began to be exerted as well, among other reasons because of the cold war. In the late 1940s Spanish America again became dependent on international capital and its markets. The memory of cultural and social self-reliance made this renewed dependency less acceptable than ever. Generated by the U.S.-sponsored coup in Guatemala in 1954 and by continued U.S. support of reactionary regimes, resentment and tension deepened.

Although many facets of modernism began to coalesce for Spanish American writers of the 1940s, the energies of modernism in the postwar United States were appropriated with considerable success by phenomena as diverse as mass culture, a mystique of psychoanalysis, and the academy. The unprecedented prosperity that followed the war produced a quantum explosion in the communications industry. The growth of the military–industrial complex and the deepening of the cold war, however, limited adversarial expression in the expanded media. These factors combined to create a mass audience that was unusually complacent and accommodating. The society was thus relatively incapable of defining or sustaining a coherent adversarv culture except, as we shall see, for a brief period in the 1960s and early 1970s. Writers who, before World War II, had been either progressive (Dos Passos and Steinbeck) or conservative (Penn Warren and Eliot) lost their critical edge and were drawn to an all-consuming center.

The mystique of psychoanalysis as it came to be popularly imagined in this period in the United States converted what had been a potentially radical critique of Western assumptions into a promise of fulfillment through adaptation. This mystique hovers over much of the new writing of this period, from Mary McCarthy (*The Company She Keeps,* 1942) to Philip Roth, however ironic their awareness. And the acutely sensitive protagonists of J. D. Salinger's fictions function less to symbolize opposition to reigning values than to confirm the reader's own values.

The academy came to preside over literary production in this period in a variety of ways. The New Criticism, which had originally served as a handmaiden to literature, came subtly to affect the manner of its writing. Writers planted symbols and ironies in their texts as if with one eye on the future student-reader. Not only the aesthetic values of the New Criticism – tightness, elegance, and emotional understatement – but also the ethics of ambivalence and the social philosophy of quietism prevailed in many writers, of whom John Updike is a prominent example. On another level, the academy became literally the setting for novels by Lionel Trilling, Randall Jarrell, Mary McCarthy, Leslie Fiedler, and others.

In general, writers who began to publish in the 1940s and 1950s introduced new materials but failed to break formal ground. Although Norman Mailer would later become one of the nation's most fecund experimenters, the remarkable war saga on which his reputation is based (*The Naked and the Dead,* 1948) did not drive him past the resources of realism. Flannery O'Connor's war-haunted apocalyptic vision found its home in the ambience of the grotesque South articulated by Faulkner.

The generally leveling effect of the culture on white writers of the United States is confirmed by its exceptions, that is, by the fact that two writers who made significant contributions to the novel as a genre in this period were an Afro-American and a Russian emigré whose identities made them insusceptible to assimilation. Ralph Ellison's *Invisible Man* (1952) achieves something tantamount to formal innovation in its synthesis of the disparate resources of jazz, dream logic, and leftist political experience and in their application to a reading of black and white relations as existentially interdependent. In *Lolita* (1955), Vladimir Nabokov revitalizes the linguistic resources of the genre and, in his fabulous game of mirrors, introduces self-referentiality as a literary resource to U.S. fiction at the same time that he reveals the deadly narcissism at the heart of the 1950s culture.

The Spanish American narratives of the 1950s demonstrate a somewhat different development. If U.S. novelists of that decade did not advance the modernism of some of the narratives of the 1920s and 1930s or the radical critique of the socially conscious writers of the same period, the Spanish American novelists moved ahead with both the traditions of their 1940s' novels *and* those of the social critiques of the 1920s and 1930s. Spanish America's dependence on the economic order of the advanced nations spurred their anatomizing of existing social orders or seeking alternative ones.

In terms of the novel, the results were narratives in which formal experimentation, multiple and unusual borrowings from established literature (European, U.S., and Spanish American), the use of indigenous resources, and a critical attention to society produced a dynamic and fruitful mix. Juan Rulfo's *Pedro Páramo* (1955) succeeds in deploying an exceedingly complex narrative pattern in a luminously lapidary but also colloquial prose. These devices articulate a striking transformation of the novelistic genre prompted by the Mexican Revolution while examining in an original way the boundaries between life and death, the vagaries of love and power, and the corruption of social institutions by force, greed, and resentment. Alejo Carpentier's *Los pasos perdidos* (1954, *The Lost Steps*) amasses the artifacts of Western high culture and the commodities favored by an intellectual bourgeoisie in great and concrete detail, juxtaposing these with the luxuriant and fabulous nature of the South American aborigine in order to essay an ambiguously unresolved quest for origins. Carlos Fuentes in *La región más transparente* (1958, *Where the Air Is Clear*) combines Mexican mythology and neorealism to portray critically the corruption of the Mexican bourgeoisie in the historical context of a failed revolution.

There are like examples from the 1950s that became a veritable flood during the 1960s and early 1970s with the advent of that complex cultural invention known as the "Boom." Just what the "Boom" was depends on the eye of the beholder and on the purposes the "Boom" was intended to serve. At the extremes this body of work was fought for by Cuban cultural institutions such as the Casa de las Américas, on the one hand, and U.S.-subsidized publishing ventures, on the other.

The "Boom," however, is an important emblem of the fluid literary relations between the United States and Spanish America. Many of the writers identified with the "Boom" – Cortázar, Vargas Llosa, García Márquez, and Fuentes – are indebted to U.S. writers of the past – Poe, Faulkner, Hemingway, Dos Passos – for the treatment of self-conscious American themes as well as their formal resources. Reciprocally, the abundance of Spanish American narratives translated and published in the United States during the 1960s and 1970s stimulated their northern contemporaries.

In the 1960s the retrospectively short-lived hegemony enjoyed by the United States abroad and internally by its white male elite began to be challenged. It had its symbolically euphoric swansong at the Kennedy inauguration, where Robert Frost announced the advent of an "Augustan age of Poetry and Power." Little did he know then that the Augustan reign would be demolished over the next twenty years in Cuba, Vietnam, and the Middle East or that the "poetry" would hardly conform to the great peaks and standards of his generation or that the power would be diffused from the national entity he celebrated into the abstraction of international capital.

Writing in the United States – insofar as it was an activity of white European-oriented men – seemed to have exhausted itself in the tensions created by the desire for mass appeal, on the one hand, and critical success, on the other. Moreover, it seemed to lack within its own cultural ambience any potential source of renewal. The great social changes that began during the 1960s unleashed many of those sources. The civil rights movement opened national discourse to black voices, which in turn articulated and revived versions of U.S. history and U.S. culture that had been ignored, forgotten, or unimagined by the mainstream. The Vietnam War inspired both a mass movement and a revision of the historical mission of the United States. The youth movement, however frivolous, provoked the expression of life-styles that for a brief time ran counter to the mainstream norms. The women's movement provoked a massive shift in power relations and, like the civil rights movement, prompted a strong challenge to the established cultural canon, both in questioning norms and in providing new provocative works.

It was in this context that the collective appearance of "new" Spanish American narratives constituted one more challenge and option for U.S. writing, both for the countertradition and the mainstream one.

Apart from the stimulus that writers like Borges and García Márquez provided, much U.S. writing in the 1960s and 1970s had some common characteristics with Spanish American writing. A cultural conservative like Saul Bellow, whose indignant and bemused reaction to radical challenges finds one symbolic parallel in a scene from one of his own novels, Mr. Sammler's encounter with a Hispanic mugger-flasher, produces novels during this period – from *Herzog* to *Humboldt's Gift* – that manifest more narrative color and resonance than heretofore, as well as greater recourse to literary and historical reflection. Afro-American writers like Toni Morrison (*Song of Solomon, Tar Baby*) and Paule Marshall (*Praisesong for the Widow*) recover and elaborate the imaginative range of their characters and their own linguistic scope. A "postmodernist" like Thomas Pynchon exposes, even as his fables are propelled by, the paranoia that is a chief product of the consciousness industry. A García Márquez-like tonality of marvelous or magical realism appears in writers as culturally diverse as John Irving (*The World According to Garp, Hotel New Hampshire*) and Maxine Hong Kingston (*The Woman Warrior*).

The growing convergence of American literatures was further advanced by two developments beginning in the 1970s. Political repression in the Southern Cone drove exiles in increasing numbers to the United States, and among them intellectuals and writers who began to lecture in U.S. universities, offer readings, and even give us back our culture in delightful new packages, as the Argentine Manuel Puig did in *Betrayed by Rita Hayworth* or the Chilean Ariel Dorfman in *How to Read Donald Duck*. Then Central America began to excite a general interest like that raised earlier by Cuba and Vietnam. Political refugees from Guatemala and El Salvador and representatives of revolutionary Nicaragua all fed concern about U.S. government intervention in the region. This is reflected in Carolyn Forché's poetry of moral outrage about El Salvador (1981, *The Country Between Us*), and there is a growing genre of fiction about the experience of Central America by writers like Joan Didion and the Canadian Margaret Atwood. Perhaps most similar to Latin American literature are works centering on the wisdom that U.S. history and policy are blindly repeating themselves, like Robert Stone's *A Flag for Sunrise,* or that culture is madly recombining its elements, like Paul

Theroux's *The Mosquito Coast,* in which a cross between the Connecticut Yankee and Captain Ahab plays Robinson Crusoe on the coast of contemporary Central America.

In summary, many of the narrative conventions to which U.S. readers have become acclimated since the 1960s, regardless of their direct provenance, were first essayed in modern form and in American contexts by Spanish Americans who in turn had transformed U.S. and European sources into devices suitable for renewing their own American traditions. All of this suggests that if U.S. culture and Spanish American culture display extraordinary historical discontinuities, by the same token they share many often unexpected elements of reciprocity, both actual and potential. Whatever dialogue results from such reciprocity, whether friendly or adversarial, cannot but illuminate our American selves and disclose them in proportions ever closer to their true ones – which is to say in relationship.

The six essays in this section present a variety of approaches to the issue of comparison. Bell Chevigny and Cynthia Steele adopt a similar approach in considering works that best reflect aspects of the problematic construction of American identity and ideology in the United States and parts of Spanish America. Both essays treat works separated roughly by a century, reflecting our argument that conditions for broaching certain critical issues developed unevenly. Chevigny finds Melville's analysis of national independence complemented by Carpentier's analysis of Caribbean dependence: In *Moby-Dick* the individual's identification with nature generates imperialism, whereas *Explosion in a Cathedral* exposes the connection between underdevelopment and over-conditioning. Steele finds in comparing the literary treatment of the Indian by Cooper in the United States and by Rosario Castellanos in Mexico an opportunity to investigate the links between political policy, national ideology, and literature. Doris Sommer's analysis of Whitman's capacity to embrace the contradictions of liberal democracy in the time of Cooper and Melville enlarges our understanding of this seminal moment in the United States and prepares us to understand why Whitman's Spanish American heirs, Borges, Paz, and Neruda, were obliged to split his legacy into mutually exclusive parts.

Susan Willis shifts the emphasis to the Caribbean and uses a geographical metaphor to explore the ways in which Caribbean poets deploy their linguistic resources to counter traditional Western images of space, culture, and domination and to set up alternative scenarios to colonial dependence. Julio Marzán, himself a Caribbean poet of Puerto Rican extraction, explores the typically U.S. case of William Carlos Williams, a striking example of cultural transmigration. Marzán indicates several ways in which Williams's Caribbean heritage contributes to the poet's tense and complex self-constitution as a "United Stateser," in Williams's own turn of phrase. Pablo Armando Fernández, also a poet and novelist, who lived in the United States beginning in the mid 1940s and returned to his native Cuba after the revolution, offers a reflection on the ideas of America and of its parallel and divergent realization in the literatures of the United States and Spanish America.

NOTES

1 The general framework of this argument draws extensively from Louis Hartz's *The Founding of New Societies* (New York: Harcourt, Brace, 1964), in particular "A Theory of the Development of the New Societies," pp. 1–122, and Richard M. Morse's "The Heritage of Latin America," pp. 123–77 (ibid.). Octavio Paz makes some fruitful comparisons on the respective religious heritages of the two Americas in "Reflections: Mexico and the United States," *The New Yorker,* September 17, 1979, p. 143.

2 Quoted by Richard Drinnon, *Facing West: The Metaphysics of Indian-Hating and Empire Building* (New York: New American Library, 1980), pp. 9–20.

3 Quoted by Edmund Wilson in *Patriotic Gore: Studies in the Literature of the American Civil War* (New York: Farrar, Strauss & Giroux, 1977), p. 186.

4 On the slave codes see Frank Tannenbaum, *Slave and Citizen: The Negro in the Americas* (New York: Random House, 1946). Eugene Genovese, in *The World the Slaveholders Made* (New York: Vintage, 1971), pp. 21–102, contends that the slave codes did not always result in humane treatment of slaves and that what the law promised the slave in theory in Latin America was often granted the slave in fact by "humane" planters in the Old South. In addition, Genovese points out instances, as in Cuba in the nineteenth century, in which economic factors transformed a relatively "humane" system of slavery into one perhaps more brutal than the one of the southern United States. However, the fact remains that the law and social institutions in Latin America allowed for the presence of large communities of free blacks from the earliest days of the colonies. Such was not the case in the Old South. See also Winthrop Jordan, *White over Black: American Attitudes Toward the Negro, 1550–1812* (Chapel Hill: University of North Carolina Press, 1968) for the connection of black slavery to white independence in the United States.

5 Domingo Faustino Sarmiento, *Facundo: Civilización y barbarie* (1845), ed. Raimundo Lazo (Mexico: Porrua, 1966), p. 22.

6 Myra Jehlen, *American Incarnation: The Infinite Spirit of Man and Its Continent* (Cambridge, Mass.: Harvard University Press, forthcoming).

7 Quoted by Jean Franco, *Spanish American Literature since Independence* (London: Ernest Benn, 1973), p. 95.

8 Since the 1960s the United States has witnessed a renewed interest in Native American literature. Native Americans like N. Scott Momaday with *House*

Made of Dawn (1969) and Louise Erdrich with *Love Medicine* (1984) have been critically well received. For a short and insightful survey of the emergence of Native American literature, see Arnold Krupat, "Native American Literature," in Robert von Hallberg, ed., *Canons* (University of Chicago Press, 1984), pp. 309–38. For Latin American Indian literature see Gordon Brotherston, *Image of the New World: The American Continent Portrayed in Native Texts* (London: Thames & Hudson, 1979).

9 J. B. Findley, *Life among the Indians* (Cincinnati, Ohio: Thompson, 1878), p. 3.

10 Quoted by David Haberly, "Captives and Infidels: The Figure of the *Cautiva* in Argentine Literature." *American Hispanist* 4 (October 1978), p. 10.

11 Harriet Beecher Stowe, Preface to *Uncle Tom's Cabin* (New York: New American Library, 1966), p. vi.

12 Pedro Barreda, *The Black Protagonist in the Cuban Novel,* trans. P. Bancroft (Amherst: University of Massachusetts Press, 1979), pp. 79, 82.

13 Quoted by G. R. Coulthard, *Race and Colour in Caribbean Literature* (London: Oxford University Press, 1962), p. 21.

14 Cities themselves had always been prominent in Spanish American life. When Baron von Humboldt visited the Americas at the turn of the eighteenth century, the cities he found most grand were not Boston, New York, or Philadelphia but Havana and Mexico City. These cities impressed him not only because of their architectural magnificence but because of the number and quality of their scientific and cultural institutions.

15 The identification of the land as female is implicit in many of these romances and appears to be a trait widely manifested in U.S. literature. See Annette Kolodny, *The Lay of the Land: Metaphor as Experience and History in American Life and Letters* (Chapel Hill: University of North Carolina Press, 1975).

16 Alfred Kazin, *On Native Grounds* (New York: Doubleday, 1956), p. 70.

17 Quoted by Larzer Ziff, *The American 1890s: Life and Times of a Lost Generation* (New York: Viking, 1966), p. 266.

18 Gordon Brotherston, *The Emergence of the Latin American Novel* (Cambridge University Press, 1977), p. 11.

19 We use the Spanish words *modernista* and *modernismo* to describe those Spanish American poets who belong to the turn-of-the-century movement. We use "modernist" and "modernism" in the manner common in English. Thus later Spanish American poets like Neruda and Vallejo are modernists, not *modernistas*.

20 Rubén Darío, "Rostand o la felicidad," in M. Sanmiguel Raimundez, ed., *Rubén Darío: Obras Completas* (Madrid: Afrodisio Aguado, 1953), vol. 6, p. 324.

21 John M. Bradbury, *The Fugitives: A Critical Account* (Chapel Hill: University of North Carolina Press, 1958), p. 259.

22 Quoted by Jean Franco, *César Vallejo: The Dialectics of Poetry and Silence* (Cambridge University Press, 1976), p. 254.

2

"Insatiable unease"
Melville and Carpentier and the search for an American hermeneutic

BELL GALE CHEVIGNY

"Lord, when shall we be done growing? As long as we have anything
more to do, we have done nothing. So, now, let us add *Moby-Dick* to
our blessing, and step from that. Leviathan is not the biggest fish; – I
have heard of Krakens."

"As long as we have anything more to do, we have done nothing." . . . In this simple and profound sentence Herman Melville sums
up all the insatiable unease – unease which is destiny – of the true artist.
– Carpentier, "Una carta de Melville," *El Nacional,* June 8, 1954

When, in 1891, José Martí entitled his influential essay "Nuestra
América" (Our America), his use of the possessive adjective announced a
double discovery and implied a comparison that is the point of departure
for this essay. With his use of "nuestra," Martí recognized and challenged the domination implicit in the appropriation by the United States
of the name of the New World, and this recognition spurred him to
identify the qualities of another and potential "America."

Martí's polemic should be located in the context of the "ideological
discourse about America" in Spanish America, which according to
Irlemar Chiampi has a vehement and obsessive quality unmatched in
North America or Brazil. The name first given the southern lands seen
by Amerigo Vespucci was used by both north and south. In the eighteenth century both regions generated a neo-utopian image of America
to counteract European charges of inferiority. The United States began
to monopolize the name when the thirteen colonies became a nation, and
its claim was reinforced in the next century by its growing political and
economic hegemony. To all this, the great leaders to the south (an America now denominated by qualifiers: Hispano-, Ibero-, Indo-, and Latino-)
gave indirect support. Bolívar's experience moved him from optimistic

Enlightenment belief in absolute democracy to skepticism about Spanish America's intellectual readiness for democracy. Education was held to be the means by which the Spanish tradition would give way to modern Western culture. As a neocolonial relation to the United States developed, so did that country become a touchstone for this project. Sarmiento then narrowed the problem to an opposition between "civilization" and "barbarism," a formulation Chiampi finds lacking in "conceptual rigor" because it confers the status of barbarism on a culture "formed of an anomalous mixture of savage and civilized elements" and the status of civilization on a minority estranged from its country and a prospective immigrant population. By the end of the century, imported positivist analysis had further reduced "América Bárbara" (barbarous America) to "América Enferma" (sick America).[1]

In this context, Martí's call for an America distinct from both Europe and the United States and united with itself both ruptured an ideological tradition and required the dismantling of a hemispheric social and economic system. Martí saw that in Spanish American republics an insidious cultural and psychological neocolonialism made its people vulnerable to North American expansionism. Subscribers to "América Bárbara" could own neither themselves nor their culture. The condition for both unification and authentic independence in "Nuestra América" was its shared recognition and valorization – its possession, in fact – of its unique *mestizo* (racially mixed) culture and the inscription of that culture in political institutions.

Ralph Waldo Emerson played an ironic role in this debate. Greatly admired by Sarmiento, he was better understood by Martí. For Martí, Emerson's spiritual independence of institutions of the past and of social constraints in the present completed his country's revolution and made him the philosopher of universal democracy. On the occasion of Emerson's death in 1882, Martí wrote, "He shed from his shoulders all the mantles and from his eyes all the bandages that the past lays upon men, and lived face to face with Nature, as if all the world were his homestead, the sun his sun, and he a patriarch."[2] Martí acutely discerned that Emerson's valorization of nature over culture sanctioned his equation of self-possession with possession of the physical world. Emerson and his contemporaries assumed that historical strife had culminated in, and been obviated by, the U.S. Revolution. Because they also tended to think in spatial rather than temporal terms, they habitually conceived of development as expansion rather than the product of internal social struggle. And, indeed, in the decade following Emerson's death, Martí saw an internal limit set on democratic struggle (dramatized in the Haymarket trial) and a growing inclination to control Spanish America.

Martí's admiration for Emerson and his idealism remained intact, but historical events moved him, as they had Bolívar, from a universalist to a relativist position. Revolution was no timeless monument for Martí; he saw it failing in the north, doubly betrayed in the south (where those who had fought were being oppressed in Yankee or French style), and waiting to be won in his native Cuba. In "Nuestra America," he uses Emerson against Sarmiento to insist that in Spanish America "the struggle is not between barbarity and civilization but between false erudition and Nature."[3] But Martí's work constituted a radical revision of Emerson's universalism in its promotion of *mestizaje* as the crucial and special essence of Latin America, and of Emerson's ahistoricity in its implicit judgment of American revolutions as processes, not achievements.

In the twentieth century, a sharpened concern for Spanish American identity gave unprecedented range and intensity to the ideological debate, which was played out in novels as well as essays. Although notions of American Latinity or indigenism sometimes prevailed, the concept of cultural *mestizaje* (as propounded by José Vasconcelos and Uslar Pietri) has proved the most stimulating to writers who continue to resist the surrender of the name "America," even while they seek its meaning. The Spanish American temper seems to be marked by permanent expectation, by a sense of "forever-not-yet-being," which may constitute an identity in itself.[4]

This essay takes as its premise that self-consciously "American" modern literature is marked in the United States by the assumption of achieved independence, and in Spanish America by the ongoing pursuit of independence in the context of dependence. I shall examine Herman Melville's *Moby-Dick* and Alejo Carpentier's *El siglo de las luces (Explosion in a Cathedral)* as works that sustain and problematize the projects of Emerson and Martí. Of course, the lapse of 110 years between the publication of the two books has enormous consequences. Melville's book defines modernism in metaphysical and romantic terms, Carpentier's in historical, ironic, and parodic terms.[5] Yet I am persuaded that the interrogation of "America" was comparably important in the mid nineteenth century to the north and the mid twentieth to the south. Moreover, I shall argue that both Melville and Carpentier used the novel to pursue an American hermeneutic, by which I mean both a means of interpreting America and an American way of interpreting.

Because Melville's work is set at the time of writing and Carpentier's is set more than a century and a half earlier than his time, both *Moby-Dick* and *Explosion in a Cathedral* treat the age of revolution, where the issues of national definition and psychological independence were critical. Both consider periods in which remarkable economic growth coincided with a strong belief in the mutative power of ideas, particularly the idea of progress. In its name, secular sanctions displaced religious ones, and human potential, individual and social, was liberated. Carpentier traces the playing out of the idea of progress in its Enlightenment phase, when dreams of reason gave birth to the monsters of the Terror. Doubtless one of Carpentier's objectives was to discredit the liberal myths of the Enlightenment and the French Revolution, in contrast to which the Spanish American bourgeoisie had drawn its image of barbarous America, which in turn justified their internal colonization.[6] His novel begins in 1789 on the eve of the Haitian and French revolutions and ends with the popular uprising in Madrid against Napoleon's invasion on May 2, 1808, which precipitated a chain of events culminating in the wars of independence in Spanish America. Carpentier reconstructed these struggles between colony and empire during the late 1950s, when this conflict was being replayed. In a nominally independent Cuba, anti–Batista forces were contesting the neocolonialism of the United States that Martí had anticipated. Like Martí, Carpentier inhabited a moment at once postrevolutionary and prerevolutionary, and his work looks both forward and backward.

Melville's narrative action, at the midpoint of the nineteenth century, is saturated with the sense of the mounting crisis and seems to anticipate the Civil War itself. Melville witnessed the high romantic, individualistic phase of the idea of progress, which sanctioned even as it tried to conceal the playing out of Manifest Destiny, the shattering dislocations of the Industrial Revolution, and the deepening rift in the Union. Melville wrote in the years, beginning with the acquisition of Mexico and climaxing with the implementation of the Fugitive Slave Law, that Michael Paul Rogin has aptly characterized as "the American 1848," because these years called to account the claim of the United States to be the home of republican ideals.[7]

In short, although both works are animated by the creative potential of progressive ideals, they also betray profound skepticism about their implementation. Both project their mistrust of idealist claims backward to the earliest "possession" of the Americas, and a disenchanted reading of Columbus is placed on a continuum with subsequent events. In *Explosion in a Cathedral,* when questioned about the presence on shipboard of the guillotine, Victor defends his mission to the Caribbean by making an invidious contrast with Columbus and the conquistadores. "For the first time a fleet is advancing toward America without bearing crosses aloft. . . . We, the cross-less, the redeemer-less, the god-less, are going there, in ships without chaplains, to abolish privilege and to establish equality."[8] In this rhapsody, Victor may forget the guillotine, but his analogy recalls it; as the sword enforced the cross in the age of discovery, so does the guillotine enforce the decree of freedom in the age of revolution. Victor's contrast is superficial: The imposition of European values on America by violence is constant.

In his chapter "Fast-Fish and Loose-Fish," Melville asks, "What was America in 1492 but a Loose-Fish, in which Columbus stuck the Spanish standard by way of waifing it for his royal master and mistress?" A loose-fish is "fair game for anybody who can soonest catch it"; the casual arbitrariness of Columbus's gesture characterizes for Melville all imperial design. He goes on: "What was Poland to the Czar? What Greece to the Turk? What India to England? What at last will Mexico be to the United States? All Loose-Fish."[9] Melville's final rhetorical question is part of his larger inquiry into the connection, which Emerson's work had unwittingly forged, between democracy and imperialism. Here Melville adds to the imperialist acts of Europe the menace of the usurpation of one part of America by another. Melville's query foreshadows Martí's, but the historical Victor Hugues antedated both. What especially attracted Carpentier to Hugues, he said, was the fact that "when others believed in the democratic spirit of the United States, he was the first to show that, with its independence barely won, that country was becoming a reactionary power, animated by imperial desires."[10] Carpentier and Melville are linked in their alertness to the double betrayal of "America": the violation of the independent ideal in the violation of territory.

How do writers so aware that ideals in general, and the idea of America in particular, may be self-serving constructs go about constructing a hermeneutic fiction that analyzes the possibility of an independent America? I propose to open the question by looking at three discrete issues that reflect the problematics of independence and dependence. These are originality and imitation, nature and social history, and prophecy.

The first issue reflects the need to articulate experience that is peculiarly American in a tongue that belongs to colonial power. American writing, Anglo and Hispanic, reflects the dilemma Juan Marinello identified: "We *are* through a language that is our own while being foreign."[11] Although *all* language is in some sense foreign, American writing, lying at the seam between the New World and the "mother tongue," is more acutely aware of its condition. The problematic negotiation of the relationship between originality and imitation may be seen as a synecdoche for the negotiation of independence from Europe.

The second issue engages the critical commonplace that European fiction locates its characters in social history whereas American fiction positions them, often metaphysically, in nature. We might expect works that examine American independence from Europe, achieved or sought, to treat the interface between these two approaches. And although Melville's work takes its name from a whale and Carpentier's from a century (in Spanish it means the century of lights, the Enlightenment), the formal construction of both narratives brings the thematics of social history and nature into mutual confrontation.

Finally, both books announce their finales with the same quotation from the Book of Job: "I only am alone escaped to tell thee." The prophetic dimension of these novels also sheds light on their authors' different interpretations of American destiny.

ORIGINALITY AND IMITATION

The writing of Melville shares two strikingly opposed and remarkably fused characteristics with that of Carpentier. It is inordinately dependent both on books and on unusual experience. The relevant experiences are those of voyage and discovery and of fascination with exotic places and providential accidents. Of course, these adventures fed their narratives: Melville's jumping ship in the Marquesas formed *Typee* and his escape from the British Consul in Tahiti entered *Omoo,* even as the chance landing of a plane in Guadeloupe led Carpentier to Victor Hugues. More significantly, the adventitious form of these discoveries fed their conception of writing and of "America" as well.

This is particularly the case with Carpentier, in whom serendipitous adventure inspired his ontological theory of "lo real maravilloso americano" (marvelous American reality). His later discussion of the baroque supplies a complementary aesthetic and a style to flesh it out. This evolving body of theory, which bears critically on issues of originality and imitation, is fraught with contradictions that Carpentier does not always acknowledge. In his Parisian exile from 1928 to 1939, he learned from the surrealists that political and cultural vanguards were interdependent, as freeing words from the meanings established by positivism was an act against dominant ideology, and that the provincial local color of the Latin American realists of the 1920s and 1930s had failed to capture the essence of America.[12]

Yet in 1949 he published *El reino de este mundo* (*The Kingdom of this World*) with a prologue that employed an attack on the surrealists to define aesthetic resources peculiar to Latin America. "The magicians are becoming bureaucrats," he charged, by erecting "codes of the fantastic." During a visit to Haiti in 1943 he had found, in sharp contrast to the premeditated fabrications of the surrealists, the presence of "marvelous American reality" in the survival of a palace once inhabited by Pauline Bonaparte and in the traces of witchcraft in the landscape. He concludes that "because of its virginal landscape, its gestation, its ontology, the Faustic presence of Indians and blacks, because of the Revelation constituted by its recent discovery, by the fruitful racial mixtures that it favored, Latin America is far from having exhausted its wealth of mythologies."[13] In short, the physical, social, and cultural *realities* of America offer the vigilant artist ready material and liberation from conventions of time and causality.

His celebration of America notwithstanding, Carpentier's polemical prologue is far from an Emersonian repudiation of Europe. First, his pleasure in startling juxtapositions betrays his debt to surrealism. Then, the anomalous presence of the European palace in Haiti and the European pretensions of Henri Christophe are essential to his theory; traces of Europe may be deformed or estranged, but they must be there. Without the European conquest there could be no marvelous American reality; it is Creole in origin. And synchronisms delight because they violate European chronology. Finally, the very need to establish American *difference* reveals dependence, Western culture remaining a necessary reference point for the American world.

By the time Carpentier published *Explosion in the Cathedral,* his claims for extreme American originality were muted, and in his elaboration of the baroque he developed a theory more accommodating to the necessary link between America and Europe. He saw contemporary American novelists afflicted by a variation of Cortés's linguistic embarrassment, when he wrote to Charles V, "Not knowing how to name these things, I don't express them." In writing of their native ceiba, they could not depend on universal knowledge, as he assumed Heine could in naming the pine or the palm. Carpentier rejected recent novelists' solution of appending glossaries to support the use of local terms for flora and fauna. He believed that only a baroque style, "created by the necessity of *naming things,*" could give unfamiliar things their "life and consistency, weight and measure" because it "surrounds the particular, detailing it, coloring it, distinguishing it, to set it in relief and define it . . . to situate it in the universal."[14] Global resources of language and metaphor will be summoned to ambush the American particular.

Cultural interdependence is at the heart of Carpentier's baroque. He revels in combinations that express American difference: synchronic events, cultural syncretisms, *mestizo* society, and the amalgamation of styles from many epochs and cultures that characterize American buildings and cities. On the Caribbean seafloor Esteban finds the "earliest baroque of Creation": "forest of coral, with its texture of flesh, lace, and wool, its blazing auriferous, transmuted trees, alchemical trees . . . flamboyant ivy, twined in counterpoints and rhythms so ambiguous that all delimitation between the inert and the palpitant, the vegetal and the animal, was abolished" (p. 176). A baroque world demands a combinatory rhetoric the most blatant sign of which is the hyphen; in the Caribbean Esteban celebrates the "verbal amalgams" that convey the formal ambiguity of things that participate in several essences at once: trees called "acacia-bracelets," "pineapple-porcelain," "tisane-cloud" (p. 178).

With his definition of culture in 1979, Carpentier signals that he has made his peace with his dilemma: "I would say that culture is the accumulation of knowledge which permits a man to establish relations, beyond time and space, between two similar or analogous realities, explaining one in terms of its likeness to another which could have been produced many centuries before."[15] The artist of Nuestra America must be a comparatist.

In the early 1950s Carpentier devoted three articles in *El Nacional* to Melville, whose work had just begun to receive serious attention in the United States. In a small way, these essays repeat the "shock of recognition" with which Melville had responded to the works of Hawthorne. Carpentier celebrated Melville's interest in hemispheric America and his comparison between Europe and America in his story of a slave insurrection, "Benito Cereno." He admired his "marvelous power of giving a mythic, universal scale to any quotidian reality of life," his "power of expressing the authentic poetry of things"; and he quoted passages from Melville's essay of 1850, "Hawthorne and His Mosses," that bear directly on the issue of originality.[16]

"Bound" as an American "to carry republican progressiveness into Literature as well as into Life," Melville adopted in his essay the grand manner of Emerson: "Let us boldly contemn all imitation though it comes to us graceful and fragrant as the morning; and foster all originality, though at first it be crabbed and ugly as our own pine knots." But Melville also warned, more subtly, that "imitation is often the first charge brought against real originality." American writers, however, need not fear imitation, for – and this is the passage from which Carpentier quotes – "the world is as young today as when it was created; and this Vermont morning dew is as wet to my feet, as Eden's dew to Adam's. Nor has Nature been all over ransacked by our progenitors, so that no new charms and mysteries remain for this latter generation to find. . . . The trillionth part has not been said; and *all that has been said, but multiplies the avenues to what remains to be said.*"[17] We note that Melville shares with Carpentier a predilection for the trope of Adam as American writer. What is of greater interest is Melville's conviction that prior creation frees up space for the next writer rather than exhausting it. What Carpentier's prologue implies against the grain of its own argument is freely asserted here: Original writing springs from a transformation of existing traditions.

In July 1850, Melville was preoccupied with the issue of originality, for his reading of Hawthorne's stories, preceded by his first exhaustive reading of Shakespeare in 1849, was firing him to devote another year to rewriting his manuscript of what he called "the whaling voyage." Melville elaborated no theory of American literature and language, but his sense of their relation to Europe can be deduced from his use of Shakespeare. Melville lamented that Shakespeare died too soon to be an American. It prevented his being "a frank man to the uttermost," he wrote, adding "who in this intolerant universe is, or can be? But the Declaration of Independence makes a difference." Charles Olsen calculates the difference thus: "As the strongest literary force Shakespeare caused Melville to approach tragedy in terms of the drama. As the strongest social force America caused him to approach tragedy in terms of democracy."[18] As we shall see, the idea of American democracy enabled Melville to fashion artistic autonomy out of European materials.

Shakespeare's language was even more decisively useful to Melville than his dramatic form. "To endow the whaling industry with a mythology befitting a fundamental activity of man in his struggle to subdue nature," F. O. Matthiessen argues, Melville had to come into possession of "the primitive energies of words."[19] Shakespeare's language helped Melville to make homely American material take on enormous significance. The idiom of European grandeur and its rhetorical brilliance are employed paradoxically to glorify democracy even as their relevance is denied. In contrasting Ahab, "a poor old whale hunter," to "emperors and kings," he says, "all outward majestical trappings and housings are denied me. Oh, Ahab! what shall be grand in thee, it must needs be plucked at from the skies, and dived for in the deep, and featured in the unbodied air" (p. 199). Although Shakespeare knew that all trappings mask individuals' common humanity, Melville has the sanction of democracy to broaden this wisdom. Thus he clothes in royal language those on whose nakedness he insists, in his imperious summoning of the democratic muse: "If, then, to meanest mariners, and renegades and castaways, I shall hereafter ascribe high qualities . . . bear me out in it, thou just Spirit of Equality, which has spread one royal mantle of humanity over all my kind!" It is "the great God absolute! The centre and circumference of all democracy! His omnipresence, our divine equality!" (p. 160) whose holy leveling entitles Melville to ransack and remake the glorious traditions of Europe. In the remaking, the European source is stripped of its hierarchical identity. Europe is subordinated, absorbed, supplanted, and the hyphen, the mark of the difference that Carpentier retains, disappears.

Melville's renaming of the epic muse is linked to a remaking of genre that poses a contrast to Carpentier. *Moby-Dick*'s mixed genre is bound up with Melville's democratic claims. As if by natural right, he usurps what he wants of Milton's and Homer's epics as well as the dramatic verse of Shakespeare and the rhetorical prose of Carlyle and Browne; he plunders encyclopedias and contrives his own. The resulting transgression and transcendence of form express the defiant assertion of originality that is his American stance; but since Carpentier lacks this democratic sanction, all his allusiveness works to underscore his interdependence. For all its Kabbalistic codes and its modernist experiments with time,[20] the form of his novel, and its historical–psychological conception of character, is solidly in the tradition of Stendhal. The originality lies in his shipping that most European of traditions back and forth across the Atlantic to see how it fares. In short, Melville was right; the Declaration of Independence was decisive. Its unprecedented and all-consuming egalitarianism entitles him to use and transgress antecedent language and form. This zealous appropriation of literary resources stands in tension with the tragedy of expansionism that it documents. With Carpentier, cosmopolitan without a country, there is a different tension between form and content. His narrative repudiates European domination, but as an American "forever-not-yet," his language depends on Europe precisely to establish his difference.

There is quite another way in which both writers investigate originality, which has to do with the prodigious bookishness of both, the modernist foregrounding of artifice in their creations, and the frequent suggestion that the texts are wholly self-referential. Whales are folios, the voyage is writing, the French Revolution exists only as formulas of words always subject to reversal; the verbal creation of reality coexists with the possibility of its cancellation at any moment. At the same time and paradoxically, both writers suggest the possibility that, precisely by means of literature, literature may be superseded, the ineffable named, or the unseekable origin found.[21] The priority of American reality and, more precisely, the sense of American nature as the matrix of meaning are the usual context for these implications. Take, for example, Ishmael's repeated discovery of meaning in the "facts" about the whale. In noting that the whale's eyes are set far back on opposite sides of his head, he asks, "Is his brain so much more comprehensive, combining, and subtle than man's that he can at the same moment of time attentively examine two distinct prospects, one on one side and the other in an exactly opposite direction?" He finds this "as marvelous a thing in him, as if a man were able simultaneously to go through the demonstrations of two distinct problems in Euclid" (p. 429). The whale's vision suggests a utopian human goal.

Similarly Esteban, at the midpoint of the novel, contemplates a snail shell, "mediator between evanescent, fugitive, lawless, measureless fluidity, and the land, with its crystallizations, its structures, its morphology, where everything could be grasped and weighed." Coming out of the flux of the sea, it "contains exactly what the Mother lacked, concrete examples of linear development, of the laws of convolution, of a wonderfully precise conical architecture, of masses in equilibrium, of tangible arabesques which hinted at all the baroquisms to come" (p. 180). The spiral of the snail shell establishes the relation of the finite to the infinite, the tangible to the intangible, the present to the future. The spiral "had been present to the everyday gaze of maritime races, who . . . still lacked eyes to appreciate it," and Esteban begins to wonder what other signs nature might have strewn around him, "already complete, recorded, real, yet which I cannot understand" (p. 180). The original of the phrase "aun sin ojos para pensarla" is literally "still without eyes to think it." The "metonymic displacement" of this striking phrase is linked to Carpentier's notion of naming as imaginative recombining of linguistic signs drawn from global resources. Culture and history also present themselves to the creative mind as repositories of meaning,[22] but when we read nature, which stands more radically outside human categories, we are closer to the ineffable, to self-transcendence, and to the peculiar discovery of America. Ishmael's and Esteban's readings of nature are privileged ones, and as we shall see, the capacity to read "with eyes to think" must be wrested from history.

HISTORY AND NATURE

The nightmares of history in both novels are countered in some measure by reveries inspired by nature. The claims of social history and timeless nature are schematically set forth in the imagery of the two-page epigraph to *Explosion in a Cathedral*. The passage evokes Carpentier's note: "*El siglo de las luces* was the theatre of a gigantic struggle between the Temporal and the Absolute."[23] The speaker is Esteban, and the moment is his return voyage to the Caribbean with Victor from Europe. "I saw them erect the guillotine again to-night. It stood in the bows, like a doorway opening on to the immense sky – through which the scents of the land were already coming to us across an ocean so calm, so much master of its rhythm, that the ship seemed asleep, gently cradled on its course, suspended between a yesterday and a to-day which moved with us." The guillotine of Europe is made strange by its American context. It is now the innocuous door through which the Caribbean landscape reaches Esteban, and, as an emblem of European experience, it is the passage through which Esteban, like Carpentier, can for the first time in full consciousness enter America. But it is more, for it seems to "go ahead of us like a guide, resembling . . . some gigantic instrument of navigation." In this aspect, it is Victor's machine and will function to estrange America. It is the door through which, as a last resort, Americans will be "Europeanized."

In the symbolic system of *Moby-Dick,* nature is not so neatly distinguished from history; rather they are fused. The vessel that seeks the whale is also a microcosm of society, and the issues of race, industry, and authority are intrinsic to its adventure. In many ways the *Pequod* suggests the ship of state, and its fate portends the wreckage of civil war, but the novel resists political allegorical interpretation, embracing all political positions and undercutting the force of any one.[24]

Again in a more schematic fashion, Carpentier's original conception of his plot sets history against nature. He introduces the historically real European Hugues into the lives of three fictitious Americans (the two most important of whom will be richly associated with nature). Moreover, the movement of the plot accentuates the polarity of the book's themes. The novel commences in a prehistory or a utopian chaos to which the fictional characters regress after the death of the father. They abandon all authoritative institutions, convert the crates of commodities in the warehouse into a terrain of play, and mock time by reversing it, turning night into day. Victor's portentous knocking announces the arrival of history, although its full implications are not revealed to him all at once. By history I mean here the compulsion to act, to move through space because of the shortage of time. Beginning in flight from death, the historical actor consciously seeks life in an action that conceals the pursuit of death. Victor eventually leads Esteban into history and Europe. When Esteban returns and breaks free of Victor, he discovers American nature. Still later, Sofía initiates a parallel adventure, which inaugurates a complex synthesis of America and Europe, nature and history.

Melville's plot, albeit on a more symbolic level, also forestalls the main action of the voyage to introduce a prehistorical, or at least a pre-Cartesian, world. In "marrying" Queequeg in New Bedford, Ishmael enters a golden age of erotic unity. Queequeg is not separated from nature; he is his own interpretation, just as his meaning is integral to his skin on which it is tattooed. The portentous appearance of Ahab on the quarterdeck announces history. Ahab's relation to history is, of course, ambiguous – he aspires to transcend it even as he represents a linear notion of historical progress. Fired by Ahab's purpose and bound in brotherhood to Queequeg, Ishmael does not voyage between nature and history but has access to both in every moment on the same ship.

As revolutionary actors, Ahab and Victor share the project of carrying the *Rights of Man* farther than any precursor had done – Victor to America, Ahab to the very face of God. It is in the narrative unfolding of these projects that Melville and Carpentier analyze the problematic destinies of their respective Americas. Ahab is the culminating and terminal figure of the American Renaissance. His project embodies the assumptions of liberal democracy that animated Emerson and Whitman. Emerson's monism permitted him to believe uncritically in the unity of Lockean individualism and Rousseauan democratic equality. Whitman intermittently perceived their contradiction but embraced them in the great swinging arcs of his verse.[25] Ahab's enactment of his project lays bare the contradiction forever.

What makes Ahab's project, his pursuit of the white whale, attractive both to the reader and to his crew, even while on another level its madness is patent, is his refusal of a whole range of splits – physical, metaphysical, economic, and social – that rational modern life had seemed to exact. As such, Ahab's project is Emersonian. Emerson believed that American independence made possible metaphysical democracy; equality with God achieved through imaginative engagement of nature would in turn protect the self from the fragmentation endemic to contemporary economic and social life. But in the creation of an Ahab who has lost his leg to the whale, Melville puts these values radically to the test.

Ahab's tragedy is that of a betrayed Emersonian who seeks to recreate unity through revenge. In the physical realm, despite the testimony of his severed leg, he refuses the split between mind and body or between self and physical nature.[26] His determination to meet the whale on his own terms, man to man, as it were, is metonymic for his desire to come into possession of God's secrets, to make them accessible to human understanding. He refuses to accept an abstract God, hurling his histrionic challenge in "The Candles": "In the midst of the personified impersonal, a personality stands here" (p. 641). In the economic realm, he repudiates the alienating splits implied by owners, markets, and profits, proposing to replace all with a transcendent purpose. Hence in the social realm, he so craftily dramatizes his project to the crew on the quarterdeck that they rally to it as one, as if rampant individualism and the democratic will were a seamless whole.

In this last episode, the deception is transparent. The crew is drawn less by Ahab's metaphysical goal than by the doubloon for the one who raises Moby-Dick. To transcend the marketplace, Ahab must use the profit motive. The quarterdeck episode also exposes the social contradiction. Ahab's metaphysical democracy requires political tyranny. Starbuck is alive to this irony when he recalls Ahab's Emersonian shout on the quarterdeck: "Who's over me? Truth hath no confines." Starbuck mutters, "Who's over him, he cries; – aye, he would be a democrat to all above; look how he lords it over all below" (p. 228).

In fact, Ahab's furious attempt to heal splits results in his driving them deeper. The effort to unite mind and body ends in the domination, and even the reification, of the body by the mind: "He whose intense thinking thus makes him a Prometheus, a vulture feeds upon that heart for ever; that vulture the very creature he creates" (p. 272). Ahab's need to deny his own nature shows most poignantly in his rejection of Pip, the only one to have experienced the profound vision that Ahab ostensibly desires. The intense exercise of the will also precludes the openness necessary for "knowledge" of external nature. Ahab reads it as a solipsist or interrogates it with rhetorical questions.[27]

As Ahab's desire to connect the natural inside and outside himself gives way to his need to dominate both, his defeat is guaranteed. Ahab's purpose comes to *depend* on his *independence*. He too glimpses the necessity in his freedom, when he asks, "What cozzening, hidden lord and master, and cruel remorseless emperor commands me. . . . Is Ahab, Ahab? Is it I, God, or who, that lifts this arm?" (p. 685). The evolution of Ahab's absolutely free self-assertion into fatalism in the metaphysical sphere suggests an analogy in the economic: The Protestant exercise of free will that gave rise to capitalism leads inexorably to rigid laws. Ahab makes the analogy himself, saying, "The path to my fixed purpose is laid with iron rails, whereon my soul is grooved to run" (p. 227).

In the social realm the "inexorable self" exacts not only the domination of the crew in general but also a particular form of domination of the darker race. When Ahab's relation with Fedallah, his alter ego or dark brother, is contrasted with Ishmael's with Queequeg, we discern an epistemological explanation of racism, here conveyed through contrasting literary means of characterization. It is as if the literary creation of each dark figure is linked to his white alter ego's perceptual mode, which in turn stems from the white man's attitudes to individualism and equality. As a character, Queequeg is created in terms of symbolic integration, of a myth of primitive self-sufficiency; he is the most whole character in the book, a man "always equal to himself" (p. 83). In knowing Queequeg, in sharing his erotic epistemology, Ishmael is freed from ethnocentric prejudice and reconstitutes democratic and Christian values.

Ishmael has access to Queequeg because of his relative indifference to a sharp-etched individualism and to the fragmenting and dominating epistemology that subtends it. Fedallah, by contrast, is an allegorical figure, a shadow who emerges from hiding only with Ahab's vengeful purpose and as a metaphor for that purpose. Never shown in three dimensions, he remains a figment of fear and superstition even for the crew. Ahab, forever denied the holistic epistemology that supposes the possibility of social equality, projects Fedallah solipsistically, a fragment of himself. If racism is a function of epistemology, Ishmael's way of knowing makes it vanish, whereas Ahab's dominative way guarantees its prevalence.

Finally, the imperialist drive has a latent life in Ahab. It is the synthesis of the domination of nature and the domination of other peoples that already drives him. Imperialism is a potential and perhaps inevitable outgrowth of Emersonian individualism when it is severed from commitment to democratic equality.

In *Explosion in a Cathedral,* Carpentier translates Ahab's metaphysical project into purely historical terms. A self-creating individualism animates Victor Hugues as well as Ahab; but whereas Ahab desires so utterly to originate his own identity that in the process he will rival or even displace the Creator, Victor desires to emulate the most perfect man he knows. Neither accepts his own specific humanity. The shapes of both their lives have been wrenched by devastating losses – in Victor's case, the loss of his property to the premonitory fires of the Haitian Revolution. Like Ahab, Victor is an actor in both historical and histrionic senses. His theatrical penchant and chameleonic opportunism first stimulate him to imitate Robespierre freely, but imitation then becomes the ineluctable organizing principle of his life.

In Victor's imitative passion, Carpentier locates the problem of dependence for Latin America as surely as Melville locates the problem of U.S. independence in Ahab. As Ahab's authority draws on his denial of all external authority, Victor paradoxically develops confidence and real political power from his dependence on it. Thus, although he learns that the English have taken Guadeloupe during his voyage there, Victor rejects pragmatic retreats in the name of obedience: "In a Republic the military do not argue, they obey. To Guadeloupe we were sent, and to Guadeloupe we shall go" (p. 130). His daring is rewarded by his nearly miraculous defeat of the British. Again, when he learns in Guadeloupe of Robespierre's death, he stands under his portrait of the Incorruptible and refuses the news: "I shall continue to recognize no other morality except Jacobin morality. . . . And if the Revolution must perish in France, it will continue in America. The time has come for us to occupy the Mainland" (p. 156). So he insists that Esteban translate the Jaçobin Constitution and *The Declaration of the Rights of Man* into Spanish.

Homi Bhabha's essay "Of Mimicry and Man: The Ambivalence of Colonial Discourse" explains Victor's stance: "If colonialism takes power in the name of history, it repeatedly exercises its authority through the figures of farce. For the epic intention of the civilizing mission, . . . 'writ by the finger of the Divine' often produces a text rich in the traditions of *trompe l'oeil,* irony, mimicry, and repetition." Colonial mimicry is "constructed around an *ambivalence*; in order to be effective, mimicry must continually produce its slippage, its excess, its difference." Furthermore, "the ambivalence of colonial discourse repeatedly turns from *mimicry* – a difference that is almost total but not quite – to *menace* – a difference that is almost nothing but not quite."[28]

When Robespierre was at his height, Victor's mimicry contained a latent menace. When it survives Robespierre's defeat, the menace in the mimicry becomes overt. He builds power in the temporal space that separates him from Europe and delays the arrival of its mandates. He continues to raid Spanish ships even after France has signed a peace treaty with Spain. He becomes disillusioned with the United States, whose siding with the British he sees as aimed at driving France out of its American colonies: "The very name of American," he says, "inspires only scorn and horror here. . . . The same men who achieved independence are now denying everything which made them great" (p. 198). He urges the Directory to declare war on the United States, and when they refuse, Victor's privateers begin to seize U.S. vessels as well as those of Spain and England. Victor becomes literally the slaver Ahab is metaphorically, instructing his captains to sell in Dutch ports slaves from the captured ships of enemies of the republic. The privateers now make Point-à-Pitre the richest town in America, causing the old India Companies to be revived. The revolutionary governments of both Americas symmetrically betray their originating principles, reverting to the rawest spirit of conquest. Responding to Victor's one-man war, the United States declares war on France in American waters.

"The Robespierre of the Isles" (p. 173), as the American newspapers styled him, is now forcibly overthrown and deported by the Directory. Although Victor again converts this loss into triumph and returns invested as the agent of the Directory in Cayenne, he does so without menace to France or the United States. He resumes his posture of mimicry, this time with virtually no ambivalence, slavishly taking dictation from Paris, whether from the Directory or Napoleon, even when it means reinstituting the slavery it was once his pride to abolish. These final ironies should not distract us, however, from the significance of the extraordinary if brief moment of "slippage," or "difference," Victor had achieved in America. Unable to eliminate the distance – in space, time, and culture – between the metropolis and the periphery, the empire cannot fail to generate slippage in every instance. Its attempts at reproduction will inevitably miscarry, and its abortions may, in part and briefly, intimate a liberation to be fulfilled at a later moment.

In the end, Victor backs out of the novel as he came, via history, but history now hypostatized, abstracted from social and ideational context. Standing under a portrait of Bonaparte in Cayenne, Victor quotes him to Sofía, "The novel of the Revolution is written; our concern is to undertake its history, and, in applying its principles, to consider only what is realistic and feasible" (p. 323). Fatalist like Ahab at the end, Victor exits the novel of life to enter linear and unadorned "history," endorsing time as finitude and death. In seeking to impose a bourgeois European revolution on America, Victor has ignored not only American history but American nature as well. In the black comedy of the finale, he enacts all these misreadings of America by ordering the newly reenslaved blacks of Guiana to build him a Versailles-like park in the jungle. When the slaves take flight in that jungle, Victor pursues them with French soldiers seasoned in Napoleon's most arduous campaigns. But the forces of American nature – blacks, Indians, jungle, and jungle fever – combine to defeat the forces of Europe. "It's not war," says Victor hoarsely. "You can fight men, you can't fight trees" (p. 330).

"I'm going to conquer Nature here" (p. 324), Victor announces on the verge of his final folly; it is his last laconic echo of Ahab. The hubris of both, based on their identification of the heroic self with progress, leads to their inability or refusal to read nature except in a solipsistic way. Conversely, the relative modesty of Ishmael and Esteban and their ultimate rejection of the Enlightenment notion of progress fit them to read in an open and holistic, and perhaps a peculiarly American, way what I call American nature: that nonhuman reality presented for both writers chiefly by the sea, which by turns exposes the limits of human understanding and points beyond them.

Ahab draws Ishmael both into history and into the quest for deeper significance. After Ahab's riveting performance on the quarterdeck, Ishmael interrogates his own "wild, mystical, sympathetic feeling" in a long meditation on why the whiteness of the whale inspires him with vengeful terror. The associative and self-contained method of this speculation resembles that of Ahab; so do some of his findings. Essentially Ishmael demonstrates that the contradictions inherent in whiteness itself constitute an intolerable affront to the categories by which the human mind orders itself. To pursue the white whale is to insist on the preeminence of human mental categories over natural mysteries, or to close the gap between them with violence.

But at his side on Ahab's fiery hunt, Ishmael has his first mentor, Queequeg, a natural mystery in himself, who begins not only with the gap closed, but ignorant of all categories and divisions. With Queequeg and their fellow sailors squeezing the spermacetti on the sunny deck, Ishmael sits at the end of all quests, or as if before they were conceived. The body of nature, the whale's spermacetti, transforms the men even as they squeeze its solids back into fluid. The utopian relation of the individual to nature becomes a utopian social relation, with eros as the solvent. The slippery stuff they squeeze, called "sperm," causes Ishmael and the men to squeeze one another's hands, first by accident then by design, and while their individuality is lost in erotic communion, so is the alienation of labor.

If this scene suggests that American nature rightly read lends its auspices to a utopian American industry, the try-works scene that follows counters that the domination of nature intrinsic to the industry makes it demonic. While the blubber is being melted, the scene of men working over the flames at night seems to Ishmael "the material counterpart of the monomaniac commander's soul." Under its spell, susceptible Ishmael has another revery, as nihilistic as the other was utopian. Reflecting on this disparity, he reaches a vantage point between hell and paradise, in which he tries to assimilate Ahab's position, including but transcending it: "There is a wisdom that is woe; but there is a woe that is madness" (p. 541).

By now we should understand that all of Ishmael's positions are provisional. He is too ready a reader of experience to settle for any singular learning; he is the reader as sailor, navigating the flux of nature. As readers of Ishmael, we must take him provisionally as well. He is too innocent of devastation – he cannot know the woe of Ahab – to assimilate his meaning. And Ahab's meaning is imperial, crowding out the understanding of others. Ishmael may know natural secrets withheld from Ahab, as at the end of "The Grand Armada," where Queequeg and Ishmael arrive at the privileged center of a herd of nursing whales, but so is Ahab's fatal drive – dramatized at the beginning of that chapter when, pursuing whales, he is being pursued by pirates – unknown to Ishmael. As Ahab cannot know Ishmael's Eros, Ishmael cannot know Ahab's Thanatos.

Esteban passes through a period of initiation by Victor roughly similar to Ishmael's with Ahab. He first celebrates the man who has rescued him from illness and boredom and taken him to participate in the French Revolution. Yet even in Paris, the revolution eludes Esteban, seeming not native but imitative, "a gigantic allegory of a revolution rather than a revolution itself, . . . a revolution which had been made elsewhere, which revolved on a hidden axis" (p. 95). The work the revolution gives him, translation, places him at a further remove. Esteban's westward voyage reverses the meaning of his first eastward one. Having been to the source of history, he can now *see* America freed of the illusion that originality lies abroad. He develops a critical propensity toward Victor when he discerns his imitative dependency. In Guadeloupe, while Victor builds his power, Esteban takes a leave from the absurdity of historic revolution to engage the revelations of American nature.

Esteban begins to see independently from the top of a ceiba tree, whose "spiral staircase" he has climbed. In this "mother of all trees," he puts behind him the bladed tree of the guillotine and loses himself in a rich dream that combines eros with regression to the mother, though it is not without its imperialist reflex: "A man who embraces the tall breast of a tree-trunk is realizing a sort of nuptial act, deflowering a secret world, never before seen by man" (p. 162). This synthesis of healing, eros, and self-loss in nature recalls Ishmael; but the image of the spiral belongs only to Esteban.

Esteban's immersion becomes literal when he sails past the dark shadow of a whale and into latitudes that seem to belong to earlier centuries. He beaches, and the very light of nature, in contrast to the delusory light of the Enlightenment, produces "a state of lucid intoxication" in which suddenly he learns to swim. His greater affinity to nature than to history, to water than to land, culminates in his desire to become a fish. Then he finds the snail shell mentioned earlier. Its spiral, foreseen in the ceiba, is like the "hidden axis" he imagined at the center of the revolution in Paris, with the difference that it is now accessible and articulate. We will not understand all of its implications, however, until the end of the novel.[29]

Esteban's desire to escape the absurdity of history is deepened by a sudden hunger for his childhood home, which now seems to him the true utopia. On his circuitous journey to Cuba, he learns from a Swiss planter at Sinnamary of the long history of black uprisings in America, of which the Haitian is simply the best known. "All the French Revolution has achieved in America is to legalize the Great Escape which has been going on since the sixteenth century," he concludes (p. 231). This invisible pattern is the social equivalent of the snail shell, another instance of marvelous American reality that Victor cannot read. It is an American history concealed from the eye of the West like Remigio's herb garden in the secret patio of the bourgeois house in Havana. There the bust of Socrates, transformed by the Afro–Cuban cult of *santería* into an effigy of the Lord of the Forest, demonstrates (to adopt Pascal) that America has reasons that Western Reason knows not. In an almost involuntary gesture, throwing copies of the inflammatory *Rights of Man* into a slave boat in Surinam, Esteban furthers this subversive history.

Esteban's taste of the marvelous real in American history and nature helps him repudiate the Enlightenment. He sums it up in his cry to Sofía upon his return to Cuba: "I have been living amongst barbarians" (p. 248). But if he can unmask "civilization" to expose it as barbarism, he is not ready to announce that American culture can be found in demystifying "barbarism." His experience points that way, but it is a direction in which Esteban cannot go. Like Ishmael's opposition to Ahab, Esteban's to Victor is powerless and provisional.

Moreover, in Esteban's case, the passion of nature is displaced by his erotic desire for his erstwhile "mother" Sofía. His love is declared and rejected on a strange evening that begins as Christmas Eve and ends as New Year's Day, the first day of the new century. This stumbling of time signals its coiling upon itself to launch another loop in the spiral. With the close of the century of Enlightenment and the dawn of the romantic era, the action will pass from Esteban, who explored the limits of the first, to Sofía, who will press the possibilities of romanticism to its limits. It is Sofía's turn to apprentice herself to Victor's revolution by way of discovering her own. In initiating this replication of the plot, the ironic images of revolution as translation or performance become positive, for Esteban's translations of *The Social Contract* have stimulated Sofía to act, and Esteban distracts the police by impersonating a revolutionary agent, until she has escaped from Cuba.

In the creation of Sofía, analogies in characterization with *Moby-Dick* break down, for she presents in some measure a synthesis of Esteban's capacity for vision with Victor's for action that has no parallel in Melville. The passion that motivates her differs from Ishmael's eros in that the core of self is not lost in it, nor is the sense of history. In her single meditation on the sea, for example, she reflects on the jellyfish: "Sofía wondered at the continual destruction which was like a perpetual extravagance on the part of creation: the extravagance of multiplying only to suppress on a larger scale; only to surrender the fruits to a world in a state of perpetual voracity" (p. 77). Evincing the "smiling wisdom" that her name betokens, her acceptance here of the annihilation at the heart of nature's dialectic prepares us for the passionate rigor that distinguishes her feeling from Esteban's sentimentality and for her reckless courage at the end.

In the character Sofía, Carpentier breaks with the tradition of female representation in Latin America by refusing to allegorize her as land (though elsewhere he presents American land as woman) and by insisting on her historical agency. Emblematically, on her voyage to Victor she contemplates the land in the manner of a historic visionary. "A fabulous smell, of the humidity of a continent not yet properly awake" enables her to foresee Bolívar's revolution, which with all his "realism" Victor cannot. She senses that she is at "the beginning of something that would find expression in great troops of horses crossing the plains, in voyages up legendary rivers, in the crossing of high mountain ranges. An age was being born which would accomplish, here in America, what had come to naught in senile Europe" (pp. 303–5).

Sofía's relationship with Victor, which Carpentier saw as a "dichotomy" symmetrical with that between Victor and Esteban,[30] begins and ends with her rejection. Though she threw him out of her bedroom in Havana, Victor's advances "made her conscious of her own being," and she later accepts him. During her marriage to the bourgeois merchant, that passionate self sustains a hidden life, like the "riot of bright materials" and luxurious garments Esteban finds concealed in baskets supposed to contain her widow's weeds. Her first days of lovemaking with Victor in Guiana seem utopian: For Sofía they are "situated outside time," and she devotes herself "to exploring her own sensuality" as Esteban had explored the seafloor (pp. 312–13). But her passion was always for Victor the revolutionist; far from blinding her, it helps her to see his multiple betrayals of her ideal. She cannot defeat Victor any more than Esteban can, but she mutinies against him in leaving him.

Sofía mutinies again when she leads Esteban into the popular revolt against Napoleon's invasion of Madrid in 1809. The meaning of her last act, however, is highly ambiguous. She moves from the last of her sheltering houses into the street, snatching up antique weapons. "We've got to do something! . . . Anything!" she is said to have cried before disappearing with Esteban into what Carpentier styles the "Day Without End." If the baroque is characterized by its breaking out of the frame and its forward movement, as Carpentier says,[31] then Sofía's gesture is quintessentially baroque, one that suggests the inception of another swing of the spiral. Clearly Sofía has opted for the Novel of the Revolution, leaving Victor to play out his bankrupt History. But what does her Novel mean?

Carpentier frustrates our curiosity by having the final scene pieced together later by the stolid Carlos, who was as distant in spirit as in space from his relatives on May 2. Carlos learns only of their sentimental bond and of their having read Chateaubriand's *René*. Whether Sofía *saw* her last act as one of romantic desperation or as a repudiation, in resisting Napoleon's troops, of Victor and of all foreign influence, and if the latter, to what, if any, end – all this, and the interpretation of Carlos's presence at the end, is left for our construction. A similar task confronts us at the end of *Moby-Dick*. We are reminded that the words assigned to both Carlos and Ishmael as epigraphs near the ends of their texts, "I only am escaped alone to tell thee," were said to Job, thus initiating his test. So do they announce ours. The terrible isolation of the survivor who speaks these words, doubly stressed ("only," "alone"), can be relieved only by the act of telling and by the listener's taking on the burden of the tale. We inventory the wreckage with him.

PROPHECY

New World literature is often apocalyptic, as if the ultimacy of beginnings inevitably calls up endings. But an apocalypse is not only an ending; it is a revelation and implies a new beginning. Apocalypse is summation and prophecy.

One's interpretation of the prophecy in *Explosion in a Cathedral* depends on the extent to which one draws out its implications. The suggestion that the popular uprising of May 1808 betokens the correction of bourgeois revolution is countered by the fact that resistance to Napoleon brought about the restoration of reactionary Ferdinand VII. Those who reply that bourgeois Creoles like Carlos then rose against the restoration are answered by those who note that the Creoles negotiated their own internal domination and a new external dependence.[32] To extrapolate from our earlier discussion of Victor, popular liberation will indeed be forestalled in the establishment of new republics slavishly imitative of foreign ones; but in the imitative discourse of the neocolonial republics of Spanish America, slippage will recur. Americans like Martí will note the slippage and argue for a conversion of mimicry to the invention of an American discourse for America, the creation of a stance that will implicitly "menace" any imperialist design.

The sign binding together these prophecies is the spiral. No such trajectory emerges with Ishmael from the downward vortex of the sinking *Pequod*. Ishmael, an infinitely weightier figure than Carlos, remains the ceaseless quester and the source of the dream of utopian fraternal labor, but he points to no historical future. If the dialectical energy in Carpentier has an outlet in an endless spiral of unstable syntheses, in Melville it mounts as an implosive pressure, but does not break through its own impasse.[33] It is tempting to read whales' eyes and their impossible dual vision as Melville's prophetic sign. In a typical utterance, Ishmael draws on this bifocal image: "Doubts of all things earthly, and intuitions of some things heavenly; this combination makes neither believer nor infidel, but makes a man who regards them both with equal eye" (p. 480). Ahab and Ishmael are each in some sense the creation of the other, but they cannot be reconciled. And we cannot choose between the utopian vision of Ishmael and the demonic imperative of Ahab, because they are inseparable in American liberal democracy. Unable to view "with equal eye" the vision of natural brotherhood and the logic of imperialism, the reader comes to suffer the "insatiable unease" of the author.

"Words do not fall in the void": Carpentier's epigraph from the *Zohar* might stand for both works. The readers who write may best decipher this prophecy, since their works constitute the net above the void.[34] In Latin America, Carpentier's successors – eminently Gabriel García Márquez and Carlos Fuentes, who have acknowledged their debt to the Cuban, but others as well – continue to seek means of converting dependency to originality, historical circles to liberating spirals. In the United States, much of American literature, from Mark Twain to Norman Mailer, continues to be inscribed in a dichotomy in which industrial, urban, military, or technological power is countered by a pastoral vision, derived from relative closeness to nature, that is as impotent as it is harmonious. Those who follow Melville have lost the innocence of their independence and, like Latin Americans, inhabit a forever-not-yet-realized "America."

NOTES

I am grateful to Carol Ascher and Doris Sommer, and especially to Donald Moss and Daniel Kaiser, for their useful suggestions about this essay. My students at Purchase have deepened my appreciation of Carpentier, especially Deborah Mullaney, Andrew Hubbard, and David Shane.

1 Irlemar Chiampi, *El realismo maravilloso: Forma e ideologia en la novela hispanoamericana* (Caracas: Monte Avila, 1983), pp. 121, 129–31, 139. Several Hispanic Americans responded to the French naturalist Georges Louis Leclerc de Buffon, whose calumnies also stimulated Thomas Jefferson's *Notes on the State of Virginia*.

2 Juan de Onís, trans., "Emerson," *The America of José Martí* (New York: Farrar, Straus & Giroux), pp. 217–18.

3 Ibid., p. 141.

4 E. Mayz Valenilla, *El problema de América* (Caracas: Universidad Central de Venezuela, 1969), p. 92. Cited by Chiampi, *El realismo maravilloso*, pp. 164–5.

5 Although ironic distancing, of course, appeared in U.S. literature of the nineteenth century (witness Melville's *Confidence-Man*), the romantic authorial premise of *Moby-Dick* and the Titanic character of Ahab could no longer appear in serious Western twentieth-century discourse. The distinction between romantic and ironic modernism corresponds to that which I am drawing between U.S. independence and Spanish American dependence; witness the treatment of the ocean in these two epics. For Melville, it is the medium of the imagination: "The open independence of the sea" embodies the democratic meaning of America as the security of the land cannot. What interests him is the immediacy of the sea, its infinitely complex life and especially its depth, the deceptive relation between its layers, and even, through Pip, its terrible floor; its breadth is incidental. For Carpentier the ocean is all breadth. Esteban swims in a cove, Sofía muses on its surface, but its depths do not engage them. It is meant to be traversed. Each of the seven chapters begins or ends with an arrival or a setting sail, and the novel draws its ironic meanings from the dislocations resulting from the effort to carry Europe to America and from the transformation of America by its assimilation and resistance to the traffic from abroad. As the conditions of independence are underscored in a romantic metaphysical discourse, so are the conditions of dependence in an ironic distanced one.

6 See Angel Rama, "Una Revolución Frustrada," *Marcha,* no. 1207 (May 29, 1964): pp. 29–30.

7 Michael Paul Rogin, *Subversive Genealogy: The Politics and Art of Herman Melville* (New York: Knopf, 1983), pp. 21, 106.

8 Alejo Carpentier, *Explosion in a Cathedral,* trans. John Sturrock (New York: Harper & Row, 1963), p. 125. Subsequent references to this edition will appear in the body of the text.

9 Herman Melville, *Moby-Dick,* ed. Charles Feidelson, Jr. (New York: Bobbs-Merrill, 1964), pp. 507–10. Subsequent references to this edition will appear in the body of the text.

10 Alejo Carpentier, *Rotograbado de Revolución* (Havana, April 15, 1963), p. 5.

11 Juan Marinello, *Americanismo y cubanismo literarios* (Havana, n.d.), p. 6; cited by Roberto González Echevarría, *Alejo Carpentier: The Pilgrim at Home* (Ithaca, N.Y.: Cornell University Press, 1977), p. 29.

12 In a 1964 interview with César Leante, Carpentier said that the Parisian experience had made him see "textures, aspects of American life which I hadn't noticed, wrapped up as we were in the wave of nativism swept in by Güiraldes, Gallegos and José Eustacio Rivera"; cited by Chiampi, *El realismo maravilloso,* p. 11.

13 Translated by González Echevarría, *Carpentier,* p. 123.

14 Alejo Carpentier, "Lo barroco y lo real maravilloso," *Razón de ser* (Havana: Editorial Letras Cubanas, 1984), p. 78; "Problematica de la actual novela latinoamericana," *Tientos y diferencias* (Buenos Aires: Calicanto, 1976), pp. 35–6. In the latter essay, Carpentier adapts Sartre's theory of contexts to locate and explain the origin of the marvelous through its various contexts.

15   Alejo Carpentier, "La novela latinoamericana en vísperas de un nuevo
      siglo," *La novela latinoamericana en vísperas de un nuevo siglo* (Mexico City:
      Siglo ventiuno, 1981), p. 17.
16   Alejo Carpentier, "Revelación de Melville," September 39, 1951; "Herman
      Melville y La América Latina," April 2, 1955; "Una carta de Melville," June
      8, 1954. All three essays appeared in *El National*.
17   Herman Melville, "Hawthorne and His Mosses," *Moby-Dick: An Au-
      thoritative Text, Reviews and Letters by Melville* (New York: Norton, 1967),
      pp. 543–6; emphasis mine.
18   Charles Olsen, *Call Me Ishmael: A Study of Melville* (San Francisco: City
      Light Books, 1947), pp. 29, 42, 69.
19   F. O. Matthiessen, *American Renaissance: Art and Expression in the Age of
      Emerson and Whitman* (London: Oxford University Press, 1941), p. 423.
20   See González Echevarría, *Carpentier*, pp. 226–56.
21   For such discussion of Melville, see especially Charles Feidelson, *Symbolism
      and American Literature* (University of Chicago Press, 1953); James Guetti,
      The Limits of Metaphor: A Study of Melville, Conrad, and Faulkner (Ithaca,
      N.Y.: Cornell University Press, 1967); and Jonathan Arac, *Commissioned
      Spirits: The Shape of Social Motion in Dickens, Carlyle, Melville and Hawthorne*
      (New Brunswick, N.J.: Rutgers University Press, 1979). For Carpentier,
      see González Echevarría, *Carpentier*.
22   See Raúl Silva-Cáceres, "Un desplazamiento metonímico," *Imán*, vol. 1
      (Havana: Editorial Letras Cubanas, 1983), pp. 219–28. Consider, for exam-
      ple, the painting Ishmael studies at the Spouter Inn and the Neapolitan
      painting that gives Carpentier's book its English title; consider the names of
      ships, how both the *Pequod* and the slave ship called the *Contrat Social* repre-
      sent the ironic return of the historical repressed.
23   Loose sheet written in Carpentier's hand found with the manuscript of the
      novel, Biblioteca Nacional José Martí, Havana.
24   In fact, the allegorical readings that abounded in the 1960s refuted one
      another: in one Ahab represents William Lloyd Garrison, in a second the
      compromising Daniel Webster, and in a third, John. C. Calhoun. See
      Rogin, *Subversive Genealogy*, p. 108.
25   See Doris Sommer's essay (Chapter 4) in this volume.
26   See Sharon Cameron's provocative argument that the desire to reunite with
      the world's body motivates Ahab, in *The Corporeal Self: Allegories of the Body
      in Melville and Hawthorne* (Baltimore, Md.: Johns Hopkins University Press,
      1981), p. 25.
27   See, for example, Chapter 70, "The Sphynx," in which Ahab interrogates
      the whale's head.
28   Homi Bhabha, "Of Mimicry and Man: The Ambivalence of Colonial Dis-
      course," *October* 29 (1984): 126–7. The logic of this formulation replicates on
      a political plane the polemical impulse of marvelous realism: to find the
      "menace" of independence by way of mimicry.
29   The spiral image, midbook, informs its structure; the second half may be
      read both as its winding backward, as many events are repeated and re-

versed, and, because of changes accompanying the repetition, as a spiraling onward.

30 Interview with Carpentier, *Granma,* April 6, 1969, p. 10.

31 Carpentier, "Lo barroco y lo real maravilloso," pp. 60, 66.

32 See Julio Ortega on the last position, in *Poetics of Change: The New Spanish American Narrative* (Austin: University of Texas, 1984). Carlos Fuentes sees in the novel a tragic dialectic, which nevertheless, because liberty is a "permanent aspiration," points to perpetual revolution; *La nueva novela hispanoamericana* (Mexico City: Cuadernos de Joaquín Mortiz, 1969), pp. 50, 55. In an essentially idealist reading, Ariel Dorfman suggests that imagination and nostalgia preserve defeated dreams; see his *Imaginación y violencia en América* (Santiago: Editorial Universitaria, S.A., 1970).

33 In "Los productivos años setenta de Alejo Carpentier," Angel Rama offers a suggestive account of Carpentier that stands between these alternatives. The symmetrical series of events in *El siglo de las luces,* he argues, are kin to the norms of baroque writing in which "proliferating nuclei . . .substitute themselves for one another . . . in an incessant expectancy which turns out always to be blocked." This "constancy of compression can be attributed to the social context and is exercised on forces that are unleashed without power to achieve their ends" (*Latin American Research Review* 16 [1981]: 230).

34 The subsequent work of the authors themselves, of course, constitutes one kind of interpretation. Melville's descent into darkness after *Moby-Dick* may be read as his confession of inability to bear buoyantly, and without the support of a reading public, the weight of his discoveries. Carpentier's fate was in some ways the reverse, since the triumph of the Cuban revolution and the ensuing celebration by Nuestra America coincided with the completion of *Explosion in a Cathedral.* Although he has said that he had expected the revolution since the days of his adolescence (González Echevarría, *Carpentier,* p. 218), its existence doubtless altered the impulses of his work in incalculable ways, which are beyond the scope of this essay.

3

The fiction of national formation

The *indigenista* novels of James Fenimore Cooper and Rosario Castellanos

CYNTHIA STEELE

Indigenista fiction, that is, fiction treating the conflicts between native American and dominant, nation-building societies, reached its apogee in the United States during the Age of Jackson (1820–60), as it did in Mexico after the revolution (1920–60). Both were nationalistic periods characterized by rapid industrialization and modernization and by the institution of definitive programs for federal Indian policy. Because of this confluence of economic, political, and cultural factors, the fiction produced in these two periods offers a singular opportunity for exploring connections among political policy, national ideology, and literature. In this essay I shall undertake such an exploration through the analysis of the social theory implicit in the works of the key *indigenista* writer of each period: James Fenimore Cooper in the United States and Rosario Castellanos in Mexico. As different as the works of these novelists are – and the products of such diverse literary and historical contexts could not help but differ greatly – they nevertheless share certain key features, as well as corresponding ideological implications. For instance, both novelists treat historical events as mediated through characters who are non-Indian and yet are somehow marginal to the dominant society. Both employ the image of what was called Savagism in Jacksonian America as a principal agent of historical causality.

In both Jacksonian America and postrevolutionary Mexico, Indian policy responded to the nation's economic needs. In the antebellum United States black slaves and white wage laborers created a labor surplus, while unprecedented immigration from Europe produced an ever increasing demand for Indian lands. The political consequences of these circumstances in the United States were Indian removal and the establishment of the reservation system. Mexico, in contrast, had depended heavily on Indian labor since the conquest; its need after the revolution

60

was to incorporate further the Indian into national society in order to ensure the continued, harmonious modernization of the country. In both national ideologies the "Indian problem" was attributed to the "fact" that Indians stubbornly remained at a stage of societal development anterior to that of those who were taking over and improving Indian lands. In Jacksonian America the paradigm of the dual society was set by the conflict of Savagism and Civilization; for Mexicans a century later it was set by the conflict of the primitive and the modern. In both cases, political decisions were understood to be responding to the imperatives of national progress.

Writing in the second quarter of the nineteenth century, James Fenimore Cooper was influenced by both Locke and eighteenth-century French and Scottish social scientists. From Locke he adopted the concept of the inevitability and desirability of social change and economic development. From the Scots (themselves influenced by Locke) he derived the stages-of-civilization theory, which held that European (and hence Euramerican) civilization had evolved out of prior civilizations based on simpler economic modes.[1] For Cooper, as for his sources, commercial and agricultural civilization represented the highest form of social development that had yet existed. Hence he believed it to be Americans' Manifest Destiny – as it was to be called – to disseminate this culture throughout the continent, thereby replacing the historically anterior, and so morally inferior, culture of the American Indians.

This "civilizing process" is represented in the Leatherstocking Tales by the succession of Cooper's three "stages of settlement" as defined in *Home as Found* (1838). Having defeated the Indian, the semibarbarian frontiersman gives way to the farmer, who in turn yields to the merchant and statesman. Leatherstocking represents the frontiersman, that traditional social type created by the clash between the New and Old World civilizations, Savagism and Civilization. He epitomizes the ideological contradictions of Cooper's age. Though he laments the passing of the noble red man, he dedicates his life to Indian fighting. As he paves the way for commercial and industrial development across the continent, he recoils from the corruption and destruction that follow in its path. As the advance guard for Civilization, he is to be its final casualty.

Critics have frequently remarked on the increasing idealization of Leatherstocking in the course of the tales; to this trajectory there corresponds an increasingly ambivalent narrative attitude toward violence. From the seasoned, half-wild hunter of *The Pioneers*, Natty evolves into the exultant killer of *The Last of the Mohicans*, then into the tired and reformed killer-cum-trapper of *The Prairie*. In *The Pathfinder* he is again the Indian fighter in his prime, ever quick on the draw and yet (as in *The*

Prairie) somewhat uneasy about the moral implications of his profession. Finally, as the novice Indian fighter of *The Deerslayer*, Natty is ostensibly concerned to justify the morality of his actions, yet he approaches his first killing reverently, almost lovingly.[2] Having tenderly laid his first savage opponent to rest (carrying him to the lake for a drink and cradling the dying man's head in his lap), Leatherstocking embarks on his violent career (ironically, precisely as his fictional career ends) confidently, even enthusiastically. The culmination of his "first warpath" is the annihilation of an entire Iroquois village.

Cooper was particularly alarmed by what he saw as the rise of the mercantile mentality in America, unchecked by adequate social controls. On the frontier (and for Cooper and his contemporaries, all of America was still a frontier) the Jacksonian profit motive encouraged lawlessness, as illustrated fictionally by characters like Ishmael Bush of *The Prairie* (1827) and Harry March of *The Deerslayer* (1841). For Cooper the only safeguards against American immorality and cultural regression could be provided by a strong civil law administered under the enlightened guidance of a landed gentry.

Yet as he progressively idealized Leatherstocking, Cooper grew increasingly pessimistic about those who would replace the frontiersman in American society. In *The Deerslayer* the standard aristocratic hero and heroine are missing altogether, and their middle-class counterparts are doubled and deformed. The middling hero is doubled into Leatherstocking and his dark underside, the Indian hater Hurry Harry. The heroine becomes a grotesque parody of the light–dark convention: the virtuous but feeble-minded Hetty and the bright yet immoral Judith. The daughters reflect the sins of the parents: their late mother, an aristocrat who succumbed to passion and deceit, and their stepfather Tom Hutter, a squatter and former pirate whose greed and lack of scruples lead him to seek the scalps of Indian women and children. Each parent suffers a punishment appropriate to his or her sin. Fallen aristocracy is buried in the anonymous depths of the American wilderness, and Jacksonian venality falls victim to the Savagism in which it has participated: Tom Hutter, merchant of human blood, is himself scalped alive.

Thus, although the tales ostensibly focus on Indian characters, their central concern is not with the Indian, whose defeat was seen by the 1820s as a fait accompli, but rather with the settlers who would displace him. Incidentally, the tales justify this process of displacement. As Roy Harvey Pearce has established, Cooper achieves a fictional justification for Indian removal and destruction in the image of the savage. Combining noble and ignoble savage qualities, Cooper's Indian characters share certain virtues and vices that were considered peculiar to savage society.

Cooper's Indians continued a long tradition in American literature; yet in his novels they were "imaged so powerfully that no one could doubt that they had to be destroyed."[3]

The massacre of Fort William Henry is a case in point. As the British women and children are leaving the fort after the French victory, Montcalm's Huron allies unexpectedly attack. Maddened by the sight of their victims' blood, the Indians drink "freely, exultingly, hellishly, of the crimson tide." Michael D. Butler has demonstrated that this passage exemplifies Cooper's view that historical events were governed by the concept of "fatal inertia"; this idea is developed in Montcalm's reflections before the massacre, to the effect that his alliance with the Hurons has set "in motion an engine which it exceeds human power to control."[4]

Because the Mexican nation was colonized gradually, over a period of centuries, the frontier never acquired the symbolic importance that it had for North Americans. There was no "westward movement" to measure the growing strength and prosperity of Mexican society. Similarly, the frontier Indian war was never the widespread phenomenon that it was in the nineteenth-century United States. Most Indian groups had been incorporated into the national economy at the time of the conquest, and the few northwestern tribes that had remained independent were subdued during the nineteenth century, through both exterminatory warfare and massive deportation programs. By the twentieth century, Indian responses to domination were uniformly those of a colonized people: acculturation, passive resistance, and, decreasingly, insurrection.

After the Mexican Revolution, policy makers and intellectuals turned to the Indian both as a source of nationalistic pride (an attitude that was popularized by the muralists) and as a bothersome impediment to national progress. During the 1930s *cardenismo* extolled the dormant virtues of noble savage *campesinos* at the same time that it deplored their "backwardness." Until the 1970s, Mexicans continued to view Indian society as frozen in the same abject state to which it had been reduced by the conquest. If Indian society had remained static for four centuries, then only sustained contact with a more "progressive" society could change it.

During the late 1950s, the nationalistic optimism and social reformism of *cardenismo* (as expressed in the works of writers like Gregorio López y Fuentes and Francisco Rojas González) gave way to disillusionment with the fruits of the revolution. During the 1940s and 1950s ethnologists and others with extensive firsthand knowledge of the Indian began to produce literature incorporating Indian language and mythology. Their fiction attempts to demystify the stereotypes of earlier *indigenista* fiction and to open itself for the first time to the referents, Indian culture and psychology.

Rosario Castellanos was the first Mexican novelist – and the only one to date – to explore seriously both the social and psychological mechanisms of race relations in Mexico. In an interview with Emmanuel Carballo that took place in 1962, the year that her second novel, *Oficio de tinieblas,* was published, Castellanos revealed that her fictional treatment of these matters was profoundly influenced by the social theories of French philosopher Simone Weil. In particular she was intrigued by Weil's explanation of the dialectical relationship between the oppressor and the oppressed, "the current of evil that goes from the strong to the weak and that returns again to the strong."[5] This theme recurs throughout the two novels and the collection of short stories that Castellanos wrote between 1956 and 1961 while she worked for the Insituto Nacional Indigenista (INI) in Chiapas.

According to Weil, oppression is an inevitable product of human nature within technological society. Oppression is created by the struggle for power, which is never absolute and so requires continual reaffirmation. Power "weighs as pitilessly on those who command as on those who obey . . . [creating a vicious circle in which] the master produces fear in the slave, by the very fact that he is afraid of him, and vice versa." When an oppressed group finally succeeds in defeating one team of oppressors, it is only to replace it with another.[6]

The influence of Weil's social theory on Castellanos's work is neatly illustrated by the short story "La tregua," which appeared in the collection *Ciudad real* (1960). In this story, when a dying *ladino* (i.e., a non-Indian) stumbles into a remote Tzotzil village, the Indians make the stranger a scapegoat for their accumulated frustration and anger. Crop failure had turned them for a livelihood to the manufacture of alcohol, for which they were violently punished by the *ladino* authorities. Degraded by a lifetime of misfortune, the Indians submitted to the *ladinos'* cruelty with a sort of eager fascination. Now, assuming the intruder to be an emissary of the same sadistic authorities, they turn themselves over to him for further violence. When the villagers realize that the dying man is in no position to punish them, their submission suddenly gives way to rage. Declaring the helpless stranger to be the evil spirit that has brought about all of their misfortunes, they proceed to beat him brutally and hack him to death. Then, having vented their anger, they calmly return to their daily routine, until the day when crop failure or an epidemic will prompt them to murder again. "La tregua" vividly illustrates Weil's concept of the vicious circle of fear and violence that is created by oppression. For Castellanos, as she explains in the interview with Carballo, social relationships are ruled not by justice but by force. When one group acquires power over another, it uses this power according to the dictates of its passions.

Whereas the marginality of Cooper's frontiersmen derives from their social position within white male society, that of Castellanos's protagonists usually derives from their sexual and/or cultural identity. In *Balún-Canán* (1957) the autobiographical protagonist is the seven-year-old daughter of an aristocratic landowning family that is threatened by Cárdenas's agrarian reform program. Initially the girl's innocence grants her insight as insight is accorded to children in Faulkner's work. She understands the subservient world of her Tzotzil nanny; yet by the end of the novel she too has adopted the attitude of the oppressors. In *Oficio de tinieblas* the two female protagonists epitomize the psychological conflicts resulting from the power relationships existing within Indian and *ladino* societies. As women they pertain to the most oppressed segment of their respective societies; yet each of them attempts to compensate for her marginal position by using culturally accepted means to acquire control over those around her. Julia Acevedo, the common-law wife of the agrarian reform agent, attempts to gain access to aristocratic society by taking as her lover her husband's principal enemy, Chiapas's most powerful landowner. Catalina Díaz Puiljá, the victim of Tzotzil sanctions against female sterility, is driven to adopt the role of shaman, and ultimately to spearhead a revitalization movement, as alternative means of winning her community's respect. In both cases the personal and social consequences of these women's actions are devastating. Julia's betrayal contributes to the violent repression of the Chamula rebellion and leads to her husband's death; Catalina's revelations lead to the massacre of innocent *ladino* and Tzotzil victims and to the grisly murder by crucifixion of her adopted son.

The revitalization movement serves as the central metaphor for the destructive power relationships between the two societies. Believing the *ladinos'* socioeconomic power to derive from their religion, the Chamulas attempt to acquire power for themselves by imitating Christianity. Eventually they carry this imitation to its "logical" conclusion by crucifying their own "savior." Ironically, the boy they choose to be their savior is the offspring of the landowner and a Chamula girl whom he raped and thus of the violent master–slave relationship the Chamulas are seeking to reproduce with themselves in the position of power.

As Castellanos explains in her interview with Carballo, she differs with writers of *cardenista* fiction in seeing the Indian as neither mysterious nor poetic: "What happens is that they live in atrocious misery. It is necessary to describe how poverty has atrophied their best qualities." At the same time that poverty has atrophied the Mexican Indians' virtues, it has accentuated their tendencies toward violence, treachery, and hypocrisy.[7] This notion of cultural atrophy recalls the Jacksonian paradigm of anterior and posterior levels of societal development. In Castellanos's fiction the modern/primitive paradigm is implicit in her treatment of history as lineal and progressive for the *ladino* characters, and yet mythic/cyclical, or simply static, for the Indians. Thus *Oficio de tinieblas* concludes with the Chamula survivors retreating to the mountains, where they regress to the Stone Age: "Naked, poorly dressed in rags or loin cloths of half cured leather they have abolished the time that separated them from past ages. Neither before nor today exists. It's always. Always defeat and always persecution."[8]

Because the Indian's memory is less constant than the *ladino*'s, the Indian's goals and purposes are easily engulfed by a wave of violence, which becomes an end in itself.[9] In *Oficio de tinieblas* this chain reaction is portrayed vividly in the description of the Chamula insurrection. The rebels quickly lose sight of their political purpose and proceed mindlessly, attacking randomly out of fear, anger, greed, and despair. When at one point they happen upon a church filled with women, children, and old people, they indulge in an orgy of rape and slaughter. One Chamula carefully quarters and dissects corpses, hoping thus to find the source of *ladino* power.

The similarity between this description of savage violence and those in Cooper is striking. As we have seen, Cooper created this image of Savagism as a symbol for all that Americans must overcome, culturally and morally, in order to achieve maturity. If Cooper's frontiersmen lament the passing of the noble red man, they are still, fundamentally, Indian fighters. In celebrating national expansion and consolidation, the Leatherstocking Tales justify the Indian's removal and destruction.

Like Cooper, Castellanos is interested primarily in the moral constitution of the dominant society; yet for her the Indian's foes are not liberators, but oppressors. If the key concept in Cooper is progress, in Castellanos it is liberty. Her concern is to elucidate the social and psychological mechanisms of oppression as it operates within Mexican and Tzotzil societies; yet at the same time that she demystifies the noble savage of *cardenista* fiction, she returns to the image of Savagism as defined by Cooper. The effect not only dehumanizes the Mexican Indian, but is also profoundly pessimistic about the future of Mexican race relations.

NOTES

1 Ronald Meek, *Social Science and the Ignoble Savage* (Cambridge University Press, 1976), p. 2; Roy Harvey Pearce, *The Savages of America: A Study of the Indian and the Idea of Civilization,* rev. ed. (Baltimore: Johns Hopkins University Press, 1965), pp. 82–91.

2 Yvor Winters, "Fenimore Cooper, or the Ruins of Time," in his *In Defense of Reason* (Denver, Colo.: Alan Swallow, 1947), pp. 188–90.

3 Pearce, *Savages*, pp. 99–101.

4 Michael D. Butler, "Narrative Structure and Historical Process in *The Last of the Mohicans*," *American Literature*, 48, no. 2 (May 1976): 118–19.

5 Emmanuel Carballo, "Rosario Castellanos: La historia de sus libros contada por ella misma," *La Cultura en México*, no. 44 (December 19, 1962) (literary supplement of *Siempre!*, no. 495, p. 3).

6 Simone Weil, *Oppression and Liberty*, trans. Arthur Wills and John Petrie, ed. F. C. Ellert (Amherst: University of Massachusetts Press, 1973), pp. 65–9.

7 Carballo, "Rosario Castellanos," pp. 4–6.

8 Rosario Castellanos, *Oficio de tinieblas*, 4th ed. (Mexico City: Editorial Joaquín Mortiz, 1975), p. 362. The ideological implications of Castellanos's treatment of time have been studied by Joseph Sommers, "Forma e ideología en *Oficio de tinieblas* de Rosario Castellanos," *Revista de Crítica Literaria Latinoamericana* 4, nos. 7 and 8 (1978): 80.

9 Carballo, "Rosario Castellanos," p. 4.

4

Supplying demand
Walt Whitman as the liberal self

DORIS SOMMER

This essay is the first of a projected series that will consider how very different readers in Spanish America have responded to Whitman's invitation to write and to justify him. The series will bear the general title "Walt Whitman, Left, Right and Center: The Contest for a Legitimate American Poetry in Neruda, Borges and Paz." Although it is only half-written, the titles of chapters announce themselves almost imperiously, leaving spaces I feel bound to fill in. One title is "Paz and Whitman: Bearing the Contradictions"; I am not yet sure, however, how to spell "baring" because that homophone suggests the double effect of time for Whitman's heirs. His project to identify self-love with the general good may be untenable, but it also may be what identifies us as Americans. Paz evidently recognizes the predatory tendency in Whitman's expansive democracy, but his own loyalties to the double goal of personal and political freedom lock Paz into an anxiety of influence. The chapter on Borges will probably be called "I Am You, You Are Me, So We Are Neither," in reference to Borges's Schopenhauerean "misreading" of Whitman. Rather than imagine democracy as the free exercise of multiple and discrete wills, Borges imagines it as the freedom from stable or coherent identities. The completed essay on Neruda already calls itself "How Neruda Rights What Whitman Left Out." In case the pun too tersely suggests my direction, or in case that direction surprises the reader to the point of doubting whether I mean what I wrote, I should explain that the essay calls into question the "leftist, democratic" quality of Pablo Neruda's poetry. His self-avowed rights to the Whitman patrimony allow him to write in all the gaps left open. Neruda's admiration for the master may have displaced Whitman's narcissism with love for others; but I argue that it did so, ironically, by re-placing self-love with the hierarchy-producing secondary narcissism of hero worship.

How can we account for this spectrum of readings and readers? That these and other admirers read Whitman as democracy's poet for the Americas suggests how plurivalent the terms "democracy" and "America" are. How did Whitman manage to keep them so broad as to assimilate the starkest differences? For an answer we should consider his literary construction of liberal democracy, which paradoxically owes more to what he left unwritten than to what he wrote, because of, rather than in spite of, the narcissism that embarrasses some of his admirers. Despite their discomfort, Whitman's cosmic self is the necessary origin of the equalizing intimacy he manages to establish with his reader in *Leaves of Grass*. By supplying this perfect self as the ideal lover for each of his readers, Whitman elicits our desire for him. By appealing to us, in both senses of that word, through a laconic and fragmentary book, Whitman invites the reader-lover to be coauthor. The empty and unpredictable spaces in the poems promise free and equal erotic exchange, and therefore also promise to level the traditional hierarchy of writer over reader. This does more than reaffirm the ideal equality of American subjects. It *constructs* that equality by seducing each reader into becoming Whitman's ideal lover and counterpart. The question I raise here is whether Whitman's construction allows for the community of differences that a liberal democracy presumes, or whether (in the spirit of Tocqueville's critique) it imagines democracy as a cloning process in which citizens all look suspiciously like the ideal Whitman.

It is probably evident that I am interested here in the relationship between literature and ideology. This has long been a focus for marxist theory, though traditional marxist criticism assumes that literature is a "reflection" of a given historical content. But since Louis Althusser's redefinition of ideology as "the representation of the subject's *Imaginary* relationship to his or her *Real* conditions of existence,"[1] political readings of literature tend to ask how poetry, for example, affects its readers and therefore effects the historical change the older criticism took for granted as determined by an economic base. To point out that Althusser's redefinition owes its terminology to Jacques Lacan's neo-Freudian psychoanalysis may indicate something of the direction this essay takes. The political will lead ineluctably to the psychoanalytic, not for particular biographical reasons but because the production of ideology involves, as Althusser illustrates in his vocabulary, an intersubjective region of the unconscious. Ideology, then, is not "false consciousness" but a shared Imaginary relationship to the world. How is it produced and modified, and how is it assimilated by groups of people? These will be the questions I pose to the example of Whitman's ideological production.

Whitman intentionally left empty spaces in his poetry, between the fragments and within the fragments themselves. He chose not to fix or finish them in the etymological sense of making perfect, because no living thing ever reaches the stasis of perfection (Preface, pp. 24, 28).[2] Some of his readers are annoyed by the sloppiness, notably Mark Van Doren, whose 1945 essay continues to introduce the widely distributed *Portable Walt Whitman.* "Whitman had the illusion, common to prophetic natures, that everything he said must be right because he said it. Poetry has a special way of exposing the error, for it demands its own kind of rightness, regardless of any other. Whitman did not regularly take the trouble to be right as a poet. He has paid the penalty" (p. xxiv). Whitman's own 1855 Preface is not an excuse for the rawness and dissonance of some of his work; it is a manifesto for it, for a new American poetry that is not always just right. The self-conscious rawness is taken up again in a preface of 1872, where, after several editions that added to, deleted from, and rearranged the book, Whitman finally defends the coherence of *Leaves of Grass.* Yet he insists, sounding almost like a Derridean reader of his own texts, that writing goes on, in "the surplusage forming after that volume." Of the current "supplementary volume" he confesses uncertainty, since "there is no real need of saying anything further. But what is life but an experiment? and mortality but an exercise? . . . If incomplete here, and superfluous there, n'importe – the earnest trial and persistent exploration shall at least be mine."[3] The model of disturbance that Whitman offers allows for variations that should make the reader an accomplice, inviting him or her to fill in the ellipses and to fit into the gaps between the fragments, so that a democratic poetry is produced every time a reader takes up Whitman's invitation to be his equal. If Whitman's Americanness meant kissing old models affectionately but unflinchingly goodbye, as he does in the first paragraph of the 1855 Preface, then his heirs should do the same. "He honors most my style who learns under it to destroy the teacher" (SOM, 47, p. 91). On the next page he repeats, "I teach straying from me," but adds immediately, "yet who can stray from me?"

This contradiction between Whitman's apparent invitation to equality and his assumption that equality, diversity, and ultimately Americanness are embodied in him is one major concern of the present essay. Another is why Whitman's disavowal of conflict in his "unfinished" pieces seems to legitimate competing political "misreadings." What does it mean for Whitman to love the American ideal by loving his ideal self, which he offers as our model too? Like Narcissus, Whitman is in love with his own mirror image repeated by the reader, who has been seduced into staring back from the other side of the poems. Are the spaces that Whitman left open the emptiness that provides the site of real dialogue with an equal counterpart? Or are they the flat and predictable surfaces already informed by a master poet who leaves room enough only to repeat himself and for whom equality can mean only an identity with his own infinite self, an equality that disavows any differences?

Ironically, an heir such as Pablo Neruda seems indifferent to the problem; he will destroy his teacher by resuscitating older models that never even tempted the reader with a promise of equality and the like of whom Whitman had kissed off in the Preface to his poems. Neruda's colossal *Canto general* (1950) writes in and closes off the spaces for the poet's interlocutor by returning the model of America's new fragmented "epic" to a familiar tradition of apparently seamless romantic narrative. It sets Whitman's rawness right; it tames the earlier and more revolutionary aesthetic until what is left of Whitman is the figure of the father, something Whitman claimed he never wanted to be. Neruda thus reaffirms the political usefulness of representative romance over a poetry of "pure possibility"[4] and reestablishes the hierarchy of poet over people that Whitman had managed (however briefly) to level.

This irony is prepared by the cultural politics of the Communist party's Popular Front, dating from the mid 1930s, when the Left stopped condemning Whitman as a narrowly nationalist, even jingoist, poet and started the revision of his career as the herald of an international democratic order. This was when Americanism again became synonymous with democracy, as Whitman had always maintained, and when struggles for national liberation became part of communism's internationalism. For obvious reasons, the American Whitman attracted Spanish American Popular Frontists like Pablo Neruda, but he attracted other Spanish American heirs as well. To give an idea of the range of these "partial" misreadings (in Harold Bloom's double sense of being both insufficient and interested) and of how contemporary Spanish American poets literally fight over Whitman's dead body, it may be enough to juxtapose the following publication events. In 1969 Borges published an exquisite, but selective translation of *Leaves of Grass* and dedicated it to Richard Nixon.[5] Four years later Neruda's *Incitation to Nixonicide and Praise for the Chilean Revolution* was published posthumously. It opens the assault by invoking Walt Whitman in the following fastidiously rhymed lines:

> Es por acción de amor a mi país
> que te reclamo, hermano necesario,
> viejo Walt Whitman de la mano gris.[6]

[From an act of love for my land
I call on you, necessary brother,
old Walt Whitman of the gray hand.]   (my trans.)

Although not all this dramatic, one could multiply examples of Whitman's inscription in Spanish American verse ever since José Martí celebrated him as the bard of both Americas.[7] There would be little point to this, however, especially after Fernando Alegría's *Walt Whitman en Hispanoamérica* (1954), where the phantom of Whitman's ubiquity is grounded in a series of concrete and weighty forms.[8] The questions I want to pose are more interpretive than bibliographical, however. First, what is it about Whitman's aesthetic strategies that allows for the ideological diversity of his readings? Some critics argue that Whitman is a precursor of revolutionary poetry, others insist that his heirs are the nihilists, and yet others point out that Whitman is the father of a mystical individualism. The disagreement is a contest with political stakes. Yet Whitman is not any one of the above; he is all of them. He cultivates their cultural space, and any attempt to read today's ideological options back into his poetry would be limiting and would probably miss the point that his democratic liberalism has no direct heirs. At most we can say that the balance Whitman manages to strike between individual freedom and social equality survives for others only as an impossible ideal. In the best case it is what Barbara Herrnstein Smith calls a "possible utterance,"[9] which suggests nonmimetic directions for future poets who may be able to construct relationships rather than merely to imitate existing patterns. In this sense, perhaps, César Vallejo was Whitman's best Spanish American reader.[10] Whitman's poetry exhibits a sensibility and an aesthetics that establish a pre-text and at the same time go beyond immediate identification with any of today's ideological options. There is no mystery in this if we recognize that Whitman's contribution to modern poetry was to forge what I call an aesthetics of liberal democracy, which fragments into various and competing options. Later readers, including the aged Whitman, lose confidence in America's experiment to coordinate Lockean liberalism, or equal market relationships and the natural right to personal property, with Rousseauan democracy that insists on equality of political participation.[11] That is why C. B. McPherson can eulogize the effort in *The Life and Times of Liberal Democracy*.[12] Some of the results of this loss of confidence in Whitman's twentieth-century partial misreaders will be a left-wing populist poetry, like Neruda's, a Schopenhauerean pessimism, like Borges's, and an erotic mysticism as Octavio Paz practices it in an attempt to fill the void left in the wake of nineteenth-century liberalism.

One way of approaching Whitman's accomplishment of fathering feuding heirs to his work is to focus on his construction of a utopian plenitude that ignores, and therefore has no need to oppose, political conflict and social hierarchies. In other words, rather than attempt to coordinate liberalism and democracy in his poetry (as he would in essays like "Democratic Vistas"), Whitman manages to sidestep the ideological competition by fixing the contestants in an uncannily static and perfect moment. Some readers have, then, been coaxed into mistaking or exchanging his celebration for dynamism, utopia for development, and the resonance of a single voice for the harmony of a nation. We may intuit a better future, but the promise comes in the form of an inviolable present. Something about Whitman's poetry puts conflict under erasure, as Derrida uses that term; it does not deny the conflict, but neutralizes it on the page. Whitman's ideal America will fuel as well as frustrate later writers, for one thing because his promise does not need or even admit the possibility of change. How, then, can he have any real heirs? In fact, the fragility of his static construct shatters as soon as time touches it.

My answer to the question of Whitman's remarkably broad dissemination in literary history will conclude with an observation of his genius in neutralizing ideological differences and thus establishing a discursive space in which all positions seem legitimate. But the answer begins elsewhere, with the first lines of "Song of Myself," where Whitman introduces himself, his reader, and their practical synonymity:

> I celebrate myself,
> And what I assume you shall assume,
> For every atom belonging to me as good belongs to you.
>
> (SOM, 1, p. 32)

Is this an invitation or a challenge? If we refuse to be his ideal readers, we are no readers at all. Then, presumably we should put the book down. But if we continue to read, we have already accepted Whitman's terms, and a deal is struck for nothing less than our bodies and souls. Whitman gives himself freely to us, claiming at times to expect nothing in return. But he does not always forget, even if the reader does, that gifts are made to circulate; in some form they ultimately return to the giver. In Whitman's case the profits he expected were enormous:

> What is commonest and cheapest and nearest and easiest is
>   Me,
> Me going in for my chances, *spending for vast returns*,
> Adorning myself to bestow myself on the first that will
>   take me,

> Not asking the sky to come down to my goodwill.
> Scattering it freely forever.
>
> (SOM, 14, p. 44, my emphasis)

Again he will expect us to reciprocate at the same time that he protests disinterestedness: "Spread your palms and lift the flaps of your pockets, / I am not to be denied . . . I compel . . . I have stores plenty and to spare, / And any thing I have I bestow" (SOM, 40, p. 80). Even if the gift economy he locks us into is not the market of dollars and cents,[13] Whitman obliges just the same, perhaps more, to return (give returns on) his generosity; and the economic vocabulary he uses to represent social relationships suggests that the market is their legitimate site. In this way, Whitman's exchange reproduces the oxymoronic economic ideal of ante-bellum America: to preserve free market trading among independent producers without promoting unequal capitalist relationships.

His offer is irresistible for at least two reasons, as Whitman himself tells us. First, as implied members of a market society we cannot refuse an offer of the cheapest and most available commodity. Whitman is as plentiful as the grass and the fresh air that he prefers over the cloying perfumes that he leaves behind immediately after the first lines, along with the regular rhymes and iambs of "Houses and rooms are full of perfumes." And he offers himself up to unlimited takers for the very reasonable price of simply recognizing his worth. The second reason is that his worth is limitless. He is the most common and also the vastest and most satisfying comrade on the market. We both want him and want to believe that we merit him. Whitman assures us that the double desire is already fulfilled: both because he is already ours and because the erotic exchange that he touches off with his initial offer makes his partners fully equal in their obligation to give vast returns for his love. By representing erotic exchange in market language, then, Whitman involves each reader individually in a market relationship that enacts the ideal of free and equal access to an American market where the best commodities are the cheapest. Each reader is a perfectly adequate buyer, because Whitman is so "reasonable" and because we all equally have the resource for exchange: our selves. Thus we enact and affirm the Lockean, liberal ideal of political equality through equal opportunity in a free market. The same ideal will find a convincing rhythm in Whitman's apparently arbitrary catalogs, where the most extreme differences of social class, profession, origin, and gender level out through the steady and ardent incantation that melts differences into mere variation.

At the same time that he is giving aesthetic form to the equalizing force of the free market, however, Whitman is also flooding the market (of ideal American comrades) by offering himself so cheaply, "Outbidding at the start the old cautious hucksters" (SOM, 41, p. 81), and by insisting that he be bought. There is no room for competition here, even though the thought of an intellectual or cultural monopoly seemed abhorrent to him. Whitman wanted to "be marked for generosity and affection and for encouraging competitors . . . without monopoly or secrecy . . . glad to pass any thing to any one . . . hungry for equals night and day" (Preface, p. 15). My concern is, of course, whether generosity is consistent with encouraging competitors. Whitman's "gift economy" may in fact undermine the very free market that Whitman assumes in his erotic transaction. In other words, his apparently disinterested initiation of the lover who reads him threatens to overcome all the healthy independence that Whitman says he admires in an ideal partner.

Whitman becomes the monopolizer, the archcapitalist whose best and cheapest wares reduce competitors to mere consumers of an Imaginary fulfilment of conflicting desires (for market freedom and for political control). Whitman's ideal of democracy, however, continued to be based on the mass participation of independent producers, even after many of America's workers had already become wage laborers. America is most firmly knit by "the aggregate of its middling property owners . . . ungracious as it may sound, . . . democracy looks with suspicious, ill satisfied eye upon the very poor, the ignorant, and on those out of business" ("Democratic Vistas" [DV] p. 339). Whitman shared his disdain for capitalism in its rapacious and centralizing manifestations with most of the political and economic thinkers of his day. Capitalism was the cancer that would reintroduce the hierarchy and antagonism of classes and undermine the participatory government that made America special. In the antebellum period, the South was understandably more tolerant of a class society, so long as the distinctions coincided with color and precluded the slave "underclass" from political participation. In the North, the "American School" of economics condemned the "capitalist" planters for demeaning the role of labor and thereby threatening the wages commanded by white independent workers. Whitman says clearly that the fate of the white working class is or should be the real concern of northern abolitionists.[14] The Civil War may well have been fought, as Allen Kaufman argues, over that fate; could democracy be consistent with class society or not?[15] Despite Whitman's definite no to that question, or maybe because of it, he will leave nothing up to chance or competition in the exchange by which his readers buy into being ideal equal Americans.

The threat of class and other social divisions is so unspeakable that Whitman enthralls us in order to overcome all differences, perhaps even the ones that his ideal liberal democracy and market thrive on. On the one hand, he endorses John Stuart Mill's definition of democracy as a polity with varied character and full play of differences (DV, p. 317). On the other hand, differences represent obstacles to be overcome by one equalizing force that Whitman calls love or sex in his poems and in "Democratic Vistas" calls the "tremendous Idea" of the true nationality, "melting everything else with resistless heat, and solving all lesser and definite distinctions in vast, indefinite spiritual, emotional power" (DV, p. 324). Why does Whitman assume that "distinctions" must be "solved," as if they were problems? And even if we grant that some solution or mediation is in order, what does it mean for democratic practice to equalize by "melting everything else with resistless heat?" Whitman's ardor may be burning up the very thing he celebrates, just as his generosity threatens to monopolize his free market ideal, unless, of course, what he celebrates is only himself, the ideal American whom we can become if we but let him love each of us.

With resistless heat is precisely how Whitman comes on to his reader in *Leaves of Grass*. He is the hottest item imaginable; we seem to enact an exchange between free and equal partners, but we cannot refuse him. How can we, when he knows that our desires are infinite (Lockean) and promises to respond to them all (à la Rousseau)? That is why I choose to call his approach a seduction. We are free to look away, and some readers manage to escape him through their indifference; but those of us who hold on to the book are held in turn by Whitman's pledge that to know him, to be him, is to know and be our best possible selves. From now on the differences between curiosity and vanity, between interest in others and self-interest, and ultimately between democracy and imperialism begin to blur.

Years after the Mexican War and right after the "Spanish–American War," otherwise known as Cuba's War of Independence, José Enrique Rodó expressed a collective worry about one thing leading to another. "As fast as the utilitarian genius of that nation takes on a more defined character, . . . so increases the impatience of its sons to spread it abroad by propaganda, and think it predestined for all humanity. To-day they openly aspire to the primacy of the world's civilization, the direction of its ideas, and think themselves the forerunners of all culture that is to prevail."[16] Passages from Whitman's "Democratic Vistas" of 1871 sound as if they were among Rodó's sources: "When the present century closes, . . . The Pacific will be ours, and the Atlantic mainly ours. There will be daily electric communication with every part of the globe. What an age! what a land! Where elsewhere, one so great? The individuality of one nation must then, as always, lead the world. Can there be any doubt who the leader ought to be?" (DV, p. 369). North America's liberalism –

in the sense of generosity and the motivation to share itself with the less fortunate (something like the motivation Plato attributed to a self-sufficient God who created the world from an excess of love) threatened to grow monstrously and to make of others what Sinclair Lewis would call the "victims" of its "generosity."[17]

When we allow Whitman to give himself to us, he not only guarantees his own returns; he also seduces us into denying the value of any will but his. Although the assaults, or appeals, are multiple, it is appropriate to talk about at least two levels as particular stages of intensity with their corresponding techniques. The first assault is that of a lover who acknowledges the possible distance between himself and the beloved (reader) only to cancel that distance through a mutual embrace. At this stage, as I suggested, Whitman and his readers enact the ideal of a democracy in which equality is reduced to identity. If each participant identifies with the poet, we repeat at the level of political subjects the same kind of equality the free market affords by being available to each citizen. What contradiction can there be here between Lockean equal economic opportunity and Rousseauan equal political participation?

At a second level of Whitman's seduction the identity established between reader and writer returns both to the moment of identity formation that Jacques Lacan's psychoanalytic vocabulary calls the mirror stage of development. This moment precedes any acknowledgment of difference outside oneself. Only a newly discovered self and the identical other in the mirror exist. This stage therefore precedes the possibility of competing ideas about how the self is related to the other. By insisting that his readers leave their autonomy at the threshold of his poem, Whitman can re-form them into reflections of his own specular image. And he can fix them there in a peculiarly American moment, before ideology pulls at the identity on either side of the glass. This movement back into what is otherwise known as infantile narcissism thus vaporizes the whole question of ideological positioning. Therefore, to combine the first and second levels of my reading, one of Whitman's accomplishments is to identify the truce he has called between the free market and democracy as the absence of ideology. Now I confess that I may be reading backward from a preoccupation with a widespread resistance among Americans to acknowledging their ideological partisanship to a text that I consider foundational. In fact there may be no relationship of cause and effect between the poem and the resistance. But the coincidence between them would be telling nonetheless; even if Whitman does not serve as a model for ideological disavowal, he certainly serves to reinforce it. Let us now consider each of these stages, or levels, in some detail.

Of the several innovative techniques that Whitman uses to court and to

conquer us on the first level, the most seductive may be his direct appeal
to a single reader, you who are reading and responding to your lover.
"This hour I tell things in confidence, / I might not tell everybody but I
will tell you" (SOM, 19, p. 51). The fact that Whitman will be just as
available and intimate with anyone else who picks him up does not
contradict the terms of his offer; it reinforces them. The important thing
is that he calls us into the relationship as individuals, not as a compact
mass who may share some characteristics. The collectivity is constructed
through our particular mergings with Whitman; it does not precede him.
In the beginning was the gift and the intimate tone of Whitman's offer.
Borges noticed the intricate mechanism of Whitman's apostrophes to the
reader: "We are touched by the fact that the poet was moved when he
foresaw our emotion."[18] An especially daring example follows from
Whitman's anticipation of our surrender, "Prodigal! you have given me
love! . . . therefore I to you give love" (SOM, 21, p. 53), as if it were the
reader who initiated the erotic exchange by the free "prodigal" gift to
which Whitman obligingly responds.

When Borges suggests that we compare this intimacy with that of
other poets, it is to illustrate the extent to which Whitman succeeded in
breaking with a European bardic tradition each time he asks, or even
demands, permission from each of his readers to represent them. Instead
of taking for granted that he, the bard, can legitimately be our collective
voice by virtue of his superior sensitivity, Whitman reconstructs the
bard's legitimacy by having each individual reader enlist him for the role.
Far from simply assuming that we will, Whitman first acknowledges the
distance between the subject and his object, poet and nation, so that he
can overcome that distance by the brute force of his love and by the
implied humility of a god who needs worshipers in order to exist. I
mentioned before that Whitman slyly begins by offering himself rather
than claiming the other; then he continues with a calculated modesty. If
his "unoriginal" thoughts "are not yours as much as mine they are
nothing / or next to nothing" (SOM, 7, p. 49). Later he will add more
aggressively: "All this I swallow . . . and it becomes mine" (SOM, 33,
p. 71);[19] and "I have embraced you, and henceforth possess you to
myself" (SOM, 40, p. 81). This direct appeal is difficult to resist because
his self-importance is not exclusive; it is contagious. By identifying the
authorial voice with the overwhelmed interlocutor, the reader cannot
help but enjoy some of Whitman's megalomania as if it reflected on the
power of the silent partner.

José Martí, for example, in the 1887 article that celebrated Whitman as
the model for all America's poets, responded to his erotic power despite
the hint that persuasion bordered on coercion. Martí wants the "other"

America, "our" America, to buy into Whitman's (i)deal. "Let us hear what this hardworking, contented people sings; let us hear Walt Whitman. Self-assertion raises this people to majesty, tolerance to justice, order to happiness."[20] Nevertheless, something about Martí's admiring language confesses his own powerlessness to refuse and a potential fear that here only heightens the awe. Whitman's poetry sometimes "sounds like a stolen kiss, *like a rape,* like the snapping of a dried-out parchment in the sun. . . . his verses . . . gallop on devouring the land; at times they neigh eagerly like lustful stallions; at times covered with lather, they trample clouds with their hoofs."[21] Whitman's seduction, in other words, makes dialogue unnecessary, but it does acknowledge the poet's dependence on the reader, just as a rapist needs a partner even though he may not be performing an act of love.

The formal innovation of Whitman's free verse works together with the direct address to incorporate the reader into the text by encouraging the idea that he or she is capable of equaling Whitman's language, since the register is so close to everyday speech. This may be why some professional English-language poets resisted him more than did foreign-language poets. The verse, threatening as it does to decompose into a prose of the street variety, tended to displease English-speaking conservatives, who, unlike Spanish Americans, were not spared any of the rudeness through the mediation of translation or the charitable indulgences toward exotic art. Even so, men like Pound and Eliot finally had to make their peace with the "pig-headed father."[22] Earlier, and without the burden of inheriting a brutish American father, Gerard Manley Hopkins had confessed to recognizing the similarity between his and Whitman's experiments in scansion. Hopkins identified them as using the prose rhythm of iambs, anapests, and a combination of these. "Extremes meet and . . . this savagery of his art, this rhythm in its last ruggedness and decomposition into common prose, comes near the last elaboration of mine."[23] The prosaic "decomposition" was a major strategic break from traditional poetry; it tended to cancel the privilege of poet over reader, of regular scansion over the flexible patterns of common speech, and generally legitimated the ordinary by blurring the boundaries between life and art. The social plenitude that Whitman achieves, then, is to a large degree produced by the free verse that levels the various registers of language into a construction of "writing degree zero."[24]

Whitman, the leveler of style and architect of an American poetics, appears impatient with all hierarchies and dichotomies: poetry versus prose; the individual versus nature; production versus reproduction. The leveling is also the product (or cause) of Whitman's self-consciously disordered catalogs as well as of the fragmentary structure given to endless permutations. Rather than privilege one term over another, Whitman consistently points to their interdependence. The subtle metaphor that gives Whitman's book its title nicely conflates the individual–nature dichotomy into one harmonious image. He simply substituted the word "leaves" for "blades." Now the image owes as much to the poet writing the leaves, or pages, as it does to the common grass he is exalting. Or should the reader go farther and imagine that the grass itself is as much the product of the poet's practice as his poem is the product of nature? Not wanting to fix the meaning of the grass, Whitman suggests that it may be the coquettishly planted "Handkerchief of the Lord, / A scented gift and remembrancer designedly dropped, / Bearing the owner's name someway in the corners, that we may see and remark, and say Whose?" (SOM, 6, p. 36). Alternatively, the grass may be the pubic-like "curling" hair of graves, transpiring from breasts of young men and laps of mothers. The remarkable thing to notice here is that one hypothesis does not cancel out another; they are not dichotomous but continuous, because in either case the leaves bind Whitman to his lovers. They also bind him, not surprisingly, to his typical and representative self, as John Irwin argues in *American Hieroglyphics*. For the transcendentalist Emerson, leaves are the ultimate hieroglyphic of Nature's writing, because they reveal the simplicity of relationships that allows for correspondences. Thoreau continues this by posing a challenge: "The Maker of this earth but patented a leaf. What Champollion will decipher this hieroglypic for us, that we may turn over a new leaf at last?"[25] Whitman simply assumed he was the man. His leaves, unlike Thoreau's, were less a "metaphysical reading" of nature than a production of it. According to Irwin, Whitman's poetry attempted to return language to the childlike natural signs made popular in the "hieroglyphic Bibles" of his day;[26] yet one astounding way that Whitman changed the commonplace goes unnoticed by Irwin. Whitman's leaves are no longer arranged in the top–down model of the trees his contemporaries were gazing up at; they make up the level ground underfoot.

The scandal of displacing heterosexual love with homoeroticism is obviously related to Whitman's appeal for the reader's surrender, to the socially equalizing quality of his free verse, and to his reaffirmation of a covenant with nature that needs no detours through a transcendental spirit. If the seduction that Whitman practices is of a reader who is his equal ("For every atom belonging to me as good belongs to you"), then that reader-lover is logically another man. The radically equal love between comrades spills over into Whitman's utopian vision of a society bound by affection:

If I worship any particular thing it shall be some of the
   spread of my
   body;
Translucent mould of me it shall be you,
Shaded ledges and rests, firm masculine coulter,
   it shall be you,   (SOM, 24, p. 57)

Homosexual love, then, becomes an allegory for a nonhierarchical and
truly democratic relationship, a point that appealed to Edward Carpenter
among other English homosexuals of the nineteenth century, as Eve
Kosofsky Sedgwick has shown.[27] Later D. H. Lawrence offered his own
gloss for the allegory. Rather than cancel the first two stages of human
love that Lawrence describes (the cohesion of family or clan and the
powerful sexual bond between man and woman), homosexuality fulfills
these in a kind of Hegelian realization of human(e) capacities: a love
beyond purpose,[28] possible only when freedom is wrested from necessity.

I doubt that Whitman's democratic ideal preceded or conditioned his
sexual preference; but I am convinced that his homosexuality allowed
him to feel what a radically democratic relationship would be, one that
overcame both masculine domination and feminine coyness. In their
place, Whitman offers an image of love between equals, a highly charged
sensuality based on sameness, not difference. "Dash me with amorous
wet," he could challenge the ocean, "I can repay you" (SOM, 22, p. 54).
Lawrence perceived that, for Whitman, in their displacement women
were reduced to mere childbearers. What Lawrence ignored, however, is
that men, even and especially as lovers, suffer a comparable reduction;
they are flattened into mirror reflections of the poet. One begins to
suspect that Whitman could fancy himself as Everyman, not only because he was typical but also because he had devoured everyone else.

Now this absorption of difference is the very feature that I associate
ideologically with liberalism (and later with populism like Neruda's and
pessimism like Borges's), the feature that appears to result in a political
ambiguity between a democratic embrace through the leveling of relationships and an imperialist, centralizing thrust that denies difference and
autonomy. It is what tempered Martí's admiration with implied fear and
what probably convinced Rodó not to complicate his criticism of North
America with any mention of a Whitman he could not help admiring.[29]
Whitman's style and his redundant message say, in effect, that we are all
equal because you are, or should be, the same as I am. He will love you,
but he may love you to death. Although his practically irresistible and
equalizing direct address offers an alternative to the traditional privilege

of the bard and of the extra-ordinary poet, Whitman achieves a comparable authority each time a reader suspends his or her autonomy in the poet's amorous, but annihilating bear hug. "My flesh and blood playing out lightning, to strike what is hardly different from myself" (SOM, 28, p. 62).

Equality here is synonymous with identity, that is, an identity with Whitman at the center of a universe that repeats him endlessly. To indicate the continuing vitality of this appeal I will mention only one rather surprising example. It comes from Gilles Deleuze and Felix Guattari's proposal for breaking out of the philosophical dualisms that not even Nietzsche, with his "cyclical unity of the eternal return," escapes.[30] The proposal is to reorganize our political imagination on the basis of the "rhyzome," "an underground stem" that proliferates without any center or goal so that each growth is equal to and connects with all others. Their primary example is the grass; and several pages later they cite Whitman's *Leaves of Grass* as the radically American work that sets the model for the "successive lateral shoots" that can loosen Europe's hold onto roots. The problem that recurs in Deleuze and Guattari, just as it surfaced in Whitman, is that proliferation requires a model or a typical element that is endlessly repeated. Who establishes what that allegedly humble model is? And how can its endless repetition even recognize the differences that a Hegelian pyramidal structure considers inessential but at least acknowledges? In other words, Deleuze and Guattari seem to imagine that by dismissing their philosophical fathers they can clear an empty space for establishing nonhierarchical relationships. But they forget what Whitman never did, that by writing they are already occupying the space of discourse and calling in their readers to model themselves after the writer, no matter how much he insists on his humility.

To review this first level of Whitman's seduction, we can say that his strategy of engaging the reader as lover and as equal, as well as his leveling of language registers, offers a form for the nineteenth-century liberal ideology of social equality based on free market relationships. Competition among equals, specifically among independent producers, was assumed to benefit each individual and allow for personal development. Therefore, each citizen could celebrate, not envy, the success of a fellow. If aristocratic literature pitted good against evil, insider against outsider, Whitman's liberal poetics overcomes this dichotomy among others by denying the *difference* of the other. In "Democratic Vistas" the mature Whitman will admonish the people of his country to internalize a spirit of democracy without which its institutions are superficial and vulnerable. That spirit would produce a culture to displace the feudal, aristocratic, romantic habits of feeling that are vestiges of Europe and limit the legal and political strides toward democracy (DV, p. 320).

> [A]s . . . it is strictly true that a few first-class poets, philosophs, and authors have substantially settled and given status to the entire religion, education, law, sociology, etc., of the hitherto civilized world, by tinging and often *creating the atmospheres out of which they have arisen,* such also must *stamp,* and more than ever stamp, the interior and real democratic construction of this American contintent, today, and days to come. (DV, p. 322, my emphasis)

The young Whitman, however, was less moved to admonish than to enact and to celebrate the triumphant democracy that the poem gives form to. "Song of Myself" is written from inside the Imaginary triumph, beyond all doubts and arguments for how to achieve it. Along with the European habits of hierarchy, dichotomy, and prosody that Whitman leaves behind in the introduction to his poem, he leaves all struggle and dialectics. He not only asserts this; he enacts it throughout a poem that never budges from an eternal present tense. In the Preface, the poet "is no arguer . . . he is judgment" (p. 9); later he insists, "Backward I see in my own days where I sweated through fog with linguists and contenders, / I have no mockings or arguments . . . I witness and wait" (SOM, 4, p. 35). That is why the "talkers" and "trippers and askers" (SOM, 4, p. 35) are irrelevant. Whitman cannot be contained by words here; he is the excess of meaning, a surplus that overcomes all distinctions and that spills over beyond the text. "Writing and talk do not prove me, / I carry the plenum of proof and every thing else in my face, / With the hush of my lips I confound the topmost skeptic" (SOM, 25, p. 60).

From inside, the ideal America is already constructed and perfected, for one thing because the fragments are left purposefully imperfect, unfinished, in a way that invites readers to write themselves in. Whitman hails us into his construction of an equality based on identity by the several seductive techniques already mentioned; but it would be hasty to assume that he would have us as we are. In fact just as the poem creates the ideal America that gives Whitman birth, it re-forms the reader into another ideal American. The act of hailing us, as Althusser describes it, produces the subject of the ideology that is calling us in. When we stop for the policeman who yells, "Hey, you," we become his subjects,[31] and when we accept Whitman's initial challenge to assume everything he assumes we become his subjects too, even if the ideology of unmediated equality that he produces looks neutral and nonideological. How, we may wonder, does the poem constitute the ideal subject it is calling in?

The range of its subjects, left, right, and center of the political spectrum, is at least one hint that Whitman's poem works at the second level mentioned above, a level more basic than, or anterior to, ideological differences. Therefore, my reading takes a detour around the narrowly political interpretations that characterize the contestants for his paternity, to consider "Song of Myself" as a re-presentation of an early moment in human psychological development, a moment before the advent of differences and struggle. This stage prepares the ground for ideology, although Whitman's poem assiduously refuses to move there. Our continuing fascination with the poem derives in large measure from its simulation of the process of ego formation. Since Whitman's is the model ego for his readers, that process is almost immediately fixed in an unabashed narcissism. One result of this kind of self-discovery or self-constitution for the reader as much as for the poet is a utopian harmony based on the identity of subject and object. Neruda's political poetry will begin with the expulsion from this originary Eden and will be motivated by the desire to catch up with an ideal, heroic, but alienated ego; Whitman never let that ego escape from his embrace. The psychoanalytic hypothesis that helps to direct my reading is less concerned with personal biography than with a general process of identity formation. I am not very interested here in studying poetry as symptomatic of particular and unusual spirits. That would only undercut Whitman's project to the extent that it demands equality between reader and writer. Nor should we assume that his poetry is merely representative of shared psychoanalytic patterns; that would miss the degree to which poetry may present and direct the collective experience of its readers.[32]

According to Lacan, the individual's self-identity originates in a "mirror stage of development."[33] This refers to the phase when an infant discovers its reflection in a mirror. Until that point it is a mass of fragmented organs that has no discrete feature, function, or identity. The mirror reflection returns a pleasing image of coherence to the infantile diffuse consciousness. By returning this totality through a reflected and thus alienated image, the mirror stage establishes the ideal of wholeness as belonging to the other, that is, to the person or image in the mirror with whom the subject identifies. The static quality of "Song of Myself" and Whitman's insistence that we have identities to the extent that we are identical to him led me to the observation that his poem works like a mirror in which the fragments of a divided nation fuse together. Instead of a mirror, we can imagine Whitman holding up a clear glass to the reader and saying, "He who looks at me looks at himself." Whitman actually does invite us to look at his poem as if into a mirror: "You shall stand by my side and *look in the mirror with me*" (Preface, p. 14, my emphasis). Later, each reflection is individual and repeats the divine model: "In the faces of men and women I see God, and in *my own face in the glass*" (SOM, 48, p. 94, my emphasis). Like the infant, narcissistically mesmerized by its own representation, Whitman seems almost paralyzed in his self-absorbed confrontation with the reader, who becomes not merely a "*frère*" or "*semblable*" (as Baudelaire daringly apostrophized his own readers) but an identical twin or the subject himself. Whitman returns the reader to this founding moment and then refuses to budge from it. Extending the celebration of this newfound totality and harmony in the mirror stage, the poet can afford to retain his fix on the fragments because they no longer threaten the coherent image that comes into focus. He makes the fragments of his poem repeat the image of a coherent doubled image, so that each piece becomes the object of his self-admiration. Whitman could not have known Lacan's theory, but he seems to come upon the same intuition, especially if we draw a parallel between this mutual mirror gazing and the poet's work to "stamp . . . the interior and real democratic construction of this American continent" (DV, p. 322). Whether the model is reproducing itself in the mirror or in the stamping of repeated images, like coins at the mint, America is the construction of the proliferated poet. Thus Whitman can insist that the alienated self in the mirror, the other, must always be identical to the self. He acknowledges the distance initially, as I mentioned above, only the better to overcome it in a heroic leap into the mirror that blissfully (or tragically) obliterates the tension on which identity depends.

What Whitman does in the series of fragments he calls "Song of Myself" is to realize the utopian dream of affirming that in America the real is already ideal. This sleight of hand has the staying power of a logical argument: If America is the dream of utopia, then to be American is to be ideal. But this begs the question of what it means to be American. Whitman's answer exceeds and precedes the sum of its celebratory parts. The enumeration of qualities and varieties of Americans makes sense only because a particular essence of Americanness is being established by the poem. And that essence is a peculiar identity that is interchangeable with other American subjects. Whitman does much more than simply make interchangeability possible (as American manufacture did in the nineteenth century). He compels it through a poem that simulates the psychological formation of the subject so that he can control the reformation and produce equal and identical subjects. Whitman, in other words, is something like America's midwife, helping America to give birth to itself. Better, he is the New World's Zeus, who insists, as the old

Zeus must have done,[34] that the more ancient Athena and Dionysus be reborn through the civilizing agency of himself. Whitman's body is so diffuse and inclusive that he can call it a cosmos.

His assimilation of America into himself is the primary way that Whitman negotiates the erotic and social tensions between imagining the individual as part of the collective and at the same time as an independent personality (see DV). The danger of his limitless love, as I have been arguing, is that it will become aggressive and monopolize the very cult of personality that he celebrates. Lacan (like Norman O. Brown) draws a connection between Freud's understanding of love as union and Sartre's notion of love as the drive for possession. That drive is motivated by a paranoid and aggressive subject's worry that follows necessarily from the mirror stage as if one said, "If I am not the only I, then others know what I am and even are or possess me."[35] At the point when the "specular I" (in the mirror) is confused with other particular "I"s, language mediates the hostility by converting them to social "I"s, so that the social dialectic can begin. For example, once the little boy stops identifying directly with his father as a rival and begins to understand the category father as that linguistic sign or social space he will be able to fill, the aggressivity of the oedipal complex can be normalized, and the child fully enters society.

But Whitman does not risk normalization. He clearly perceives a repetition of an oedipal or competitive social order to be the problem, not the solution; so he winds the psychological clock back to the zero hour and then stops it where he and we fix our respective loving gazes on one another. That is, his American subject is born through a cloning, an apotheosis of self-reliance. It finesses any need for legitimating founding fathers. They are precisely what Whitman, as an American, considers illegitimate; he excludes them from our process of self-birth so they cannot become our models in an endless desire to be them. The great irony and accomplishment are that this specular embrace that seems to equalize reader and writer in an Imaginary stasis is engineered by unstable and unfixable Language, the system that Lacan calls the Symbolic realm, the Law and also the realm of the father.[36] Whitman's feat, I believe, was never repeated, not even by his most devout disciples, for as soon as they touched the glassy text to pull it in some ideological and therefore narrative direction, they set language back into its characteristic conflictual motion.

NOTES

My thanks for encouragement and suggestions for this essay go to the editors of the volume and especially to my colleague Andrew Parker.

1 Louis Althusser, "Ideology and the Ideological State Apparatuses," *Lenin and Philosophy* (London: Monthly Review Press, 1971), p. 162.

2 Page numbers for "Song of Myself" (SOM), the 1855 Preface, "Democratic Vistas," and Van Doren's "Introduction" refer to *The Portable Walt Whitman,* ed. Mark Van Doren, enlarged by Malcolm Cowley (Middlesex, England: Penguin Books, 1981).

3 Walt Whitman, Preface to *As a Strong Bird on Pinions Free and Other Poems* (1872), quoted in John C. Broderick, ed., *Whitman, the Poet,* (Belmont, Calif.: Wadsworth, 1964), p. 9.

4 See Donald Pease, "Blake, Crane, Whitman, and Modernism: A Poetics of Pure Possibility," *PMLA* 96, no. 1 (January 1981): 64–84; esp. p. 81: "A poetry of pure possibility neither imitates nor represents what is or has been. It is not anchored in any past perception and does not anticipate any specific future one; a free projection of the imagination, it preconstitutes, through a unique use of repetition what might be. As we have seen, because possibilities can never be represented, they must continually be repeated before they can possess even a formal quality." I thank Jonathan Arac for pointing out this article to me and for his comments and criticisms.

5 Roberto Fernández Retamar, *Calibán: Apuntes sobre la cultura en nuestra América,* 2nd ed. (Mexico City: Diógenes, 1974), p. 55.

6 Pablo Neruda, "Comienzo por invocar a Walt Whitman," *Incitación al nixonicidio y alabanza de la revolución chilena* (Ediciones Grijalbo, 1973), p. 12.

7 José Martí, "Walt Whitman," trans. Luis Baralt, in *Martí on the U.S.A.* (Carbondale: Southern Illinois University Press, 1966), pp. 3–16.

8 Fernando Alegría, *Walt Whitman en Hispanoamérica* (Mexico City: Fondo de Cultura Económica, 1954).

9 Barbara Herrnstein Smith, "Licensing the Unspeakable," *On the Margins of Discourse* (University of Chicago Press, 1978), pp. 107–24. The "possible utterance" refers to the capacity of poetry to call into existence, through the agency of repetition, that which cannot yet be represented. For my purposes, this suggests that poetry may be the appropriate medium for ideological production, since it can formulate rather than merely imitate.

10 This impression should be developed, as some readers, such as Jean Franco, have begun to do. See her *César Vallejo: The Dialectics of Poetry and Silence* (Cambridge University Press, 1976) and a forthcoming article by Gari Laguardia, "Digesting Modernismo: Peristalsis and Poetic Paternity in Vallejo," where he argues convincingly that Whitman was Vallejo's lead out of *modernista* preciosity.

11 See J. Roland Pennock, *Democratic Political Theory* (Princeton, N.J.: Princeton University Press, 1979). For a succinct, but less satisfying discussion of the double tradition see Alan Wolfe, "The Predicament of Liberal Democracy," his Introduction to *The Limits of Legitimacy* (New York: Free Press, 1977), pp. 1–10.

12 C. B. McPherson, *The Life and Times of Liberal Democracy* (London: Oxford University Press, 1977). In the first two pages of the Introduction he makes clear that the definitive biography can now be written because the subject has long been dead.

13   Lewis Hyde, "A Draft of Whitman," *The Gift: Imagination and the Erotic Life of Property* (New York: Vintage, 1983), pp. 161–215.

14   Mauricio González de la Garza, *Walt Whitman: Racista, imperialista, anti-Mexicano* (Mexico City: Colección Málaga, 1971), p. 176.

15   Allen Kaufman, *Capitalism, Slavery, and Republican Values* (Austin: University of Texas Press, 1983).

16   José Enrique Rodó, *Ariel* (1900), trans. F. J. Stimson (Boston: Houghton Mifflin, 1922), pp. 120–1.

17   See Sinclair Lewis's *Babbit* and Jorge Luis Borges's jibe at a North American philanthropist, in "Pierre Menard, Author of Don Quixote" – "Simon Kautzsch, who has been so inconsiderately slandered, alas! by the *victims of his disinterested maneuvers," Labyrinths,* ed. Donald A. Yates and James E. Irby (New York: New Directions, 1964), p. 36 (my emphasis).

18   Jorge Luis Borges, "Note on Walt Whitman," *Other Inquisitions,* trans. Ruth L. C. Simms (Austin: University of Texas Press, 1964), p. 70.

19   Compare this with Melanie Klein's work on infantile subject formation as a process of "introjecting good objects" and "projecting bad ones," "Some Theoretical Conclusions Regarding the Emotional Life of the Infant," in *Developments in Psycho-Analysis,* ed. M. Klein, P. Heimann, S. Isaacs, and J. Rivera (London: Hogarth Press, 1952), esp. p. 200.

20   Martí, "Walt Whitman," p. 8.

21   Ibid., pp. 14–15.

22   Ezra Pound, "A Pact," in *Selected Poems of Ezra Pound* (New York: New Directions, 1957). p. 27. "I come to you as a grown child / Who has had a pig-headed father."

23   Gerard Manley Hopkins, in a letter to Robert Bridges, October 18, 1882, from *Walt Whitman: The Measure of His Song,* ed. Perlman, Folsom, and Campion (Minneapolis, Minn.: Holy Cow Press, 1981), p. 13.

24   This term was coined by Roland Barthes to describe a "universal language" that would not cultivate individual style but anticipate a homogeneous social state (*Writing Degree Zero and Elements of Semiology,* trans. Annette Lavers and Colin Smith [Boston: Beacon Press, 1967], esp. p. 87).

25   John Irwin, "The Symbol of the Hieroglyphics in the American Renaissance," *American Quarterly* 26 (1974): 103–126, esp. pp. 112, 116–17, and his *American Hieroglyphics: The Symbol of the Egyptian Hieroglyphics in the American Renaissance* (New Haven, Conn.: Yale University Press, 1980), pp. 37–9.

26   Irwin, *American Hieroglyphics,* p. 40.

27   Eve Kosofsky Sedgwick, *Between Men: English Literature and Male Homosocial Desire* (New York: Columbia University Press, 1985), pp. 206–8.

28   D. H. Lawrence, "Whitman," in *Walt Whitman: The Measure of His Song,* ed. Perlman et al., pp. 43–51.

29   See Gordon Brotherston's introduction to Rodó's *Ariel* (Cambridge University Press, 1967), p. 14. "He [Rodó] certainly had second thoughts about Whitman because next to the phrase [incorporated into *Ariel*] about 'Excelsior,' originally he wrote: 'Tiene en Walt Whitman el acento de los evangelistas! . . . Inmensa expansión de amor'" (Archivo Rodó, armario 2, 8A 7, 20508).

30 Gilles Deleuze and Felix Guattari, "On the Line," trans. John Johnston, in *Semiotext(e)* 6, no. 1 (1983): esp. pp. 9, 43, 48.

31 Althusser, "Ideology," p. 174.

32 Shoshana Felman, for example, assumes that poetry works like the unconscious and that it reveals a shared system rather than a peculiar pathology. See her "On Reading Poetry: Reflections on the Limits and Possibilities of Psychoanalytical Approaches," in *Psychiatry and the Humanities,* ed. J. H. Smith, vol. 4 (New Haven, Conn.: Yale University Press, 1980), pp. 199–248.

33 Lacan wrote both the "The Mirror Stage" (1949) and "Aggressivity in Psychoanalysis" (1948) (*Ecrits: A Selection,* trans. Alan Sheridan [New York: Norton, 1977], pp. 1–29) in order to fill the lacunae of Freud's daring and admittedly introductory essay "On Narcissism" of 1914 (Sigmund Freud, *Collected Papers* [New York: Basic Books, 1959], vol. 4, p. 56). If Freud observed the universality of narcissism, which indicated for him the psychic immaturity of human infants, who must constitute their egos through a perceptual process, Lacan claims to describe just how the process works. It begins with a kind of experience that Köhler called the *Aha-Erlebnis,* the surprise of discovery when an infant recognizes its form in a mirror. Any discovery of a human image will do, however, as long as the child recognizes that the object is alienable and can be lost. Fascinated by its image, the child stops at the mirror to play hide and seek with itself. This is love at first sight, and the child becomes fixed in a self-absorbed dyad of lover and beloved. The dyad of self-identification can be repeated between child and mother, although Freud considered love for the mother to be sexual rather than narcissistic. Lacan calls this closed and reciprocal system the Imaginary realm. Its hermeticism denies the possibility of ambiguity because it posits a coalescence of signifiers and signifieds. It denies, in other words, the unconscious, where words and things are in an endless process of displacement. But the child's entry into language, the Symbolic order that repeats the structure of the unconscious, breaks the child out of the narcissistic dyad. And the mark of its expulsion from Paradise and entry into a world of mutability and language is the unrealizable desire for the originary harmony. That desire constitutes the subject as human. Sexual love, therefore, is a result of the subject's being forced, by language and the father, out of an incestuous, narcissistic stasis into the unstable economics of libido exchange.

34 George Thomson, *Aeschylus and Athens: A Study in the Social Origins of Drama* (London: Lawrence & Wishart, first in 1941), especially the chapter "Exogamy," pp. 21–34.

35 In this way, Whitman resolves the threat to harmony posed by that aggressivity, which Lacan calls the correlative tendency of narcissism. Since Whitman refuses to advance beyond the point of self-discovery, he keeps the social implications of that discovery at some distance. Lacan's essay "Aggressivity in Psychoanalysis" indicates, then, the extent of Whitman's departure from "shared" psychological experience.

36 If the Imaginary is the realm of mother and child, self and mirror image, even readers unfamiliar with Lacan can guess that the father dominates the

Symbolic order, otherwise known as the Law or Language, that sends the child out of Eden. The agent of displacement is more specifically the phallus, that signifier of signifiers and harbinger of the rest of the Symbolic system. As the object of the mother's desire, the phallus disrupts the Imaginary realm and sends the child out into the world of unstable signifiers, where it attempts to become the object of the mother's desire so that harmony can be restored. Another way of plotting the shift from the Imaginary into the Symbolic is to observe that, once the child learns that the image in the mirror or the mother can be absent, the child tries to compensate for the loss by language, that is, by the very intrusion that both corrupts the harmony and seems to promise a restitution.

Despite Lacan's ethical commitment to (a paradoxically imaginary) maturity of language, in which we would leave behind the intolerant Imaginary delusion that words mean things in a fixed and unproblematic way, the Imaginary and the Symbolic realms coexist in a tension, or a competition. Readers like Derrida and DeMan point to this constitutive struggle in language when they insist on the ambiguous or split nature of the linguistic sign: On the one hand, it affirms the immediacy of meaning; on the other, it draws attention to its own fictionality by being unavoidably figural. Ambiguity, then, is not the result of a particular trope but a general feature of language because it always, to use Austin's terms, performs speech acts. That is, it does things, but does them theatrically.

The constitutive tension between Lacan's realms, in which the Symbolic is already inscribed in the Imaginary, and the Imaginary is the unattainable object of desire for the Symbolic, gives us a vocabulary for reappraising Whitman's poetic and ideological accomplishment. It was to conquer the displacements of the Symbolic with a diffusion that simulated the undifferentiated harmony of the Imaginary. Beginning with an acknowledgment of the gaps and the distances between two subjects of Language, Whitman insists that the distance is literally a mirage, a single image refracted and doubled through a mirror. Starting from the Symbolic, divisive order that both he and his readers have inherited and that is caught in the contradictions between particular and general interests, he embraces the field of battle to the breadth and width of any one subject's capacity and ushers it backward, or forward, to recover an Imaginary utopia through a language that will seem to be transparent and static. Although his medium is the fallen realm of Language, Whitman cunningly organizes it to re-present an earlier, preverbal and formative stage when love identifies the ego with its other, before the phallus and the Law of the father convert love into insatiable desire. Law has been subsumed here into the Imaginary stasis, and as a result Whitman succeeds in erasing the boundaries of harmonious narcissism. The phallus is no longer a threat; instead it becomes the medium of fixing meaning. Now the originary dyad can be infinitely multiplied without any fear of loss or castration. There are no margins from which the Symbolic realm could disrupt the mirage, no enemies, no foreign or extraneous element to set the poem into a dialectic of struggles and displacements. The self is the other and the Other, the unconscious itself. And the mother is the phallus, because Whitman has subordinated phallus to mother, desire to plenitude. Irwin's very similar argument concludes that Whitman drowns out the phonetic distinctness of spoken language by "the fusing power of song, to turn the phallic tree of spoken language back into the cosmic tree of the language of natural signs." "Song of Myself" is a singularly undialectical poem, as static and utopian as only narcissism or death could be.

5

Caliban as poet
Reversing the maps of domination

SUSAN WILLIS

. . . by the authority of God omnipotent granted to Us through blessed Peter, and of the vicarship of Jesus Christ, which we exercise upon earth, by the tenor of the presents give, concede, and assign for ever to you, and to the kings of Castile and Leon, your successors, all the islands and main-lands discovered and which may hereafter be discovered, towards the west and south: drawing however and fixing a line from the arctic pole, viz from the north, to the antarctic pole, viz to the south; which line must be distant from any one of the islands whatsoever, vulgarly called the Azores, and Cape de Verd Islands, a hundred leagues towards the west and south . . .

– Papal Bull "Inter cetera," 1493

Be not afeard, the isle is full of noises,
Sounds, and sweet airs, that give delight, and hurt not.
Sometimes a thousand twangling instruments
Will hum about mine ears; and sometime voices,
That, if I then had wak'd after long sleep,
Will make me sleep again; and then, in dreaming,
The clouds methought would open and show riches
Ready to drop upon me, that, when I wak'd,
I cried to dream again.

– Caliban, in Shakespeare's *The Tempest,* act III, scene 2

When Caribbean poets describe their world, the image they depict is strongly influenced by geography. Whereas we in the First World are apt to conceive of the Caribbean as a hodgepodge of discrete islands, the poets see it as a whole, often referring to it as a basin, a cradle, or a trough that is held in place by a dynamic relationship to the Americas and Africa and the external limits of which commence with the Atlantic

92

Ocean. Individual islands are thought of, not in isolation, but in relation to others. The result is a poetic topography, externally bound by a sense of closure and internally defined by geographic configurations. Often the poetry evokes fertility as one island in a chain of islands engenders the next. When, in his poem "The Star-Apple Kingdom," Derek Walcott asks, "What was the Caribbean?" the reply is:

> islands that coupled as sadly as turtles
> engendering islets, as the turtle of Cuba
> mounting Jamaica engendered the Caymans, as
> behind the hammerhead turtle of Haiti–San Domingo
> trailed the little turtles from Tortuga to Tobago;[1]

Taking another point of view and grappling to define the position of Third World artists with respect to the culture of their origins, Aimé Césaire, in "Return to My Native Land," demonstrates that geography is not a static projection when seen from the Third World vantage point. His description of the Caribbean traces expanding and contracting relationships, beginning with the broad sweep of archipelago and isthmus, then narrowing to pinpoint specific islands, and finally reaching outward to embrace whole continents:

> mine, too, the archipelago bent like the anxious desire for self-negation as if with maternal concern for the most frail slenderness separating the two Americas, and the womb which spills towards Europe the good liquor of the Gulf Stream, and one of the two incandescent slopes between which the Equator funambulates towards Africa. And my unfenced island, its bold flesh upright at the stern of this Polynesia, and right before it, Guadeloupe slit in two at the dorsal line, and quite as miserable as ourselves; Haiti, where Negritude stood up for the first time and swore by its humanity; and the droll little tail of Florida where a Negro is being lynched, and Africa caterpillaring gigantically up to the Spanish foot of Europe, its nakedness where death cuts a wide swath.[2]

Although Walcott and Césaire share a language in which rich natural imagery conjoins with a sense of fertility, Césaire's portrayal is rooted in history. Fertility suggests the economics of the Caribbean, the tremendous wealth of which was siphoned off by Europe as smoothly and "naturally" as that continent draws the Gulf Stream. When Césaire traces a line from his homeland, Martinique, to Florida, he transforms geographic space into a series of reference points in the history of black struggle. Then, by referring to his own "unfenced island," he refutes the commonly held belief in the First World that islands are of necessity isolated, and instead defines the particular in terms of the universal.[3]

I would like to emphasize that nowhere in the above discussion have I used the term "map." The tendency to grasp geographic relationships as mapable space is alien to this poetry and pertains, instead, to a world view conditioned by European colonial history. Caribbean writers are well aware of the function of the map as a sign for the history of their domination. In George Lamming's mythic novel of the era of "discovery" and conquest, *Natives of My Person* (1972), rival European powers vie for the possession of maps with the same vigor as they contended for newly charted territories. From the perspective of the Third World, the science of cartography paved the way for slave trade and the expropriation of wealth, and the map itself is identified as the sign for the abstraction of cultural reality as well as topography.

In its portrayal of geographic relationships, the poetry of the Third World challenges the First World to imagine a topography without reducing it to a map. The immediate result is a richer notion of spatial configurations, where topography is deeply infused with natural imagery.

For many Third World poets, and Césaire is clearly one of these, the redefinition of geographic space is not an end in itself. Geography, freed from abstraction, gives structure to a very different world view: the oppositional poetics of dependency.[4] Rather than a map, geography is a figural representation of the complex system of economic and historical relationships that define the periphery in relation to the First World. For these writers, geographic lines and contours produce a dynamic figure for a concrete dialectic.

Rich geographic imagery combined with the sense that geography is a metaphor for economics occurs throughout the literature from areas of economic dependency. In the United States, Faulkner, as narrator for the semiperiphery of the South, demonstrates the peripherality of Yoknapatawpha County in direct proportion to its distance from the economic core, be it the southern metropolis, Memphis, or the more distant and more central New York City. In his short story "The Bear," geography produces a diagram for the economics of dependency, where the chainlike relationship of satellite to metropolis follows the path of the logging train from wilderness to sawmill, thence to Memphis, where a change of trains leads inevitably, like the flow of wealth, to the North.[5]

Faulkner's geography depicts the dialectic of expropriation as a series of confrontations between satellite and metropolis on an economic continuum that binds the least developed, most peripheral area to the advanced centers of production and finance. His is a literary translation of

Gunder Frank's analysis of the *Development of Underdevelopment.*[6] This particularized view of dependency is possible only from the Third World point of view and represents a markedly deeper understanding of economic expropriation than the First World point of view, which tends to see massive economic wholes. The perspective of the First World is reductionist, typified by its notion that the Near East is an exclusively "Arab world," the only exception being Israel. The same point of view overlooks the Second World, apparently unaware of the economic presence and productivity of Eastern Europe, and imagines the entire Third World as an undifferentiated whole – its economic opposite: the source of unskilled, cheap labor and a market for its surplus.

In its view of global economics, the Third World has access to a far deeper understanding of history as defined by the expropriation of surplus than its potential class ally in the First World: the industrial proletariat. As Dahrendorf explains in his book *Class Conflict in Industrial Society,*[7] the proletariat sees through the bourgeoisie's complex notion of multiple social strata and instead defines history as a dramatic polarization of "them versus us." Although it is true that class struggle inevitably produces the polarization of social classes, a worldview reduced to a "them versus us" equation is simplistic. When the industrial proletariat of the First World sees the Third World in such reductive terms, as it has done in the case of Iran and the PLO, then its worldview has been inscribed within the optic of domination.

Whereas the Third World comprehends its exploitation as a series of moments and modes, the First World, because it defines the rest of the world in terms of the demands of capitalism, sees only its "other." The worldview of domination, so clearly inscribed in Sartre's analysis of "The Look," objectifies all that it beholds, abstracting the vital human presence of the Third World and reducing its cultural richness to assimilable forms. The dialectic of domination, defined phenomenologically by "The Look" and the notion of "otherness" has its economic equivalent in the history of expropriation and the map.

For the Third World intellectual, whose education and development often include years spent in exile in the metropolises of Europe, the map comes to be a highly charged symbol for the individual's alienation. In his moving *L'Enfant noir,* Camara Laye describes his personal alienation, caught between wholly different social worlds, in terms familiar to all artists and intellectuals from the Third World. When as a student, having just arrived and not yet integrated into the life of Paris, Camara Laye looks back to describe his African childhood, he structures his narrative on a binary opposition between the plenitude and familiarity of his family's compound and the empty, impenetrably abstract map of the Paris metro, which as an immigrant he carries in his pocket at the conclusion of his tale.

The unequal development between the First and Third Worlds, reproduced in cultural imperialism, inevitably separates the Third World intellectual from the community and culture of his or her birth. In all the great autobiographies of the Third World the "I" writing the narrative is never the same "I" being described. Writers and critics alike have attempted to define the alienation of the Third World intellectual, and many, like Derek Walcott, see it as a form of schizophrenia.[8] For Sylvia Wynter, whose terminology is less psychological, more sociological, alienation is produced by the individual's inscription in parallel social processes peculiar to colonial society. As she sees it, the "I growing up" in relation to traditional social practice is also the "I growing away" in relation to European institutionalized education. The result is the artist's (often permanent) inscription in a cultural Middle Passage.[9]

Perhaps the most graphic and complex rendering of alienation in the exiled Third World artist occurs in George Lamming's highly allegorical novel, *Water with Berries* (1971). The title is derived from Shakespeare's *The Tempest*[10] and evokes the plight of Caliban, who decries Prospero's previous kindnesses and the gift of language and who, in the recent literature of the Caribbean, has come to be associated with all artists from the Third World who must grapple with the languages of their domination. Lamming's modern-day Caliban, an exiled West Indian painter, curtains the windows of his London flat with maps of his Caribbean homeland. Gazing through the windows, the protagonist beholds the abstracted representation of the Caribbean superposed on the real, but for him alien, skyline of London. When the rising sun, which calls Londoners to their work, streams through the exile's windows, it illuminates the maps, making the island appear to float in an "ink blue ocean." The image is a complex figure for double estrangement. It is also oppositional, because the interplay between reality and abstraction evokes the history of colonial domination. What might be thought of as real, the London skyline, is for the exile unfamiliar, and because we perceive it through his eyes, cast as alien. In contrast, what was formerly familiar, the rich natural world of his birth, has been reduced to ink and abstracted to its geographic configurations.

The movement of *Water with Berries* is toward the ultimate reversal of the exile's alienation. This is achieved when, at the novel's conclusion, the terms of the narrative have been redefined. The artist returns to his island home, not as a repatriated immigrant, which would only reaffirm his oppressed status as "other," but as a revolutionary leader. The protagonist's political transformation of necessity negates those forces that in the novel sought to maintain the dependence all exiles feel toward their adoptive nations. The two characters – the one excessively protective and the other aggressively hostile – who attempt to hinder or prevent the protagonist's return, are killed. Their deaths liberate the exiled artist to assume his revolutionary mission. The elimination of these characters, embodiments of domination, cancels the equation of domination that defined the First World as real and the Third as a mappable abstraction. Piloting a stolen boat, the revolutionary sets out without charts, relying only on the position of the sun and stars to plot his course back to the Caribbean. Geography is now a statement of the concrete rather than the abstract, as the receding coastline and distant horizon define the revolutionary's movement toward the future.

Because *Water with Berries* is a novel, the reversal of abstraction is produced in relation to the specific nature of the narrative. Characters are introduced, events contribute to their development, and their relationships change – all of which defines the eventual polarization between the exile and his oppressors as process.

The situation is very different when the same sort of reversal occurs in a poem. Metaphoric language, compressed images, and closed form create a potentially explosive context for the reversal of domination inscribed in the First World point of view.

The great universal poet of the Third World, Nicolás Guillén, demonstrates in his poem "Soldiers in Abyssinia" that when a writer from the periphery uses a form charged with the history of domination – like the map – he does so fully aware of its ideological function and determined – like George Lamming – to fling the demystified content of ideology back in the face of the First World.

The poem opens with the dramatic confrontation between First and Third Worlds:

> Mussolini
> On his fist, his beard.
> On the table, like a cross,
> Africa
> bleeding
> Greenish-black and bluish-white Africa
> of geography and the map.

Hunched over a map of Africa, Mussolini embodies fascist imperialism. Domination is made brutally concrete in the masculine images of fist and beard, whereas a crucified Africa, its reality bleeding out, is abstracted in ink and paper.

Developing the metaphor of abstraction, Mussolini jabs at and pierces his paper Africa:

> His finger, son of Caesar,
> pierces the continent:
> the paper waters
> do not speak,
> nor do the cities of paper.
> The map, impassive, is paper,
> and his finger, son of Caesar,
> with its bloody nail, is fixed
> on a paper Abyssinia.[11]

The dramatic antithesis between the physically concrete Mussolini and the reductive and abstract representation of Africa is, however, based on a contradiction, inherent in power, that Guillén will use to reverse the terms of domination in the poem. The impassivity of the map and the poet's insistence on the word "paper" underscore the fact that the map is only a representation and that a real Africa exists, which escapes abstraction – like the black skin under a white paper mask – waiting to seize and reconstitute the terms of oppression. Moreover, no matter how physical the description of First World domination, it does not constitute a concrete whole, but a dismembered and fragmented notion of power, the separate parts of which – finger, fist, and beard – are themselves reductive and tend toward abstraction.

The last stanza fully develops the contradiction of power. The once integral whole, captured and framed by the name "Mussolini," which has undergone fragmentation, is finally disintegrated and redefined in myriad faceless surrogates – the soldiers:

> Ah, but the soldiers
> will fall and stumble!
> The soldiers
> will not travel on a map,
> but on the ground of Africa,
> under Africa's sun.
> There they will not find paper cities;
> the cities will be something more than dots that speak
> with little green topographical voices:
> a swarm of bullets,
> submachine-gun coughs,
> canefields of lances.

Then the soldiers,
(who did not travel on a map),
the soldiers,
far from Mussolini,
alone;
the soldiers
will roast in the desert,
and much smaller, of course,
the soldiers
will then slowly dry up in the sun
the soldiers
come back,
the soldiers
in the excrement of buzzards.[12]

The poem's definition of power is very similar to the understanding the Third World brings to bear on global economic relationships. Whereas the First World imagines a direct confrontation between massive global wholes – Mussolini and the continent of Africa – the Third World knows that real struggle takes place in the concrete geography of countryside and cities and is waged against the oppressor's army of stand-ins. In setting the soldiers down amidst the real terrain of Africa rather than placing them like so many pawns on a chessboard, Guillén reverses the hypocrisy of colonialism's original moment: the 1885 conference in Berlin, where the dominant powers of Europe convened to carve up the map of Africa for their separate colonial ventures. Ever since this historic meeting, the economic development of the First World has depended on seeing the Third as its abstract and exploitable "other."

Guillén's radical reversal of the First World point of view lifts the poem out of the imagery of domination. He neither recreates images of brute physical force nor abstracts his object. Rather, he employs a language derived from nature to suggest the unity and strength of Third World opposition. The sun that roasts the soldiers, reducing them to dried bits of buzzard fodder, and the buzzards themselves, who return to Mussolini his attenuated selves, thus rendering to Caesar what is his, define the poem's oppositional stance at a new level. By replacing the language of domination with subversive images derived from nature, Guillén departs radically from the tendency in more assimilable Caribbean writing to romanticize natural description. Rather than pastorals of domination, Guillén's natural imagery gives voice to the spirit of liberation.

The use of nature also creates a space for Guillén's truly universal perspective. Imagining "canefields of lances" breaking through the map of Abyssinia, rupturing the abstraction, the poet alludes to his own nation's history. Images derived from the centuries of sugar production in Cuba inform all of Guillén's writing, from the very sensual to the stridently political, defining its perspectival base in the Caribbean. In his "Cuban Elegy," Guillén offers this brutal epigram, which combines sugar production and the map to demonstrate the link between exploitation and abstraction:

> Cuba: sold-out palm grove,
> Drawn and quartered dream,
> tough map of sugar and neglect . . .[13]

When in "Soldiers in Abyssinia" Guillén envisions resistance in the form of "canefields," this specifically Caribbean image functions as a highly compressed metaphor, bridging geographic and historical space. This image facilitates the linking of Africa and Cuba precisely because it is not a purely natural figure, as are the sun and the buzzards, but a figure associated with production in the field. The metaphor works on the basis of a shared mode of economic oppression wherein Cuba and Abyssinia were historically defined as single-crop economies for the world capitalist system. In the space of this single metaphor, Guillén demonstrates that he speaks for all oppressed peoples and that the struggle for liberation in any one nation of the Third World concerns the whole of the Third World.

The most striking feature of a reversal of the First World optic is that it causes the entire content of a poem to undergo redefinition. As a literary device, reversal is not epiphenomenal, influencing only the line or stanza in which it occurs, but a radically explosive moment that dramatically separates the envisioned future from the past as it has been conceived within the system of domination. Reversal negates power and defines liberation in terms of a new, universalizing perspective. The bold expansive movement of Césaire's "Return to My Native Land," where negritude comes to be synonymous with liberation, is intimately structured on the same reversal of abstraction we found earlier in Lamming and Guillén. As the poem draws to its conclusion, negritude emerges as a tremendously virile force, alive in the poem's hyperbole of nature and culture. Not gratuitously, and as its historical contradiction, negritude is defined against the most reductive of abstractions, the content of which is so clearly understood that the word "map" need not even be mentioned:

islands, cheap paper torn upon the waters[14]

To reverse the First World optic, which so inferiorizes and disdains its Third World object, Césaire imagines the map made for his own use; and in so doing, he negates the dialectic of domination between First and Third Worlds:

> And my original geography also: the map
> of the world made for my use, not painted the
> arbitrary colours of scientists, but with the
> geometry of my shed blood.[15]

By placing the Third World in the position traditionally ascribed to the First, Césaire does not institute a new form of domination – a Black Power antithesis of white colonialism; rather, he suggests a humanized universality. In replacing ink with blood, the poet empties his view of the world of abstraction and envisions human relationships as the basis for global relationships that have traditionally been defined by geography and geometry. Because Césaire's concept of human relationships is rooted in the history of struggle – the "shed blood" is remembered even at the moment of liberation – his definition of universality is not a negation of history but a transcendence of the way history has been determined and defined by the First World.

Césaire's greatness as a poet of the Third World can be grasped only when negritude is understood in the fullest sense as a form of cultural revolution. Lamentably, our apprehension of negritude in the First World has been influenced by the function of dominant ideology to reduce negritude to a purely racial category. In writing the introduction to the Présence Africaine edition of Césaire's poem, André Breton exemplifies the way negritude has been bracketed in First World thought:

> when art itself is on the verge of being stultified in obsolete forms and values, the first new breath of life that can give us back our trust and vigor comes from a black poet. A black man it is who masters the French language as no white man can today. A black man it is who guides us today through unexplored lands building as he goes the contacts that will make us progress on sparks.[16]

As a corrective to the centuries of white political domination that is incapable of renewing itself in fresh cultural forms, Breton equates negritude with black supremacy and imagines that Césaire's writing will breathe new life into decayed European forms. In marveling at Césaire's mastery of the French language, Breton displaces the reader's attention from the fact that Caliban has no other language to work with but the language of domination and, by implication, diminishes the rest of the Third World. By imagining that Césaire's use of the French language gives new life to the European model and congratulating Césaire for somehow being more French than the French, Breton defines negritude as an assimilable form.

Negritude is assimilable only so long as ideology in the First World continues to function on the basis of its political and economic domination to make it impossible for cultural revolution in the Third World to be realized in political terms. This does not negate the fact that, for the Third World, negritude signifies liberation – and not just the liberation of blacks, former slaves, but the universal liberation of colonial subjects.[17] The representative relationship between the history of Black slavery and the degradation of all colonized populations is clear in the final pages of Césaire's poem, where he offers the description of a "poor-old-Negro," the caricature of inferiority, who unexpectedly stands up:

> the seated "poor-old-Negro"
> unexpectedly standing
> upright in the hold
> upright in the cabins
> upright on the bridge
> upright in the wind
> upright under the sun
> upright in the blood
>   upright
>   and
>   free

The image is twofold. As a black man, he embodies the history of slavery. As a "poor-old-Negro," the apotheosis of degradation, he represents the way neocolonialism maintains the impoverishment of the Third World. In standing up, the black man overturns the history of slavery, which sought to inscribe his race forever in inferiority. And in standing up, the "poor-old-Negro" divests himself of modern-day connotations of cultural inferiority.

Once the colonized subject stands,

> unexpectedly upright
> in the rigging
> at the bar
> at the compass

at the map
under the stars
upright
and
free[18]

his appropriation of the ship of history signals the coming into being of unified historical perspective.

NOTES

1   Derek Walcott, *The Star-Apple Kingdom* (New York: Farrar, Straus & Giroux, 1979), p. 56.
2   Aimé Césaire, *Cahier d'un Retour au Pays Natal* (Paris: Présence Africaine, 1977), pp. 65–7.
3   The relationship of the particular to the Third World's understanding of universality is at the crux of Césaire's famous letter of resignation from the French Communist party:

> . . . Je ne m'enterre pas dans un particularisme étroit. Mais je ne veux pas non plus me perdre dans un universalisme décharné. Il y a deux manières de se perdre: par ségrégation murée dans le particulier ou par dilution dans l'"universel."
>
> Ma conception de l'universel est celle d'un universel riche de tout le particulier, riche de tous les particuliers [letter to Maurice Thorez, 1965].

In a 1967 interview with the Haitian poet René Depestre, Césaire criticizes many fellow negritude poets who were also Communists for being "abstract Communists"; that is, "there was nothing to distinguish them either from the French surrealists or from the French Communists." For these poets, negritude was not a process of "disalienation" as it was for Césaire, but a means of their "assimilation."

When told, "You have tried to particularize Communism . . . ," Césaire responds, "Yes, it is a very old tendency of mine. Even then the Communists would reproach me for speaking of the Negro problem – they called it my racism. But I would answer, 'Marx is all right, but we need to complete Marx.' I felt that the emancipation of the Negro consisted of more than just a political emancipation" ("An interview with Aimé Césaire," in Césaire's *Discourse on Colonialism* [New York: Monthly Review Press, 1972], pp. 65–79).
4   My understanding of dependency is derived from Immanuel Wallerstein's *The Modern World System* (New York: Academic Press, 1974). According to Wallerstein, capitalism is a global economic system, historically defined by three modes of labor control that produced three areas of production: the Third World periphery, originally defined by slave labor; the Second World

semiperiphery, defined by coerced labor; and the First World core, where wage labor came into being. Wallerstein's notion of the semiperiphery is particularly important, for it expands the notion of the dialectic of expropriation–accumulation between Third and First Worlds. As I see it, this expanded dialectic is the essence of the Third World's global optic and the basis for its deeper understanding of economic dependency.

5   For an expanded description of dependency in Faulkner, see my article, "Aesthetics of the Rural Slum, Contradictions of Dependency in 'The Bear,'" *Social Text,* no. 2 (Summer 1979): 82–103.

6   The terms "satellite" and "metropolis" were coined by André Gunder Frank, whose definition of dependency describes a chain of relationships starting from the most underdeveloped rural satellite areas, whose wealth is expropriated by the immediate village metropolis, which in turn serves as a satellite to some more advanced urban metropolis – and so on from the Latin American hinterland to the cities of North America and Europe.

7   Ralf Dahrendorf, *Class Conflict in Industrial Society* (Stanford, Calif.: Stanford University Press, 1959).

8   Derek Walcott, "What the Twilight Says: An Overture," *Dream on Monkey Mountain* (New York: Farrar, Straus & Giroux, 1970).

9   Sylvia Wynter, "History, Ideology and the Reinvention of the Past in Achebe's 'Things Fall Apart' and Laye's 'The Dark Child,'" *Minority Voices* 2, no. 1 (1978): 43–61.

10   When thou cam'st first,
          Thou strok'st me, and made much of me; wouldst give me
          Water with berries in't. And teach me how
          To name the bigger light, and how the less,
          That burn by day and night: and then I lov'd thee.

The figure of Caliban has served in different guises as a central symbol in many Caribbean and Latin American discourses of identity, from José E. Rodó's *Ariel* (1900) to Roberto Fernández Retamár's *Calibán: Apuntes sobre la cultura de nuestra América* (1971). The latter provides a useful overview of Caliban as variously drawn by New World and European writers.

11 Nicolás Guillén, *The Great Zoo* (New York: Monthly Review Press, 1972), pp. 180–2.

12 Ibid.

13 Robert Márquez and David Arthur McMurray, eds., *Man-Making Words* *(Amherst: University of Massachusetts Press, 1972), p.78.*

14 Césaire, *Cahier,* p. 138.

15 Ibid., p. 135.

16 Ibid., pp. 13–15.

17 It is important to note Césaire's use of the term "negritude," which throughout the poem is equated with a class historical position rather than a purely racial category. The word "negritude" is used sparingly and first occurs more than halfway through the poem, where Césaire uses it to define a huge, almost grotesque, impoverished old Negro seated on a train:

A Negro big as a pongo, who tried to make himself small on the tram bench. He tried to relax his gigantic legs and trembling hungry pug's fists on the dirty bench. And everything left him, left him. His nose seemed a peninsula adrift, his very Negritude paled under the action of a tireless tawing. And the tawer was Poverty.

Here "Negritude" is a compressed metaphor, a bridge between a sign for race (the shape of his nose) and the experience of a class ("Poverty").

For Césaire, negritude is a dynamic force, rather than a solidified and static concept:

> my Negritude is not a stone, its deafness
> thrown against the clamour of the day
> my Negritude is not a speck of dead water
> on the dead eye of earth
> my Negritude is neither a tower nor a cathedral

18   Césaire, *Cahier,* pp. 147–9.

6

Mrs. Williams's William
Carlos

JULIO MARZÁN

William Carlos Williams's *Autobiography* opens with the following disclaimer:

> Nine-tenths of our lives is well forgotten in the living. Of the part that is remembered, the most had better not be told: it would be of interest to no one, or at least would not contribute to the story of what we ourselves have been. A thin thread of narrative remains – a few hundred pages. . . . They constitute our particular treasure. That is all, justly, that we should offer.[1]

Only Williams, of course, had the right to select the pertinent "thin thread of narrative" he would weave into his autobiography, and only he was qualified to reveal that behind the story he chose to tell lay a "secret," the proverbial "secret of our lives," that should remain untold:

> We always try to hide the secret of our lives from the general stare. What I believe to be the hidden core of my life will not easily be deciphered, even when I tell, as here, the outer circumstances. (p. 1)

What part of his *remembered* life "that had better not be told" belongs to his "hidden core" is left unclear. That core, we are told, is indecipherably encoded in the "outer circumstances" described in *The Autobiography*.

On the surface, Williams's prefatory caveat appears to describe a principle universally adhered to by autobiographers: that the process of culling autobiographical details assumes a necessary demarcation of the poet, the literary "person we ourselves have been," from the less significant historical person in whom readers would be less interested. After reading *The Autobiography* and his other autobiographical writings, however, one must conclude that Williams's caveat – reminiscent of Jorge Luis

Borges's fictive division in "Borges y yo" – literally posits the coexistence of two distinct personae whose relation to each other Williams leaves nebulous and which, in fact, are depicted as separated by a subdued metaphorical wall, like the one in the opening to *The Autobiography*. In front of that cracked wall stands Williams the poet, *The Autobiography*'s secret-possessing protagonist; behind it stands William Carlos the man, whose biographical particulars the protagonist carefully selects or encodes.[2] Williams's keen sense of this division is evident in much of his autobiographical writings. In general, he portrays the mature poet as the persona that broke free from an earlier romantic influence. What is missing from that portrait, however, is the whole Williams, the dichotomous, composite Williams who went to some lengths (occasionally stretching the facts) to preserve the image of his literary persona. That Williams was either unequipped or unprepared to comprehend the lifelong influence on the mature poet of the person whom, by his own admission, he least understood: the "foreigner" in his life, his mother, Elena.

Raquel Helene Rose Hoheb was born in Mayaguez, Puerto Rico, to a mother originally from Martinique and a Puerto Rican father, both of whom had died by the time she was fourteen. Elena's marriage to William George, the poet's father, was a link in a chain of unfortunate coincidences. While studying art in Paris, she received word from her brother Carlos that, owing to his personal financial losses, she would have to discontinue her studies and return to live with him and his family in Puerto Plata, Dominican Republic. Anglo-American literary history might have been different if shortly before her departure she had not discovered that, out of love for her, her Spanish lover had jilted another woman. Incapable of accepting a love so tainted by deliberation, she broke with the Spaniard – a decision that, judging from Williams's tone, the entire family lived to regret.

> From Paris she returned to those meager islands. She married at the home of one of those same Monsantos and pretty soon has two boys on her hands. I call it her vicarious atonement.[3]

In 1882, at her brother Carlos's home in the Dominican Republic, Elena met William George Williams, who at the age of five had been taken from England, after a brief period in New York City, to St. Thomas. Williams grew up in the Caribbean, moved about by his mother's marriages or traveling to other islands in search of employment. While on a stop in the Dominican Republic before going on to the United States, he met and soon proposed marriage to Elena. Still bitter with herself for having left her Spaniard and with little to look forward to in Puerto Plata, she accepted his proposal. She followed him to Rutherford, where they married, and in 1883 gave birth to William Carlos Williams.

Elena was destined to have a greater influence on William Carlos than his father. First there was the necessary deference paid to her culture and language. Elena spoke no English and her husband spoke fluent Spanish. In *Yes, Mrs. Williams,* Williams described the household into which he was born as "Spanish-speaking":

> My father spoke Spanish quite as easily as he spoke English. . . . So that when I was a child Spanish was the only language spoken in the household, except by Mrs. Wellcome, my father's mother, who employed what was called *español de cocina,* pig Spanish, which was not pretty to hear.
>
> So that as children my brother and I heard Spanish constantly spoken about us. A steady flow of West Indians, South Americans and other speakers of Spanish language came to visit us, to stay sometimes the entire winter if it so fitted their fancy or the necessity of the case. (p. 45)

From an interview with Walter Sutton, we gather that both he and his brother started out as bilingual or monolingual Spanish speakers before they "dropped" the language at some unspecified time:

> We've dropped it in our day, curiously enough, but my parents spoke Spanish, preferable to English, and my brother and I heard it and understood it because they said things in Spanish that they didn't want us to understand.

This version of Williams's linguistic formation contradicts the linguistic emphasis in his earlier *Autobiography,* in which his years as a Spanish speaker – years presumably irrelevant to his life as an English speaker – remain unmentioned: "Spanish and French were the languages I heard habitually while I was growing up" (p. 15). Williams's vacillations, which his critics largely tolerate unexamined, explains Paul Mariani's contradictory descriptions of Elena in his *William Carlos Williams: A New World Naked.*[4] On page 2 of that book Mariani describes Elena as a "mother who spoke French first and then Spanish and – when necessary – a very broken English." On page 17 he tells us that at home she was a Spanish speaker who "practiced her beloved French" whenever she received someone who spoke it.

Two other, related reasons for Elena's greater influence on her son are her personality and her husband's prolonged and frequent business trips to Central and South America (once for an entire year). The paternal vacuum left by Williams's usually deferential father permitted Elena's powerful personality to reign unchallenged. In *The Autobiography,* Williams tells us that the strong-willed Elena successfully resisted his grandmother's attempt to take over his upbringing:

> Grandmother took me over or tried to. But once Mother lost her temper and laid the old gal out with a smack across the puss that my mother joyfully remembered until her death. Her Latin blood got the best of her that day. (p. 5)

The reference to Latin blood is significant. First, it characterizes the writing persona as non-Latin. Second, it generates a symbol: Mother symbolizes Latin and thus, implicitly, Grandmother symbolizes English. The importance of Williams's attachment to his grandmother as symbol cannot be overstated. Grandmother descended from the Godwins, making Williams remotely related to Shelley and consequently – through his language at least – in direct line of great English-language poets. Williams appeals to his reader's unconscious, resorting to his pattern of contradictory syntax: The words "Grandmother took me over" prominently stand out before he concedes she had not in fact; the persona is aware that his ideal reader, being Anglo-American, sympathizes with the persona's wish to be saved by his grandmother from being raised a Latin "foreigner."

Elena impressed Williams with her artistic sense and her refinement. As James E. Breslin observes:

> Into a largely sterile environment, Mrs. Williams introduced an early and important impetus toward artistic activity. Because of her, Williams was at first interested in painting. But the direction of her influence was not immediately creative, since it inspired a sense of beauty that was dreamily nostalgic: it was she who led him to Keats. Behind all of Williams' later attraction to the elegant, his frequent squeamish distaste for the common, lies the refined and remote figure of his mother.[5]

Williams confirmed Elena's importance to him during his early years as a writer in *I Wanted to Write a Poem:*

> I was conscious of my mother's influence all through this time of writing, her ordeal as a woman and as a foreigner in this country. . . . I was personifying her, her detachment from the world of Rutherford. She seemed an heroic figure, a poetic ideal. I didn't especially admire her; I was attached to her. I had not yet established any sort of independent identity.[6]

As should be evident from that statement, Williams's feelings toward Elena were ambivalent. After his youthful idealization of her, he later felt the need to be free of her influence. Then, after years of estrangement, he rediscovered her, especially – characteristically – her manner of expressing herself: her accent, her Spanish aphorisms, and her nostalgic anecdotes about Puerto Rico – traits that had surely also influenced the young Williams.

Williams eventually came to resent Elena's romantic nostalgia and idealism as mere tactics to insulate her from coarse reality. This resentment prompted his writing "All the Fancy Things," in which his persona admonishes "ma chère" to forget "All the Fancy Things" she idealized in her past and to "withstand rebuffs / from that which returns to the beginnings –."[7]

Their relationship was also strained by Elena's spiritualism. In "Eve," Williams confesses that seeing her entranced, as well as seeing her being seen by others, shamed him:

> I realize why you wish
> to communicate with the dead –
> And it is again I
> who try to hush you
> that you shall not
> make a fool of yourself
> and have them stare at you
> with natural faces – . . .
> It not so much frightens
> as shames me.

As Williams acknowledges in "Eve," however, her spiritualism was not the only reason for their estrangement; there was Elena herself or, more accurately, how Williams perceived her:

> It is as though
> you looked down from above
> at me – not
> with what they would describe
> as pride but the same
> that is in me: a sort
> of shame that the world
> should see you as I see you, . . .

Williams leaves unexplained why Elena should look at him with the shame he feels. What is clearest about the poem is its thrust, Williams's plea to be forgiven for having "been a fool" who, until "Adam" (his father) died, failed to see in her a passion stifled by the circumstances of her life. Whatever Williams perceived in her after his father died, however, did little to erase the original shame that doubtless accounted for his painting Elena as a difficult old woman. More than a decade later, in his *Autobiography*, a book in which she is frequently and condescendingly referred to as "poor Mother," any significant discussion of her as a young woman usually turns to pathetic examples of her nostalgia or her spiritualism, two tributaries to his original shame. Nowhere in *The Autobiography* do we get a sense of the young woman to whom he was so attached, as if to suggest that that woman belonged to the life of the person and not of the poet. Similarly, his original shame appears to underline Williams's inclination to exaggerate his English grandmother's hand in his upbringing or his underplaying Elena's.

In short, Williams gives signs of being psychologically blocked from writing about Elena's life in a manner that does not hint of either the historical persona's shame or the poet's condescension. An extreme example of this block is found in *Yes, Mrs. Williams*, the book he had promised to write about her. Even though intended as a biography of Elena, very few pages are passed before Williams drifts into a biography of his father, whose remarks about his wife are apparently quoted to support Williams's own ambivalent feelings toward her: "He confided to me just before the end that she was strange and cautioned me that I would have my trouble with her." Then, self-conscious of his extended evasion of the subject of his book, he adds, "But this is merely an excuse for speaking of him here" (pp. 18–19).

Williams never does elaborate on why William George (who sometimes shared Elena's spiritualist beliefs) saw her as strange. In *Yes,* however, we learn another reason for Williams's increasing estrangement from her as he grew older: In addition to his shame, he suffered from a sense of being betrayed by those qualities about her that as a boy he most admired. Her idealistic standards of beauty, art, and love and her dreamlike world of pleasant memories in Puerto Rico were things on which the boy Williams had also counted and that when he tried to harmonize them with his surroundings, failed him:

> She died with a tranquil smile on her face, just went to sleep from pneumonia. What dream she was following at the moment of course we will never know. The truth and its pursuit was always at the front of my mother's mind. It was a long time before I came to realize how her romantic ideas had deceived her and me in the modern world which we in our turn had to push behind us to come up fighting or smiling, if we could make it, or just to find some sunny spot where we could stretch our bones. (*Yes,* p. 20)

Left unexamined, all these particulars of the "outer circumstances" of Williams's biography obscure that what most distanced Williams from his mother was that she deprived him of a cultural lineage in his own country. In his eyes, which saw only through the filter of Anglo-American cultural and linguistic conventions, Elena's being Puerto Rican or Spanish made her a cultural "foreigner," a word whose true meaning for Williams must be properly defined. Contrary to today's stereotype of post–World War II working-class immigrant Puerto Ricans, Elena belonged to the island's gentry. Williams himself confirmed that the Hohebs had lost count of how many of their generations had lived in Puerto Rico (*Yes*, p. 52). Because at the time Elena emigrated Puerto Rico had yet to become a colony of the United States, she was officially Spanish. But whatever Elena's citizenship was in fact meant little to Williams, except that her being Spanish allowed him to identify with the more prestigious "Spanish" – as many maligned, immigrant Latin Americans were wont to do in his time. The stream of "West Indians" in their home and Elena's terrifying spiritualist trances imprinted in his mind unpleasant symbols of his unprestigious heritage.[8] Those symbols, among which Elena herself was the central one, caused Williams to perceive her as a "foreigner," and her foreignness haunted him:

> It was all in a great yard with a painted wooden fence of boards, cut out into a scroll design and painted green and red – that stood above his head – but he could peek through and see the people passing. Behind him his smaller brother, six years old or less, came following while the mother leaned upon the balustrade of the balcony that encircled the house and watched them play.
>
> There above them, as they played, leaned nothing of America, but Puerto Rico a foreign island in a tropical sea of earlier years – and Paris of the later Seventies. (*Yes*, p. 116)

Being a product of his spoken language, Williams the man looked up at the balcony and saw the foreigner. Williams the *poet*, however, tried not to see the foreigner, seeing instead a universal, abstracted image of her: the poetic truth of the details of his life. Elena became a poetic image that belonged to a system of stereotypes (which were already provided by his language) about Latins – and Anglo-Saxons. In the poem "The Marriage of Souls," his parents are abstracted into a powerful juxtaposition of opposite forces:

> That heat!
> That terrible heat

That coldness!
That terrible coldness

Alone!
At the flame's tip
Alone!
In the sparkling crystal

So they stay
Adjacent
Like to like
In terrible isolation

Like to like
In terrible intimacy
Unfused
And unfusing

In *Adam and Eve in the City,* his parents became the allegorical Adam and Eve who came to the city banished from their Caribbean paradise. In those poems the social stereotypes are explicit – William George was the cold, passionless Englishman; Elena the warm, passionate Latin – except that for Williams these were not equal opposites. Because she was Latin, Elena was flawed by a romanticism that, according to Williams (and the conventional Anglo-American view of Latins), the Latin employs to avoid confronting reality. Conversely, Williams interprets Latin romanticism as the source of the intolerable "lying" he accuses Latins of doing with their popular music in the "The Desert Music":

> What else, Latins do you yourselves
> seek but relief!
> with the expressionless ding dong you dish up
> to us of your souls and loves, which
> we swallow. Spaniards!

One has to wonder who "we" are who swallow this "Spanish" (probably Mexican) music. If he was writing as an Anglo-American, he stepped out of character. Then, sensing his remark too sweeping, Williams adds a parenthetical, characteristic retraction:

> (though these are mostly
> Indians who chase the white bastards
> through the streets on their Independence Day
> and try to kill them)

Even more important, however, is his retraction of his own posturing:

What's that?
Oh, come on.
But what's that?
the music the
music! As when Casals struck
and held a deep cello tone
and I am speechless

Casals was an artist and a Latin whose music Williams esteemed. Besides Williams's identification with Casals as a fellow artist, the cellist and he had something else in common: Casals's mother was Puerto Rican.

This Mexican episode in *The Desert Music,* in which Williams's Anglo literary persona thoughtlessly (and conventionally) labels Spanish anyone whose language is Spanish, also illustrates Williams's practice of converting his cultural past to a system of symbols, as he did with Grandma, his father, and especially Elena and the adulterating "Latin" heritage he was condemned to bear. In *The Autobiography,* for example, he summarizes his stopover at Ciudad Trujillo, Dominican Republic: "Here only a moment. Spanish again." This language symbol also reiterates that Williams defined persons and societies by their spoken language. The language and the person were synonymous. Hence he, insofar as he spoke English and had "dropped" Spanish, was "American." His English-speaking father, who refused to become a U.S. citizen, was never seriously seen by Williams's literary persona as a "foreigner," despite the occasional allusions to his being English or cold. Elena, however, would be congenitally foreign, despite the Jones Act of 1917, which made her a U.S. citizen. To this point, Linda Wagner's observations concerning Williams's stories are also applicable to his life:

> For Williams, any person's identity rested on his spoken language. Many of his short stories open with a character speaking: we hear the words with no introduction or setting given.[9]

His only history, then, was that of his spoken language, which if pursued too scrupulously would lead him to Europe, the pedigree that the convention of bigotry accused him of lacking. Understandably, therefore, he perceived that his language's past, like his own, was less important than its future, the most important tense of the American experience. Despite Williams's fervent delving into his parent's genealogy, he was careful to dissociate that past, which produced the man from his pastless literary persona. Between his foreign past and his persona stands a wall, which explicitly appears in the poem "An Eternity," on the death of his mother:

> I,
> turn my face to the wall,
> revert to my beginnings and turn
> my face also to the wall.

Then, responding to the harshness of that statement, he retracts it in the following line: "And yet, mother, that isn't true."

This metaphorical wall reappears as the subdued metaphor that separates the mature poet from the impressionable youth and the public from the private Williams in his *Autobiography*. From all evidence, Williams believed that the creator of that wall was Elena, whose language was not only foreign but a stream of unreal memories and abstract ideas that gradually congealed to barricade her from the tangible world of "things," William Carlos Williams among them.

Williams's critics have skirted the implications of his nonliterary biography on the literary "person we ourselves have been." Had they overstepped that tacit boundary, however, Anglo-American letters would have discovered that Williams's analysis of Latins and of Elena's influence on him were fallacious and, more important, that far from breaking from her influence, his Latin half accounts for the mature style of the literary persona. To begin with, his stereotypical view of Latins was a weak basis on which to erect an antithetical self-image. Elena's idealism and dreamy nostalgia may have appeared to him dishonest or ridiculously anachronistic when measured against the modernity of industrial Rutherford, but she was the product of a belated romantic period in Latin America generally and therefore concordant with her time. Her romanticism was unsymptomatic of a genetic Latin flaw.

Despite Williams's implicit celebration of his Anglo-Americanness as the antidote to her (Latin) romanticism, his literary reaction to her romanticism was identical to that of contemporaneous Puerto Rican writers to the same romantic traits in Puerto Rican society. In 1896, Manuel Zeno Gandía broke with romanticism by realistically imaging the lives of the rustic *jíbaros* in the novel *La charca* (*The Stagnant Pool*). In that novel, at one point the protagonist Juan del Salto reflects on his son Jacobo, who, typical of his social class and like Elena Hoheb, studied in Europe. After reading Jacobo's letters gushing with patriotic nostalgia for his homeland, Juan describes Jacobo's perception of Puerto Rico in words that could have described Elena: "Apart from that he kept his homeland printed on his soul: he dreamed it more than he experienced it. He gazed at it through the prism of his romantic soul."[10]

Williams's preoccupation with language as a measure of a society parallels twentieth-century Puerto Rican writers' theme of the failure of their country's language to grasp reality. Antonio S. Pedreira (1898–1939) voiced this concern in his essay "Insularismo" (1934), in which he chastised Puerto Rican society for its *retoricismo,* or its penchant for euphemism and circumlocution. Highly relieved by the closing of the period of romanticism, which he generally dismissed as a long "poetic pneumonia," he specifically rapped the poet José Gautier Benítez, whose popular poems epitomized the romantic lyric in Puerto Rico, in words that aptly parallel Williams's criticism of Elena:

> He turned his lyricism into a nostalgia and perceived Puerto Rico as a reflection in a mirror of water, on the verge of a departure or a return, "like the memory of a deep love," with that lover's emotion that impedes a man's arriving with sharp penetration at the heart of things.[11]

These parallels,[12] along with others that can be made with other contemporaneous Latin American writers, make more sense if we consider that Williams and Latin American writers faced the same challenge: to define an American future of cultures composed of both European and non-European legacies. It was the same quest that in the late twenties and throughout the thirties produced the major introspective Latin American essays, as well as the novels of the jungle and the pampa. The writers of these works shared with Williams the need to define their respective countries' Americanness. Williams's reaction to Elena's romanticism, therefore, was an expression of his own Americanness as a Latin and not, as Williams presents the dualism, a question of his Anglo half overtaking him as he outgrew his Latinness (as he envisioned Grandma English taking over his upbringing). In summary, even though Williams was convinced that he had fashioned a literary identity purged of Elena's influence – or though he felt the need to convince the literary world of that purgation – one cannot accept at face value, as critics almost unanimously have, his portrayal of himself as entirely the product of his spoken language.

This analysis of Williams, of course, is not intended to argue that Williams denied Elena's personal or cultural influence. That I can quote so extensively from Williams's writings demonstrates that he probably made more of it at times than others would have liked. In *The Autobiography,* Ezra Pound is described as always insisting that Williams placed too much emphasis on his mother's influence:

> Ezra's insistence has always been that I never laid proper stress in my life upon the part played in it by my father rather than my mother. Oh, the woman of it is important, he would acknowl-

edge, but the form of it, if not the drive, came unacknowledged from the old man, the Englishman. (p. 91)

But Williams never really understood Elena's culture or its influence on him as much as he gave the impression that he did. Instead, he perceived Elena as sociolinguistic conventions colored her, as a "West Indian" and "foreigner," two words whose combined meaning in Williams's day prefigured today's sense of "minority." These were the very linguistic conventions Pound employed to tease Williams in a jocular discussion of some of Williams's poems, a revealing jocularity that Pound doubtless knew touched Williams's most sensitive nerve:

> And America? What the h...l do you a blooming foreigner know about the place. Your *père* only penetrated the edge, and you've never been west of Upper Darby, or the Maunchunk switchback . . .
> I was very glad to see your wholly incoherent unamerican poems in the L.R. . . .
> You thank your blooming gawd you've got enough Spanish blood to muddy up your mind, and prevent the current American ideation from going through it like a blighted colander.
> The thing that saves your work is opacity, and don't forget it. Opacity is NOT an American quality. Fizz, swish, gabble, and verbiage, these are *echt americanisch*.[13]

Perhaps because Hilda Doolittle also detected Williams's dissatisfaction with himself she saw the need to touch that sensitive nerve in a rejection note:

> I don't know what you think but I consider this business of writing a very sacred thing! – I think you have the "spark" – am sure of it, and when you speak *direct* are a poet. I feel in the hey-ding-ding touch running through your poem a derivative tendency which, to me, is not *you* – not your very self. It is as if you were ashamed of your Spirit, ashamed of your inspiration! – as if you mocked at your own song. It's very well to *mock* at yourself – it is a spiritual sin to mock at your inspiration –. (*Imaginations*, p. 13)

After citing this note in his preface to *Kora in Hell*, Williams's persona characteristically took the offensive: "There is nothing in literature but change and change is mockery." Doolittle's emphasis, of course, was on the archetypal permanence of literature, whereas Williams defended the irreverence of style. Williams depended on style to translate the particulars of his exotic autobiographical situation into universal truth. Being an artist and knowing that his life was as microcosmic as any other, Williams developed an aesthetic of a *poetic* truth pruned of superfluous details that make up *natural* truth and stripped of the "associational or sentimental values" we attach to natural things:

> The true value is that peculiarity which gives an object a character by itself. The associational or sentimental value is the false. . . .
>
> The imagination goes from one thing to another. Given many things of totally divergent natures but possessing one-thousandth part of a quality in common, provided that it be new, distinguished, these things belong in an imaginative category and not in a gross natural array. To me this is the gist of the whole matter. (*Kora in Hell,* p. 14)

Consistent with that aesthetic vision, Williams expurgated the Latin side of his life from his autobiographical persona because it did not constitute a "peculiarity which gives an object a character by itself." Or to use Williams's device of retraction, he *tried* to repress that side, managing instead to sublimate it. Ultimately, his sublimation of those repressed feelings impelled him to arrive at the quintessential function of art. He universalized, sometimes abstracted, his subjects, turning them into allegories that permitted him to reflect on essential human experience, with the enduring results belonging to the world of outer circumstances described in *The Autobiography*. "The Marriage of Souls," is an example of this kind of abstraction. "Wide Awake, Full of Love," a poem possibly about the ailing Elena dreaming of going "South" (to Puerto Rico) could easily have been about an elderly patient.

This formula of universalizing particulars is also evident in poems with an apparently remote autobiographical connection. Who, for instance, can extricate the contemplative poem from the ethnic tone in "El Hombre"? The Spanish title transforms the poem into a metaphor of the way Williams viewed that strain of his cultural formation, as a remote element, present yet having no recognizable effect on him:

> It's a strange courage
> you give me ancient star:
> Shine alone in the sunrise
> toward which you lend no part!

But higher poetic truth too often clashes with the biographical particulars, and we find Williams trapped in more than one contradiction.

Williams the poet, a man of mixed ancestry and with a remote European heritage, could find his literary niche only in the future of a mythological pluralistic America. Pound may have been right about what was American before Williams came along, but Williams's "America" was also a poetic ideal: Williams the poet lived in an America that should be. In fact, as Pound's comment suggests, Williams's visionary Americanness constituted a unique foreignness. Williams himself raises the question of his inadaptability to his time in the poem "Sub Terra" (using the symbolic, subliminal Latin title):

> Where shall I find you,
> you my grotesque fellows
> that I seek everywhere
> to make up my band?
> None, not one
> with the earthy tastes I require . . .

In the process of rebelling against the European standard in Anglo-American arts and letters, Williams flaunts his own earthiness, playing Elena's scion more than his cool father's. More important, of course, are his expressed feelings of alienation. The country he inherited did not share his past. Its literature denied its true, as yet undefined identity. America had yet to be discovered – the real America that would naturally understand that Williams was a genuine product of its fresh history, the ideal America in which the poet could explicitly identify himself as Williams the man.

Williams the poet prevailed, however, ingratiating himself with the sociolinguistic conventions by identifying his Anglo-Americanness with a high moral purpose of seeing a greater truth. Moreover, his Anglo-Americanness nurtured with righteousness his hatred for the self-deception of Latin romanticism, his tacit justification for claiming to have overcome the influence of those social traits that might have tainted him with that kind of foreignness. In other words, as part of his characterization of himself as an Anglo-American, he adopted the Anglo-American's arrogance toward Latin America. Even more important, he acted out its ignorance. Thus by his tone he attempts to convince us that he never seriously pondered the idea that Elena's Caribbean background also made her a "pure product of America."

Of course, neither Williams the poet nor Williams the man identified with later working-class Puerto Rican immigrants[14] who, along with Elena, shared the commonality of the American hemispheric experience. Whatever thoughts Williams harbored of that immigration were doubtless sublimated and incorporated into his expressed notions of Latins; the subject remained part of his solitude, his "hidden core."

Juxtaposed, the Williams of the poetic vision and the ingratiating Williams form a composite very closely resembling the one described by Denis Donoghue: ". . . despite all contrary indications, Williams is a Paleface, very much a highbrow . . . but a Paleface dissatisfied with this condition becaue it seems a bit thin, a bit too English, too far removed from a local immediate American context. Hence his rush to exalt the Redskin, the frontiersman, taking this warmer role unto himself by *fiat*." Hence

> his reluctance to effect a direct entry to ideas – except in neces-
> sary polemic. Hence his distrust of urbanity, his distaste for
> "Rev. Eliot," his snarling essays (sounding off), his insistence
> on making discussions of literature earthy, barbaric, sexy. It is
> my understanding that Williams, by temperament, is closer to
> Henry James than to Whitman, and that his dissatisfaction with
> his temper makes him adopt the accouterments of Daniel
> Boone. [15]

If Williams was closer to James, it was because he emulated Elena. If he exalted redskins it was because of a spiritual identification with them: That same aristocrat who was his mother had to suffer the ignominy of being genetically identified with "savages," as the *Morning Sun* in 1912 described immigrants arriving from Latin America. This tense, dichotomous Williams, whose enduring image will be one of solitude, understood the harsh terms of the real Anglo-America and tried to be true to both it and to himself. He was keenly aware of Elena's permanent cultural influence on him, of his inherited Latin traits, and unprepared to allow himself to comprehend it. He read Latin American writers and had a greater curiosity for that past than his literary persona felt free to record. This Williams, ever striving to live up to Elena's idealistic standards, identified with the ideal United States, campaigning on its behalf even while, contradictorily and reflexively, ingratiating himself with its prejudices. Finally, embodying the most profound vision of what is *American,* this composite Williams imparts the true beauty and breadth of the American experience that was his heritage through Elena:

> In the West Indies, in Martinique, St. Thomas, Puerto Rico,
> Santo Domingo, in those days, the races of the world mingled
> and intermarried – imparting their traits into another and forget-
> ting the orthodoxy of their ancient and medieval views. It was a
> good thing. It is the best spirit of the New World. (*Yes,* p. 30)

NOTES

1 William Carlos Williams, *The Autobiography* (New York: New Directions, 1967), p. 1.
2 Together man and poet comprise a complex psyche deserving of a more complete treatment than can be compressed into this introductory discussion. This essay is based on a work in progress.
3 William Carlos Williams, *Yes, Mrs. Williams* (New York: New Directions, 1973), p. 5.
4 Paul Mariani, *William Carlos Williams: A New World Naked* (New York: McGraw-Hill, 1981).
5 James E. Breslin, *William C. Williams: An American Artist* (University of Chicago Press, 1985), pp. 6–7.
6 Edith Heal, ed., *The Autobiography of the Works of a Poet* (Boston: Beacon Press, 1958), p. 16.
7 Editions from which Williams's poems have been quoted are *Collected Earlier Poems* (New York: New Directions, 1950), *Collected Later Poems* (New York: New Directions, 1963), *Paterson* (New York: New Directions, 1963), and *Selected Poems* (New York: New Directions, 1969).
8 Caribbean *espiritismo,* ironically, was a product of the belated romantic influence of French spiritualists on Latin sophisticates and not of the primitiveness of the "West Indies," as Williams probably feared.
9 Linda Wagner, *Interviews with William Carlos Williams: Speaking Straight Ahead* (New York: New Directions, 1976), p. xiii.
10 Manuel Zeno Guardía, *La charca* (Rio Piedras: Edil, 1973), p. 104.
11 Antonio S. Pedreira, "Insularismo," in *Obras de Antonio S. Pedreira,* vol. 1 (San Juan: Instituto de Cultura, 1970), p. 63.
12 I have found evidence of a direct literary influence of, among others, the poet Luis Palés Matos. This will be discussed at length in my book.
13 William Carlos Williams, *Kora in Hell,* in *Imaginations* (New York: New Directions, 1970). p. 11.
14 Elena, owing to the differences in social class, doubtless did not either. See *The Memoirs of Bernardo Vega,* ed. C. A. Iglesias; trans. J. Flores (New York: Monthly Review Press, 1984), in which Vega confirms that, earlier, skilled middle-class immigrants shunned the poorer people of their country.
15 Denis Donoghue, "For a Redeeming Language," in J. Hillis Miller, ed., *William Carlos Williams: A Collection of Critical Essays* (Englewood Cliffs, N.J.: Prentice Hall, 1966), p. 130.

7

Dreams of two Americas

PABLO ARMANDO FERNÁNDEZ

"Every social condition," José Martí tells us, "expresses itself through literature and in fact through literature's many facets the history of peoples can be told with greater truth than through their chronicles and annals."[1] This causes us to take a closer look at the following questions. How does the present-day literature of the Americas interpret and reflect the history and societies of this hemisphere? To what extent do writers reveal a full, lucid vision of this part of the world and its inhabitants? What has been their contribution and how has it become part of our life experience? Such questions demand more than one answer. I shall try to offer a few here.

In the fifteenth century, Europe was forced to find new trade routes between the European countries and India. Don Quixote's proverbial stew, more beef than lamb, boiled on without spice.[2] There was no nutmeg, no pepper; no cinnamon for chocolate or for rice pudding; no ginger and no fragant cloves. Storms would often wash ashore exotic pieces of wood or bones. "¿Qué enigma entre las aguas?"[3] as Nicolás Guillén asked – "What mystery across the waters?"

There was a need for precious metals, since European veins were almost exhausted; a need to maintain and increase trade with Eastern countries – an implacable reality. And there was the glitter of Marco Polo's book, which accompanied the Discoverer on his first voyage, each page meticulously annotated in the margin. All this took place from the very start of the enterprise, a curious interaction between the real and the fabulous. The Navigator's fascination for Marco Polo made such a mark on his imagination that when he reached the beaches of Yucayas he truly believed he had come to "the island of Cipango of which marvelous tales are told."[4]

The territory Columbus discovered for the Europeans had no name,

122

until a German cosmographer by the name of Walseemuller, after reading the travelogues of the Italian Amerigo Vespucci, proposed that the continent be called America. So here we have another superimposition of European fiction on aboriginal reality, just as there was on the natives of those lands. The Maya, Aztecs, Quechua, Aymara, Arawakane, Guaraní, among others, and all of their geographic surroundings were to lose their autochtonous names with the arrival of the conquistadores. From the sixteenth century to the present day, their descendants, whether of pure lineage or *mestizo* descent, were to be "Americans."

The historical and cultural values of the indigenous civilizations were to remain occult for centuries, only to reappear when those born in this part of the world felt the need to search for an identity of their own. The same thing happened when the Pilgrim fathers reached the cold shores of North America: The Iroquois, Sioux, and others suffered the same fate. The aborigines were to lose not only their land and civilizations, but also their lives. Europe imposed its languages, religions, and cultures on those who survived. The Spanish and Portuguese odyssey was to spread the Christian faith among the aborigines in exchange for the extraction of their riches.

Conquistadores and chroniclers sought in the lands they ravaged, the land of the Amazon women warriors, the Seven Cities of Cibola, full of gold, silver, and precious stones; the Fountains of Youth and Eternal Life; Eldorado. And the conquered land became a trail of blood and tears, of weeping and bloodshed.

In the age of the conquest, chroniclers exalted by tales of chivalry, Marco Polo, and Greek and Latin mythology set about reconciling the pretensions of their imagination with the virgin reality before their eyes, a landscape of civilizations based on golden corn, on the stones of war, on precious metals, and on solar dynasties. This is what gave rise to the discourse of suggestive hyperboles that give form to the baroque in our milieu. The real and the unreal reinforce one another and gain strength in doing so. These are the antecedents of magical realism that still characterizes the "American" voice.

Alejo Carpentier argues "that our art was always baroque, from the splendid pre-Columbian sculpture and the Codices through the colonial cathedrals and monasteries of the continent up to the best of the present-day American novel. Even physical love becomes baroque, as in the obscure Peruvian 'guaco.' "[5] Daniel Boorstin, speaking of North America, has said, "No language could be American unless it was elastic enough to describe the unusual as if it were commonplace, the extravagant as if it were normal. The extravagance of the American experience and the inadequacy of the traditional language made tall talk as necessary a vehicle of the expansive age of American life as the keel boat or the covered wagon."⁶ José Lezama Lima adds that "in no other culture has fable so taken on the force of reality as it did among the Incas."⁷ Hyperbole, the baroque, and the fable penetrated the American language and has dominated the works of such diverse authors as Sor Juana Inés de la Cruz, Twain, Melville, Poe, Faulkner, Asturias, Borges, Rulfo, Carpentier, Lezama, and García Márquez.

The age of the conquest was the age of Cortés, Pizarro, Ponce de León: the age of Cuauhtemoc, Viracochi, Túpac Amaru; the age of the sword and the cross, of priests and warriors, of repartition and land concessions, of Quetzacoatl and Kukulkan; the age of Las Casas and Oviedo, of Sahagún and Cabeza de Vaca, of Los Alvarados and Luis de Velazco, of La Malinche and Díaz de Castillo, of Pachacamac and Cintli, of Montecuhzoma and the sun god. Myth and reality go hand in hand; and individuals born of European and aborigine, of European and African look to both as they begin to see themselves in a context and culture with which they can identify and that allow them to realize themselves historically.

Spain and Portugal were the first to endow the aboriginal people with their languages; later England and France did the same. Their lands were usurped, their riches plundered, their autochthonous culture destroyed; the aborigines became "outcasts on their own soil."⁸ It is no secret that those languages were imposed solely for the purpose of annihilating those that belonged to the conquered peoples. This ensured the severance of any thread that united them and might enable them to resist and fight the oppressor. "Language is the handmaiden of Empire," the Spanish humanist Antonio de Nebrija told Queen Isabel of Spain, commending to her his grammar of Spanish, the first of a modern European language.

Spanish, English, and French have served as intermediaries for our knowledge of indigenous and African cultures, since those peoples lacked an alphabet and, without the linguistic contributions of the European cultures, would have had no means of literary expression. The Popol Vuh, the Annals of the Cakchiqueles, Quechua poetry, the books of the Chilam-Balanes, and the legacy left to us by the Nahuatl people of their own vision of the conquest were translated into Spanish by Spanish priests. As for the African contributions to our literature, it has been in Cuba with the work of Fernando Ortiz and Lydia Cabrera, Nicolás Guillén, Rómulo Lachatañeré, Pedro Dechamp Chapeau, and Miguel Barnet, and in the English- and French-speaking Caribbean with the work of Jean Price Mars, C. L. R. James, Aimé Césaire, Claude McKay, Jacques Stephen Alexis, Jacques Roumain, René Depestre, George Lamming, Wilson Harris, Andrew Salkey, and Edward Braithwaite, among

others, where, out of recognition of black people, or obeying an eager-
ness to investigate the cultural roots of their peoples, have been revealed
the values of a culture that among us remained, like the aboriginal American, submerged in a shameful anonymity.

With the conquest, pre-Columbian cultures were buried; indigenous
peoples were enslaved, condemned to live as, and made to feel like,
inferior beings; their religions and their beliefs were maligned, persecuted as the work of the devil and so doomed to disappear; culture
centuries old was destroyed. The Spaniards built on the ruins of the cities
they had razed. They took the age-old foundations and on them erected
their own dwellings and churches, thus proclaiming their superiority
over the conquered. Martí describes this period as a "historical misfortune and natural crime,"[9] which, as Marx remarked, helped to accelerate
in giant strides the transformation of the feudal mode of production into
the capitalist order. He adds that the discovery of gold and silver and the
subsequent crusade of extermination, enslavement, and burial of the
aboriginal population in the mines, the conquest and sacking of the West
Indies, and the conversion of the African continent into a hunting ground
of slaves were all events that announced the advent of the era of capitalist
production. The booty obtained outside of Europe by means of out-
rageous plunder, slavery, and slaughter flowed into the metropolis to
convert itself into capital.[10]

Hegel, who located America in prehistory because its people had not
formed a state, did not recognize – his imperial rationality prevented him
from knowing it – that there is history in the stones transformed into
warriors to fight by the side of Viracochi, warriors who after the victory
returned to their natural condition of stones. There is history also in the
monumental ruins of temples and palaces that would have awakened not
only the envy but also the greed of the kings and pharaohs of antiquity,
on whose civilizations Hegel bestowed history; temples and palaces
raised by a great human mass that suffered the oppression and exploitation of a dominant priestly class. There is history in the fortresses and
military roads, in the aqueducts and terraced mountains, in the open
galleries, in the rocks and in the bridges suspended in the air; works that
would confound the most capable engineers of our time and that were
carried out by the Incas with great success. There is history in the development of the art of agriculture and the mysterious industry of spinning
and weaving. There is history in the agrarian laws and the application of
justice, in the books and the schools, in the music and the dance, and in
the painting and the poetry of those great civilizations. And there is
history in the indigenous rebellions against the conquistador and the
colonizer and in the rebellions of the Africans enslaved in those lands

against their masters and in those of their masters against the metropolises. There is nothing as moving and serious as the actions for independence of the peoples of America, actions that were a living present in the time of Hegel. For him, America belonged to the future, and to that future he entrusted American historicity.[11]

When in December 1620 the Pilgrim fathers disembarked from the *Mayflower* on the coast of Massachusetts, more than a hundred years had passed in the history of the Spanish and Portuguese conquest of the lands that today make up Latin America, countries that in large part constitute a linguistic community and the history, ethnic composition, cultural formation, and economic development of which are very similar. Hegel establishes a significant difference between North and South America. Of the first he says, "It has been colonized; it is guided by the principle of industry and of Protestantism: it upholds the freedom of the individual."[12] In contrast, "South America has been conquered; in it predominance belongs to military power, clericalism, the accumulation of treasure, and the vanity of titles and honors."[13] On this point his observations are not far from those of José Martí: "North America was born from the plow, Spanish America from the hunting dog."[14] Hegel foresees a possible confrontation between the two Americas; Martí warns us of the danger posed by the strength and power and expansionist ambitions of European America to its *mestiza* sister in the south. From the moment the British colonies of the north obtain their independence and form themselves into a nation, the differences between the North American and the Latin American can only become more acute and intense.

Since the nineteenth century, the North American states have developed to the point of becoming the richest and most powerful nation on earth. The nations of South America, however, have grown poorer and their possibilities for development have been so limited that the colonial condition imposed on them by the conquest has – whether one admits it or not – failed to disappear. Their natural riches gone and those that remain completely or almost completely undeveloped, their role in the international world has not ceased to be more or less that of a servant. First Europe and later the North American states made use and continue to make use of our increasingly depleted reserves (except oil) of iron, meat, fruit, copper, coffee, sugar, cacao, rubber. The spectacle could not be more discouraging, even if one hears that Latin America "represents one of the most dynamic ideas in the world today" because its demographic explosion "threatens to be converted, in its turn, into a political explosion."[15]

Two currents of European thought powerfully influence North American culture: puritanism and rationalism. The rationalist current can be detected in its social and political institutions and influences the thinking of its politicians, philosophers, and jurists.

In the nations of *mestizo* America, Iberian irrationality can be observed in the conflict between civilization and barbarism and in the struggle between tyranny and freedom. Company-town countries, they live in the most absurd and shameful isolation and backwardness (we shall return to this), subjected constantly to civil wars and to dictatorships generated by savage *caudillismo;* subjected to violence and disorder, to foreign dependency, to flattery, lying, and crime as a political system, until the day when, rising in arms, the people will recover their independence and political and economic power.

Such is the history of Latin America; what is its literature? Let us consider only those works that set out to reflect a vision of their societies and history. We have said that the nineteenth century established the lines of divergence between South and North America; these differences should consequently be reflected in their literatures.

In North America the nineteenth century produced five classic novels, three of which rank among the world's greatest: *Moby-Dick* (1851), *The Scarlet Letter* (1850), and *Huckleberry Finn* (1884). The other novels are *The Narrative of Arthur Gordon Pym* (1838) and *The Last of the Mohicans* (1826). In addition there is the most fertile and seminal book of poetry produced on the continent: Walt Whitman's *Leaves of Grass.*

The first novel written in Spanish in America is *El Periquillo Sarniento* (1838, *The Itching Parrot*), and its major effect consists of the description of the wicked habits of Mexico City. Others are *Cecilia Valdés* (1839), *El Matadero* (1840), *Amalia* (1851), and *María* (1857).

It is certain that Latin American novels of this period in Spanish do not transcend romanticism. If something can be distinguished in them, it is the fact that they are political novels. At least those of Mármol and Echeverría most certainly are, and Villaverde's is to a certain extent. What is truly significant in Latin America is the political thought of men like Bolívar, Hostos, Montalvo, Sarmiento, and Martí, some specimens of gaucho poetry, and the romantic poetry essayed by the Cuban José María Heredia. In this context Martí deserves special consideration. I do not think that any string of adjectives, however original and recondite, are sufficient to describe a work whose size, importance, and transcendence still offer an unsuspected depth of thought. It is enough to say that Martí is the greatest poet in Spanish of the nineteenth century and that his prose and political thought outdistance anything that came before. Otherwise, it was not until the twentieth century that Spanish American literature produced works and writers that compare with those of the nineteenth century in the United States.

If I refuse to make qualitative comparisons between the literatures of north and south, it is because I find it unfair to do so. The nations of South America have lived under the tutelage of the states of North America, which have been able to count on the complicity of our native oligarchies. They have lived, as we have said, in the dialectic between "civilization and barbarism," and I stress that this is not solely a question of the abyss between the city and nature, between the "European" and the "natural," as Sarmiento describes it in the pages of his *Facundo*. Martí puts it best:

> The battle is not between civilization and barbarism, but rather between false erudition and nature. Natural man is good, and he honors and rewards superior intelligence as long as it does not take advantage of his submission to harm him, or offends him by dispensing with him, for this is something natural man does not forgive, ready to recover by force the respect of whoever wounds his sensibilities or jeopardizes his interests. Through this conformance with the scorned natural elements the tyrants of America have risen to power, and they have fallen the moment they betrayed them. Through their tyrannies the Republics have purged themselves of their inability to recognize the true elements of the nation and to derive from them their form of government and govern with them. Governor, in a new people, means creator.[16]

From the novels of Mármol and Echevarría to the recent trilogy of Carpentier, Roa Bastos, and García Márquez, tyranny, *caudillismo,* and dependency have obsessed our writers. The arduous and desperate struggle to wrest from nature the raw materials that are the economic basis of our societies is witnessed in Latin America's first classic novels, *La vorágine (The Vortex), Don Segundo Sombra,* and *Doña Bárbara,* which, notwithstanding the whims of chance, the acuity of their commentators, and the pecuniary interests of publishers and distributors, have become international novels in their own right.

The infernal exploitation of *heves brasiliensis,* the tree that produces latex, reached its culmination in 1878 and its decline around 1913 with the catastrophe that befell Brazilian rubber. The jungle and the nightmare world of the rubber workers are the essential matters of *La vorágine,* by the Colombian José Eustasio Rivera. The exportation of livestock was the principal industry of Argentina, and the way of life of its cattle-herding gauchos was its greatest source of richness. Ricardo Güiraldes's *Don Segundo Sombra* is a farewell to the world of those cowhands charged "with their own skills and greatest powers, to drive the herds of cattle from ranch to ranch, from ranch to slaughterhouse."[17] According to Alejandro Bunge, that was the last generation of importers and ranchers. In the next, predominance would belong to the farm and to industry. Rómulo Gallego's *Doña Bárbara* picks up the theme outlined by Sarmiento, the opposition between civilization and barbarism, from a new perspective, to the point of resolving it, but more in line with contemporary progressive thinking. The secular discord between nature and the individual yields to the reforming will of the latter.

In these novels the characters disappear, devoured by nature – pampa, plains, jungle – a nature that does not forgive those who break the relentless laws of its domains unless they yield to it, integrating themselves within it. "I saw him ride away at a gallop," Fabio tells us of his godfather's farewell in *Don Segundo Sombra.* "What faded in the distance was more an idea than a man. And brusquely he disappeared, leaving my meditation without an object." Later on: "I don't know what strange suggestion the limitless presence of that soul proposed. . . . I left, like a man bled white."[18] In *Doña Bárbara* the news runs from mouth to mouth: The boss of the Arauca has disappeared.[19] As for Arturo Cova and his companions in *La vorágine:* "Clemente Silva has been looking for them in vain for five months. Not a trace of them. The jungle devoured them!"[20]

Can *Don Segundo's* pampas exist without a nation of cattle and wheat that satisfies the appetites of distant consumers? In *Doña Barbara,* does not the hard, malicious hand that exploits the *llanos* do so in full knowledge that those lands are the ultimate resource, eternally negotiable? Can the exterminating hell of *La vorágine* exist without the fever for rubber, in the delirium of which appears now the thirst of fortune satisfied by a miraculous find, now the resignation of living in the shadow of a foreign company? The jungle has provided material for other writers. Asturias, Quiroga, Vargas Llosa depict, within the economic context, the exploitation of its riches and of the men who, extracting the rubber sap, worked in conditions close to those of slavery.

The cacao plantations of Brazil found their chronicler and fabulist in Jorge Amado: *Sao Jorge dos Ilhéus* and *Gabriela, Clove and Cinnamon.* *Sao Jorge dos Ilhéus,* where "the Coronel Maneca Dantas lit his cigars with five hundred milreis notes,"[21] repeating the gesture of all the rich landowners in the country during the boom times of coffee, rubber, cotton, and sugar, is today a faded postcard. The splendor and decadence of Ilhéus, the extravagance, ostentation, and prodigality of its oligarchs, the wretchedness and suffering of its landless recall other cities with the predictable fate of disappearing when their natural resources are exhausted: Potosí, Manaos, Sucre, Vila Rica de Ouro Preto – dead, ghostly cities where one survives on decayed memories alone. Juan Rulfo's Co-mala, with its air full of dead voices, and the Macondo of García Márquez in its august, dynastic solitude are less fictional than those actual cities in their heyday of splendor whose fabulous riches were the cause of their present impoverishment and ruin. There has been no lack of critics who have tried to legitimize these woeful inventions of García Márquez and Rulfo, seeking for them a Faulknerian paternity. We do not wish to deny that Faulkner's work has contributed powerfully to the enrichment of our literature. His world and ours bear multiple correspondences: a plantation culture based on an agrarian economy; racial conflict with all its consequences; nostalgia for a splendid past and uncertainty before the future; an expressive baroque style; a memory divided, in his case, by the Civil War and, in ours, by the wars of independence and the struggles against successive tyrants and the colonialist metropolises; and, finally, the irreducible mixture of myth and reality.

It is not only Faulkner. Other writers have exerted an influence on our letters: Cooper, Poe, and Whitman; Eliot, Pound, and Hemingway; O'Neill, Dos Passos, and Henry Miller; and more recently Mailer, Salin-ger, and Bellow. The influence has been natural and organic, like the food we import from North America, the clothes and automobiles, the medicine, electrical gadgets, machinery, industries, spare parts, and all the trinkets produced by North American light industry. This seems fine to me; what seems wrong is that the trade is generally one-way: One side is mostly benefited, the other mostly injured. With equitable exchanges, both sides would gain not only materially, but in respect and mutual dignity.

At a writers' congress in the Bahamas, Edward Albee said that the participants from South America believed they should have closer ties with the North Americans. Albee, however, was not so sure that such could be the case, because South Americans "are closer to the European tradition than are North Americans." "They are," Albee continued, "not in an intellectual sense but in their expressive means, their ability to find an authentic, natural voice, fifty to seventy-five years behind the United States. But the South Americans believe that there is or should be intense relations between the writers of the two continents."[22] I may not agree with Albee, and I should point out that he said this more than fifteen years ago. However, to admit that we are more attached to the European tradition than are North Americans would be to approve a widespread but nonetheless fallacious contention. Both North and Latin American writers have suffered from the European fetish. That we Latin Americans are fifty or seventy-five years behind North Americans in breaking away from this fetish seems logical, infamously logical. Those years, and four hundred more to boot, are the years we have spent in underdevelopment, producing raw materials for capitalist monopolies, suffering an almost total political and economic dependency. It is precisely these facts that have served as the theme for some of the greatest novels produced in this century in Latin America.

In fact, I do not believe that we are now fifty or seventy-five years behind Anglo-American literature as Albee suggested. I do not deny that from 1850, when Hawthorne published *The Scarlet Letter,* until the 1920s, when Güiraldes, Rivera, and Gallegos published their novels, such a gap may have existed; but these novels covered the ground for Latin America that the classic novels of Hawthorne and Melville, among others, covered for the United States. The critic Enrique Caracciolo has compared Güiraldes to Melville: "Like Ishmael, Fabio is an orphan. Ishmael goes to sea on the Pequod, Fabio flees to a life with meaning. Melville has the sea, Güiraldes the sea of land of the Pampa. Ishmael returns wiser from his metaphysical voyage, Fabio comes back a man."[23] I should add from *Don Segundo Sombra:* "Everything I learned in my adventurous childhood constitutes a miserly sum of experience for the existence I was about to begin. Why the hell did they take me away from mama's side at the outpost, sending me to school to learn the alphabet, arithmetic, and history, that today are of no use to me?"[24] So thinks Fabio upon fleeing his aunt's house. Like Huck Finn, Fabio opts to be and feel free. For him liberty resides in the pampa under the open sky, for Huck in the Indian territories: "But I reckon I got to light out for the Territory ahead of the rest, because Aunt Sally she's going to adopt me and civilise me, and I can't stand it. I been there before."[25]

This quest, shared by both Faulkner and Hemingway, points to one of the problems that, ever since the time of the conquest and colonization, has been posed over and over by individuals born on this continent, whatever their bloodline: that of their own identity, a theme so common in our literatures that I need not pause to name authors and works. The list would be interminable, although there are certain cases that deserve particular attention: those of writers predominantly Amerindian or predominantly African (especially in the Caribbean). The case of black writers, linked as it is to slavery, has very special features. Blacks, removed from slave labor and converted to instruments of production, not only were stripped of their history, culture, psychological integrity, and personal identity, but found imposed on them the historical, cultural, and racial values of whites, condemning them to feel alienated from themselves, their faces, their black skin, and their origins. In all of the literature produced in the Caribbean and on the South American coast it washes, we find as a basic intent the pursuit and assumption of racial identity. The works of Nicolás Guillén and Aimé Césaire, indispensible poets in their respective languages, have transcended the ethnic problem and its conflicts, situating it on a universal level. In such works one finds a deliberate attention to the destruction of the myths and stereotypes of blacks. It is a poetry that embodies the revolutionary thinking of our time. The syncretism of the cultural elements drawn from Europe and Africa is resolved into a synthesis that expresses the true, full, and diverse spirit of nationhood.

In Cuba, for instance, with the transformation of economic and social structures, a change has taken place that permits the black, white, or racially mixed to free themselves, however gradually, from the alienating dogmas of colonial society; racial dogma has begun to disappear. Referring to this, René Depestre has said, "All the initiatives of the Cuban Revolution in the various fields of culture and education, are at the same time dynamic elements of racial integration."[26]

Indigenism, in contrast, has had its devotees ever since the nineteenth century, some of them memorable only for their unfortunate designs. The image of the Indian from the remote times of Oviedo so tainted, so lamentably adulterated with nativism, indigenism, and Creolism, so simplified, exalted, impoverished, and idealized in good, bad, or middling poems, stories, and novels, found in Argüedas and Roa Bastos its most faithful vindicators. With the Mexican Revolution the reappraisal of aboriginal values spread over the entire continent, culminating in the work of two masters of our literature: José María Argüedas and Roa Bastos. In the context in which we are dealing, these authors interest us for their contribution to the conclusive formation of what can and should be called the American language, for a language is the most authentic and vital expression of the spiritual character of a people. Both authors find their identity by expressing in Spanish, by means of a vocabulary, syntax, and rhythm parallel to those of their aboriginal idioms, Quechua and Guaraní, the sensibility, psychology, and cultural peculiarities of the Indian.

I do not know with what anticipation the Puritans in their old Elizabethan houses read Chapter 60 of Isaiah, where islands await the ships of Tarsis, who with the faithful Pilgrims will bring the Word of God to virgin lands. Every prophecy is a dream – a dream that launches thousands of people over unknown seas in search of a promised realization. In this case the dream would become a nightmare for the Amerindian, one that still visits its effects on their dispossessed inheritors. Lionel Trilling's well-known sentence "Ours is the only nation which prides itself on a dream and gives it a name: 'the American dream'"[27] will guide our elaboration of the themes we have already touched.

I do not believe that all of us aspire to achieve what is understood in North America by the "American Dream"; we Latin Americans have our own dream, a dream quite distant from the pretensions that drove the North American to territorial and economic expansion and toward the building of an empire. Walt Whitman, the singer of democracy in his country, fears the dangers that begin to lurk and makes the necessary admonitions. Nevertheless, Whitman champions the growth of his country to the point of its transmutation into a colossal empire:

> I say that our new world democracy, however great a success in uplifting the masses out of their sloughs, in materialistic development, products, and in a certain highly-deceptive superficial popular intellectuality, is, so far an almost complete failure in its social aspects, and in really grand religious, moral, literary, and esthetic results. In vain do we march with unprecedented strides to empire so colossal, outvying the antique, beyond Alexander's, beyond the proudest sway of Rome. In vain have we annex'd Texas, California, Alaska, and reach north for Canada and south for Cuba. It is as if we were somehow being endow'd with a vast and more and more thoroughly-appointed body, and then left with little or no soul.[28]

Whitman was not wrong; his mournful prophecies were fulfilled, to the misfortune of his America. One of his most faithful descendants, Hart Crane, would have to confront the violent and hard reality of modern life:

> This was the Promised Land, and still it is
> To the persuasive suburban land agent
> In bootleg roadhouses where the gin fizz
> Bubbles in time to Hollywood's new love-nest pageant.
> Fresh from the radio in the old Meeting House
> (Now the New Avalon Hotel) volcanoes roar
> A welcome to highsteppers that no mouse
> Who saw the Friends there had ever heard before.
> . . . .
> Who holds the lease on time and on disgrace?
> What eats the pattern with ubiquity?
> Where are my kinsmen and the patriarch race?[29]

Crane wanted to extend a bridge between past and present – "really building a bridge between so-called classical spirit and the many divergent realities of the seething confused cosmos of today." He wanted to find in the Brooklyn Bridge the symbol of the "initial impulses" of the North American people, but he forgot that with capitalist development those impulses were getting lost. Capitalization was burying in disillusion some of the most precious ideals of the country's first settlers. The inability to confront a civilization where the law of the most powerful ruled along with the worship of richness for its own sake hurled the most illustrious descendants of the Pilgrim fathers into a European exodus.

The superstitious attachment of value to the European, as I have argued, is a phenomenon that affects equally the writers of the two Americas. The diaspora began in the nineteenth century with Darío, Henry James, and many others. In this matter what distinguishes the Latin Americans from the North Americans is that the first group sought in emigration new political horizons, which they sometimes found in one or another of their kindred nations, whereas the North American voyagers acted out of a rejection of the society in which they lived, without proposing changes that might make it match their aspirations. It is in this context that the Latin American Europeanism stressed by Albee and so many others should be understood. There is an essential difference between the voyage that in the nineteenth century drove writers across the lands of Europe, the United States, Mexico, Central or South America and the voyage in the twentieth century that reunited in Paris or London the members of the so-called lost generation or their contemporaries. This diaspora has repeated itself time and again in the present century. *Rayuela* (*Hopscotch*) of Julio Cortázar offers an account of the life of the South American expatriates in Paris. *The Sun Also Rises* of Hemingway and Fitzgerald's *Tender Is the Night,* to give two examples, address the same theme. Nevertheless, Latin Americans, such as Asturias and Cortázar, feel in Europe the Eros of distance, whose emanations are embodied in works that reveal an America until then unknown by them. This discovery grants them an identity that has not yet found its full definition but draws them near to the American essence of action: the dream – dream of liberty, of independence. Trapped in the alienation that North American society and the individual suffer, U.S. writers have lost the dream that inspired the first generations of colonizers. Having lost the American dream, these writers have lost their America. As their history still eludes them, so does the wholeness of the nation, and they live constantly whipped by the lash that impels them to creation: the blow of history. They respond to it, they confront it, they explore and express it, because they affirm it and contest it in themselves, seeking themselves, seeking their own identity, their place and role in the world. The work of Carlos Fuentes is the best example we can offer them.

Martí and Whitman plead for a literature of foundation. Faulkner does too. Though he does not speak for contemporary North American writers, let us listen to him: "I believe that man will not merely endure; he will prevail. He is immortal . . . because he has a soul, a spirit capable of compassion and sacrifice and endurance. The poet's, the writer's duty is to write about these things. It is his privilege to help man to endure by lifting his heart, by reminding him of the courage and humor and hope and pride and compassion and pity and sacrifice – which have been the glory of his past. And, I would like to add, of his future."[30]

NOTES

This chapter was translated from the Spanish by Chris Kearin, Gari Laguardia, and Bell Gale Chevigny.

1 José Martí, "El poeta Walt Whitman," *Obras completas* (Havana: Editorial Lex, 1953), p. 1137.
2 Miguel de Cervantes, *Don Quijote de la Mancha*, trans. S. Putnam (New York: Modern Library, n.d.), p. 25.
3 Nicolás Guillén, "El apellido" *Obra poetica*, vol. 1 (Havana: Instituto Cubano del Libro, 1972), p. 396.
4 Cristobal Colón, *Diario de la navegación* (Havana: UNESCO, 1961), p. 70.
5 Alejo Carpentier, "Problemáticas de la actual novela latinoamericana," *Tientos y diferencias* (Mexico City: Universidad Nacional Autonoma, 1970), p. 32.
6 Quoted by Walter Allen, *The Urgent West: The American Dream and Modern Man* (New York: Dutton, 1969), p. 70.
7 José Lezama Lima, "Sumas críticas del Americano," *La expresión Americana* (Madrid: Alianza, 1969), p. 188.
8 Jacques Roumain, "La poesía como arma," *Gaceta del Caribe*, no. 1 (January 1944).
9 Martí, "Gestación de América," *Obras*, p. 98.
10 Karl Marx, *El capital*, vol. 1 (Havana: UNEAC, 1965), pp. 688–9.
11 Quoted by José Ortega y Gasset, "Hegel y América," *El Espectador* (Madrid: Revista de Occidente, 1950), p. 794.
12 Ibid., p. 789.
13 Ibid.
14 Martí, "Gestación," p. 98.
15 Cesar Fernández Moreno, "Introducción," *América Latina en su literatura* (Mexico City: Siglo XXI, 1972), p. 5.
16 Martí, "Gestación," p. 107.
17 Quoted by Dardo Cúneo, "La crisis del '30 en Güiraldes," *Serie valoración multiple* (Havana: Casa de las Américas, 1971), p. 262.
18 Ricardo Güiraldes, *Don Segundo Sombra* (Havana: Casa de las Américas, 1971), p. 262.
19 Rómulo Gallego, (Havana: Ediciones la Tertulia), p. 349.

20 José Eustasio Riveras, *La vorágine* (Havana: Casa de las Américas, 1966), p. 317.

21 Jorge Amado, *Gabriela, Clove and Cinnamon* (New York: Avon, 1974), p. 2.

22 Digby Diehl, "Conversación con Edward Albee," *Casa de las Américas Revista Bimestral* 4, no. 24 (January–April 1964), pp. 88–98.

23 Enrique Caracciolo, "Otro enfoque," *Serie valoración multiple* (Havana: Casa de las Américas, 1971), p. 254.

24 Güiraldes, *Don Segundo Sombra,* pp. 41–2.

25 Mark Twain, *The Adventures of Huckleberry Finn* (New York: Collier, 1912), p. 405.

26 René Depestre, "Problemas de la identidad del hombre negro en las literaturas antillanas," *Casa de las Américas Revista Bimestral* 9, no. 53 (March–April 1969), pp. 19–28.

27 Quoted by Allen, *The Urgent West,* p. 85.

28 Walt Whitman, *Leaves of Grass and Selected Prose* (New York: Modern Library, 1950), p. 468.

29 Hart Crane, "The Bridge: Quaker Hill," *The Complete Poems of Hart Crane,* ed. Waldo Frank (Garden City, N.Y.: Doubleday, 1933), pp. 50–1.

30 Quoted by Robert Coughlan, "The Private World of William Faulkner," *Prize Articles 1954* (New York: Ballantine, 1954), p. 156.

II

The lives and fictions
of American women

8

Introduction

BELL GALE CHEVIGNY

The comparative study of American women's literature is both problematic and inevitable. It is problematic because the kind of scholarly archeology and multidisciplinary theoretical work on women that has been done in the United States has barely begun in Spanish America. Understandably, the women's movement that would support such research there is much smaller and younger. In Third World countries where the dominant facts of daily life include war, denial of human rights, illiteracy, massive unemployment, runaway inflation, and exploitation, the issues of gender that have preoccupied U.S. feminists have seemed secondary.

Comparison is also problematic because the enormously divergent social and cultural conditions of the Americas affect women in powerful but elusive ways. We do not yet have a theory with which to account in hemispheric comparative studies for the ideological impact of differences in class and religion. Class in Latin America is perceived as a more crucial variable than it is in the United States and as a more decisive factor than gender in analyzing the experiences of women;[1] in the United States there is a complementary distortion as the ideology of egalitarian individualism blinds us to the realities of class. The influence of Catholic beliefs in Spanish America confirms and complicates the ideology of gender in ways unparalleled by other religions in the United States.

Since 1975, the "Year of the Woman," the commitment of the UN and other agencies to support research projects and seminars on women has sponsored a flowering of women's organizations in Latin America. Major research institutions have made women a central area of scholarly concern, and women's centers for local organization and education as well as for international conferences have proliferated. International newsletters have grown up side by side with comic books and instruction manuals designed to mobilize poor urban women; women's concerns are reflected in the electronic media, and major universities have begun to offer courses on women. In some areas, liberation theology has undertaken attacks on machismo and a reconsideration of the meanings of the Virgin Mary. Much of this activity, though by no means all, has been inspired by the feminism of European and North American women.

Inevitably, the comparative study of American women's literatures will be pursued in coming years. As a movement of women, feminism must evolve globally; it must devise means to cross the boundaries not only of class, race, and religion but also of nations. By the inner logic of a comprehensive social movement, the test of any descriptive or theoretical articulation will be its ability to accommodate variation; yet extensive spadework must be done country by country, even region by region, before the most meaningful comparisons can be drawn.

It is worth noting that Latin American women's writing is more cosmopolitan than that of women in the United States. Of the writers mentioned in this essay, the vast majority have lived out of their native land for extended and decisive periods of their lives – seeking better education or broader culture, on diplomatic missions or in political exile. Though their language is still sharply marked by place of origin, the experience of exile may make them more kindred than would otherwise be the case. Consequently, a comparison of women from one country with those from more than twenty may be less peculiar than it may seem at first glance.

The simplest justification for comparison is the fact that American women's experience in the past two centuries can be viewed as a single story, at once historical and literary, of women's emergence as self-conscious subjects. My approach in this introduction is to sketch a map of that emergence, beginning with a survey of suggestive features of women's historical experience from the independence period to the present.

In the independence period in Spanish America, which ended with the battle of Ayacucho in 1824, the participation of women was fuller and more varied than that of their northern counterparts. For example, in Argentina and Gran Colombia, women led or supported intellectual activity in the conspirators' *tertulias* (political salons) and were jailed for circulating revolutionary literature. Women's batteries defended cities, and female soldiers served under Bolívar. Yet when independence was won, women resumed their former status. Bolívar's letter in 1826, warning his sister María Antonia "not to mix in political business nor adhere to or oppose any party" because "a woman ought to be neutral in public business," recalls John Adams's derisive refusal fifty years earlier of his wife's request that he "remember the ladies" in shaping his "new code of laws."[2] An ideology of femininity grew up in the Americas to block women's pursuit of their own independence by making it seem freakish. After Margaret Fuller invoked the Declaration of Independence in her *Woman in the Nineteenth Century* (1845), Edgar Allan Poe divided humanity into three classes: men, women, and Margaret Fuller. In the same period, the work of the boldly independent Cuban writer Gertrudis Gómez de Avellaneda won her the equivocal praise "es mucho hombre esta mujer" (this woman is a real man).

Whereas the struggle for independence was a principal catalyst for Spanish American women, the cause of abolition of slavery mobilized women in the United States. Fighting for the liberty of others fed women's awareness of their own condition, especially when they were denied the right to speak in public about what they knew to be just. In 1838 Sarah and Angelina Grimké linked their own political impotence to the subjugation of the slave; ten years later, Lucretia Mott and Elizabeth Cady Stanton, abolitionists who had been granted secondary status by their own cohorts, helped organize the first woman's rights convention.

In general, the activities open to women in Latin America were sharply divided by class from the colonial period on into the nineteenth century. Whereas the poor woman worked at whatever she could to survive, the aristocratic lady was confined to the respectable alternatives of child rearing or membership in a religious order. By the early nineteenth century, her education, if she got one, was shaped so as to benefit her influence on her children and did not necessarily include literacy. In the United States, the class divisions were never so sharp, because the actual middle class was much larger, and its ideology, reinforced by the promise of upward mobility, was rarely challenged. The productive labor expected of women generally in the colonies continued under frontier conditions; but by the early nineteenth century much of their work had been usurped by new industry, from which, for the most part, women were excluded, with the convenient justification that women's "sphere" was domestic. Some thinkers like Catherine Beecher embraced domesticity, seeing in it an opportunity to wield influence from within the home.

Regardless of these important differences, the view that women were by nature maternal and selfless was fundamental to social order throughout the hemisphere. Hence "good works," the extension of one's maternal concern beyond the family, continued to offer middle-class white women in the United States the chief passage from private to public life in the nineteenth century. In Latin America, similar opportunities presented themselves only in certain areas and among the wealthy. In Buenos Aires, for example, the secular reformer Bernardino Rivadavia in 1823 enlisted thirteen socially prominent women to administer a girls' public elementary school; this Society of Beneficence eventually supervised social services for women and children for 125 years. To the north, the cult of domesticity fed Catherine Beecher's argument in the 1840s that teaching was the "true" profession of unmarried women: In forty years public education was converted from a stopgap choice for men to a profession for well-educated women. The schoolmarm gained not only self-esteem but also such adventurous opportunities in the 1860s as educating black freedmen during and after the Civil War and accepting the invitation of President Domingo F. Sarmiento to teach and set an example for Argentine women.[3] In the relative absence of the confining cult of domesticity and relieved from housework by servants, upper-class women in Latin America, especially in Argentina, Uruguay, and Chile, had begun by the end of the century to enter such professions as medicine, law, engineering, and architecture with greater ease. In the United States, "social housekeepers" developed political organizing skills and became increasingly controversial as they moved from settlement houses to temperance crusades, social purity movements, and trade union organizing.

With the turn of the century, the National American Women's Suffrage Association became the leading U.S. feminist organization, but it won the vote in 1920 by shrewdly adopting racist and xenophobic rhetoric when necessary and by alienating free-love anarchists like Emma Goldman and pacifists like Alice Paul, not to mention birth-control advocate Margaret Sanger. A feminist movement that accommodated most of these factions flourished at the same time in the Yucatán, where the spirit of the Mexican Revolution was complemented by foreign ideas brought to its busy ports. Between 1915 and 1922, socialist governors launched campaigns for literacy and against Catholic ideology (the "defanaticization" campaign), gave women the vote, and elected them to office. But the advocacy of "free love," easy divorce, and birth control – and especially the publication in 1922 of Margaret Sanger's pamphlet on contraception, interdicted in the United States – was too extreme for Mexican feminists.[4]

The battle for suffrage in Latin America varied from country to country. Although feminist parties were formed in a few countries and international congresses were held in several, all suffrage movements were subject to the rise and staying power of democratic governments and to the vicissitudes of other political struggles. Thus in Peru in the 1930s even Magda Portaì, novelist, poet, and leader of the influential Popular Revolutionary Alliance of America (APRA), argued that only privileged women would qualify as voters, whereas from its inception in 1896 the Argentine Socialist party included in its platform demands for universal suffrage.[5] In the twentieth century, the struggle for women's rights in Argentina was led by women as different as Victoria Ocampo, aristocrat and cosmopolitan editor of the magazine *Sur* and mortal antagonist of Juan Perón, on the one hand, and, on the other, Eva Perón herself, a provincial working-class actress who, once in power, worked for her class and sex and won women the vote. In Hispanic America the struggle for suffrage lasted four decades longer than in the United States; it was won first in Ecuador in 1929 and last in Paraguay in 1961. During this period, U.S. feminism entered what Elaine Showalter has called its awkward age.[6] Although women were active during the 1930s in movements of the Left and during World War II, they were less unilaterally feminist.

The 1960s represent a sharp turning point, for different reasons, in the experience of women throughout the hemisphere. In the United States, the "second wave" of feminism was triggered by the concerted discovery in the late 1960s of female activists in the civil rights and antiwar movements that they were consistently discriminated against by the male members of the New Left. Although segments of the new movement often work with issues that are not gender specific and some are working to build a socialist feminism, this wave of feminism finds its roots in its severance from the Left. By contrast, in Latin America, political parties and movements have provided the context for the later growth of feminism in Latin America. Moreover, women's organization has to be seen in the context of the Cuban Revolution of 1959, which by fulfilling the promise of many defeated revolts sharpened the desire for autonomy throughout Latin America. Perhaps the most important factor distinguishing women's struggles in the United States from those in Latin America has to do with the relative peace and prosperity in the United States; this has permitted the flourishing of a feminism that is often relatively isolated from other political crises.

Very divergent political realities inform contemporary women's experience of Latin America. Countries that have won or are engaged in popular revolutions have sought to correct discrimination against women, and each revolution learns from its predecessor. Although the Cuban Revolution began in the mid 1970s to institutionalize equality for women through a Family Code and "popular power," the much greater participation of women in the Nicaraguan insurrection resulted in much swifter legislation of equality. According to the reports of the Women's

Association of El Salvador, discrimination against women is being systematically addressed during the struggle itself by more equal sharing of responsibilities within the zones controlled by the rebels.

In countries where conservative forces have been strong, women's experience ranges widely. In Chile in the early 1970s, for example, the right wing exploited traditional notions of women as defenders of the home to enlist their aid in opposing Salvador Allende, while making that aid seem devoid of political content. Stereotypical female values were used to "naturalize" and even "sanctify" opposition to the Popular regime. Thus, after the coup, women could again be closed off from the public arena and restored to the pedestal as tutelary "angel of the family, fatherland and property."[7]

The ability of dictatorial regimes to identify their causes with ideological invocations of mother and of home, however, has been steadily eroded by their own violation of women and of homes (in the uprooting of indigenous communities in Guatemala or of working-class populations in the Southern Cone, for example). Consequently, as Jean Franco observes, the moral meanings that had been assigned to particular territories or genders are rapidly being altered both by the military and by new oppositional forces. In this change women are finding new sources of power. For example, in the late 1970s mothers of the "disappeared" in Argentina began to meet each week in front of the government palace to demand the return of their loved ones. In this repeated act, the Mothers of the Plaza de Mayo simultaneously put behind them their definitive domestic, private space to create themselves anew in public space, translating the meaning of "mother" from biological reproducer of individuals to protector of the community.[8] They were thus called locas, madwomen, and became a political force; in 1982 they were among the very few who protested the war in the Malvinas. It might be instructive to compare the several groups of mothers of the disappeared, whose lives have been shaped by disaster, with women's antiwar movements in the United States, whose projects are shaped rather by anticipation of disaster. The latter range from the Women's Strike for Peace, which in the early 1960s concerned itself strictly with military issues, to the Seneca Women's Encampment in the 1980s, which contends that only the end of patriarchy itself can make disarmament meaningful.

The story of the emergence of women in literature is retold with difficulty because, in the first place, an inventory of American women's literature has not yet been fully taken or even designed. In the second place, the measures of emergence are more ambiguous and its stages less separable in literature than in history.

On the assumption that narratives are the most direct indices of social values, this discussion is limited literally to story, or fiction. (A comparative study of poetic production should be undertaken, especially since in Latin America, until recently, women poets were more important numerically and many of them more overtly feminist than prose writers, and in certain epochs women poets have received greater recognition in Spanish America than in the United States.)[9]

Before turning to women's construction of their own story, let us consider their literary use of the concern for others so long and widely attributed to them. Presumed to be naturally and essentially maternal or selfless, women were expected to devote themselves to others. When they wrote about others who were oppressed, their writing potentially broached, symbolically or by analogy, the question of their own status. Sometimes this writing issued in protest against the production of woman, and at other times in exploitation of it, in the sense that women made something for themselves of the ways they had been made. Thus, in the Cuban novel *Sab* (1841), Gertrudis Gomez de Avellaneda linked the causes of feminism and antislavery by making slavery an overt metaphor for marriage as experienced by the white woman. In *Uncle Tom's Cabin* (1852) Harriet Beecher Stowe sought also to reconcile the causes, but with diametrically opposed assumptions about "woman's sphere." She fused the antislavery tract with the dominant literary from of U.S. women in the nineteenth century, the sentimental novel, which sought female supremacy through domesticity. Uncle Tom has the qualities of an ideal woman, and Rachel Halliday's Quaker community is a harbinger of a superior matriarchal order.[10] Both these rival political strategies – a liberal feminism that seeks to increase women's power within existing systems and a radical feminism that seeks alternative systems – persist in literatures of the hemisphere.

Despite their differences, both works announce a tradition of pursuit of female self-expression through imaginative engagement with a member of another group, oppressed by race or class. This "other" would resemble less the "other" de Beauvoir describes in *The Second Sex* – by contrast with whom men know themselves – than the "other's" own "other," a partial alter ego, empathetic analysis of whom would generate self-understanding and, potentially, authority. Such "others" continued to spur women to write in both Americas, and the dialectic between concern for others and recognition of one's own oppression continued. Although many men wrote similar works, it is worth noting that Clorinda Matto de Turner portrayed the lives of the Peruvian Indians and the abuses visited on them by the oligarchy and the priests in *Aves sin nido* (Birds Without a Nest) in 1889. Her white female characters suffer too at the hands of the socially ambitious and the clergy; but the ideal, celebrated in her abundant essays, remains the traditional maternal woman. Although her novel won approval from the president, she was later driven into exile by conservative forces.

In a very different context, half a century later Rosario Castellanos wrote about the Tzotzil Indians in Chiapas, also exposing oppression by the governing whites. As Cynthia Steele argues in this volume (Chapter 3), Castellanos refuses to romanticize either the Indian or the oppressed white woman. Yet Stacey Schlau shows, by focusing on the parallel between "Indian enclosures in a cycle of oppression and destruction" and "female enclosures in a cycle of silence and thwarted voice" in *Oficio de tinieblas* (The Service of Shadows, 1962), how the Indian Catalina gains power from her transformation of the enclosures of church and cave. Though Catalina is defeated, Schlau suggests that the power of transgressive speech remains as memory and prophecy.

When the 1960s brought a new impetus in Latin America to uncover the unrecorded reality of the region and the revolutionary potential of the peasants and working classes, testimony and the testimonial novel emerged as genres of a major importance for both men and women writers. In *Si me permiten hablar* (1976, *Let Me Speak*) and *Me llamo Rigoberta Menchú* (1983, *I . . . Rigoberta Menchú*), social anthropologist Moema Viezzer and ethnographer Elizabeth Burgos-Debray act as midwives and translators for the revolutionary experiences of the indigenous Domitila and Rigoberta. (Burgos-Debray says she became Rigoberta's "instrument, her double.") Elena Poniatowska anticipated their work in her fictional adaptation of the testimony of Jesusa Palancares, *Hasta no verte Jesús mío* (1969, Here's Looking at You, Jesus). Poniatowska has spoken and written about the way this imaginative engagement helped her to constitute her own voice and identity as a writer.[11]

In the United States, white middle-class writers have attended intermittently to black characters in the South and to native Americans in the Southwest. The working class began to be used as the middle-class writer's "other" on the day that Rebecca Harding Davis fancied that the miner passing by her Virginia window was a secret artist (*Life in the Iron Mills*, 1861). Gertrude Stein rang interesting changes on this approach when in *Three Lives* (1907) she explored the lives of immigrant German servants and a restless black woman through the invention of their secret languages. The problematic articulation of class consciousness with feminist consciousness was broached in the writing of turn-of-the-century socialists like Charlotte Perkins Gilman and Susan Glaspell and the Old Left writers of the 1930s like Josephine Herbst and Tess Slessinger. In Spanish America, as far as we can tell, working-class and peasant "others" were probably not treated until later.[12]

Earlier than in Latin America, the white middle-class woman's "other" in the United States would begin to speak on her own behalf. Meridel Le Sueur, Tillie Olsen, and Agnes Smedley analyzed their own working-class and radical backgrounds from a woman's point of view. The scattered black voices of the nineteenth century (e.g., Harriet Wilson and Frances Harper) became a chorus in the "Harlem Renaissance" of the 1920s and 1930s with the works of Nella Larsen, Jessie Fausset, and especially Zora Neale Hurston, whose bountiful legacy is still being discovered by such writers as Alice Walker and Toni Morrison. To the south, writing workshops in Cuba, Nicaragua, and Mexico have cultivated the writing of workers and peasants in recent years.

Writing by working-class or minority women who experience multiple oppression or redoubled "otherness" sometimes occasions penetrating analysis of the social construction of women. Such analysis provides the route from object status to subjecthood. Zora Neale Hurston's novel *Their Eyes Were Watching God* (1937) is paradigmatic. Learning from her grandmother that "de nigger woman is de mule uh de world," protagonist Janie explores her options through a series of relationships that reveal how, materially and ideologically, the forces of racism, capitalism, and patriarchy are interlocked. This novel goes beyond deconstruction to point toward a construction of self rooted in the rich alternative culture and language of black folk. To some extent Rigoberta Menchú's testimony and that of Jesusa Palancares achieve the same effects.

If we turn to the unfolding story told by writers who attend to the self without mediation of the "other," we find that women writers began by fighting their way out of the romance plot. As Rachel Blau DuPlessis describes it, romance converts the "female hero," a figure whose energy and insight promised growth, into the "heroine," the passive "object of male attention or rescue," and confirms her reduced identity in marriage. The romance plot is "a trope for the sex–gender system as a whole" and bears an "uncanny resemblance" to "the telos of 'normal femininity' as the proper resolution of the oedipal crisis" of Freudian theory. Nineteenth-century romance established that *Bildung* and romance, or quest and love, could not be integrated for the heroine at the resolution of the plot.[13]

The pioneering classics of American women tell a single tale of a woman who awakens to her condition and imagines a freed self she is powerless to realize. She submits as sacrificial victim to marriage, as in Venezuelan Teresa de la Parra's *Ifigenia* (1924), or she escapes it in death, as in Kate Chopin's "The Awakening" (1899) and Edith Wharton's *House of Mirth* (1905), or marriage reveals itself as death, as in Chilean María Luisa Bombal's *La última niebla* (1935, The Final Mist).[14]

Despite the enduring popularity of romance in popular culture, many women writers, whether or not they consider themselves feminist, have sought narrative strategies that challenge the hegemony of romance. By "breaking the sentence" and "breaking the sequence," in Virginia Woolf's words, they criticize or revise the social scripts assigned them by a patriarchal culture.[15] Though many writers have continued to explore the natural habitat of romance, heterosexual love, they subvert the plot, beginning with divorce rather than ending with marriage, or subject it to irreverent playfulness.[16]

When they move beyond the scene of the heterosexual couple, writers can interrogate more sharply the production of "woman." One narrative strategy is the story of the female child, a kind of "wild child," who, standing at what might be called "the site of production" of gender identity, can subvert its assumptions. Carson McCullers's Frankie in *A Member of the Wedding* (1946) identifies with freaks and the underclass before she comes of age, whereas coming of age itself is denied the black Pecola of Toni Morrison's *The Bluest Eye* (1970) for whom the social scripts of her culture are hopelessly out of reach. In Latin America, Argentine Silvina Ocampo and Colombian Albalucía Angel suggest that the taboos of Catholic socialization can be escaped only by physical and psychic violence; they construct narratives of girls who, by virtue of their sexual molestation by servants, achieve the problematic freedom conferred by the sense of evil.[17]

Another circumvention of the romance plot can be found in texts that center on the daughter's relation to the mother, implicitly evoke the preoedipal bond between them, and, by granting it dominance, work to "neutralize, minimize, or transcend" the oedipal script.[18] An extreme example of this narrative strategy in the United States is Marilynne Robinson's *Housekeeping* (1980), in which the protagonist's bond to her drowned mother so galvanizes the imaginative energy of the narrator that she refuses socialization and becomes a vagabond. Surrogate mothers who are servants, usually women of color, have functioned in Spanish American women's texts to offer alternative ideologies to white girls growing up. It would be interesting to compare this phenomenon with the role played by black slaves or servants in the southern United States.[19]

Often, of course, the mother is an agent, complicit or reluctant, of patriarchy. The daughter's formative ambivalence is at the heart of a great deal of recent U.S. writing,[20] and the same issue is examined from the point of view of the mother in such works as Tillie Olsen's "I Stand Here Ironing" and "Tell Me a Riddle" (1961) and E. M. Broner's fanciful *Her Mothers* (1975).

In lieu of this ambivalence about mothers, Latin American writers have often engaged in unequivocal assault, perhaps because the cult of the Virgin Mary has proved more durable than the U.S. cult of domesticity. The ideal of female purity is onerous enough, but when it is coupled with haut-bourgeois pretension, it draws the creative fire of writers like Puerto Rican Rosario Ferré. In the 1960s and 1970s, writers like Uruguayan Cristina Peri Rossi in *El libro de mis primos* (1965, The Book of My Cousins) read the mother's subservience to patriarchy (they polish the very bones of the paternal corpse) as a metonym for support of dictatorship. Peri Rossi anatomizes the violence at the heart of the bourgeois family to show how it is creature, bulwark, and epitome of the totalitarian regime. In the symbolic central chapter, some boy cousins secretly carve a hole between the legs of a doll of their girl cousin, stare into its emptiness, stuff it with keys and other things, and bury it. In this multiple violation of the powerless, they discover their power, with the complicity of the women in the family. Political texts intrude in the narrative, even as political violence intrudes on the growth of a young woman, in Colombian Albalucía Angel's *Estaba la pájara pinta sentada en el verde limón* (1975, The Painted Bird Was Sitting in the Green Lemon Tree), an inverse *Bildungsroman* that systematically desacralizes all family institutions. Both these works so construe social alternatives that armed struggle becomes the only reasonable recourse.[21]

However, the institution of motherhood is changing, and the exodus of mothers from the home in concerted action for the disappeared in Mexico prompted Poniatowska to celebrate them in a personal chronicle in *Fuerte es el silencio* (1980, Silence Is Strong). And reports of the Madres of the Plaza de Mayo stirred Marta Traba to write a novel, *Conversación al sur* (1981, *Mothers and Shadows*) in which a young working–class guerilla and a middle-aged bourgeoise build a fragile community in response to their shared loss.

Such bonding of women, like the relationships in what Nina Auerbach has called "communities of women," draw on the psychodynamics of mother–daughter relations.[22] Attention to these social bonds constitutes a related narrative strategy, to which Afro-American writers have made a particularly rich contribution. The growing body of lesbian writing, of course, offers the most radical rejection of the romance script.[23]

In connection with the community of women, Spanish American writers have painted on large canvases communities in which women's experience is central to illuminate definitive epochs of their national history. Mexican Elena Garro's *Los recuerdos del porvenir* (1963, *Reflections of Things To Come*) is a novel in which collective memory and narration, magic, and a circular theory of time are made to organize and interpret history. In contrast to writers whose novels assess critically what the

Mexican Revolution has produced (like Carlos Fuentes's contemporaneous *The Death of Artemio Cruz*), Garro charts what was lost in it. As the revolution promised the women freedom, its defeat locked them in a state of permanent unrest. Garro finds in the duality of the position of women – frozen by centuries of institutionalized repression, but freer than men to imagine all possibilities – the source of her aesthetic. All things are fraught with absence, with their lost but imaginable alterity. Calendar time becomes a fiction of dominance: Women live by anatomizing desire and memory, which thus become predictive. Despite the great difference in their contexts, this largely conceived and resonant novel is in some ways a precursor of Isabel Allende's *La casa de los espíritus* (1982, *The House of the Spirits*), although Garro's book has been largely ignored and Allende's was praised upon publication as the first book by a woman to make it into the "men's club" of contemporary classics. Allende's sweeping account of three generations culminates in the sinister violence of the Pinochet regime. In the torture chamber, the youngest, urged on by the ghost of the eldest, makes her survival out of the act of writing. Her book of memory, the house of spirits itself, develops a cyclical view of history and a moral of political reconciliation. Another large-scale work based in political history, though without the focus on women's experience, is Luisa Valenzuela's fantastic black comedy *Cola de lagartija* (1983, *The Lizard's Tail*).

Large historical themes have been elaborated by writers in the United States from Stowe through Edith Wharton (*The Custom of the Country*, 1913) and Willa Cather to the contemporary Beulah quintet of Mary Lee Settle and Paule Marshall's *The Chosen Place, The Timeless People* (1969). Utopian histories have attracted women writers since Charlotte Perkins Gilman invented *Herland* (1915), whose community of mothers-and-daughters by parthenogenesis gave the ultimate quietus to romance. Gilman's heirs include Joanna Russ, Marge Piercy, and Ursula Leguin.[24]

A final strategy for breaking the sequence of romance, which Garro and Allende and others mentioned employ, is to write the story of the female hero as artist. This may take one of two forms. The protagonist may be an artist literally or figuratively, as the narrator of her story. The former approach particularly attracted the "New Woman" of the United States at the turn of the century, because it offered a means of exploring the conflict between work and marriage.[25]

When the protagonist is the narrator, a potential artist, she can inscribe her own lack of (and desire for) authority in the act of constituting herself as author, or play with the interrelation between social scripts for "woman" and the ever-potential script of the self. "The Yellow Wallpaper" and *Ifigenia* present themselves as letters and diaries of the protagonist in which the protagonist herself cannot authorize her own understanding. Recreating the 1920s in *Querido Diego, te abraza Quiela* (1978, Dear Diego, with Hugs from Quiela), Elena Poniatowska elaborates and extends the real and unanswered correspondence to Diego Rivera in Mexico from Angelina Beloff, his mistress abandoned in Paris. In this epistolary novel of dead letters, this duet for one instrument, Poniatowska finds the form that follows the contours of unrequited love and baseless but enduring hope, in order perhaps to exhaust and exorcise that perennial female script. Willa Cather explores a transitional solution by engaging in authorial cross-dressing. She presents *My Ántonia* (1918) as the writing of a man, who, like the Trojan horse, smuggles immigrant women characters through the gates of literary respectability; like a ventriloquist's vessel, he also voices her attraction to women.

In the 1970s, writers in the United States were suggesting that, to elude their social scripts, protagonist-narrators would have to transgress them. Thus Maxine Hong Kingston's novel of Chinese-American girlhood, *The Woman Warrior* (1975), begins, " 'You must not tell anyone,' my mother said, 'what I am about to tell you.' "[26] As the Chinese mother offers her daughter a heritage of secrecy, silence, and death, a heritage that denies and invalidates her existence, the child must bear herself into the world by violating the heritage that would cancel her, betraying all the secrets. Epistolary narrator Celie in Alice Walker's *The Color Purple* (1983), opens with the self-imposed mandate: "You better not never tell nobody but God. It'd kill your mammy."[27] Herself violated, Celie feels she has transgressed and must write her life in hiding from her mother until she comes by its means to inherit everything. One of Puerto Rican Rosario Ferré's most ingenious stories, "La bella durmiente" (The Sleeping Beauty), sets anonymous letters against such social scripts as wedding-picture albums, shower invitations, and ballet reviews to spring woman free of the haut-bourgeois world that cages her. This story is one of the *Papeles de Pandora* (1976, Pandora's Papers), a volume that, once opened, its title suggests, will let loose all the evils that afflict the human race – and hope.

This survey suggests two more general points of contrast, one thematic, concerning the relation of the self to society, the other formal. It is a commonplace that U.S. writing by men is fueled by the drive to identify and develop the self, often in social isolation. Their female compatriots participate in this tendency, though the urge for transcendence makes a rare appearance (often to be fulfilled by death, as in "The Awakening"), and isolation usually needs correcting by relationship. Latin Americans, male and female, assume a more necessary relation between self and society. Recent events have intensified this distinction in women's work. The contemporary phase of the U.S. women's movement has generated greater attention to self-definition and self-development, whereas the more intrusive political developments in Latin America have made women's writing generally more overtly political. This is not to ignore either the political strain in works by U.S. writers like Marge Piercy, Grace Paley, Rosellen Brown, Alix Kates Shulman, and most women of color, or the ongoing private concerns of writers like Julieta Campos and Silvina Ocampo. Writers like Luisa Valenzuela and Elvira Orphée, for example, have testified to the fact that they would not deal with political unrest or torture had not the daily life of Argentina in the 1970s obliged them to do so.[28]

Our other contrast concerns form. In general, women of the United States have favored realism in fiction for several reasons. At the turn of the century, for example, women found the conventions of naturalism serviceable in charting the forces that confine women.[29] Later, as Sandra M. Gilbert and Susan Gubar point out, women's regionalist writing was cultivated not, like men's, to provide romantic color but to record the conditions and qualities of women's lives otherwise lost to history. In the exploration of sexual freedom in the 1970s, as Ann Snitow notes, realism was found to be appropriate, as it often is to "first phases," where demystification is perceived to be the most pressing need.[30] Again, without ignoring exceptions on both sides of the Rio Grande, there appears to be a greater tendency toward literary experiment to the south. (Experiment is, of course, not to be equated with originality; Hispanic American experiment began with imitation of Europe, especially France, and goes on with self-mirroring.) One thinks of the linguistic play of Rosario Ferré and Ana Lydia Vega, the fragmentation of narrative of Valenzuela, Julieta Campos, and González de León, among others.

To approach these observations another way, it is an arresting fact that Latin American experimentalists have flourished (especially in the contemporary period) under conditions of political exile, in internal exile at home, or in a way of life that precludes fixed addresses. Moreover, many of the experimental writers of the United States, like Stein, H.D. (Hilda Doolittle), and Djuna Barnes, did the bulk of their work abroad. When we recall that the latter writers were also lesbian (hence in a kind of social exile) and that many Latin Americans are breaking out of the prisons of social as well as of literary convention, promising topics for further inquiry present themselves. When does the need to write in code become a new literary resource? What is the relation between realism, relative security, and relative social and literary convention, on the one hand, and social deviation, exile, and literary innovation, on the other?

In the pages that follow, we offer no examples of conventional literary criticism. Rather, the five contributions to this section represent five ways in which feminist criticism questions assumptions implicit in canonical thinking. In her play, *This Life Within Me Won't Keep Still,* and in her introduction to it, Electa Arenal, of Mexican and U.S. descent, offers an example of feminist "re-visioning" of literary history. By juxtaposing and hence equalizing the first female poets published in New England and New Spain, she bypasses issues of hierarchy and influence, ignoring the much greater intellectual and artistic power of Sor Juana Inéz de la Cruz, because her interest is in exploring American female expression at its origin. Margaret Randall, of U.S. parentage, has also built bridges in her own experience in several Spanish America countries and in most of her prolific work. Her own biography dramatizes the early feminist maxim that the personal is political, and our use of the interview to offer her testimony is a growing tradition among feminists.

Lisa Davis's essay compares the information made available by Elena Poniatowska and Alice Walker, whose works give voice to women who have been socially oppressed and historically ignored. These writers' use of the *novela testimonio* and the epistolary novel challenges canons of genre by stretching or combining them to produce new forms. Luisa Valenzuela's essay shifts the ground of discussion from the oppression and suppression of women to their repression and its psychological roots in the origin of language. An innovative writer of fiction herself, Valenzuela's thought, like that of many Latin American writers, has more in common with the current French school of feminist theory – with figures like Julia Kristeva, Luce Irigaray, and Hélène Cixous – than with U.S. theorists or fiction writers. Improvising on Lacan, who sees the attainment of the symbolic order, figured by the phallus, as grounded in loss and censorship, she proposes that women's double loss is redressed in the transgressive linguistic strategies of writers who consume the stuff of censorship.

Finally, Jean Franco's essay represents two trends in cultural criticism that feminist scholars have strengthened. Feminists have begun to validate and examine forms outside the canon, such as diaries, letters, reminiscences, beyond the limits of elite canons; by contrasting the U.S. Harlequin romance with Mexican comic books, Franco assumes the significance of all cultural signs. Her analysis also ties her work to reception theory: She traces the female consumer's response to the Harlequin plot, showing how it plays on her individual needs and anxieties, and she asks why an apparently emancipatory plot in Mexican comic books emerges at a time when potential readers are being incorporated into the work force.

NOTES

I am indebted to the following people for their generosity in sharing their work and making useful suggestions in connection with this essay: Marjorie Agosín, Electa Arenal, Carol Ascher, Gwenda Blair, Magda Bogin, Jean Franco, Judith Friedlander, Gabriela Mora, Bobbye Ortiz, Nancy Porter, Mary Pratt, Ann Snitow, Doris Sommer, Elizabeth Wood.

1   Helen I. Safa notes in her paper "Women in Latin America: The Impact of Socioeconomic Change" that since 1975 there have been many feminist activities in research, action, service provision, and training that "cross-cut the class distinctions that appeared to be insurmountable during the early years of the women's movement." Forthcoming in *Women in Latin America: A Decade of Change,* ed. Jack Hopkins (New York: Holmes & Meier).

2   See Evelyn Cherpak, "The Participation of Women in the Independence Movement in Gran Colombia, 1780–1830," in *Latin American Women: Historical Perspectives,* ed. Asunción Lavrín (Westport, Conn.: Greenwood Press, 1978), pp. 229–30, and Miriam Schneir, *Feminism: The Essential Historical Writings* (New York: Vintage, 1972), p. 3.

3   Cynthia Jeffress Little, "Education, Philanthropy, and Feminism: Components of Argentine Womanhood, 1860–1926." in *Latin American Women,* ed. Lavrín, pp. 236, 238. See also Nancy Hoffmann, *Woman's "True" Profession* (Old Westbury, N.Y.: Feminist Press, 1981).

4   Anna Macías, "Felipe Carillo Puerto and Women's Liberation in Mexico," in *Latin American Women,* ed. Lavín, pp. 286–301.

5   See Robin Morgan, ed., *Sisterhood Is Global* (New York: Anchor, 1984), p. 549.

6   Elaine Showalter, *These Modern Women* (Old Westbury, N.Y.: Feminist Press, 1978), p. 9.

7   Michele Mattelart, "Chile: The Feminine Version of the Coup d'Etat," in *Sex and Class in Latin America,* ed. Nash and Safa (New York: Praeger, 1976), p. 291. More recently, on the Left, some Chilean women who have returned from years of European exile are questioning the hierarchical structures and procedures of leftist political parties and seeking autonomous organization. Many are actively organizing women in urban slums.

8   See Jean Franco's "Beyond Ethnocentrism: Gender, Power, and the Third World Intelligentsia," unpublished manuscript, Columbia University, New York, 1983.

9   Although the example of Emily Dickinson towered for nearly a century over her versifying female compatriots, four powerful figures born in the Southern Cone between 1886 and 1905 were enormously successful in their own time and have subsequently been accepted into the canon. They are the Chilean Nobel Prize winner Gabriela Mistral, the Uruguayans Delmira Agustini and Juana de Ibarbouru, and the Argentine Alfonsina Storni. The work of the last-named and a Puerto Rican poet of the next generation, Julia de Burgos, is boldly feminist.

10 See Jane P. Tompkins, "Sentimental Power: *Uncle Tom's Cabin* and the Politics of Literary History," *Glyph* 8 (1981): 79–102. It is telling that Stowe's book was an influential best-seller of unprecedented scope, whereas *Sab* was written in Europe, drew heavily on European romantic models, and was not allowed entry into Cuba. See Beth Miller, "Gertrude the Great," *Women in Hispanic Literature: Icons and Fallen Idols* (Berkeley: University of California Press, 1985), p. 209.

11 See Bell Gale Chevigny, "The Transformation of Privilege in the work of Elena Poniatowska," *Latin American Literary Review*, no. 26 (July–December 1986), 49–62.

12 Gabriela Mora points to Sara Gallardo's *Enero* (1958, January) and Marta Brunet's *María Nadie* (1957) for their treatments of a peasant woman and a working-class woman, respectively ("Narradoras hispanoamericanas: Vieja y nueva problemática en renovadas elaboraciones," *Theory and Practice of Feminist Literary Criticsm,* ed. Gabriela Mora and Karen S. Van Hooft [Ypsilanti, Mich.: Bilingual Press, 1982]).

13 Rachel Blau DuPlessis, *Writing beyond the Ending: Narrative Strategies of Twentieth-Century Women Writers* (Bloomington: Indiana University Press, 1985), pp. 3, 5, 35, 200.

14 More radically, in Charlotte Perkins Gilman's "The Yellow Wallpaper" (1892) and in María Luisa Bombal's "The Tree," the protagonists' inability to name, locate, or even miss their own subjectivity results in their displacing it obsessively onto the object named in the title and in their enacting the drama of subjectivity in interaction with that object. Until it is cut down, Bombal's "tree" keeps Brigida a child, obscuring her capacity to know her real feelings, and Gilman's wallpaper figuratively "papers over" or mystifies the "wall" or barrier patriarchy builds between the protagonist and her self, a wall so sturdy that, to know her condition, she must become insane.

15 I am indebted for this interpretation of Woolf to DuPlessis, *Writing beyond the Ending,* chapter 3. The importance of Woolf's theory to Latin American women writers cannot be overstated; Victoria Ocampo, Rosario Castellanos, Silvina Bullrich, Albalucía Angel, and Ulalume González de Léon are among those who have written about it.

16 Attacks on the double standard came first. (Consider the best-selling novels of Argentine Silvina Bullrich, *Bodas de cristal* [1952, Crystal Anniversary], and Marilyn French in the United States, *The Women's Room,* 1977.) In Spanish America, endemic female passivity has elicited satiric flights in recent years. Woman's servility, and even her suicidal inclination, is ridiculed in Uruguayan Ulalume González de León's *A cado rato lunes* (1970, Every So Often on Monday; cited by Mora, "Narradoras hispanoamericanas," p. 162). In Rosario Ferré's fantastic comedies, a wife becomes a doll, or the wife and prostitute of a man meet after his death to collapse the double standard (*Papeles de Pandora,* 1976). Mary McCarthy's corruscating satire of sex (*The Company She Keeps,* 1942) and the jaunty abandon of Grace Paley's abandoned mothers generate new possibilities for both literary style and life-

style. For articulating the heroics of sexual liberation, Erica Jong's *Fear of Flying* (1973) may be the hemispheric champion. It has an ironic counterpart in the play of language and of voraciously masochistic fantasy in Luisa Valenzuela's *El gato eficaz* (1970).

17 Helena Araujo, "Ejemplos de la 'niña impura' en Silvina Ocampo y Albalucía Angel," *Hispamérica* 38 (1984): 27–35.

18 DuPlessis, *Writing beyond the Ending*, p. 37. Nancy Chodorow's study of the role preoedipal relations play in the formation of women's psychology in *The Reproduction of Mothering: Psychoanalysis and the Sociology of Gender* (Berkeley: University of California Press, 1978) has exerted an extraordinary influence on women scholars in the United States and has probably contributed to the greater attention in the United States than in Spanish America to mother–daughter relationships.

19 McCullers's *A Member of the Wedding* and Castellanos's *Balún-Canán* are examples.

20 See, for example, Paule Marshall, *Brown Girl, Brownstones* (1959); Rosellen Brown, *Autobiography of My Mother* (1976); Helen Henslee, *Pretty Redwing* (1982): Susanna Moore, *My Old Sweetheart* (1982); and Jamaica Kincaid, *Annie John* (1985).

21 See Gabriela Mora, "Un *Bildungsroman* femenino y la Violencia colombiana," *Selected Proceedings, Pacific Coast Council on Latin American Studies* 10 (1982): 73–79. Female characters take up the gun in many novels of this period, for example, María Esther de Miguel's *Puebloamérica* (1974) and Iverna Codina's *Los guerrilleros* (1968).

22 Nina Auerbach, *Communities of Women: An Idea in Fiction* (Cambridge, Mass.: Harvard University Press, 1978).

23 Afro-American writing on female bonding includes Toni Cade Bambara's "The Johnson Girls," in *Gorilla, My Love,* Alice Walker's *Meridian,* and Toni Morrison's *Sula.* Among North American lesbian writers are Rita Mae Brown, Kate Millett, June Arnold, and the Canadian Jane Rule. Spanish American lesbian writing ranges from Silvia Molloy's discreet *En breve cárcel* to Peri Rossi's openly erotic *La nave de los locos* (1984, Ship of Fools).

24 Daphne Patai offers the interesting finding that, although many women conceive of utopias peopled only by women, she has found no utopia that posited a society entirely of men ("Beyond Defensiveness: Feminist Research Strategies," *Women's Studies International Forum* 6 [1983]: 177–89).

25 Elizabeth Stuart Phelps's *The Story of Avis* and Willa Cather's *Song of the Lark* are examples. See also Nancy Porter's Afterword to Mary Hunter Austin, *Woman of Genius* (Old Westbury, N.Y.: Feminist Press, 1985).

26 Maxine Hong Kingston, *The Woman Warrior* (New York: Vintage, 1977), p. 3.

27 Alice Walker, *The Color Purple* (New York: Washington Square Press, 1983), p. 11. See Margaret Homans's discussion of "ambivalence concerning appropriation of the dominant discourse" in writers marginalized by race and nationality as well as gender (*Signs: Journal of Women in Culture and Society* 9 [1983]: 186–205).

28 This is the case in Luisa Valenzuela, *Aquí pasan cosas raras* (1975, *Strange Things Happen Here*) and Elvira Orphée, *La última conquista de El Angel* (1977, *El Angel's Last Conquest*). See Bell Chevigny, "Ambushing the Will to Ignorance: Elvira Orphée's *La última conquista de El Angel* and Marta Traba's *Conversación al sur*," in *El Cono Sur: Dinámica y dimensiones de su literatura*, ed. Rose S. Minc (Upper Montclair, N.J.: Montclair State College, 1985), pp. 98–104.

29 Consider the many fetters of talented Lily Bart in Edith Wharton's *House of Mirth* (1905), a novel that may be read as a feminist (and realist) correction of Henry James's creation of the independent Isabel Archer (*A Portrait of a Lady*, 1882), a figure shaped as much by self-projection as knowledge of women.

30 Sandra M. Gilbert and Susan Gubar, eds., *The Norton Anthology of Literature by Women* (New York: Norton, 1985), p. 968; Ann Snitow, "The Front Line: Notes on Sex in Novels by Women, 1969–1979," *Signs: Journal of Women in Culture and Society* 5 [1980]: 705.

9

This life within me won't keep still

ELECTA ARENAL

INTRODUCTION

Anne Bradstreet's first book of verse was published in London in 1650; Sor Juana Inés de la Cruz's came out in Madrid in 1689. The titles of both volumes referred to the authors as "the Tenth Muse."[1] These titles were composed not by the poets themselves but rather by admiring supporters who served as intermediaries and editors seeking to avoid censorship and to please the public. The epithet "muse" reveals more than the era's penchant for mythological analogy. Even a woman who was clearly an autonomous intellectual and poet was immediately cast as helpmeet to the inspiration of others – therefore a "tenth muse." In fact, however, Bradstreet's work is considered to have launched poetry in New England, whereas Sor Juana Inés de la Cruz caps and closes the baroque period of Hispanic letters.

Both women defended the intelligence, reason, art, and power of their sex. A female tradition, reaching back through biblical and mythological literature, gave wing to their aesthetic ambitions; it made persuasive their assertion of the right to wield not only the needle but the pen. In both, irony often hid behind deference, and wit frequently masked disdain for the narrow-mindedness and injustice of their detractors. Markedly different, however, were the physical and sociopolitical settings in which the two women lived and the roles they played in those settings. Bradstreet, the first English-speaking North American poet, was born and brought up in England on the estate of landed gentry (in whose service her father was employed) who looked favorably on education for women, and she lived out her adult life as the respectful and respected daughter and wife of two of the most prominent citizens of the Massachusetts Bay Colony. In contrast, Juana Ramírez, daughter of an unmarried *criolla* (women of Spanish descent born in the colonies), was a child prodigy who created her own supportive milieu among the books in her grandfather's library, refused marriage, took the veil, and at eighteen became Sor Juana Inés de la Cruz. By becoming a Bride of Christ she entered a subculture of women; paradoxically the cloister provided a degree of solitude and independence the outside world could not.[2]

Salem, Charlestown, Ipswich, Newtowne (Cambridge), and Andover, Massachusetts, where Anne Bradstreet and her family successively settled, were relatively new villages carved out of the wilderness. The bonds of marriage and dedicated motherhood inspired some of Bradstreet's poetic work, though they also curtailed the possibility of autonomous development. The Puritan communities held mundane hard work in high esteem. All members participated in the labor of building and maintaining the new settlements and institutions. Woman's place was in the home and in church, where she was to be subservient if not silent. Although Anne Bradstreet and her mother Dorothy Dudley, like other prosperous householders, were aided in domestic tasks by servants, neither in their homes nor in their towns did the servant population far outnumber the masters.[3]

It would seem that, whereas the Puritans were to get to heaven on a road paved with circumspection and unadorned pewter, the Catholics of New Spain were to do so on roads of penitence and elaborately ornamented gold and silver. Mexico City, capital of the Spanish colony, was a thriving metropolis built on the ruins of the Aztec capital, Tenochtitlán. For fifteen thousand Spanish colonizers, some eighty thousand Indian serfs and fifty thousand black and mulatto slaves and freed women and men provided a labor force to attend to every need.[4] Both Sor Juana and her mother, Doña Isabel Ramírez de Santillana, lived surrounded by servants. Despite vows of poverty, nuns in most convents brought their entourage with them. Sor Juana attributes her abandonment of secular life to her wish for unencumbered study and to her "absolute refusal" to marry. The graceful, spacious Renaissance convent she joined – after an unsuccessful attempt to embrace the most ascetic life of the Carmelite order – was run by a complex hierarchy (not unlike the social structure *extra muros*): at the top, nuns of the black veil, fully dowered, supposedly legitimate of birth and pure of blood; in the middle, *mestizo* and Indian servants; and at the bottom, mulatto and black slaves, some belonging to the community at large, some to individual nuns.[5] It was here that for more than two decades Sor Juana produced texts for the highly elaborate ceremonial life of the viceroyalty and the church. In her salon-like convent quarters she often entertained prominent visitors. Her exceptionality and the favor of the viceroyal couples and of some church dignitaries allowed her to keep those (in the ecclesiastic hierarchy) who would persecute her daring at bay until four years before her death.

It is impossible, indeed, to separate religious from secular life, so intimately intertwined were they at the time in both the Catholic and Protestant worlds. Anne Bradstreet spoke in a personal voice about the joys and tribulations, the certainties and doubts she encountered on the path to salvation and eternal bliss. Some of her finest prose and verse, the *Meditations* and *Contemplations,* were inspired by her religious experience and quest for unhesitant surrender to divine will. She shared with Sor Juana an Aristotelian concept of the world: The spheres were ordered; the cosmos theocentric. At times, both cast the divine power in the role of a strict parent concerned with the upbringing of children; there is something motherly about the God they describe, whose aim is lovingly but firmly to correct the misguided, confused, or misbehaving. For Bradstreet, nevertheless, that divine spirit was always male – although his very existence she admittedly, if timidly, questioned. Sor Juana's use of the prevalent Marian cult allowed her to place Mary sometimes above, sometimes next to God. She made brilliant use of Catholic values and baroque aesthetics to develop an overarching historical and mythical feminist ideology. She replaced the male metaphors that defined nature and evil as female: Adam, not Eve, became the first sinner. Thus she revised patriarchal concepts.

What was virtue to one was often vice to the other, both in terms of theology and of aesthetics. Ornamental artifice was part and parcel of Sor Juana's religious-literary expression; such literary adornment was anathema to Bradstreet's contemplative ideal. At certain points each, in accord with the edicts of her faith, categorically denounced the religion of the other. Bradstreet feared damnation, Sor Juana the Inquisition. And yet the Mexican poet, although surrounded by a sharply antiintellectual climate, aimed unrelentingly at promoting respect for intelligence (which for women went against Counter-Reformation decrees), at stimulating changes in the social relations between the sexes, and at publicizing images of women as a powerful force in Catholicism, in history, and in culture. She found in the Virgin Mary, the "Queen of Wisdom," her ultimate court of appeal. Anne Bradstreet, in turn, was emboldened by Queen Elizabeth, the "Phoenix Queen," "She [who] hath wiped off the aspersion of her Sex, / That women wisdom lack to play the Rex." It is in this paean that Bradstreet most resembles Sor Juana in image, tone, and discourse. And yet, though the Puritan too evolved a woman-inspired vision of the world, her strategies in life and in art were inherently less feminist than those of her Mexican counterpart, her revisions less fundamental.[6]

Bradstreet wrote about faith and the difficulty of its attainment; about marriage, love, childbirth, and death; about the awesomeness of creation; and about the destructiveness of men's wars – about power and powerlessness. She refused to subordinate nature to reason as was common in her day, in which a mechanistic view of the world was beginning to gain ground.[7]

Her society permitted leeway for questioning religious ideas. In describing her spiritual struggles Bradstreet speculates on the possible correctness of the papist creed, as opposed to her own. She confesses past bouts with nonbelief. It was, of course, a foregone conclusion that she would end up on the side of faith. The doctrine of conversion, implicit in Catholicism, was a lifelong project for Protestants. Debate was used, traditionally, to strengthen decision.

At the end of her life Anne Bradstreet made unqualified peace with the tenets of her Protestant sect. Earlier, rebellion and protests were on her lips, as, for example, in poems of grief at the death of grandchildren, in which she came close to shaking her fist at God, if not denying him. We do not have a record of her response to her father's disinheritance of her sister for straying from the path of devotional rectitude or to his role in the prosecution and expulsion of that courageous speaker and leader, the religious dissenter Anne Hutchinson. Lines avowing submission to the will of God in poems that at the same time express resistance, protest, or rejection of orthodox resignation indicate stress: She was wary of stepping too far out of bounds. She knew too well that women who spoke out and taught and preached did so at great risk.

The stereotype of Puritan life and ethics, however, has led to misconceptions. True, what could be written and published was more limited than what one could say, and even read, in one's circle of family and friends. According to booksellers' lists and orders, for instance, much frivolous and erotic literature was consumed in the English colonies.[8] Bradstreet's love poems to her husband are sparked by unveiled references to sexual arousal and pleasure. Direct affirmation of potency and desire are interlaced with ardent affection for the children conceived by their sexual union – a union she also celebrates with words.

Not only the conception of new human beings but artistic creativity, and the earthly planet too, provoke Bradstreet's imagination. Strong sentiments regarding the preservation of life and livelihood surface in verses about her family and in historical poems such as "A Dialogue Between Old England and New," in which she laments and censures civil strife for its destruction of towns and houses, crops and merchandise, and lives, young and old. Mother England and her daughter New England converse; the mother speaks with anguish of "plunder," "devastation," and "dearth of grain" caused by wars waged among different factions of her own groups of men: "I," she asserts, "am now destroyed and slaughtered by mine own" (*Works,* p. 338). But it was when "mine own" meant literally her immediate kin, in poems of love and pain and grief and fear – personal poems about illness, childbirth, marital union, and domestic calamity – that Bradstreet displayed unprecedented originality.[9]

Sor Juana Inés de la Cruz possessed a more independent woman-centered vision. Her feminist understanding of scholastic tradition, her concept of reason, wisdom, and conciliation, as well as her psychological insights led to far-reaching interpretations.[10] Drawing on her classical and Christian reading and on her life experience in colonized Mexico, she spoke out against male rage and aggression. While criticizing human sacrifice among the Aztecs, she denounced the bellicosity of her Spanish and *criollo* compatriots. In the following lines she censures men for encouraging animosity to turn into brutality:

> . . . for men themselves
> are crueler to the marrow
> than the cruelest beasts –
> for beasts you'll find not one
> who'll turn his fearsome claws
> against another of his species;
> whereas among men we see
> not only hate, but enmity
> become a trade
> and cruelty an art.   (*OC,* III, p. 186)

Sor Juana accomplished a revolutionary reversal of the gender identifications typical of her culture. Base nature, usually incarnated by Eve, she saw as Adam; eliminating Eve altogether, she placed the conception of the Word in the terrain of female creativity. This accomplishment gave her an extraordinary vantage point from which to treat the issues of power and powerlessness, subservience and domination, and resistance to domination.

A metaphorical womb becomes the center of universal creation. This vision underlies her writing, including the many works dedicated to celebrating the birth, life, deeds, and death of Mary, Christ, Joseph, and some of the most venerated saints, as well as secular poems of love, art, intellectual pursuit, and philosophical speculation.

Although Sor Juana left no written expression of doubts about her faith, in some of her works she offers a comparatist viewpoint, tracing ancient usages and misinterpretations of words and symbols, and contrasting belief systems. Although filtered through orthodox Catholic texts, much of her inspiration came from pre-Christian and heterodox early Christian sources. Significant, too, was the encounter between pre-Columbian and Spanish cultures, initiated a little more than a century before her birth. Sor Juana dramatically recreated that encounter.

In the *Loa* (or prelude) to her great religious drama, *El Divino Narciso,* the character America rejects the firearms of the conquistadores and the deceptive compassion of the priests, both serving the state's organized repression of indigenous peoples:

> If your pleading for my life
> while you show me your great mercy
> arises in your hope that I
> will be beaten by your proud strength
> – as before with physical weapons,
> now with intellectual arms –
> you are certainly mistaken:
> for though, as prisoner, I mourn
> my freedom, my free will
> with liberty grown still larger
> will worship and adore my Gods!   (*OC,* III, p. 12)

The stratagems Sor Juana wrought for artistic and intellectual survival were so subtle that, given the continuity and pervasiveness of patriarchal values up to the present, the magnitude of her reinterpretations has often been missed or distorted even in our times. Her command of all aspects of the canon – the ease and skill with which she versified – gave her literary mobility: On occasion she reproduced the language of the Indians and blacks who were among those who attended the great cathedral celebrations on the numerous holy days that dotted the calendar; a few poems demonstrate her ability to versify in Latin; she even imitated Basque and Portuguese accents in Spanish. In her theatrical and musical texts she elaborated the biblical and liturgical subject matter in such a way as to offer passages of highly cultivated syntax and allusions, and others of simple, salty popular jargon and crude or cunning metaphor. It was this talent that provided a vehicle for her critique of sexual politics.

As an illegitimate daughter, Sor Juana observed and experienced directly the abusive and hypocritical relations between the sexes. Although nothing is concretely known about Sor Juana's human loves, speculations have abounded. Octavio Paz assigns her the dubious label "intersexual." What critics agree upon is that some of her most powerful and direct courtly love verse was addressed to two vicereines. In her poems, plays, and prose, female characters were rarely placed in a secondary or subservient position. In her secular verse, she wittily criticized the stupidity of palace games of love; the injustice of male attitudes toward sexual sin; and men's self-flattery in objectifying women.

She humorously defended herself against warnings that her secular poetry might damn her, claiming that sins against art (the only ones she could commit in her nonreligious work) were not punishable by the dreaded Holy Office (Inquisition). Her one incursion into formal theological discourse, which was printed against her expressed wishes, precipitated her final silencing. A year before her death, with Mexico suffering economic and social crises, she found it necessary to divest herself of her library, her musical and scientific instruments and to begin leading an entirely ascetic life. But her theological critique also precipitated her most famous prose work, an essay of self-vindication, a declaration of the intellectual traditions and rights of women in which she asserted her intention to renounce the use of the written word in the face of envy, persecution, and betrayal.[11]

Although Sor Juana in the cloister was more limited than Anne Bradstreet in how far she could roam physically, she lived in an immensely rich and sophisticated social and cultural milieu. Anne Bradstreet's milieu was starker, her concerns individual and innerdirected, although family, home, and community were primary in her life.[12] The Papist and the Puritan were on opposite grounds in terms of religious and social substance and style; and yet, as *This Life Within Me Won't Keep Still* illustrates, the contrasts are balanced by numerous points of similarity.

Anne Bradstreet was most concerned, finally, about the redemption of her soul, Sor Juana Inés de la Cruz about her inalienable right to reason freely and seek knowledge. Both scrutinized themselves to understand their hearts, their minds, and the restless spirit that moved them to words.

THIS LIFE WITHIN ME WON'T KEEP STILL[13]

A dramatic re-creation of the life and thought of Anne Bradstreet (1612–72) and Sor Juana Inés de la Cruz (1651–95), by Electa Arenal. Translations from the Spanish are by Amanda Powell.

Overture	Secular and religious music of New and Old England and New and Old Spain. A twenty-minute tape is played as people enter the theater and wait for the play to begin.

Act I

Scene 1	ANNE BRADSTREET – Looking Back
	(The story of her life and work: family and religion)
Scene 2	SOR JUANA INÉS DE LA CRUZ – Looking Back
	(The story of her life and work: court and convent)
Scene 3	ANNE BRADSTREET – The Published Poet
Scene 4	SOR JUANA INÉS DE LA CRUZ – The Published Poet

| Intermission | A ten-minute tape is played of music heard in colonial Massachusetts and colonial Mexico. |

Act II

Scene 1	SOR JUANA INÉS DE LA CRUZ – Crisis/The Flames of Persecution and Betrayal
	(The events, thoughts, attacks, reactions that led to her final silence and renunciation)
Scene 2a	ANNE BRADSTREET – Crisis/The Fire and Affirmation
2b	(Fame/Woman/Lineage and Tradition)
Scene 3	SOR JUANA INÉS DE LA CRUZ – Affirmation
	(Fame/Woman/Lineage and Tradition)

Before the play begins, as the audience is seated, taped music of Renaissance Spain/New Spain and England/New England is played for twenty minutes. As this "overture" ends, the projection scrim is raised or relit to reveal a backdrop or hanging: colonial Spanish on SJ's side (stage right) and colonial English on AB's side (stage left). The center of the stage could have a solid velvet hanging, as the neutral area where costume and character changes take place and where both protagonists perform. In the absence of appropriate hangings for the two sides, one solid velvet backing could be used for all three areas.

Each side has appropriate chair, table, possibly candleholder, container with quills, and sundry other props; chairs are especially differentiated as a symbol of the diverse cultures of the two women. In the center is a long table on which headpieces and other elements of costume are laid as actor portrays one personality and then the other.

Act I, scene 1

ANNE BRADSTREET:

What you have been, ev'n such have I before
And all you say, say I, and somewhat more.
Babes innocence, youths wildness I have seen,

And in perplexed middle Age have been:
Sickness, dangers, and anxieties have past,
And on this stage am come to act my last.
I have been young, and strong, and wise as you.

[161][14]

My dear Children, –

(goes to her chair, opens her book and reads)

Being ignorant whether on my death bed I shall have opportunity to speak to any of you, much less to All – thought it the best, whilst I was able, to compose some short matters (for what else to call them I know not) and bequeath to you, that when I am no more with you, yet I may be dayly in your remembrance . . . that you may gain some spiritual advantage by my experience.

[3]

[I was born Anne Dudley – in Lincolnshire, England, on the estate of the earl of Lincoln, to whom my father was steward.][15]

My dear and ever honoured Father, Thomas Dudley, Esquire, deceased July 31st, sixteen hundred and fifty-three, and of his age 77.

(standing behind her chair)

He was my Father, Guide, Instructor, too
To whom I ought whatever I could do:
Who heard or saw, observ'd or knew him better?
Or who alive than I, a greater debtor?
Let malice bite, and envy knaw its fill,
He was my Father, and Ile praise him still.
Well known and lov'd, where ere he liv'd, by most
Both in his native, and in foreign coast,
One of thy founders, him New England know,
High thoughts he gave no harbour in his heart,
Nor honours pufft him up, when he had part:
Those titles loathed which some too much do love
For truely his ambition lay above.

[365]

. . .

My dear and ever honoured Mother, Mrs. Dorothy Dudley, deceased December 27th, sixteen hundred and forty-three, and of her age 61.

(downstage)

A loving Mother and obedient wife
A true Instructor of her Family
The which she ordered with dexterity.
To servants wisely aweful, but yet kind,
And as they did, so they reward did find.

The publick meetings ever did frequent.
Religious in all her words and ways
Of all her Children, children lived to see.

[369]

(indicating pregnancy)

My mothers breeding sickness I will spare
Her nine months weary burthen not declare.
To show her bearing pains, I should do wrong,
To tell those pangs which can't be told by tongue:
(cradling her arms)

With wayward cryes I did disturb her rest,
Who sought still to appease me with the breast:
With weary arms she danc'd and By By sung.
When infancy was past, my childishness
Did act all folly that it could express,
My silliness did only take delight
In rattles, Baubles and such toyish stuff
Yet this advantage had mine ignorance:
Freedom from envy and from arrogance.
My quarrels not for Diadems did rise,
But for an apple, plum, or some such prize.
This was mine innocence, but ah! the seeds
Lay raked up of all the cursed weeds
Which sprouted forth in mine ensuing age.
Thence I began to sin as soon as act:
A perverse will, a love to what's forbid,
Oft stubborn, peevish, sullen, pout and cry,
Then nought can please, and yet I know not why.

[149–52]

In my young years, about 6 or 7 as I take it, I began to make conscience of my
ways, and what I knew was sinful, as lying, disobedience to Parents, et cetera, I
avoided it. If at any time I was overtaken with the like evils . . . , I could not be
at rest 'til by prayer I had confessed it unto God.

[4]

But what is best I'll first present to view
And then the worst in a more ugly hue:
My education and my learning such
As might my self and others profit much;
With nurture trained up in virtues schools
Of science, arts and tongues I know the rules,
The manners of the court I also know,
And so likewise what they in'th Country do.
The brave attempts of valiant knights I prize,
That dare scale walls and forts reared to the skies.

I can insinuate into the breast
And by my mirth can raise the heart depressed

[152–4]

(An aching head requires a soft pillow; and a drooping heart a strong support.)

[53]

Sweet musick raps my brave harmonious soul,
My high thoughts elevate beyond the pole:
My wit, my bounty, and my courtesy
Make all to place their future hopes on me.
This is my best, but Youth is known, Alas!
To be as wild as is the snuffing Ass:

[153]

As I grew up to be about 14 or 15, I found my heart more carnal, and sitting loose
from God; Vanity and the follyes of youth take hold of me.

[4]

I know no law nor reason but my will
All counsel [I] hate, which tends to make me wise,
And dearest friends count for mine enemies.
If any time from company I spare,
'Tis spent in curling, frisling up my hair.
Such wretch, such Monster am I, but yet more,
I have no heart at all this to deplore,
Remembering not the dreadful day of doom
Sometimes the frenzy strangely mads my brain,
That oft for it in Bedlam I remain,

(almost funny)

Too many diseases to recite
That wonder tis, I yet behold the light.

[154–6]

(picking up a Bible from her table)

I . . . found much comfort in reading the Scriptures, especially those places I
thought most concerned my condition, and as I grew to have more understanding, so the more solace I took in them.

[4]

About sixteen, the Lord layd his hand sore upon me and smote me with the small
pox. When I was in my affliction, I besought the Lord, and confessed my Pride
and Vanity and he was entreated of me, and again restored me. But I rendered
not to him according to the benefit received. After a short time I changed my
condition and was married [to Simon Bradstreet] . . .

[5]

If ever two were one, then surely we.
If ever man were loved by wife, then thee;

(addresses women in the audience)

If ever wife was happy in a man,
Compare with me ye women if you can.

[394]

. . . [I was 18] And [from England we] came into this Country where I found a new world and new manners, at which my heart rose.[16]

[5]

In my distress I sought the Lord
When nought on Earth could comfort give

["Another Sore Fit," 63]

But after I was convinced it was the way of God, I submitted to it and joined to the church at Boston.

(sits in chair; covers herself with her shawl)

After some time I fell into a lingering sickness like a consumption, together with a lameness, which correction I saw the Lord sent to humble and try me and do me Good: and it was not altogether ineffectual.

[5]

Twice ten years old, not fully told
Since nature gave me breath
My race is run, my thread is spun,
Lo here is fatal Death.

[391]

. . . I have had abundance of sweetness and refreshment after affliction and . . . circumspection in my walking . . .

[6–7]

I have often been perplexed that I have not found that constant Joy in my Pilgrimage and refreshing which I supposed most of the servants of God have, although he hath not left me altogether without the witness of his holy spirit.

I have sometimes tasted of that hidden Manna that the world knows not. . . . Yet have I many Times sinkings and droopings. Many times hath Satan troubled me concerning the verity of the Scriptures, many times by Atheism how I could know whether there was a God; I never saw any miracles to confirm me, and those which I read of, how did I know but they were feigned. That there is a God my Reason would soon tell me by the wondrous works that I see, the vast frame of the Heaven and the Earth, the order of all things, night and day, Summer and Winter, Spring and Autumn, the dayly providing for this great household upon the Earth. . . . But how should I know he is such a God as I worship in Trinity, and such a savior as I rely upon? When I have got over this Block, then have I another put in my way, that admit this be the true God whom we worship, and that be his word, yet why may not the Popish Religion be the right? They have the same God, the same Christ, the same word: they only interpret it one way, we another.

[7–9]

Here, there [my] restless thoughts do ever fly,
Constant in nothing but unconstancy.

[140]

Where shall I climb, sound, seek, search or find,
That *summum bonum*[17] which may stay my mind?

[387]

The eyes and the ears are the inlets or doors of the soul, through which innumerable objects enter, yet is not that spacious roome filled, neither doth it ever say it is enough, but like the daughters of the horseleach, crys give, give!! and which is most strange, the more it receives, the more empty it finds itself, and sees an impossibility, ever to be filled, but by him in whom all fullness dwells.

[61]

It pleased God to keep me a long time without a child, which was a great grief to me, and cost me many prayers and tears before I obtained one, and after him gave me many more . . .

[5]

"To [my] Husband, absent upon Publick Employment"

(intimate in tone)

My head, my heart, mine Eyes, my life, nay more
My joy, my Magazine of earthly store,
If two be one, as surely thou and I,
How stayest thou there, whilst I at Ipswich lye?
Return, return sweet *Sol* from *Capricorn:*
in this dead time, alas, what can I more
Than view those fruits which through thy heat I bore?
Which sweet contentment yield me for a space,
True living Pictures of their Father's face.
Flesh of thy flesh, bone of thy bone,
I here, thou there, yet both but one.

(addressing the Sun – Phoebus – with sweep of her arm to indicate its course)

Phoebus make haste, the day's too long, be gone
Commend me to the man more loved than life,
Shew him the sorrows of his widdowed wife;
My dumpish thoughts, my groans, my brakish tears
My sobs, my longing hopes, my doubting fears,
And if he love, how can he there abide?
My interest's more than all the world beside.

Nought but the fervor of his ardent beams
Hath power to dry the torrent of these streams.

[394–7]

(makes nest out of her shawl)

I had eight birds hatched in one nest
Four Cocks there were, and Hens the rest,
I nursed them up with pain and care,
Nor cost, nor labour did I spare,
Till at the last they felt their wing,
Mounted the Trees, and learned to sing;

(stands)

Chief of the Brood then took his flight
To Regions far, and left me quite:
My mournful chirps I after send,
Till he return, or I do end.
My second bird did take her flight,
And with her mate flew out of sight,
A prettier bird was no where seen,
Along the Beach among the treen.
I have a third of colour white
On whom I placed no small delight
Coupled with mate loving and true,
Hath also bid her Dam adieu.
One to the Academy flew
To chat among that learned crew:
Ambition moves still in his breast
That he might chant above the rest,
Striving for more than to do well
That nightingales he might excell.
My fifth, whose down is yet scarce gone
Is 'mongst the shrubs and bushes flown
And as his wings increase in strength
On Higher boughs he'll perch at length.
My other three, still with me nest,
Until they're grown, then as the rest
Or here or there they'll take their flight
As is ordained, so shall they light.
My cares are more, and fears than ever,
My throbs such now, as 'fore were never.

(said as if to young children)

Sore accidents on you may light.
O to your safety have an eye.
When each of you shall in your nest
Among your young ones take your rest,

In chirping language, oft them tell,
You had a Dam that loved you well.
She showed you joy and misery;
Taught what was good, and what was ill,
What would save life, and what would kill.

[400–3]

(transition: said to audience)

Diverse children have their different natures; some are like flesh which nothing but salt will keep from putrefaction; some again like tender fruits that are best preserved with sugar: those parents are wise that can fit their nurture according to their Nature.

[50]

(back to her book to close the narrative to her children)

My dear Children:

This book by Any yet unread,
I leave for you when I am dead,
That, being gone, here you may find
What was your living mother's mind.
Make use of what I leave in Love
And God shall blesse you from above.

[3]

A pilgrim I, on earth, perplexed
with sins, with cares and sorrows vexed
Oh how I long to be at rest
and soar on high among the blessed
Lord make me ready for that day
then Come, dear bridegroom, Come away.

[43–4]

Yet a little while and he that shall come will come, and will not tarry.

[22]

Mean while my days in tunes I'll spend
Till my weak layes with me shall end.
In shady woods I'll sit and sing,
And things that past, to mind I'll bring.
My age I will not once lament
But sing, my time so near is spent.
And from the top bough take my flight,
Into a country beyond sight,
Where old ones, instantly grow young,
and there with the Seraphims set song:

[402–3]

(to audience)

What you have been, even such have I before:
And all you say, say I, and somewhat more.
. . . Private changes oft mine eyes have seen,
In various times of state I've also been.
I've seen, and so have you for 'tis but late
The desolation of a goodly state.
Plotted and acted so that none can tell
Who gave the counsel but the Prince of Hell.

I've seen base men advanced to great degree
And worthy ones, put to extremity.
I've seen a state unmoulded, rent in twain,
But ye may live to see it made up again.
I've seen it plundered, taxed, and soaked in blood,
What are my thoughts this is no time to say.
[We] may more freely speak another day.

[161–5]

(spot out stage right, comes up stage left; transitional (ghost) light center and music up as actor changes costume center stage with back to audience)

Act I, scene 2

SOR JUANA INÉS DE LA CRUZ:

I [, Juana Ramírez de Asbaje,] was born
where the solar rays
. . . gaze directly down

[I, 146(125–7)][18]

in America the abundant,
compatriot of gold, countrywoman of the precious metals.

[I, 102(82–5)]

[The river's wave, its foam, its coursing, and
its sound were a lullaby to my ears.]

[Arroyo, 5]

Listen, that I may succeed,
while entertaining your pleasure,
in transforming my past hardships
into another's repose;
or that in the unburdening
my sad cares may find,
from the suffering of experience,
the relief of being told.

I was of gentle birth [but without fortune];
this was the first step of my downfall,
as it is no small affliction
to be born a noble beggar; . . .
because plebeian misfortunes
together with honored attentions,
existing in a single person,
repel each other as contraries. . . .

[IV, 36(263–82)

I will only say . . . Here I would wish
not to be the one to tell this tale,
for either in silence, or in saying,
two obstacles present themselves;
for if I say I was from the first
applauded as a miracle
of intelligence, I am belied
by the foolishness of saying so;
yet if I keep silence, I do not tell
of myself; at the same time
I prove myself false if I affirm it,
but you will not know if I do not say.

(287–98)]

I was not yet three years of age, when my affection and mischievousness carried me after my older sister whom my mother sent off to learn to read. The desire to learn so caught fire in me that, believing I was deceiving the teacher, I told her that my mother wished her to teach me also. She did not believe this, for indeed it was not credible; but to humor my fancy she gave me lessons. I continued to go and she to teach me, now no longer in fun, for experience had undeceived her.

I learned to read in such a short time, that I already knew how, when my mother found out. My teacher had kept it from her to let her enjoy it fully and at the same time to win praise; and I had kept still, thinking that I would be beaten for having done this without permission.

[IV, 445(216–32)]

When I was about six or seven, having already learned to read and write, along with other skills such as embroidery and dressmaking which were considered appropriate for women, I heard that in Mexico City there was a university and schools where one could learn science. I began to torture my mother with insistent and annoying pleas that she dress me in men's clothing so I could study at the university. She refused, and was right in doing so. But I satisfied this desire for learning by reading a great variety of books that belonged to my grandfather, and neither scolding nor punishments could prevent me.

I began to learn Latin, and I believe I took less than twenty lessons. My concern was so acute, that although in women (and especially those in the bloom of

youth) the natural adornment of the hair is so appreciable, I would cut off four to
six fingers in length, measuring how long it had been before, and imposing upon
myself a rule that if by the time it had grown back to the same length I did not
know such and such a thing, which I had proposed to learn, that I would cut it off
again, as punishment for my dim-wittedness . . . for it did not seem just that a
head should be covered by hair that was so bare of ideas – the more desirable
adornment.

[IV, 445–6(237–68)]

[I then came to Mexico City to live with my aunt, and later became lady-in-
waiting to the vicereine, in the court of the viceroy of Mexico, where I continued
to study and wrote many verses, plays, and songs. The viceroy, intrigued by my
knowledge, set up an examination in the court, where I was questioned by all the
learned men of Mexico. It was said that I handled the examination like a royal
galleon being attacked by small canoes.]

People marveled not so much at my ingenuity as at my memory and the diversity
of facts I had accumulated at an age when it seemed I had scarcely had occasion to
learn to speak.

[Arroyo, 27]

> I became the venerated object
> of my entire homeland,
> receiving all such kinds of adoration
> as popular acclaim creates;
> and, as whatsoever I said –
> be it good or bad –
> could no longer tarnish my face
> nor impair my charm,
> the superstition of the people
> reached such lofty extremes,
> that now as deity they adored
> the very idol they had formed.
>
> Away then flew the gossip Fame
> discoursing through foreign realms . . .
> Passion placed lenses before all eyes
> deceptively enlarging
> the appearance and the size
> of my modest talents.

[IV, 37–8(321–40)]

> Wherefore of [my learning] so much praise?

[I, 158(5)]

> I inclined myself to studies
> from my earliest years
> with such ardent wakefulness,
> with such earnest care,

that I reduced to the space of a moment
tasks of great extent.
Industrious, I beguiled the time
by the intensity of my work;
and in the briefest space of time
I was the admired target
of the attentions of all people,
so that all, at last,
worshipped as innate what were
merely acquired laurels.

[IV, 37(307–20)]

Wherefore of [my verses] so much praise?

[V, 158(6)]

What magical infusions
did the Indian herbalists
native to my Country, pour
to enchant my lines?

[I, 160(53–6)]

For if the theme at hand
were priase of such as Clio,
of an Artemis, of a Sappho,
of Corrina, or of Minerva . . .

[I, 110(173–7)

I depict in verse, the lovely form of the
vicereine, countess of Paredes.

(171–2)

(gestures as if to a life-sized portrait she is painting)

May the sky serve as canvas for your portrait: . . .

(5)

your long hair weaves prisons; . . .
your cheeks, lessons of April; . . .
Dawn's tears bedew your mouth. . . .

(25)

Passage to the gardens of Venus,
your throat is an ivory organ
that imprisons even the wind
in sweet ecstasies, in lyrical music. . . .
Dates of alabaster, your fingers
fertile, spring from your two palms,
cold to eyes that look at them,
to souls that touch them, warm.

(29–30; 37–40; 45–8)]

[Lines that express feelings for one absent]

> My Love, My Lord
>
> . . . my lamentations echo from my pen;
> since my rough voice does not reach you
> hear me deafly, for my complaint is mute. . . .
> When you see that, weeping sadly,
> a turtle-dove, her own hope faded
> moans upon a verdant branch,
> may both recall to you my grief:
> the branch my hope, the turtle-dove my sorrow.
>
> [I, 313–14(1; 7–12; 25–30)]

(picks up sheet of paper from her table and reads)

Señora, my lady . . .

Oh! how maddened I became
in the happiness of your love,
for, even if feigned, your favors
easily drove me mad.

Oh! how in your lovely Sun
my ardent affection, enflamed,
so kindled by your brilliant light
lost any thought of danger.

Pardon, if it was bold of me
boldly to woo your pure ardor;
for even in prayer there is no stronghold
against sins of thought. . . .

And though to love your beauty
is a transgression without pardon,
I would sooner be punished for sinning
than for indifference. . . .

If you fault my irreverence
blame also your permission;
for if my obedience is wrong
nor was your mandate just . . .
for to love you is a sin
of which I will never repent.

[I, 226(1); 227(25–6; 45–9; 53–6)]

For one must lose
the love which strives
to last eternally . . .
I know well of nature's
great fragility

that her sole constancy
consists of having none.

[I, 188(25–8); 190(77–80)]

. . . And within myself I [must] possess
all the joy that I desire.

[I, 227(39–40)]

[At court] amidst all the applause,
with my attention floundering
amongst the clamoring multitude,
I could not love one man,
seeing myself beloved by so many.

[IV, 38(359–64)]

My parents, vainly reassured
by my steady manner,
were careless of my honor:
what an erring judgment –
for that was to remove the outer
keepers and the locks
from a force that, in herself,
enclosed so many contraries!
And as they were foolishly
careless with their daughter,
I of necessity met with danger
where their care lost me.

[IV, 39(373–4; 375–84)]

My saying that I was born beautiful
I presume will be excused,
for your eyes will attest to the fact,
and my tribulations prove it.

[IV, 36(283–6)]

You foolish and unreasoning men
who cast all blame on women,
not seeing that yourselves are cause
of the same faults you accuse: . . .

But who has carried greater blame
in an erring passion:
she who falls to constant pleadings
or he who pleads with her to fall?

Or which more greatly must be faulted
though either may do wrong:
she who sins for need of pay
or he who pays for sinning?

[I, 288(1–4); 229(49–56)]

Without fear in these contests
I defended my virtue,
with menace, from that menace,
and with hurt, from harm.

[IV, 38(365–8)]

(lighting change: goes to center table to get headpiece)

(February 24th, 1669)

(said with headpiece across her arms like an offering)

I, soror Juana Inés de la Cruz, take vows and promise God, our Lord, and your Excellency, in whose hands I take the veil, to live and die for all the time and space of my life in obedience, poverty, chastity . . .

[IV, 522(17–18; 1; 6–15)]

(puts on headpiece)

I became a nun because, although I knew I should find in that condition certain things . . . which would be distasteful to my mind, it would, in view of my absolute refusal to marry, be the least unfitting and the most decent state I could choose, considering the assurance I desired of my salvation.

[My true] desire . . . to live alone and avoid obligations that would disturb my freedom to study . . . made me vacillate somewhat in my decision [to become a nun] until I was enlightened by knowledgeable people as to my temptation, and with divine favor I vanquished it, and took the state which I so unworthily hold.

[IV, 446(268–74)]

I thought I was fleeing myself; but unfortunate me! – I brought myself with me, and in my [scholarly] inclination, brought my greatest enemy, which I know not whether to take as a Heaven-sent favor, or as a punishment . . .

[IV, 446–7(277–87)]

(row or pile of books can be used as prop)

On one occasion when the doctors prohibited me from study because of a severe stomach ailment . . . I suggested to them that it was less damaging for them to allow me my books, because my speculations were so strenuous and vehement they consumed more vitality in a quarter of an hour, than the reading of books in four days . . .

[IV, 460(817–23)]

On another occasion a very religious and innocent mother superior succeeded in having me prohibited from study, for she believed that study was a matter for the Inquisition . . . And I obeyed (for the three months she lasted in office) . . . but even though I didn't study in books, I studied all the things that God created, taking them as letters and the whole scheme of creation as my book.

Nothing could I see without reflecting upon it, nothing could I hear without pondering it, even in the most minute, most material things; because there is no creature, no matter how lowly, that does not stagger the mind . . .

(center stage, using the theater as example)

I would often take a walk in the front of one of the dormitories (a very large room) and I would observe that though the lines of its two sides were parallel and the ceiling was flat, the eye perceived the lines as though they approached each other, and the ceiling as though it were lower in the distance than close-by; from which I inferred that visual lines run straight, but not parallel, and that they form a pyramidal shape. And I would consider whether this were the reason the ancients were obliged to doubt whether the world were spherical or not. Because, even though it seems so, it could be a visual deception, displaying curves where there were none.

(during speech kneels to watch the imaginary top)

Two little girls were playing with a top in front of me and no sooner had I seen the motion and shape, than I began, with this madness of mine, to observe the easy movement of the spherical form. I had [a servant bring] some flour and sifted it on the floor, so that as the top danced over it, we could know whether its movement described perfect circles or no. And I found they were rather spiral lines that lost their circularity as the top lost its impulse.

[IV, 458 (736–49; 758–70; 777–87)]

This kind of observation has been continual in me . . . without my having control over it; rather I tend to find it annoying, because it tires my head, and I believed this happened to everyone, as with thinking in verse, until experience taught me otherwise . . . even my sleep [is] not free from this continual movement of my imagination but rather my mind asleep labors even more freely and unfettered, discoursing, and composing verses, examining with greater clarity and calm the day's offering of images and occurrences.

[IV, 458–9(771–5); 460(824–31)]

> . . . I was born so much a poet
> that like Ovid, when whipped
> my cries are heard in rhyme and meter . . .
>
> [I, 93(22–4)]

Yet most of my verses have been in response to requests and commissions from the viceroy and the Church. . . . I had wished to live alone and to avoid any of the noise of a community which might interrupt the tranquil silence of my books. [But this could not be.]

[IV, 470–1(1264–5); 446(276–80)]

(pause and change of tone)

> Nevertheless, in the convent
> . . . [I] went about copying
> the images of all things
> and [my] invisible brush formed,
> without light, bright colors
> of [my] mind, figures
> not only . . . of all sublunary
> creatures, but also of those

clear stars of intellect;
and making possible the conception
of the invisible
in [myself], skillfully, [I] recreated them
and displayed them to my soul.

[I, 342(280–91)]

(lights out on SJ side, softly up on AB side, transitional lights center, music up; costume change – habit off, apron on)

Act I, scene 3

ANNE BRADSTREET:

(walking downstage with book in hand)

[My poems were taken to London by my brother-in-law, the Reverend John Woodridge, and published in 1650, with the title:] *The Tenth Muse lately sprung up in America, or Several poems, Compiled with Great Variety of Wit and Learning, Full of Delight . . . By a Gentlewoman of Those Parts.*

The author to her book:

Thou ill-form'd offspring of my feeble brain,
Who after birth did'st by my side remain,
Till snatcht from thence by friends, less wise than true
Who thee abroad, expos'd to publick view;
Made thee in raggs,[19] halting to th' press to trudg,
Where errors were not lessened (all may judg)
At thy return my blushing was not small,
My rambling brat (in print) should mother call,
I cast thee by as one unfit for light,
Thy Visage was so irksome in my sight;
Yet being mine own, at length affection would
Thy blemishes amend, if so I could:
I wash'd thy face, but more defects I saw,
And rubbing off a spot, still made a flaw.
I stretched thy joynts to make thee even feet,
Yet still thou run'st more hobbling than is meet;
In better dress to trim thee was my mind,
But nought save home-spun Cloth, i'th'house I find.
In this array, 'mongst Vulgars mayst thou roam
In Criticks hands, beware thou dost not come;
And take thy way where yet thou art not known,
If for thy Father askt, say, thou hadst none:
And for thy Mother, she alas is poor,
Which caus'd her thus to send thee out of door.

[389]

[Stanzas from my "Contemplations":]

> Silent, along, where none or saw, or heard,
> In pathless paths I lead my wandering feet
> My humble Eyes to lofty Skies I rear'd
> To sing some Song, my mazed Muse thought meet.
> My great Creator I would magnifie,
> That nature had, thus decked liberally:
> But Ah, and Ah, again, my imbecility!

[372]

> I heard the merry grasshopper then sing,
> The black clad cricket, bear a second part,
> They kept one tune, and played on the same string,
> Seeming to glory in their little Art.
> Shall Creatures abject, thus their voices raise?
> And in their kind resound their Makers praise
> Whilst I as mute, can warble forth no higher layes?

[373]

[From "A Letter to my Husband, absent upon Publick Employment":]

> As loving Hind that (Hartless) wants her Deer,
> Scuds through the woods and Fern with harkning ear,
> Perplext, in every bush and nook doth pry,
> Her dearest Deer, might answer ear or eye;
> So doth my anxious soul, which now doth miss,
> A dearer Dear (far dearer Heart) than this,
> Still wait with doubts, and hopes, and failing eye,
> His voice to hear, or person to discry.
> Or as the pensive Dove doth all alone
> (On withered bough) most uncouthly bemoan
> The absence of her Love, and loving Mate,
> Whose loss hath made her so unfortunate:
> Ev'n thus doe I, with many a deep sad groan
> Bewail my turtle true, who now is gone.

[397]

> *(lights off on AB side, softly up on SJ side, transitional lights center for costume
> change; music up)*

Act I, scene 4

Sor Juana Inés de la Cruz:

> *(walking downstage, book in hand)*

[My poems were taken to Madrid at the insistence of the ex-vicereine, countess
of Paredes, and published in 1689 with the title:] *Plenitude of the Muses by the
Singular Poetess, The Tenth Muse . . . who in various meters, languages and styles*

enriches Various Subjects with elegant, subtle, clear, witty, useful verses, to teach, enter-
tain, and amaze . . .

[Prologue]

My dear reader, to your delight
I dedicate these lines:
Alas, their only merit lies
in my knowing they are bad . . .

I do not expect you to be pleased:
for in truth there is no reason
that you should hold in high esteem
what was never meant for your hands.

I leave you at your liberty
To censure them, if you please;
that you are at liberty, in the end
I thoroughly comprehend.

Nothing is more free than is
the human understanding;
then why should I attempt to force
what is not forced by God?

[I, 3(1–4)]

Say of my poems whatever you like
for the more cruelly and deeply
you sink your teeth into them, you see,
the more you're beholden to me:

for my muse will have given you a taste
of the most savory dainty
(which is gossiping complaint),
according to a courtly saying.

And in either case I serve you
whether I please or disappoint you,
if I please, you are entertained;
if not, you may complain.

I could well tell you as excuse
that time has not permitted,
in the hast of the poems' dispatch
opportunity to correct them;

that they are written in motley form,
and some, the most childish sort,
have murdered all sense that was in the words
leaving each a lifeless corpse;

and I have composed them only
in those fleeting moments
afforded to leisure by endless duties
attending on my state;

that I am plagued by woeful health
and constantly distracted,
so that, even as I make this claim
I carry my pen at a trot.

But all this serves no useful end,
for you will think I am boasting
that they might have been improved
had I composed them slowly;

I do not mean to say such a thing,
for by offering these lines
to the press, I do no more
Than obey my Lady's command.

And now adieu, for this is naught
but a sample of the cloth:
if you do not like the fabric,
do not unroll the bolt.

[I, 4]

["On a Portrait"]

This picture which you see, this painted snare
exhibiting the subtleties of art
with clever arguments of tone and hue,
this is deception set against your sense;
in this a cunning flattery has tried
to overlook the horrors of the years,
and, hiding here the cruelties of time,
defeat oblivion and conquer age:
This is care's emptiest artifice,
a fragile blossom in a raging wind,
a useless guard against the common fate,
an erring work of senseless diligence;
it is a futile labor which, clearly seen,
is a corpse, is dust, is shadow, is nothing.

[I, 277]

["In Which I Answer a Suspicion with the Eloquence of Tears"]

This afternoon, my darling, when we spoke,
and in your face and gestures I could see
that I was not persuading you with words,
I wished you might look straight into my heart;

and Love, who was assisting my designs,
succeeded in what seemed impossible:
for in the stream of tears which anguish loosed,
my heart itself, dissolved, dropped slowly down.
Enough unkindness now, my love, enough;
don't let these tyrant jealousies torment you
nor base suspicion shatter your repose
with foolish shadows, empty evidence:
in liquid humor you have seen and touched
my heart undone and passing through your hands.

[I, 287]

["Although in Vain, I Wish to Reduce the Sufferings of a Jealous Man to a Rational Process"]

What's this, Alcino? How could your good sense
allow its own defeat by jealousy,
and show the world, in wild extremes of rage,
this spectacle of one gone mad, or worse?
How then has Celia hurt you, if she grieves?
Or why do you blame love of false deceit
if he has never promised, for all his power,
lasting possession of such loveliness?
Our possession of temporal things
is temporal as well; it is abuse
to wish to guard them always as they were.
Your ignorance or error I accuse:
because both Fate and Love, of things like these
have given us not ownership, but use.

[I, 292]

(lights down; intermission – ten minutes of music; then lights up stage right)

Act II, scene 1

SOR JUANA INÉS DE LA CRUZ:

(standing)

It is bold of me to oppose Vieyra? My mind is not as free as his, though it derives from the same source?

[IV, 468(1169–73)]

. . . but withal, I live always so wary of myself . . . not in this or in anything else do I trust my own judgment . . .

[IV, 460(838–41)]

. . . it will not do for the human mind with its free will, that necessarily assents or dissents to that which it judges to be true or untrue, to surrender that will, and, out of mere prudence, plunge into flattery.

[IV, 413(41–5)]

(sits and reads)

[To the bishop of Puebla:] My very dear Sir: From the generalities of a conversation of mine, which, in your kindness, you considered witticism, there was born in Your Grace a desire to see in writing some discourses that I had produced extemporaneously: most of them being on the sermons of [the Portuguese Jesuit Vieyra,] an excellent orator, some in praise of his premises, some disagreeing with his views.

[IV, 412(1–6)]

I am writing inasmuch as my objections [to putting this refutation on paper] are, in a measure, modified in that Your Grace will be the sole witness of this discourse.

[IV, 412(21–5)]

With this, it seems to me that, even in view of my coarseness, lack of wit, and limited study, I have obeyed Your Grace.

The too great haste in which I am writing has not given me the opportunity to polish the discourse more, and so I remit it in embryo, as the she-bear is wont to bring forth her unformed cubs.

[IV, 434(899–905)]

. . . God desired to punish, by means of so weak an instrument [as I,] the pride of that premise [of Vieyra's] which stated that "no one can cite better than he the greatest goodnesses of Christ." With this he believed himself able to excel the talent of the three holy Fathers [Augustine, Thomas, and Chrysostomus]. And thinking that God had not stretched forth His hand to guide [them,] he judged that it was extended to him!

[IV, 434–5(924–31)]

[Now, to give an instance of my objections:] Saint Thomas said: "To leave Himself in the Sacrament was Christ's greatest act." Father Vieyra replies that it was to remain in the Sacrament without the use of His senses. What manner of argument is this? The saint proposed the whole; and Father Vieyra replies in a particular thereof. Therefore the syllogism does not have the proper form or sequence – which renders the argument invalid.

[IV, 421–2(353–63; 375–8)]

(with irony and sense of control)

. . . It should be sufficient mortification for a man – so distinguished in all ways, that I believe there has not been a man who has ventured to reply to him – to see that an ignorant woman, in whom this kind of study is so inappropriate and distant from her sex, does dare it. But there are also Judith who wielded arms, and Deborah, the judge. And withal, if this extravagance in me does not seem licit, by destroying this paper Your Grace will erase the error of its having been written.

[IV, 435(933–41)]

You must think that I have forgotten that other point you ordered me to write about: [namely,] what is, in my opinion, the greatest goodness [or favor] of

Divine Love. The greatest goodness of the Divine Love, in my belief is shown in the benefits that God does not give us, because of our ingratitude. I shall prove it. God is infinite excellence and the sum of all good. Moreover, God has infinite love for men; therefore He is always very ready to give them infinite benefits. Therefore, when God does not make benefits for man, it is because man would convert them to his own harm. God checks the stream of his immense privilege; He restrains the ocean of His infinite love and stems the course of His absolute power. Therefore, following this manner of thought, we know that it costs God more not to grant us benefits than to grant them.

[IV, 435(948–51; 958–71)]

Thus when God ceases being liberal, His natural condition, it is so that we may not become ingrates, which is our natural requital.

[IV, 436(972–4; 991–4)]

(goes to table)

[A letter to me from the Bishop of Puebla, November 25, 1690, signing himself as "Sister Filotea de la Cruz," and my critique.]

(shocked and alarmed)

[Published! He has betrayed my expressed wish!]

[He writes:]
I have seen your letter and admired your proofs, and the clarity of your arguments. Consequently I have had your letter printed.

[IV, 694(¶1,2,3)]

. . . what you call the greatest goodness, I see as punishment . . .

[IV, 695(¶5)]

I suggest you continue your studies, but you ought to better the books you read, for knowledge should enlighten us towards salvation. Subordinate profane letters to sacred letters: you must study the latter more.

[IV, 695(¶3)]

. . . take care that the Lord who has showered you with such abundant favors in the natural world . . . may not concede to you only negative ones in the hereafter . . .

[IV, 696(¶5)]

Oh! unhappy eminence, exposed to so many risks! target of envy, and object of contradiction. These are the wages suffered by eminence, whether of dignity, or nobility, or wealth, or beauty, or learning; but it is high intelligence that experiences all this with greatest force: first, because it is more vulnerable, for wealth and power punish those who confront them, but intelligence does not . . . secondly because . . . the advantages of such understanding are essential qualities of being.

[IV, 454–5(606–17)]

. . . as the ambitious burning flame
rises heavenward

so the human mind
aspiring always to know the First Cause

[I, 345(404–8)]

(looks at his letter again)

His publication of this letter of mine which he called "Atenagórica" ["Worthy of Athena"] . . . is a special way of shaming and confusing me . . .

[IV, 441(44–8)]

. . . causing me to be the judge who condemns and sentences myself . . .

[IV, 441(52–7)]

(first anguished, then marshaling decisiveness)

Then, by my very downfall vivified
plunging in ever more precipitous ruin,
with renewed rebellion . . .

[I write my] "Reply to 'Sister Filotea'"

[I, 359(961–2;965)]

(goes toward desk; ironically)

Very illustrious lady, my lady: . . . in view of how favored I am by you . . . who had the letter published, unbeknownst to me, who titled it, and underwrote its cost . . . What will you not do? What not forgive? [I wish] only to give full account of my nature . . .

[IV, 442(104–10)]

. . . I receive in my very soul your warning that I apply my study to sacred books. . . . I have always [directed] the steps of my studies toward the peak of holy theology; [but] it seemed to me necessary to ascend by the ladder of the human arts and sciences in order to reach it . . .

[IV, 443(117–20)]

I confess that often the fear of *sacred* subjects has whisked my pen out of my hand, and made the subject-matter retreat toward the very mind from which it flows; which obstacle I did not encounter with *profane* subjects, for a heresy against art is not punished by the Inquisition . . .

[IV, 443–4(154–9), emphasis added]

(standing; forcefully, reconvincing herself)

if intelligence turns its back because – in cowardice – it fears comprehension will come poorly, or never, or late, how undertake the task of studying [the world]?

[I, 354(757; 759; 769–71; 780)]

(resumes reading)

I do not wish (nor would I be capable of such foolishness) to claim that I have been persecuted because of my knowledge, but rather only because of my love for learning and letters . . .

[IV, 457(710–14)]

I confess that it has led me closer to the flames of persecution.

[IV, 457–8(730–3)]

. . . the difficulty of responding almost caused me to leave this matter in silence . . . ; but since silence is something negative, although it explains much,
emphasizing by leaving it unexplained . . . I [needed] to name it, so that what
my silence signifies be understood. My decision is to keep still. . . . I shall never
in my own defense take up the pen again.

[IV, 441(68–75); 442(79–83); 472(1321–2); 471(1303–4)]

Keep me in your [good favor] so that you can implore Divine Grace in my
behalf, that the Lord keep you. . . . [Signed] in this Convent of St. Jerome, of
Mexico, the first day of the month of March of the year 1691 . . . Juana Inés de la
Cruz.

[IV, 475(1433–8)]

(overwrought)

[Three years after my reply to the bishop,] weighed down with dreadful fears,
though still [I] strove to rally [my] proud force, opposing . . . while this ill-
rewarded daring could scarcely hide the fright it masked knowing too well [my]
weakness at this test . . .

[I, 358(925–33)]

(kneeling; alternately prayerful and detached)

I, the most abject and ungrateful creature your Omnipotence ever created . . .
convict myself before your tribunal of the most serious, enormous, unequalled
sins . . . recognize that I do not deserve pardon . . .

[IV, 520(1–2; 8–10; 17)]

all the years that I have lived in religious life, I have lived not only without
religion, but worse than a pagan might . . .

[IV, 521(36–8)]

withal, knowing your infinite mercy . . . I wish once more to take the veil . . .

[IV, 520(18–19)]

I offer my dowry, [my books, my instruments,] all that belongs to me for
charity . . .

[IV, 521(41; 45–51)]

And as a sign of how ardently I wish to shed my blood in defense of the ultimate
truths, I sign this in my blood the fifth of March of the year 1694.

[IV, 519(57–9)]

(music; lights down stage right, up stage left and center for costume change)

Act II, scene 2a

ANNE BRADSTREET:

> If to be rich or great it was my fate,
> How was I broyl'd with envy and with hate

Greater than was the greatest was my desire,
And thirst for honor, set my heart on fire:
And by Ambition's sails I was so carried,
That over Flats and sands, and Rocks I hurried.
Then thought my state firm founded sure to last,
But in a trice 'tis ruin'd by a blast.

Sometimes vain glory is the only baite
Whereby my empty Soul is lur'd and caught.
Be I of wit, of learning, and of parts,
I judge I should have room in all men's hearts.
And envy gnaws if any do surmount.
I hate not to be held in high'st account.

[159]

(to desk to read)

The Fire, Air, Earth and Water did contest
Which was the strongest, noblest and the best,
That Fire should first begin, the rest consent,
The noblest and most active Element.
What is my worth (both ye) and all men know
The benefit all living by me find
Ye Husband-men your Coulters made by me
Your Hoes, your Mattocks, and what e're you see
Ye Cooks, your Kitchen implements I frame
Your Spits, Pots, Jacks, what else I need not name
Your daily food I wholsome make, I warm
Your shrinking Limbs, which winter's cold doth harm
Ye *Paracelsians* too in vain's your skill
In Chymistry, unless I help you Still.
And you Philosophers, if e're you made
A transmutation it was through mine aid.
Ye silver Smiths, your Ure I do refine
What mingled lay with Earth I cause to shine;
But let me leave these things, my flame aspires
To match on high with the Celestial fires:
The Sun an Orb of fire was held of old,
Our Sages new another tale have told:
But be he what they will, yet his aspect
A burning fiery heat we find reflect
And of the self same nature is with mine
What famous Towns, to Cinders have I turn'd?
What lasting forts my kindled wrath hath burn'd
The stately Seats of mighty Kings by me
In confused heaps, of ashes you may see.
And stately *London,* (our great *Britain's* glory)

My raging flame did make a mournful story,
But maugre all, that I, or foes could do
That *Phoenix* from her Bed, is risen New.

The rich I oft make poor, the strong I maime,
Not sparing Life when I can take the same;
And in a word, the world I shall consume.

To finish what's begun, was my intent,
My thoughts and my endeavours thereto bent;
Essays[20] I many made but still gave out,
The more I mused, the more I was in doubt
The subject large my mind and body weak,
With many more discouragements did speak.
All thoughts of further progress laid aside,
Though oft persuaded, I as oft deny'd
At length resolved when many years had past,
To prosecute my story to the last;
And for the same, I hours not few did spend,
And weary lines (though lanke) I many penned.
But 'fore I could accomplish my desire
My papers fell a prey to the raging fire.

[103–8]

["Upon the Burning of Our House, July 10th, 1666"]

In silent night when rest I took,
for sorrow near I did not look,
I waken'd was with thundring noise
And Piteous shreiks of dreadfull voice.
The fearfull sound of fire and fire,
Let no man know is my Desire.

(watching)

I starting up, the light did spye,
And to my God my heart did cry
To strengthen me in my Distresse
And not to leave me succourlesse.
Then coming out beheld a space,
The flame consume my dwelling place.

(resigned, perhaps with a note of irony or exaggeration)

And, when I could no longer look,
I blest his Name that gave and took,
That layd my goods now in the dust:
Yea so it was, and so 'twas just.
It was his own: it was not mine;
Far be it that I should repine.

(re-creating her sorrow and finally accepting)

He might of All justly bereft,
But yet sufficient for us left.
When by the Ruines oft I past,
My sorrowing eyes aside did cast,
And here and there the places spye
Where oft I sat and long did lye.

Here stood that Trunk, and there that chest;
There lay that store[21] I counted best:
My pleasant things in ashes lye,
And them behold no more shall I.
Under thy roof no guest shall sit,
Nor at thy Table eat a bit.

No pleasant tale shall e'er be told
Nor things recounted done of old.
No candle e'er shall shine in Thee,
Nor bridegroom's voice ere heard shall be.
In silence ever shalt thou lye;
Adieu, Adieu; All's vanity.

Then streight I gin my heart to chide,
And did thy wealth on earth abide?
Didst fix thy hope on mouldring dust,
The arm of flesh didst make thy trust?
Raise up thy thoughts above the sky
That dunghill mists away may flie.

Thou hast an house on high erect
Fram'd by that mighty Architect,
With glory richly furnished,
Stands permanant tho' this be fled.
It's purchased, and paid for too
By him who hath enough to doe.

A Prize so vast as is unknown,
Yet, by his Gift, is made thine own.
Ther's wealth enough, I need no more;
Farewell my Pelf, farewell my Store.
The world no longer let me Love,
My hope and Treasure lyes Above.

[40–2]

Act II, scene 2b

ANNE BRADSTREET:

I studious am what I shall do.

[23]

I now speak unto all, no more to one
Pray, hear, admire, and learn instruction.

[140]

(thoughtful)

By Art [I] gladly found what [I] did seek
A full requital of [my] striving pain

(outgoing)

I am obnoxious to each carping tongue
Who says my hand a needle better fits,
A Poet's pen all scorn I should thus wrong,
For such despite they cast on Female wits:
If what I do prove well, it won't advance,
They'll say it's stolen, or else it was by chance.

But sure the Ancient Greeks were far more mild
Else of our Sex, why feigned they those Nine
And poesey made, Calliope's own child.

[101]

Let Greeks be Greeks, and women what they are
Men have precedency and still excell,
It is but vain unjustly to wage war;
Men can do best, and women know it well
Preeminence in all and each is yours;
Yet grant some small acknowledgements of ours.
And oh ye high flown quills that soar the Skies,
And ever with your prey still catch your praise,
If e'er you deign these lowly lines your eyes
Give Thyme or Parsley wreath, I ask no bayes,
This mean and unrefined ore of mine
Will make your glistering gold but more to shine.

[102]

["In Honour of that High and Mighty Princess QUEEN ELIZABETH of Happy Memory"]

Although great Queen thou now in silence lie
Yet thy loud Herald Fame doth to the sky
Thy wondrous worth proclaim in every Clime,
And so hath vowed while there is world or time.
So great's thy glory and thine excellence,
The sound thereof raps every human sense,
That men account it no impiety,
To say thou wert a fleshly Deity:
Thousands bring offerings (though out of date)
Thy world of honours to accumulate,
'Mongst hundred Hecatombs of roaring verse,

Mine bleating stands before thy royal Hearse.
Thou never didst nor canst thou now disdain
T'accept the tribute of a loyal brain.
Thy clemency did yerst esteem as much
The acclamations of the poor as rich,
Which makes me deem my rudeness is no wrong,
Though I resound thy praises 'mongst the throng.

No Phoenix pen, nor Spencer's poetry
No Speed's nor Cambden's learned History,
Elizah's works, wars, praise, can e're compact,
The World's the Theater where she did act.
The 'leven Olympiads of her happy reign:
Who was so good, so just, so learn'd, so wise,
From all the Kings on earth she won the prize.
Nor say I more than duly is her due,
Millions will testify that this is true.
She hath wiped off the aspersion of her Sex,
That women wisdom lack to play the Rex:
Spain's Monarch says not so, nor yet his host:
She taught them better manners, to their cost.
The Salique law, in force now had not been,
If France had ever hoped for such a Queen.
But can you Doctors now this point dispute,
She's Argument enough to make you mute.

Since first the sun did run his nere run race.
And earth had once a year, a new old face,
Since time was time, and man unmanly man,
Come show me such a Phoenix if you can?
Was ever people better ruled than hers?
Was ever land more happy free from stirs?
Did ever wealth in England more abound?
Her victories in foreign Coasts resound,
Ships more invincible than Spain's her foe
She Wracked, she sacked, she sunk his Armado:
But time would fail me, so my tongue would too,
To tell of half she did, or she could do.

She was a Phoenix Queen, so shall she be,
Her ashes not revived, more Phoenix she,
Her personal perfections, who would tell,
Must dip his pen in the Heleconian Well,
Which I may not, my pride doth but aspire
To read what others write, and so admire.

But happy England which had such a Queen;
Yea happy, happy, had those days still been:

But happiness lies in a higher sphere,
Then wonder not Eliza moves not here.
Full fraught with honor, riches and with days
She set, she set, like Titan in his rays.
No more shall rise or set so glorious sun
Until the heavens great revolution,
If then new things their old forms shall retain
Eliza shall rule Albion once again.

(light irony)

Now say, have women worth? or have they none?
Or had they some, but with our Queen tis gone?
Nay Masculines, you have thus taxed us long,
But she, though dead, will vindicate our wrong.
Let such as say our Sex is void of Reason,
Know 'tis a slander now, but once was Treason.

[357–61]

Now Sisters pray proceed, each in your course
As I, impart your usefulness and force.

[108]

So proudly foolish I, with Phaeton strive
Fame's flaming chariot for to drive.

[350]

(lights down stage left, up center and stage right for quick costume change)

Act II, scene 3
SOR JUANA INÉS DE LA CRUZ:

[In *my* life's work]
I turned my attention
to the shining example of [Phaeton]
lofty impulse, flaming spirit

the roads of daring open

[I, 355(792), emphasis added]

new wings engendered for each flight
of the ambitious spirit

[I, 355(805–6)]

["Lines Written to Me by a Gentleman Recently Come to New Spain"]

"Mother, who makes seem little
men of gigantic wit:
Mother who may not be a mother,

"What Phoenix will live longer
than your fame in the annals?"

[I, 139(1–4); 140(6); 142(125–6)]

(angered and amused)

I had thought of no such thing;
but if he wishes to raise me
to Phoenix, shall I be the one
to throw this honor away?

And this may be why I was born
where the fiery solar rays
might gaze directly down at me,
not cross-eyed as on other lands.

What has given me greatest pleasure
is knowing, from now on,
that I and only I must be
my entire family.

(ironic)

Is there anything like the knowledge
that now I depend on no one,
that I am to be my own death and my life
when it appeals to me?

[I, 146(125–36)]

That now I need no longer figure
in common relationships;
that no relative shall ever bore me,
nor companion annoy me?

That I compose my entire species,
and need therefore incline towards none,
for one's obligation is solely
to love one of one's own kind?

[I, 146–7(137–44)

That my inkwell is the blessed pyre,
where I must go to burn,
substituting my cotton blotters
for the sweet oils of the East?

That the quills with which I write
are those that beat the wind,
as much to sustain me in this life,
as to revive me again?

(149–55)]

He says that I am she, the Phoenix
. . . – outwitting the Ages –

[I, 144(53–4)

the first-born daughter of the Sun
who, displaying her splendor,
has a beak inlaid by Ceylon,
and plumage curled in the land of Ofir;

(65–8)]

He says Arabia is the blessed land
where "an evil night and a girl-child's birth"
fell to my mother's lot,
as we hear in the proverb.

[I, 145(81–4)

That I am she who is used to walk
among elegant similes,
loading the length and weight of the lines
and adorning rhymed *romances*.

(93–5)]

Thanks be to God that no longer
must I grind the cocoa,
nor will I have to be ground down
by whomever comes visiting me!

[I, 147(161–4)

from now on I must honor myself
and I will not tarry an instant
in assuming the etiquette of Phoenix.

(166–8)

What would the mountebanks not give,
to be able to seize me,
and carry me 'round like a monster,

(177–9)

Not that! You will not find your fortune
with that Phoenix, you merchants.
This is why she is enclosed,
behind thirty [convent] locks.

(189–92)

and . . .
I wish that no one may,
without my express permission,
compare me to anything else.

(197–200)]

(sits at desk; conversationally)

As I have said . . . I had no need of books – nevertheless, the many that I have read have not failed to help me, in sacred as well as secular studies.

[IV, 460]

For there I see a Deborah issuing laws, military as well as political, and governing the people among whom there were so many learned men. I see the exceedingly knowledgeable queen of Sheba, so learned she dares to test the wisdom of the greatest of the wise with riddles, without being reprehended for it, but rather on this account becoming the judge of the unbelieving. I see so many and such outstanding women: some adorned with the gift of prophecy, like an Abigail; others, of conviction, like Esther; others, of piety, like Rahab; others of perseverance, like Anna, mother of Samuel; and infinite numbers of others, with other kinds of qualities and virtues.

[IV, 460–1(848–59)]

I see a Gertrude read, write, and teach. And to seek examples no further than my [own order], I see my own most holy mother Paula, learned in Hebrew, Greek and Latin languages, and an expert interpreter of the Scriptures. [Of her, St. Jerome says,] "If all the parts of my body were tongues, they would not suffice to proclaim the learning and virtue of Paula."

[IV, 461(884–93)]

. . .

Without mentioning others whom the books are full of and whom I omit so as not merely to copy what others have said (which is a vice I have always abhorred). I see the Egyptian Catherine studying and commanding all the branches of knowledge of Egypt.

[II, 461(881–4)]

> By a woman all the sages
> of Egypt have been vanquished,
> to serve as proof that sex
> is not the essence of intelligence.
>   Victory! Victory!
>
> A wonder it was, even miracle –
> the wonder being not the fact
> that she should triumph over them,
> but that they should admit defeat.
>   Victory! Victory!
>
> How well we see that they were wise
> in confessing they were beaten,
> for it is a triumph to concede
> the supremacy of reason.
>   Victory! Victory!

[II, 171(9–23)

Never by a famous man
have we been shown such victory,
and this, because God wished through her
to honor womankind.
        Victory! Victory!

                                                  (49–53)]

(returning to her list of predecessors)

If I [turn to the ancients], the first I meet are the Sybils, chosen by God to prophecize the principal mysteries of our Faith, in such learned and elegant verses that they fill us with amazement. I see, adored as goddess of the sciences, a woman such as Minerva, daughter of Jupiter and mistress of all the knowledge of Athens. I see Pola Argentaria, who helped Lucan, her husband, write the *Battle of Pharsalia*. I see the daughter of the divine Tiresias, wiser than her father. I see Zenobia, queen of the Palmerians, as learned as she was courageous. An Arete, daughter of Aristomache most learned. A Nicostrata, inventor of Latin letters and exceedingly erudite in Greek. An Aspasia Milesia, who taught philosophy and rhetoric and was the teacher of the philosopher Pericles. An Hispania who taught astrology and for many years was a reader in Alexandria. A Leontion, Greek, who contested the philosopher Theophrastus and vanquished him. A Julia, a Corinna, a Cornelia; and, in sum, the immense crowd of those who merited titles, now as Greeks, now as muses, again as Pythonesses. For they were but learned women, held, celebrated, and also, indeed, venerated as such in antiquity.

                                          [IV, 461(850–81)]

A lofty impulse, a flaming spirit

                                                  [I, 355(789)]

not being able to grasp
in a single act of intuition all creation
rather by stages, from one concept
to another ascending step by step

                                              [I, 350(590–4)]

. . . if there were anyone so daring . . .
in the rapid chariot bathed in light
she would accomplish it all

                                              [I, 279(#149)

new wings engendered for each flight
of the ambitious spirit!

                                              [I,355(805–6)]

. . . it being ordained [her] godlike flight
should cast,
even as the sun, a girdle round the world.
Eagle . . .

drinking the rays of the Sun, in an effort
to make a nest among its lights.

[I, 343(317, 324, 330–2)]

(blackout; music; lights up for curtain call)[22]

NOTES

1 Anne Bradstreet, *The Tenth Muse Lately sprung up in America, or Several Poems, compiled with great Variety of Wit and Learning, full of delight. Wherein especially is contained a compleat discourse and description of The Four Elements, Constitution, Ages of Man, Seasons of the Year. Together with an Exact Epitome of the Four Monarchies, viz. The Assyrian, Persian, Grecian, Roman. Also a Dialogue between Old England and New, Concerning the late troubles. With Divers other pleasant and serious Poems. By a Gentlewoman in those parts* (London, 1650); Sor Juana Inés de la Cruz, *Inundación Castálida de la Unica Poetisa, Musa Dézima . . . (Plenitude of the Muses by the Singular Poetess, The Tenth Muse, Professed Nun in the Monastery of St. Jerome of the Imperial City of Mexico, who in various meters, languages and styles enriches Various Subjects with elegant, subtle, clear, witty, useful verses, to teach, entertain and amaze . . .* (Madrid, 1689). For modern editions see, for Anne Bradstreet, John Harvard Ellis, ed., *The Works of Anne Bradstreet in Prose and Verse* (1867; reprint, Gloucester, Mass.: Peter Smith, 1962); hereafter referred to as *Works*. For Sor Juana, *Inundación castálida*, ed. Georgina Sabat de Rivers (Madrid: Editorial Castalia, 1982); *Obras completas* (Mexico City: Fondo de Cultura Económica, 1951–8), vols. 1–3, ed. Alfonso Méndez Plancarte; vol. 4, ed. Alberto Salceda; hereafter referred to as *OC*. Anne Bradstreet's *Works* comprise 413 pages of her texts, including an eight-page spiritual autobiography dedicated to her children, the initial selection of the first section of the book, known as "Religious Experiences and Occasional Pieces" and composed of twenty-four other pieces in prose and verse; seventy-seven short, aphoristic "Meditations Divine and Moral" dedicated to her son Simon Bradstreet; the "Poems" as they appeared in the first and second editions (1650, 1678), including the five long poems listed in the title above and eleven other poems, among which are the fifty-five "Contemplations," each written in a seven-line stanza; fourteen poems, among them five elegies, make up the last section of *Works*. Sor Juana's *OC* comprises 1,737 pages of her texts, including sixty-five sonnets; sixty-two *romances* (ballads); numerous poems in other metric forms; the 975-line "*Sueño*" (Dream), considered the greatest philosophical poem in the Spanish language; three sacramental *autos* (plays) and two comedies (one a collaboration), along with the farces that preceded and divided the acts; thirty-two *loas,* sung and performed for religious or viceroyal holidays; fifteen or sixteen sets of *villancicos* (carols) for Matins, each with eight or nine songs, all elaborations of religious themes such as the Nativity, the Assumption, the Immaculate Conception, and Saint Catherine; her thirty-five-page intellectual autobiography, known as "Reply to Sor Filotea de la Cruz"; the "Athenagoric Letter" (or "Letter Worthy of

Athena"), the theological critique, spoken of both in my play and in this introduction to it as significant because its publication motivated the writing of the "Reply" and was a factor in her ultimate silence and renunciation.

2 Electa Arenal, "The Convent as Catalyst for Autonomy: Two Hispanic Nuns of the Seventeenth Century," in *Women in Hispanic Literature: Icons and Fallen Idols,* ed. Beth Miller (Berkeley: University of California Press, 1983), pp. 147–83. Three other pieces in which I develop my ideas on Sor Juana and place her in a feminist context, giving fuller bibliographic references, are "Comment on Paz's 'Juana Ramírez,'" *Signs* 5, no. 3 (Spring 1980): 552–5; "Sor Juana Inés de la Cruz: Speaking the Mother Tongue," *University of Dayton Review* 16, no. 2 (Spring 1983): 93–105; "Sor Juana Inés de la Cruz: Foundations for a Feminist Enlightenment" (unpublished paper delivered at the Modern Language Association Convention, New York, December 1983).

3 See Raymond Williams, *The Country and the City* (New York: Oxford University Press, 1973); Perry Miller, *Errand into the Wilderness* (Cambridge, Mass.: Harvard University Press, 1956); Sacvan Bercovitch, *The Puritan Origins of the American Self* (New Haven, Conn.: Yale University Press, 1975).

4 Irving Leonard, *Baroque Times in Old Mexico* (1959; reprint, Ann Arbor: University of Michigan Press, 1973), p. 72.

5 See Asunción Lavrín, "Values and Meaning of Monastic Life for Nuns in Colonial Mexico," *Catholic Historical Review* 58 (October 1972): 367–87; Luis Matin, *Daughters of the Conquistadores: Women of the Viceroyalty of Peru* (Albuquerque: University of New Mexico Press, 1983), chaps. 7, 8, 9.

6 Adrienne Rich, "When We Dead Awaken: Writing as Re-Vision" (1971), *On Lies, Secrets and Silence: Selected Prose 1966–1978* (New York: Norton, 1979), pp. 33–49. See also her preface to *The Works of Anne Bradstreet,* ed. Jeannine Hensley (Cambridge, Mass.: Harvard University Press, 1967), included with an introductory note in the first-mentioned volume as "The Tensions of Anne Bradstreet" (1966), pp. 21–32.

7 See Carolyn Merchant, *The Death of Nature: Women, Ecology, and the Scientific Revolution* (New York: Harper & Row, 1983); Herbert N. Schneidau, *Sacred Discontent: The Bible and Western Tradition* (Berkeley: University of California Press, 1978).

8 See Leonard, "On the Book Trade, 1683," *Baroque Times,* pp. 164–71.

9 See Wendy Martin, "Anne Bradstreet: 'As Weary Pilgrim,'" *An American Triptych: Anne Bradstreet, Emily Dickinson, Adrienne Rich* (Chapel Hill: University of North Carolina Press, 1984), pp. 15–16.

10 See note 2 and Octavio Paz, *Sor Juana Inés de la Cruz o las trampas de la fe* (Barcelona: Seix Barral, 1982,), pp. 499, 500; translation forthcoming, Harvard University Press. Paz sees Sor Juana as an initiator of the modernist tradition in poetry. Translations of Sor Juana by Amanda Powell.

11 By 1690, when Sor Juana was 39, criticism and pressure against her role as a writer and scholar had been mounting. A furor attended the circulation by Fernández de Santa Cruz, bishop of Puebla, of her critique of famous Father

Vieyra's Maundy Thursday sermon, which she had never intended for publication. The bishop entitled it "Carta Atenagórica" (Letter Worthy of Athena) and published it together with an admonitory letter to her, signed with the pseudonym Sor Filotea de la Cruz. Threatened, angered, hurt, and jolted, within four months of having received the tract and its accompanying letter, Sor Juana composed "La respuesta a Sor Filotea" (Reply to . . .), dated March 1, 1691. Although it was not until three years later that she made her final retreat into ascetic and fervent monastic dedication, thus renouncing her worldly artistic life with the convent, she wrote very little after the "Respuesta."

12   See Mary Mason, "The Other Voice: Autobiographies of Women Writers," in *Autobiography: Essays Theoretical and Critical,* ed. James Olney (Princeton, N.J.: Princeton University Press, 1980), pp. 207–35.

13   Susan Stevens played the role of the two women in the first public performance of *This Life Within Me Won't Keep Still,* on December 28, 1979, in the California Ballroom of the St. Francis Hotel in San Francisco. It was a featured event of the Annual Convention of the Modern Language Association. Subsequent performances were presented on January 4–6, 1980, at the People's Marina Theater of the Fort Mason Foundation in San Francisco. On April 11, 1980, the play was performed at a SUNY-Purchase conference entitled "Modern Literature in the United States and Hispanic America." It was also performed at Sweet Briar College on September 25, 1980. A Spanish version of the Sor Juana section was performed in San Jose, California. It received a staged reading at the College of Staten Island/CUNY in March 1985.

The title of the Spanish version of the play is *No me callarán, No me callaré!*

14   Citations in brackets refer to *Works.*

15   Brackets in the text indicate words added by the author. Sometimes there is merely a substitution of pronouns; sometimes a few words of explanatory narrative or identification have been added. Poem titles are also bracketed.

16   Rose: meaning that she was rebellious and angry.

17   *Summum bonum:* "the highest good or supreme good."

18   Citations refer to *OC* (roman numerals indicate volume numbers; numbers following indicate page numbers; numbers within parentheses indicate lines unless otherwise noted) and to Anita Arroyo, *Razón y pasión de Sor Juana* (1952) (Mexico City: Editorial Porrua, 1971), cited as Arroyo.

19   Raggs: a printing term that means "printer's errors."

20   Essays: in the sense of attempts and even practice.

21   Store: "furniture."

22   Given the character of this volume, some production notes on staging, costuming, and characterization and scene-by-scene comments have been eliminated.

10

Interview with Margaret Randall

BELL GALE CHEVIGNY

Margaret Randall's writing career has carried her from New York in the fifties to Mexico in the sixties, to Cuba in the seventies, to Nicaragua in the early eighties, and finally, in 1984, back to the United States. The story of her movements is in many ways as expressive as the more than thirty books and numerous poems, translations, and essays she has produced. In each place she sought not only the new story but also the literary means to connect the new cultural, political, and social situations to the ones she had left behind. Thus, although her gender or nationality made her an outsider among the beatniks or in Mexico, Cuba, and Nicaragua, she turned difference to advantage: With a variety of literary activities, she mediated the cultures, or provided a bridge between them.

In New York she wrote as a member of a small countercultural community, but in Mexico she sought to put American cultures into communication with one another at a peculiarly open, rich, and volatile moment, by cofounding the little magazine *el corno emplumado/The Plumed Horn*. For the first time, as Ernesto Cardenal wrote to the editors of *el corno*, "poets are writing in different languages, but all speaking in one Pentecostal tongue. . . . You are creating the true Pan American union . . . if poets don't do this, no one will." Moving to Cuba in the late sixties, Randall devoted her prolific writing to breaking the blockade of information about Cuba. In these years, she also traveled to Peru, Vietnam, Venezuela, and Chile, recording these experiences as she went. In 1979 a visit to Nicaragua to interview women active in the revolution there resulted in her move to Nicaragua, where she worked until 1984. In January of that year she returned to enter a fifth phase of her writing life in her home country.

Although Margaret Randall has always had her ear to the ground in whatever country she has lived, she has never lost contact with the social and cultural realities of the United States, especially the women's movement. Witness to and participant in each society she inhabited, she constructed her writing life around writers – as an editor, translator, interviewer, and member or teacher of poetry workshops. Because she has always tried enthusiastically to make the cultures she has known intelligible to one another, she may be said to be a comparatist by instinct and vocation. Randall was asked, therefore, to talk about each of the four places and periods of her writing life in terms of how they shaped her definition of the writer and her sense of literature's compelling tasks.

This interview was conducted in New York on April 30 and May 1, 1984, and also incorporates some written responses Randall supplied to further inquiry.

When I came to live in New York in 1958, I was twenty-two. I had already moved around a lot. I had been raised in Scarsdale until I was eleven. Then my family moved to New Mexico, and I had traveled in Europe with my first husband. But I was really very provincial. I had just been divorced. I had had no college education, and I took a series of odd jobs: working in a feather factory in the garment district, sitting in galleries, being a secretary, a waitress, an artist's model. But I had come to New York to be a writer. I was taking my writing seriously for the first time.

I was influenced by lots of people. Back in Albuquerque in 1957, someone read "Howl" at a party, and I wrote a letter to Ginsberg offering to meet him at a park in San Francisco on a certain date. I drove all the way there from Albuquerque and waited and was extremely disappointed when he didn't show up! That's the way I was in those days. In 1959, I was waitressing at Amagansett when Jack Kerouac came in and sat down at a table. I had the audacity to go get a chapter of a novel I was working on then and ask him to read it. He read it right there – what choice did he have? – and I took the suggestions he made to heart.

Paddy Chayevsky gave me advice too. He said the way to learn how to write dialogue was to stand on a corner on Forty-second Street without a notebook, to listen and see how much you could retain, and then go home and recreate it. I would do that day after day. I was very earnest. I knew some writers in New York, some of the Deep Imagists, Robert Kelly, Jerome Rothenberg, George Economou, Rochelle Owens. Near the end of my three years in New York, I went out to Rutherford, New Jersey, several times to see William Carlos Williams. His work was about solid, everyday objects and events. I was moving toward a need in my life and work to be more specific, to ask real questions and get real answers, and in that respect Williams was essential. Later, back in New Mexico, I met Robert Creeley and was influenced by him and other Black Mountain people.

But for the most part in New York I was much more stimulated by the painters of the abstract expressionist school than by writers. The painters were more carnal; they were dirtier. Everything was out there; you could touch it; the textures were rougher. Their speech was very simple. I understood them and felt I could participate and communicate things that were solid. Elaine DeKooning was my closest friend, and every time I see her, even now, it's as if we had never stopped talking. There was the Artists' Club that met in a loft on the Lower East Side on Friday nights. Certain abstract expressionist ideas were hashed out at those meetings, and sometimes people read poetry – I did years later – and the ideas discussed affected my work by a kind of osmosis.

I also used to spend a lot of time at the Forty-second Street library with book lists from people I considered important. I would then discuss what I'd read with these people and ask questions. I was getting my own brand of college education. It's interesting: I read few women and had absolutely no women's consciousness. I and many like me were really groupies in those movements. I had strong ideas about myself as a woman and as a writer, but they were the ideas that cocky middle-class Americans often have about themselves, that they can do anything; if other women were not able to do what I could, I would have assumed it was because they weren't good enough.

Gradually I began to wake up politically. I was working for Nancy MacDonald at Spanish Refugee Aid, helping people in bad physical and financial shape who had remained in France and northern Africa after the Spanish Civil War. I was also influenced by the Catholic Workers, and I began to go to demonstrations.

Very hesitantly, I started to organize my ideas about revolution and marxism. When the Bay of Pigs was invaded, four of us, Leroi Jones, Marc Schleifer, Elaine DeKooning, and I, wrote a protest which was signed by hundreds of artists and writers. I began to have differences with Nancy MacDonald and her group, which had come out of Trotskyism and moved to anarchism and had become disillusioned with every kind of "ism." I was more radical. I loved Fidel in an intuitive way. I liked the fact that poor people without power were rebelling against the powers that be. In the United States, I was acutely aware of the forces of oppression, of repression, but I didn't know how those forces worked. I did a lot of things in opposition to them – personal, meaningless things. I dressed in a scandalous way. I wore black stockings. I painted my eyes. I smoked a lot of pot. I wrote things as a personal rejection of society. We were a subculture, and we refused to go beyond it. We used to make jokes about living exclusively below Fourteenth Street. We went uptown only to visit the galleries and museums. We worked only to get enough to write or paint, or we got unemployment, and we scorned those who wanted to get ahead.

But among ourselves, there was a lot of cameraderie. We all lived in lofts or in those apartments with the bathtub in the kitchen. My first apartment was on First Avenue and Seventeenth Street and the rent was seventeen dollars a month. My second rent, which was an enormous leap, was thirty-five dollars a month. The third and last in New York was a hundred and twenty-five dollars on Third Street between Avenues A and B. That was when I was pregnant with Gregory and was forced to get an elevator apartment. Gregory's father was Joel Oppenheimer, the poet. There was no real relationship between us at that time (although we have since become friends) – I simply wanted to have a child.

It was a struggle here in New York. By the time that Gregory was ten months old, I no longer thought one had to live in New York to be a writer. I was sick of New York, sick of the Cedar Bar, and sick of having the one-night, one-week, one-month relationships with the men one met there. Then I wanted to be with Gregory more; it was really a battle to support him and actually be with him. I had thought it very natural to want to have a baby, but at that point in history it wasn't really a very usual thing to do your own. I knew nothing about Mexico except that I had been there once for two weeks, but I had some strange idea – and I used to grab onto ideas and just act on them – that somehow in Mexico I would be able to be with Gregory more, support him more easily. I knew Spanish; I had lived in Spain for two years, in '55 and '56, with my first husband. We had attempted to go on a motor scooter to India. We'd gone broke in Spain and gotten jobs there.

So I went to Mexico City in the fall of 1961. I found work translating essays, teaching English, translating comic books – the kinds of jobs young Americans were getting in Mexico at that time. We translated everything from *Superman* to *The Lone Ranger,* whatever was popular at that time, bringing American anticulture to the Third World. I very quickly got in with a group of people through the visionary Catholic poet Philip Lamantia, whom I had met in New York. A lot of people who were expatriates of one sort or another from the United States met at his apartment on Rio Hudson – Bonnie and Ray Bremser, who had skipped bail, Harvey Wolin, Howard Frankl. Ernesto Cardenal was also around at that time. He wasn't yet a priest. He had come from his experience with Thomas Merton and the Trappists at Gethsemani in Kentucky, and he was on his way to another experience with the Benedictines in Cuernavaca.

That scene was laced with dope. I never used anything but pot, but a lot of other people were into hallucinatory drugs, especially Lamantia, who was Grand Master of all that – he had a strange mixture of mysticism and antimaterialist politics. Leonora Carrington, the English surrealist painter, was sometimes part of our group, and our mentor was León Felipe, the great Spanish poet in exile in Mexico. Some of them, like Sergio Mondragón, had had a more solid participation in protest movements such as the great electrical workers' strike and the railway workers' strike in '58 in Mexico. Some were effete loners, like Homero Aridjis; some were political, like Juan Bañuelos; some were born leaders, like Ernesto; and some were beautifully crazy, like Raquel Jodorowsky, the Peruvian poet.

It was an interesting, motley crew. We got together and read to each other a lot. Out of those readings came a very strong feeling that Latin American poets had no idea of what North American poets were writing or feeling or thinking, and had no knowledge of our mentors, people like Williams and Pound, Creeley and Blackburn; and in the same way, we had heard of Neruda and Vallejo but had never read their work. We became aware of the need to make some kind of vehicle through which that separation could be broken down. It was all in the interest of some wild, daring, exciting, all-encompassing dream that we were all brothers and sisters, that the most important and purest thing in the world was poetry, and that we were kings and queens of that world of poetry.

Some of us had that dream and that need more than others, and those who had it the most were Sergio Mondragón and myself, Harvey Wolin, and Ernesto, and we decided to create a magazine called *el corno emplumado/The Plumed Horn,* which of course combined the jazz horn of U.S. culture and the plumes of Quetzalcoatl. We just set out and did it. It seemed totally plausible and possible to us, and it became much more than a magazine; it became an institution, part of a movement. That was the decade of the flowering of little magazines in the United States. There was the classic *Black Mountain Review* to be drawn on, and the *Evergreen Review, City Lights Journal, Trobar, Kayak, Kulchur,* and *I-Kon,* and Robert Bly's *The Sixties* later showed an interest in the great voices from Latin America. In Latin America in 1961, there were only a few little magazines.

We translated and published Vallejo and Paz, and Ginsberg was translated for the first time into Spanish – all of "Kaddish" and part of "Howl" and "Supermarket in California" – and Williams and more. And then we helped organize the First American Gathering of Poets in Mexico City in February of 1964, to which poets came from the United States and all over Latin America. People sold their pianos to come; they joined "fly now and pay later" plans, which were new at that time in the world. They sold their last possessions to come to Mexico City and sleep on the floors of people's houses. This was a joint enterprise with Thelma Nava, who was editing *Pájaro cascabel* in Mexico, and Miguel Grinberg, who had a magazine in Buenos Aires called *Eco contemporaneo,* and the group from the Caracas magazine, and Jaime Carrero from Puerto Rico, Edmundo Aray and Juan Calzadilla, Raquel Jodorowsky from Peru, people from Chile, Colombia, Ecuador. It was amazing. The National Press Club in Mexico was donated to us by the Mexican presidency, and we had huge marathon readings in Chapultepec Park. I met Roque Dalton there for the first time, fresh from his escape from a firing squad in Salvador, thanks to an earthquake that loosened the walls of his makeshift jungle prison. There was a Panamanian poet, Roberto Fernández; he weighed about three hundred pounds. I remember that he was so fat that he broke one of those free-form steps riveted to the wall in our house. He had to sleep on the floor, because there was no bed that would hold him. So our idea of our own grandeur was great. We thought we were having a profound influence all over the world, and in fact, within this limited but exciting circle of poets and writers, we were!

All over Latin America, the value of poetry and artistic expression has been greater than in North America, and as a consequence, it's traditional in Mexico – except in the late sixties during the Díaz Ordaz administration – for government and institutions like Bellas Artes, the Ministry of Education, and the presidency to support culture. They all gave *el corno* money, and individuals in the government gave us money. *El corno* was at least two-thirds supported by the government until the crash, until we took the side of the students in 1968, and that money was withdrawn.

Harvey Wolin dropped out after the first issue or two, and Sergio and I slowly made the magazine into an absolute institution. We fell in love and we got married. We had two kids, Sarah and Ximena, but our personal relationship was quite oppressive from very early on. I thought Sergio was a more advanced political person, because he had taken part in those strikes in '58. He became a vegetarian on the day our first daughter, Sarah, was born in April 1963. He began to do yoga; he became involved with a sect called the Great Universal Fraternity. He also developed a series of ideas that were extremely antiwoman, like women can't reach nirvana. When I think of things like that, I wonder how I stood it as long as I did, but of course I had had my own social conditioning.

Meanwhile the experience of living in a Third World country, a country dependent on the United States, pushed me further to the political Left. A lot of this was intellectual. In issue number 7, as early as 1963, we published a large section of Cuban writing starting with a fragment of

Fidel's talk to the intellectuals in 1962. And I was also in touch with poets and writers in the forefront of the struggles in several Latin American countries; they also made me aware of the relationship of the U.S. to these countries. But some of it was more immediate. After I left Sergio I also became a midwife, learning from another midwife, working exclusively in the poverty-stricken districts around Mexico City, and I was closely involved with very poor women in really terrifying situations.

But while Sergio was becoming more mystical and I more leftist, we were creating a very solid institution which somehow involved the magazine, our lives, our kids, our house, the way we were, the picture we presented to the world. So even as I suffered the oppression of my personal relationship, it became harder and harder to break away from it. And he, in fact, was very threatening about my need eventually to break away from him. "You're just a castrating North American female" – that was one of his favorite phrases. He said, "You'll never find another man," as if finding a man was the only way that I might have a life.

The magazine, of course, was bilingual. Sergio edited the Spanish part of it, and I the English. Sometimes we made a supreme effort and did a real bilingual issue with the same work published in both languages (such as number 18, which was dedicated to Mexican literature, and number 23, dedicated to Cuban literature), but more often we didn't have the energy for that. After the first issues, Sergio and I did almost all the work, from raising the money, reading the work, accepting or rejecting it, to answering all the letters, correcting page proofs and galleys, finding a printer and distributing the magazine, eventually to more than twenty countries. But because of our personal and political differences, Sergio and I moved further apart, and the magazine really became two magazines under one cover with two different points of view. On the English side the writers' political and human perspective became as important as the quality of the work. Form and content were inseparable to me. Sergio tended more toward the mystic and saw the magazine as a place where different political perspectives short of fascism perhaps could be expressed.

For example, I published a number of long poems by a poet from the South in the United States. Then I read a letter of his and realized he was totally racist and would never publish him again. That would not have been enough to discourage Sergio. Sergio was extremely excited by a group of Colombian writers called the Nadaistas – the Nothingists – who were total nihilists. The leader of the group, Gonzalo Arango, was later accused of being a CIA agent by a number of young writers in Colombia, and in fact when Camilo Torres (the first guerrilla priest) was killed, these same writers told us that, while Arango claimed to be a revolutionary writer, he had produced a play that was very derogatory about Torres's life and death. I was furious and would never again have published Arango, but Sergio felt that it was important to keep on publishing him. For me, it was becoming increasingly clear that the writers I valued had a moral responsibility to life.

We both made our first trip to Cuba in January of 1967 to a meeting of poets held on Varadero Beach to commemorate the one hundredth anniversary of the birth of the Nicaraguan poet Rubén Darío. Going to Cuba put into perspective the fragmented feelings I had been grappling with for a number of years. It was my first experience in a socialist country. It was extremely romantic and intense, and when I came back from that trip, I was more than ever convinced that *el corno* would have to be a vehicle not only for the vanguard of writing but for the vanguard of struggle on the continent, and that there was an intimate connection between the two. I went to Cuba again, without Sergio in 1968, to the Congress of Third World Intellectuals. There I began to grapple for the first time consciously with the questions: What is the role of the intellectual, of poetry, of art in the Third World? The second trip to Cuba gave me the strength to leave Sergio. We did one or two more issues of the magazine together, and then I took the magazine on myself.

In New York I had been witness, not participant, and witness in an unformed, intuitive way. Poetry in New York was part of the counterculture, and the less importance it had the better, whereas in Mexico I saw myself, as a poet, as having a more important role in the world socially, and I became imbued with the notion that poetry could change the world. I still think it can make its mark on the world, but then I thought it could really change the world concretely. And in Mexico I still had no sense of feminism or of the importance of my own condition as a woman.

Soon after I returned from Cuba I met Robert Cohen, who had come from New York to Mexico to find his Sierra Maestra, as he liked to say. We fell in love. He was nine years younger than me. I was thirty-one, with three kids. We began to live together, he began to help with the magazine, and we decided to have a child. Then the student movement started in July of 1968. It was part of the global student rebellion emerging at that time in Columbia University in New York, and in Paris. The Olympics were to be held in Mexico, and the student movement was part of a social, political, and economic crisis almost unequaled in Mexico's modern history. Hundreds of peaceful demonstrators were murdered on October 2 in Tlatelolco by government forces, and the massacre was covered up, because the Olympics had to be held – at all costs. *El corno* took a stand, and so we were cut off from government funding, and we began to fight to survive by readings and benefits and letter campaigns, and it worked. We had a tremendous support network by that time all over the world, but especially in the United States and in many Latin American countries. All the other literary magazines in Mexico took the side of the students and were cut off, and they went under. We were the only magazine that managed to stay afloat.

We refused to die when they told us to die, and I think that infuriated the Mexican government. I was no leader in the events of '68. My participation was that of any normal thinking, feeling human being – marches, demonstrations, information brigades. I worked with some of the medical students at the School of Medicine, and then after the second of October, I hid and fed people who were underground. That, plus my trips to Cuba, was enough. The repression never really came down on Sergio or on Robert, but it certainly came down on me. By the middle of 1969, Anna had been born, Robert and I were solidly together, the first anniversary of the events of '68 was approaching. People came to our house with false identification, and armed, and stole my passport. I had to go underground for about four months. Trying to hide a three-month baby, Anna, and three other kids, the oldest only eight, was too hard. So we sent all four of them to Cuba. I had to stay underground until I could find a way out of the country, which was very difficult at that time, because the movement was virtually destroyed. It was hard to know what might happen. The *Halcones,* the paramilitary squads, were kidnapping and killing or torturing people. People were being imprisoned. I took out an *amparo,* which is a legal recourse through which one asks the different dependencies and police forces of the government if there is any charge against one. That came back negative, so it was clear that it wasn't the Mexican government per se that was persecuting me; it was these paramilitary organizations and/or the CIA, with the *beneplácito* of the Mexican government, of course.

I had relinquished my American citizenship to become a Mexican citizen because it was easier to get a decent job as a Mexican. I was married then, had kids, and expected to stay forever. It was a mistake, but I didn't know it at the time. So what they stole was a Mexican passport. I tried to get it back, and they wouldn't give it to me. It was a mess. I finally found a way to leave the country illegally. I went as far as Czechoslovakia to get to Cuba. That's where I was for the next eleven years.

The Cuban Revolution supported art and creativity in a way that made the United States pale and that made the Mexico of '68 and '69 pale. There was a certain amount of control on what one wrote in Cuba, but it wasn't coming from the government; it was self-imposed. There had been problems with writers in the sixties, with the stances some writers took, which resulted in a kind of self-censorship at certain periods. That also changed a lot in the years I was in Cuba – there were tough moments and relaxed moments – and the openness was in direct relation to the amount of defensiveness that the Cubans felt about their revolution because of their proximity to the United States, their isolation from the rest of Latin America, and the enemies they saw and felt – and also imagined – as a result. The Cubans had opened their archives and life to many intellectuals from the States and were burned severely by several of them.

I lived in Cuba through all of those years of problems around homosexuality, and problems around culture at the time that Luis Pavón and the National Culture Council were in control. I lived in Cuba during the Padilla episode. There's a lot of misunderstanding about that case, but the Cubans made a mistake in their handling of Heberto Padilla. His troubles began in 1968 when he submitted his volume of poems, *Fuera del juego* (Out of the Game), to the UNEAC [Artists and Writers Union] contest. The international jury gave him the prize, but UNEAC as an institution considered the work counterrevolutionary and published the volume with a note that voiced its disapproval. Then, in 1971, Padilla was arrested as a counterrevolutionary and detained for a little more than a month in an elegant house on the beach, according to what Padilla himself later said, publicly and privately. He said they attended to his health (he had a kidney problem), he swam every day, and he had constant discussions with people from Cuban security. When he was released, he made a public confession in front of the UNEAC writers, saying that he had acted wrongly, out of a desire to be an *enfant terrible,* always the center of attention. To me the confession was quite appalling because it was so childish. It showed no sense of process, it had no context, it was all black and white. In Cuba people believed Padilla said all that, of his own free will, and that he was absurd, but outside Cuba it had the effect of making people believe he had been mistreated or coerced. Anyway you cut it, Padilla comes out weak and self-serving. But that's not the issue. The Cubans overreacted; they shouldn't have arrested or detained Padilla. I can understand historically why they did it, but they shouldn't have made such a figure of him.

In the midseventies, the Ministry of Culture was created with Armando Hart at its head, and that was a liberating development. A lot of the mistakes that had been committed began to be corrected. That loosening-up process is still going on, and I think it has to do with the coming of age of the Cuban Revolution.

Robert and I were given an apartment, and we lived as much as possible as the Cubans lived. Foreigners at that time were offered special ration books – rationing was very tough then – but we refused that privilege. Robert went to work for the English-language section of Radio Havana, and I got a job at the Book Institute. During my four months underground in Mexico I had written my first book about women, *Las mujeres* (The Women), an anthology of writings out of the U.S. women's movement, with a long introduction. Siglo XXI published that in 1970; that house had already published *Los hippies: Analisis de una crisis* (The Hippies: Analysis of a Crisis). Those were my first forays into essay, social analysis. When I went to Cuba, it was very natural to make my first project a study on Cuban women. *Cuban Women Now* took two years, and it was the beginning of my deep relation to myself as a woman and as a feminist. The feminist movement in the States had made me see how in my own life my oppression as a woman had held me back – how the different men in my life, and I myself, had fed that oppression. Robert and I began to struggle with that so hard over a period of seven years that we struggled our way right out of the relationship. But it was crucial for me to deal with how a woman might retain her integrity in a relationship with a man and with the kind of sexism that is part and parcel of our lives. I think we both grew out of that experience.

To the Cubans we looked like oddballs in that struggle; but there was a growing Cuban feminism. I proposed doing a book on women in 1970. It was hardly a propitious time for such a project. Those were the years of the 10 million ton sugar harvest, the failure of that harvest, the Cubans coming to grips with their economic errors and making a tremendous effort to get back on their feet. But my boss at the Book Institute, Jaime Rivera, a young man, was absolutely enthusiastic and supportive of this project. In this country we see the military as a very conservative, oppressive force, but when a people's army has fought a guerilla war, you often find the most daring and advanced thinking in the military. The Cuban Revolution was committed to making women's equality more real. It didn't emerge in a verbalized, articulated, feminist form until 1974, with the people's power elections in Matanzas, where only three percent of the delegates were women, and with the writing of the Family Code. The Cubans had lost a lot of time thinking that economic equality would carry the whole thing forward, but their tremendous advances in economic, legal, and educational equality for women certainly laid the groundwork for change. They now know as well as anyone else that, although that *is* the base, a whole new consciousness has to be implemented to deepen and consolidate that process.

In Cuba I began also to write in Spanish. Sergio had always told me that I would never be able to write or to judge work in Spanish. And I accepted that! I read in Spanish, wrote letters in Spanish, spoke only Spanish with my children and Sergio, but my literary activity was only in English. The problem went from slightly unhinging me to a deep frustration that came to a head in Cuba, where it became more and more painful that I could not share my most intimate expression – poetry – with those closest to me. I remember that in a meeting of the Hermanos Sáinz Brigades (the brigades of young writers in Cuba), I blurted out, "How I would love to read!" and Bladimir Zamora, then president of the brigade, passed me a note saying, "Just name the date!" That's how my first reading in Cuba came about.

A number of other things contributed to my becoming confident in Spanish. Being a judge at the Casa de las Américas contest in 1970 along with Roque Dalton, Ernesto Cardenal, Cintio Vitier, and a Peruvian named Washington Delgado helped, and the fact that I was the first to come across what would be the winning book. I translated that a year later; it was Carlos María Gutiérrez's *Prison Diary*. It's never been published, but I think the translation is very good. Things I translated that were published: *Let's Go!*, a book by Otto-René Castillo, a Guatamalan poet, and poems by Ernesto, Violeta Parra, Roberto Fernández Retamar, César Vallejo. Vallejo has been supremely important to me, more than any other poet in the language, because he brought mysticism and communism together. I've never been a member of any party, but Vallejo's use of language in that merging of the mystical and the political has been essential to me. I carry his book on every trip I take, and hardly a week passes that I don't read some of the *Poemas humanos*. I didn't really get to know Vallejo until I lived in Cuba. Roque Dalton, who became a close friend of mine in Cuba and an important influence, helped me understand Vallejo – Roque and a Guatemalan poet named Arqueles Morales. They helped me find the courage to try to translate Vallejo. I got completely smashed on rum; I spent a week just with Vallejo and this rum in a very isolated communion and later went over the language carefully; and those ten or twelve poems were good and have been published in little magazines.

My own idea of poetry was changing in Cuba. I had split up with Robert in 1975 and began to live with a poet and singer, a musician named Antonio Castro, a Colombian who had grown up in Venezuela. He had come to Cuba to nurse a Venezuelan guerrilla named Domingo León, who was a paraplegic as a result of a failed bank expropriation in 1964. Antonio was a very active poet, a kind of troubadour really. He lived traveling around Cuba, singing his own poetry and that of others. We did that together during the five years we lived together. Antonio was never too tired to go to hospitals, to schools, to factories, to peasant bases.

Antonio and I also got together every Saturday morning with a group of ten to twelve poets on the lawn of the University of Havana, where they were all students. Sometimes a foreigner, like Uruguayan Mario Benedetti, would join us, but mostly it was these young Cubans, and my contact with them was very instructive. Up until then, I had known Cuban poets only through *el corno,* people like Roberto Fernández Retamar, Miguel Barnet, Nancy Morejón, people who were wonderful writers but whose life and poetry bridged two social systems, before and after the revolution. I was in some ways like them. I had been formed in a capitalist society in the States, and Mexico was also a capitalist society. Cuba was my first experience of socialism, and like Retamar and Barnet, who had not fought in the revolution, I had come to it along an intellectual path. Some of them had taken a stand against Batista, and many of them felt a kind of guilt for not having fought, like that evidenced in Retamar's poem "El otro." I was closer to their experience, but this experience served only to highlight the questions. It intensified the self-consciousness, the anguish, the difficulty of coping with action, but it didn't offer an answer.

And it was with the young poets those Saturday mornings that I found the answer. Alex Fleites, Marilyn Bobes, Reina María Rodríguez, Bladimir Zamora, Victor Rodríguez, Arturo Arango, and others – they didn't have these questions. They didn't need to make statements about the revolution's values: They were born in it; they *were* the revolution. They could write about their own interior landscapes, but from the perspective of people born into a society which was attempting to be just. The defensiveness and self-consciousness about being a poet and revolutionary at the same time was eliminated. All this opened a new world to me. I realized a revolutionary poet did not have to write about tractors or raised fists. It had to do with seeking a new life, a new ethic, from which writing proceeds in a new way, one that serves life rather than death.

And at the same time I was beginning to write my own books in Spanish, books of oral history. The first was in 1975, about Doris Tijerino, a Sandinista leader. I didn't think of myself as an oral historian. I didn't even know that such a category existed. But I did know that people's voices were becoming increasingly important to me. Nineteen seventy-five was International Women's Year, and the Sandinistas were fighting like hell in Nicaragua. Few people in other parts of the world were aware of that, much less of the role of the FSLN. So my interest in telling that story came together with my desire to go deep with a single woman, hear her voice, record it, and produce it, bring that life that in many ways paralleled twenty years of the history of Nicaragua to the eyes and ears of readers.

As I began to understand and value history more, I understood that it was ordinary people who made history. Most historians have never understood that, not being ordinary people themselves. I continued to seek out people's testimony in *Sueños y realidades de un guajiricantor,* which is a book about a Cuban peasant who composed peasant theater in verse form from the age of ten, though he only had a third grade education, and in a book about Puerto Rican patriot Dominga de la Cruz, called *El pueblo no sólo es testigo* [The People Are Not Merely Witnesses]. As the title implies the people are actors as well as witnesses. Dominga is the one who picked up the flag during the Ponce massacre in 1937. She was living out her old age in Cuba. I also did oral histories with Vietnamese women, with Chilean women, with Peruvian women, and with Nicaraguan women — *Sandino's Daughters.* The book *Christians in the Nicaraguan Revolution* and the one I've just finished about Nicaraguan writers, *Risking a Somersault in the Air,* are both oral history.

One thing that's exciting about this kind of work is that literature becomes a more public property, no longer reserved for the select few. The magic of the verb is everywhere. One can sit and listen for hours to a woman in the hills of northern Nicaragua. It's not simply what she says that's fascinating: Her use of language is precise, magical, evocative, sometimes astounding. You are consumed by the responsibility of providing an adeduate vehicle for this voice to reach the world, both to reveal the unique creation of a single human being and open a window onto a vision previously hidden although shared by hundreds of thousands of peasant women in northern Nicaragua. I grow impatient with much that passes for "new" and "innovative" literature. Oral history informants will speak freely, once they trust the historian. And their stories — so often a silent monument to an almost indescribable heroism — have been amulets for me in my life.

In the Cuban years, people's voices, and especially women's voices, real and imagined, were creeping into my own poetry — into those long poems like "Attica," "Wounded Knee," "Catching up with Moncada," and even "Motherhood." So all these things — translating the work of Latin American poets, listening to people's voices in a new way, using them both in oral history and in my own poetry — came together with the changes in my understanding of what it meant to be a poet and activist in the world, and the Cuban respect for culture, despite *all* the problems, was essential to that. In the last five years I lived in Cuba, after I left the Book Institute, I earned a salary simply for writing whatever I wanted to write, and I was not the only person in Cuba who had that privilege, and throughout that period, my poems and articles and essays were published in *Bohemia, Prensa Latina, Unión, Mujeres,* and *Casa de las Américas.*

But my work in oral history and with men led me to Nicaragua, especially my work with Doris. After the triumph of the revolution in Nicaragua, Ernesto Cardenal, my old friend from the Mexico days, became minister of Culture. He invited me to come and do a book on women. That invitation produced two big changes in my life. The first is that I began to take pictures of the women I interviewed in Nicaragua. I came to photography as a kind of answer to some of the frustrations I still felt about the language barriers, because although photography has its own language code, it is universal and it bridges my close friends who speak only English and those who speak only Spanish. For *Sandino's Daughters* I did the interviewing and photography in Nicaragua, then returned to Cuba to put the book together. I worked with the women's testimony in the daytime and with the images of those same women at night. There was a time when we could use the darkroom only at night because the door didn't shut properly! It became a reciprocal process. Each kind of work shed some light on the other. I understood the testimony better through the image and knew what I wanted to do with the image through the testimony. Now I want to find other projects in which the photographic image and the configuration of words can be combined, in still other ways.

The other big change came because I fell in love with Nicaragua and decided to move there at the end of 1980. People often asked, Why did you leave Cuba? – almost as if leaving Cuba meant some kind of denial, which it never was. I continue to feel very strongly about the Cuban Revolution, but it was exciting to be able to experience a new revolutionary context where everything was beginning, where I had been so close to many of the people who had died for that process, where the situation with women and with culture was for historical reasons qualitatively and quantitatively new and deeper.

The relationship between poetry and ordinary human activity is unique in Nicaragua. Poetry *is* an ordinary human activity there. It's hard to explain. Nicaragua produced so many poets, of whom the most influential was the great modernist Rubén Darío, that people wonder whether Darío was the poet he was because of that violent expanse of volcanic strength called Nicaragua, or whether poetry is important to Nicaraguans because of Darío. Not just poetry, but dance, song, and street theatre have deep popular roots in Nicaragua, and local religious festivals in Granada, León, Diriamba, and Masaya have distinctive cultural expressions, like costumes, masks, collective games, ritual verses, and the very presentations of the saints themselves. Sociodramas were used throughout the years of popular struggle, and the *pintas* (graffiti) were another collective and poetic art form, developed during the war. There were little infrastructures – one person kept the paint, another hid the brushes and stencils, one painted while another stood guard – because while sometimes they were slogans like "In the mountains we'll bury the enemy's heart," at other times they painted whole poems, either by martyred poets like Rigoberto López Pérez or Leonel Rugama or by the combatant him- or herself.

I have a book coming out soon on the *pintas*. The idea originated in 1979 when I was interviewing Dora María Téllez (a guerrilla commander in the Nicaraguan revolution) for *Sandino's Daughters*. She said, "You know, Margaret, while you're going around the country interviewing women, you should take pictures of the *pintas* because they're going to disappear." So I did. And over the four years, I tried to get her to write the text for that book – oh, yes, she's a wonderful poet; of course, she's not writing any poetry, she's making a revolution – but she never had the time. But four nights before I left Nicaragua, a bunch of women, my close friends, had a wonderful goodbye dinner. I took my tape recorder, we all got smashed, and I got them to talk about the *pintas,* and they gave a joint history, which I've edited as the text.

The Ministry of Culture was set up just days after the 1979 victory, in the mansion of Somoza's wife. Ernesto Cardenal was made minister of Culture, not only because he is a great poet, but because at his contemplative community at Solentiname he had shown formerly marginalized peasants how to paint primitive paintings, do crafts, and write poetry. Earlier, in the fifties, he had translated United States poets, including Pound, and he used Pound's ten rules for writing poetry in the workshops. Cardenal was asked to extend to the entire nation his island vision of a people's creativity. One of his pet projects has been installing poetry workshops in factories, neighborhoods, even police stations and army bases. Once, talking at Harvard in 1982, he claimed, "Our army can offer advisers to any army in the world – in matters related to poetry."

And, as a poet, Cardenal has been the most influential among living Nicaraguan poets. His open, conversational style, which he calls *exteriorismo,* the voice of the everyday, of the real objects around us, has had an impact on hundreds of writers. In a way Nicaragua's attention to oral history is an extension of Cardenal's *exteriorismo,* where people's voices are powerfully present. It also comes from the experience of extraordinary emotions during war, which have already produced such classic testimonies of combat as Tomás Borge's *Carlos, el amanecer ya no es una tentactión* (Carlos, The Dawn Is No Longer Beyond Our Reach) and Omar Cabezas's *La Montaña es algo mas que un inmensa estepa verde* (The Mountain Is More Than a Great Expanse of Green).

Oral history has a longer history in Cuba, and it was important too in

Vietnam, but Nicaragua has taken it to a new level, linking personal and national identity to history and cultural expression as never before. Perhaps because of the almost half-century of Somoza dictatorship, people knew little of their real history nor of Sandino. To have had a photograph of Sandino in your house at periods during the Somoza regime could cost you your life. So Sandino was not taught in the schools, was not part of people's consciousness – except in some deep collectively retained way. History was distorted. The revolution has made a supreme effort to discover its history as a people and to enable people to move with that history in a way that informs their own sense of identity. For example, during the literary campaign in Nicaragua – and this was not true in Cuba or anywhere else – all the literacy *brigadistas* took oral histories of the people, the peasants, the workers to whom they were teaching reading and writing. Those thousands of tapes are kept in an institute in Managua called The Institute for the Study of Sandinismo. The study of Sandinismo embraces the whole saga of the Nicaraguan people's life. Cultural brigades which now go under the auspices of the Sandinist Cultural Workers Association, the ASTC, to the war zones to perform for men and women fighting there, are at the same time recording the oral histories of these fighters.

It's interesting that with all the limitation of resources, with long hours and wartime conditions – these are not ideal conditions for an artist, although they provide a lot of food for artists – the ASTC found a way of addressing the needs of professionals at this moment. And by the way, the unions are unique in linking the idea of writers' and artists' unions of socialist countries, which are essentially professional associations, with the capitalist country's trade union concept, through which copyright laws, retirement, and other social benefits are being developed.

Some of the things the ASTC has done are quite amazing. For example, in countries like Nicaragua, there's a great tradition of Sunday marching bands in each little town. These people had no social security, no salaries. They passed on their skills from father to son, but many of them didn't really want to pass them on because there was nothing in it but misery. The ASTC has managed to get those bands hooked into the city or town administration so they now have retirement, salaries, vacation time. The same is true among the circus workers, who were really *lumpen* in the old Nicaragua. They had no one's respect, there were twenty-four flea-bitten circuses, and now there is a national circus and one of the seven unions is for circus artists.

Sometimes it seems as if everything about the arts is up for discussion in Nicaragua. Take, for example, the case of Claudia Gordillo, who is generally considered to be the best photographer in Nicaragua. She's young, maybe twenty-eight, and when the photographers' union was formed at the ASTC, we decided that the first show should be of her work. She had a wonderful series of pictures taken from inside the ruins of the Managua cathedral. They were moonlike landscapes, weeds growing everywhere, and you see different aspects of the center of Managua through the vacant windows, very strange and beautiful. We hung the show, and almost immediately Rudolf Wedel, a Costa Rican photographer, wrote a devastating criticism of the show in *Barricada* (the Sandinist paper), saying that it was not humanistic enough – where were the people? – it wasn't revolutionary art. This was a pseudo-social-realist attack and, I thought, stupid. Gioconda Belli came back in *Barricada* with a blast of his review and a defense of the pictures. Then Wedel answered, and I answered him, and so on. The result was that about thirty of us were writing for about a month and a half, in *El nuevo diario,* too, and some of the broader articles on the role of art in revolution began to appear in the cultural supplements of both papers. It was a wonderful discussion and the talk of the day.

Claudia wasn't working then but wanted a job. At the end of this discussion, *Barricada* offered her a job as part of their photographic staff. For many of us, that was the FSLN's way of making a statement, but we were also concerned because she seemed a sort of spiritual woman, not very tough, and we thought, "What will happen to this free spirit working at a daily newspaper which is a party organ where you work about fifteen or sixteen hours a day?" She accepted the job, and all the photography at *Barricada* has improved enormously through her influence on that collective. But *her* photography has also changed. She went to the front last year for two months, and with other *Barricada* photographers did a book of war photographs. I have never seen such work. It's a breakthrough in the history of war photography on an international level, the way Robert Capa's was during the Spanish Civil War.

If you look at Mexico, Cuba, and Nicaragua and the parts of three decades I spent there and the way women writers inhabited those times and places, it's very revealing. In Mexico in the sixties, Thelma Nava or Elena Poniatowska, for instance, were isolated because, as women writers, they were so unusual. Of course, Elena eventually made it in what was very much a man's world, not a woman's world; but Thelma as a poet was almost eaten up by the world of Mexican men and Mexican poetry, and she no longer writes much poetry or edits, and she has dedicated herself completely to support work for struggles in Central America. If you look at even relatively recent anthologies in Mexico, you see few women. The Mexican male presence still dominates or obliterates. It's going to take years for Mexican women to break through in any significant numbers. Of course, there are others, like Rosario Castellanos, Elena Garro, but the percentage of women is phenomenally low.

Then you have the case of Cuba. In the seventies when I lived there, there was a range from older women like Fina García Marruz, still an amazing poet, to women like Nancy Morejón, Milagros González, Georgina Herrera, who are somewhat younger, and finally to much younger women, like Reina María Rodríguez and Marilyn Bobes. I lived through a period in Cuba in which these women moved from tokenism to being recognized by many of the men and women as among the finest writers in Cuba. They were winning all the important prizes, from the UNEAC and the Casa de las Américas prizes to the prizes for younger poets. I write about this shift in *Breaking the Silences*. In 1977 and '78 I put together an anthology of fifteen young Cuban poets, of which only two were women, *These Living Songs*. Then I noticed in a meeting of poets in Santiago that women were the most exciting presences, having the most original things to say, and I did that second anthology, of only women.

When I moved to Nicaragua in the eighties, everything jumped still further ahead. There, women are not only exceedingly good poets in a country of poets, but they're among the leadership. Gioconda Belli today is in charge of the whole electoral process that's being shaped now. Daisy Zamora was for a long time vice-minister of Culture. Rosario Murillo is the secretary general of the ASTC, one of the most important cultural institutions in the country. Michele Najlis was the head of media control for the Ministry of the Interior and earlier the head of Immigration; it's out of her own choice that she has stepped down to work on *El nuevo diario* in order to devote more time to her own work. Vidaluz Meneses, another fine poet, is head of the country's library system.

Some of this difference can be explained by the fact that the Nicaraguans have had their revolution most recently, twenty years after the Cuban Revolution. And the most recent phase of the movement in the world against women's oppression was born and nurtured during these twenty years, and that change found expression in women's participation in the Nicaraguan Revolution and in the institutions that followed it. Here's a comparison: In Cuba Milagros González wrote a poem called "Diálogo primero." It's a strong feminist poem which is very critical of a certain kind of position that many men hold, in which they hide their sexism behind a revolutionary attitude. She charges her comrade with wearing "a red shadow in his pocket," a reference to his party card, while refusing to help clean the house. That poem raised havoc in Cuba; Milagros was called every name in the book for that poem. Some people tried to make trouble for Milagros, suggesting that she should lose her job, but the official reaction of the Cuban party was clearly in her defense. It was a big mess, but of course it came to nothing, and it's worth noting that that happened six or seven years ago, and I doubt that it could happen today. But in Nicaragua, Gioconda Belli wrote a poem called "We Want Our Men to Be" – it was published on the editorial page of *Barricada*. It's a much stronger feminist poem than Milagros's, and yet the poem was practically made the national anthem! Plenty of people in Nicaragua would have liked to make as big a stink about that poem, but they didn't dare.

One thing I have noticed about professional women writers in Cuba and Nicaragua is that when their work is strong, when they come into their own, they seem to concentrate much more courageously on the real problems people face. They are less concerned about current literary trends. They care less about promoting themselves. They are closer to the discovery of new literary forms through their content than through the experimentation of innovative play.

All of this is not to say that everything in Nicaragua is perfect, but to expect a revolutionary process to be perfect may be the greatest disservice you can do to that process. Some sectors of the Left here search for a perfect model of revolution, and they decide that Cuba or Nicaragua is *it,* but as soon as that country doesn't fit their preconceptions, the model is dropped and another is sought. Revolutions are made by human beings. Some are brilliant and innovative, some are good at jobs as long as someone tells them how to do it, some make little mistakes that can be corrected, and some make terrible mistakes. Revolutionary processes are enormously difficult and disruptive social changes which radically alter the lives of the people involved, and they also face obstacles from countries whose sphere of influence or control is involved. They must make changes under conditions of threat and even invasion, and this makes the revolutionaries defensive. And defensiveness prevents thinking things through with the care one might ordinarily be capable of. It's necessary to look at the particular situation of places like Cuba and Nicaragua closely, and crucial that we look as closely at our own. In the United States, we must begin with our own peculiar history and situation and devise approaches appropriate to it. It was hard to leave Nicaragua, especially in the middle of a war; but I am close to fifty, and I've been coming to a decision to devote myself to writing and photography in a way that I can do only here. I want to live in New Mexico near my parents, whom I've seen so little in these thirty years. My children are grown now. Gregory is married to a Uruguayan woman. They are currently studying in Europe. Sara is living in Cuba, almost finished with her degree in Chemical Engineering. Ximena and Anna lived with me in Nicaragua, but now Ximena is with Sergio, her father, going to the University in Mexico City in psychology, and Anna is in New York with her father. I need the space and time I've never had. I need to close myself off a bit, work harder, go deeper. And the greatest gift Nicaragua has given me is the courage to turn all I've learned there and in Cuba and before Cuba, all this stumbling, this literary, political, personal, public history, back on itself. In my particular case, I feel the most important thing I can do is *not* continue to participate in a daily struggle in places like Cuba and Nicaragua which have given me half my life, places I would feel unwhole without. My role is no longer to work there on a daily basis, but finally face the fact that I have something in me that is going to be useful to the world. I have to come home to create it. It's born of my roots in this country as well as of the vast life I've learned in Mexico, Cuba, Nicaragua, Peru, Vietnam, Venezuela, and Chile. I now feel I have the courage to attempt that.

11

An invitation to understanding among poor women of the Americas
The Color Purple and Hasta no verte Jesús mío

LISA DAVIS

We shall overcome. / Venceremos

At the outset of a conversation with Shug, which will range far afield to include the sex, color, and nature of a supernatural being roughly defined as God, Celie in *The Color Purple* (1982) protests that if this God, who seems to her as "trifling, forgitful and lowdown" as other men, "ever listened to poor colored women the world would be a different place."[1] Laying aside the thorny metaphysical problem of divine response to the plight of those here below, and particularly of those far removed from the seats of power and influence – as Albert admonishes Celie when she leaves for Memphis, "Look at you. You black, you pore, you ugly, you a woman. Goddam, he say, you nothing at all" (p. 187) – we recollect that, on an earthly plane, Alice Walker has listened from childhood to the voices of poor black women, her relatives and her neighbors, women often invisible, unknown, and beneath the consideration of the world of white or male consciousness.[2] It is no accident that she collects in *In Search of Our Mothers' Gardens* (1983), among other startling pieces, fragments of the writings of black women who taught in Headstart programs in Mississippi in the 1960s. Generally they describe with dignity and candor the savagery of the violent racist society they had lived in all their lives.[3] In the essay that lends its title to the collection, Alice Walker recalls listening to her mother's stories, the influence of that oral style on her own writing, and, as a motivating force throughout, "something of the urgency that involves the knowledge that her [mother's] stories – like her [mother's] life – must be recorded."[4]

In *The Color Purple,* Celie's liberating discourse grows out of Alice

224

Walker's convictions about being a spokeswoman for generations who could not speak for themselves. Although her story is not her own, Alice Walker's psychological and emotional proximity to Celie and her other characters stems from her childhood and achieves consciousness through her experiences as an active participant in the civil rights movement.[5] She previously contributed valuable works to the tradition of black women writers, now some decades old, in the United States, but as several recent anthologies and critical collections attest,[6] with *The Color Purple* she has expanded again the literary space where the voices of women like her mother can be heard in North American letters. Moreover, the wrenching portrait of Celie written in the character's own hand and style achieves a radical new intimacy and, we feel, authenticity.[7] Like the other characters in *The Color Purple,* Celie bears witness that such things, which Alice Walker must have seen and heard about as a child, did happen in the violent, rural segregated South of the 1940s and that she and other black women of her generation bore abuse from all sides and survived. The novel is an affirmation of Celie's right to be and of her survival as a poor black woman in a barbarous racist society where her enemies include whites and black men – just as when in answer to Albert she said, "I'm pore, I'm black, I may be ugly and can't cook, a voice say to everything listening. But I'm here" (p. 187).

It seems apparent that a similar desire to preserve the experience of poor women as a particular group among the oppressed, to make their voices heard and to record their survival, inspired the composition of the testimonial novel *Hasta no verte Jesús mío* (1969, Here's Looking at You, Jesus) by Elena Poniatowska, Mexico's most widely known living woman writer. This first-person narrative, which tells the story of Jesusa Palancares, a poor Mexican woman interviewed by Poniatowska over a period of more than two years, contains innumerable references to Jesusa's solitude from childhood and to the fact that no one talked to her, except occasionally to give her orders,[8] and she talked to no one. Recalling incidents from a life of constant hard work, Jesusa, who at ten or eleven had responsibility for the care of several small children relates: "I had no one to talk to but the children, because my only friend was my grinding stone. That's where I learned to keep to myself. I've only started to talk a little now that I'm an old woman" (pp. 55–6). That is to say that Jesusa has been freed to speak by the timely intervention of Elena Poniatowska, much as Alice Walker has served Celie and the other characters of *The Color Purple* as "author and medium."[9]

In this context, it seems more than coincidental that commentators on Poniatowska have chosen to define her not only as an author, "in the sense of an original and originating voice, but . . . [as] a medium, a recorder and transmitter of oral history,"[10] and her work as "an effort to give a voice to those who have none [. . .]: peasants, workers, members of the political opposition, women."[11] Of all Poniatowska's writings employing the interview technique and denouncing a plethora of social ills,[12] the extensive self-portrait of Jesusa Palancares that is *Hasta no verte Jesús mío* remains one of her most significant accomplishments, an early and notable example of the testimonial literature that has become in the past fifteen or so years an important genre in Latin American letters. In fact, the rise of testimonial literature in Latin America deserves comment in and of itself, but here for its relation to Poniatowska's career as a novelist and especially as the author of *Hasta no verte Jesús mío*. Since Miguel Barnet's early *Biografía de un cimarrón* (1968), we suggest that the composition of most testimonial literature in Latin America follows the pattern of the bourgeoisie joining its literacy skills to the historical impetus of the largely illiterate but politically active masses. In one sense the nature of this literature testifies to the enormous class differences that divide most Latin American countries, governed for centuries by elitist minorities, but in another sense it reflects on a literary level the potent new nationalism that cuts across class lines in revolutionary societies like Cuba and Nicaragua.[13] In the case of Poniatowska, the daughter of European emigrants, her contacts with Jesusa – poor, illiterate, but above all realistic and energetic, like the Mexican masses in general – obviously fed the author's personal sense of identification with her adopted country. Taking Jesusa as the prototype of the defiant woman of the people, Poniatowska reported that, after their interviews, "I was strengthened by everything I had not lived. What was growing or perhaps had been there for many years was my Mexican being, my becoming Mexican: feeling that Mexico was inside me and that it was the same as Jesusa's and that it would come out if I just opened the gate."[14] The article from which this statement is taken, which appeared in *Vuelta* (1978), though informative, was published at almost ten years' remove from the original appearance of the novel and does not explain completely how Poniatowska dealt with the material reluctantly provided her by Jesusa. It is significant that in the more recent work of individuals like Elizabeth Burgos Debray, *Me llamo Rigoberta Menchú* (*I, . . . Rigoberta Menchú*), the author deals more scientifically with the question of the authenticity of her text and how it was composed.[15] But in the field, Poniatowska, like Miguel Barnet in Cuba, was a pioneer and wrote when there were no models for comparison, so that although she may idealize her protagonist somewhat, emphasizing qualities dear to Poniatowska's own feminist aspirations ("I wanted to highlight the personal qualities of Jesusa that distinguish her from the traditional image of

Mexican women: her rebelliousness, her independence"),[16] we recognize in Jesusa as authentic a portrait of a poor working woman in Latin America as we are likely to get from any novelist in the near future. Illiterate like the great mass of the Latin American continent, she is nevertheless gifted with a dynamic and succulent vernacular, which Poniatowska faithfully records,[17] and the stories Jesusa tells – from her participation in the Mexican Revolution through her survival as an independent working woman to the present day – constitute the authentic history of a poor country with a chaotic past. In a special relationship of author to subject, Poniatowska has habitually turned the preparation afforded her by her class and background into a tool for the creation of a national history as told by the people who made it but whose lack of instruction and marginal situation had condemned them to centuries of silence.[18]

Obviously, the relationship of Alice Walker to her protagonist is more direct, and she is able to tell her own story, or at least the story of her mother's generation. Specifically, by virtue of the changes forced on a recalcitrant social order by the civil rights movement, which began some twenty years ago to demand basic human rights a century overdue, Alice Walker has been able to rise up and speak where her forebears were condemned to silence. In that regard, we feel at times in *The Color Purple* an optimism tending toward the utopian in the portrayal of human potential for growth, especially the flexibility of her characters' attitudes toward sexuality; Nettie's return with Celie's children and their remarkable reunion after so much hardship is a classical happy ending. Allowing for creative license and what we sense is a deep and positive desire to see prejudice and abuse overcome now, nevertheless very real political and social changes have made Celie's suffering no longer obligatory for all poor black women. In short, Alice Walker has seen doors open in her lifetime that will never be closed again. Nowhere is the relative strength of her political and economic position within the North American system more apparent than in contrast with the contemporary situation of the impoverished masses of Latin America – like Jesusa, as Poniatowska says, "millions of men and women who do not live, only survive."[19] In their case, civil rights protests and reformist efforts are most likely snuffed out by swift military repression. In too many countries eons of elitist minority rule, generally by violence, of economic exploitation, and of a nonexistent or repressive political system usually operating in collusion with foreign business interests have spawned a society without any functioning institutions open to changes of the magnitude necessary to secure for the majority of the population even the token trappings of citizenship in a supposedly modern republic. Although none of these inferences are new in regard to most of Latin America, Elena Poniatowska's career has been remarkable because of her determination to liberate broad segments of the Mexican population by telling their story, and with increasing intensity in the last few years. For that reason, despite class and cultural differences, the similarities in character, theme, and development have made the comparison of her first-person narrative based on the life of Jesusa Palancares with Alice Walker's re-creation of Celie's voice in *The Color Purple* both provocative and rewarding.

We consider both novels to be thoroughly typical of some of the most gifted writing about women being done in the Americas. Furthermore, when seen comparatively, the unsolicited parallels between the stories of Celie and Jesusa stike us as very revealing about the experiences of poor women north and south. Even in rather humorous details, they do not conform to the stereotyped notions of what women should do and be. Neither of them is particularly domestic: Celie says she "can't cook" (p. 187), and Jesusa recounts that "my sister-in-law used to beat me because I never learned how to throw tortillas . . . but the truth is I wasn't born to make tortillas and I never did" (pp. 28–9). Their maternal instincts languish since Celie's children are taken from her, and Jesusa's caring for other people's children leads her to the conclusion that "washing is hard work, but as I see it, it's harder looking after kids" (p. 280). On Celie's wedding day to Mr. _____ she spent the day "running from the oldest boy. He pick up a rock and laid my head open" (p. 21).

In a more serious vein, the stereotyped advantages of a woman's lot also elude them. They are not cared for, protected, graciously accompanied by loving husbands and children nor respected and admired by a community of their peers. On the contrary, the common note in the lives of Celie and Jesusa is abuse by men: Their husbands beat them as a matter of principle, and Celie's stepfather rapes her over a period of years while her mother is slowly dying in the next room. Jesusa's mother dies and leaves her to the care of a father who, though not abusive, is often absent seeking work. From the beginning, although Celie's world is poor in this world's goods, economic necessity plays a greater role in Jesusa's life, a sort of indirect comment on the grinding poverty of Latin America.[20] In that sense, the relentless obligation to work that falls on both heroines takes different forms: In Celie it becomes another form of sexist abuse, whereas Jesusa does not seem to look beyond economic survival; as she says toward the end of *Hasta no verte Jesús mío,* "And that's the only thing that matters, not being hungry" (p. 308). In brief, Celie wages her battles against sexism within her own small world, and the treatment of the public sphere speaks volumes about politics north and south. Jesusa is much more the political animal who has participated in a major revolutionary movement and preserves a keen interest in Mexican affairs despite her poverty within that system. Meanwhile, the isolation and help-lessness of blacks – without any political recourse in the racist, segre-gated South before the civil rights movement – have seldom been more poignantly portrayed. With scant notice accorded the larger world, which is at any rate out of reach, Alice Walker's politics here are more personal and sexual: Her main concern is the black woman and how to eliminate abuse within her own community. Jesusa's sexual politics also reflect very real abuses that have become thoroughly internalized and that will change with the future of Latin America, a model *machista* society where females have consistently been at the service of men for centuries. Therefore, although they share some experiences of poor women of color across geographic boundaries, the stories of Jesusa and Celie tend to highlight those facets of the struggle peculiar to north or south. We weigh here some of those parallels together with the dif-ferences we consider to be of great importance for the mutual under-standing of women of the Americas.

The full impact of the male-dominated society in which they will grow up to womanhood falls early on both Jesusa and Celie, who lose their mothers when they are still children. Jesusa is very small when her mother dies, and Poniatowska depicts the burial in all its pathetic poverty as the first incident in the novel: "My mother's funeral was as poor as the dirt they laid her in. They wrapped her up in a straw mat and I saw them throw her in and shovel earth on top of her just like that. I was standing next to my father, but he was busy talking to his friends and guzzling tequila so he didn't see me jump into the hole and put my dress over her head to keep the dirt from falling on her face" (p. 17). Subsequently, Jesusa often recalls the sadness and abandonment she ex-perienced at the graveside and during her father's absences, feelings that were indicative of her hard and lonely life.

Celie's relationship to and loss of her mother are more psychologically complicated and twisted because she is sexually abused as a child by her stepfather, whom she believes to be her real father. Weak from a long illness and too much childbearing, Celie's mother is never a refuge for her but someone for her to protect, even against a lustful husband, just as she will later protect her sister Nettie. In fact, the novel owes its epistol-ary form to Celie's determination that her mother will not know of her incestuous relations, which have already brought her two babies together with terrible guilt and shame: "*You better not never tell nobody but God. It'd kill your mammy*" (p. 11).[21] But her mother dies anyway, and Celie falls victim to the same abuse and hard labor in a loveless marriage.

Work is a universal reality for the poor. In Jesusa's case, the obligation to work came when she was about ten, under the tutelage of her stepmother, who cooked for the inmates of a prison: "There everybody works from four in the morning until seven or eight at night. . . . So I never had time to run off and play or sit around shooting the breeze. . . . It's been work, work, work, ever since I was a little girl" (pp. 35, 36–7). In that fashion she was perhaps best prepared for the rigorous, unrelenting life of work that was to follow when she hired out for an extraordinary variety of jobs to maintain herself alone after the death of her father and her husband in the revolution. Toward the end of Jesusa's life, she was still supporting herself, although painful inflammations from washing mountains of laundry and chronic rheumatism from washing floors plagued her: "My bones hurt so bad I can hardly pull myself up on the bus, but I never stopped working even when I was falling on my face" (p. 307). Although Jesusa displays great mobility and versatility, many of the harsh tasks she accepts are typical marginal occupations that do not require even the basic educational skills that she lacks.[22]

As for Celie, work becomes another form of sexist abuse when her stepfather recommends her at age twenty to Mr. _____ as a wife on the grounds that "she can work like a man" (p. 18); and Harpo, Mr. _____'s oldest boy, excuses himself from helping Celie with "women work. I'm a man" (p. 29). This seems to be a doctrine he learned at his father's knee, because Mr. _____ displays the same behavior: "He wake up while I'm in the field. I been chopping cotton three hours by time he come. [. . .] Mr. _____ pick up a hoe and start to chop. He chop bout three chops then he don't chop again" (p. 34). Nettie hates to leave Celie in such a situation – "Here with these rotten children. Not to mention Mr. _____. It's like seeing you buried"; Celie replies, "If I was buried, I wouldn't have to work" (p. 26). A life of brutalizing housework together with sundry hours in the fields does not, however, prove to be Celie's lot. She finds an aesthetically satisfying and rewarding occupation sewing custom-made pants and under her own label, "Folkspants, Unlimited" (p. 192). She achieves all this through Shug's intervention, who says initially that Celie needs pants for herself because "you do all the work around here. It's a scandless, the way you look out there plowing in a dress" (p. 136), and then supports her in the business.

Shug, in fact, resolves for Celie many problems, not least among them the frequent beatings Albert inflicted on her "cause she my wife. Plus, she stubborn. All women good for –" (p. 30). With the latter statement, all the men in these novels, north and south, would seem to be in agreement since wife beating is the one characteristic they all share. Accustomed to humiliation – "He beat me like he beat the children. [. . .] He say, Celie, git the belt. The children be outside the room peeking through the cracks. It all I can do not to cry. I make myself wood. I say to myself, Celie, you a tree" (p. 30) – Celie confesses her shame to Shug, who declares, "I won't leave until I know Albert won't even think about beating you" (p. 77). By contrast, in revolutionary Mexico, there is little support from the other women in Jesusa's company, who are themselves regularly and barbarously beaten. Married at fifteen to the seventeen-year-old Pedro Aguilar, Jesusa suffers daily physical abuse as a bride: "Pedro hit me whenever he felt like it, like all the other men in his company, who spoke to their wives through the snap of their whips" (p. 97). At some fifty years' remove, Jesusa remembers vividly the savagery of the beatings her young husband gave her, reminiscent of the earlier treatment of her stepmother: "He beat me until he had had his fill. I remember counting fifty blows from the side of his machete. . . . I was used to it from when my stepmother used to beat me when I was a child" (p. 98). At last, when she has had enough of Pedro's abuse, she pulls her pistol on him and, despite her history of silence, tells him off. "I don't know where I got all that nerve. Probably from desperation. I whipped out my gun and right away I could see how scared he was" (p. 99). It was a turning point in her development, and, as she explains it, from then on no one could take liberties with her. She grew stubborn and willful, and began consciously to defend herself: "That's how I was anyway, because even as a child I was very mean. That's how I was born, but up till then Pedro hadn't given me a chance to show my colors. I wised up thanks to our beloved Revolution" (p. 101).

Here and in many other references throughout her story, Jesusa at-tributes the formation of her resilient character, her courage and reck-lessness, her taste for freedom and wandering to her experience of the Mexican Revolution: "I was cured of fear when I joined up with my father" (p. 11). By the same token, despite her illiteracy and economic marginality, Jesusa consistently demonstrates concern for national issues together with an intimate knowledge of Mexican history – from Juárez's anticlericalism (pp. 208–9) to Lázaro Cárdenas, who despite other defects "always walked on his own two legs, even when he was President. . . . He's the only President I've seen sideways marching down the street" (p. 266). Among the principal figures of the revolutionary era, she calls Pancho Villa a bandit (p. 95) and finds Venustiano Carranza – "Old Goat Face" – reprehensible (p. 137), whereas she respects Madero and Zapata (p. 78).

Her appraisals of the Mexican Revolution are consistently negative: "If you ask me that whole war was a mistake, because the idea of everybody killing everybody else, fathers against sons, brothers against brothers, Carrancistas, Villistas and Zapatistas, was half-cocked to begin with: we were all one, all part of the same half-naked, half-starved, barefoot tribe"

(p. 94). "The Revolution hasn't changed things worth a damn. We're just hungrier, that's all" (p. 126). It is, nonetheless, apparent that Jesusa feels herself part of a tradition that is nationalistic if not political in an orthodox sense.[23] Often contradictory, Jesusa denies she has a country because she is poor – "if I had money, I'd be Mexican" (p. 218) – but her pride in Mexico often outweighs her class alienation. In the face of heretical theories of evolution, Jesusa has a healthy popular disregard for European rationalism: "Monkeys, ha! Maybe over in France they believe all that monkey business, but here in Mexico we're Christians, we're natural-born human beings and we have an open mind" (p. 308).

Indeed, one of the sharpest contrasts between the two novels emerges on this level of involvement with the public, or political, sphere. For example, in *The Color Purple,* an understated portrait of black isolation and powerlessness in rural racist Georgia in the 1940s emerges from Celie's narrative. Outside the limited sphere of the farm, which itself is not always hospitable to Celie, all contact with the larger world means contact with the white power structure, which enjoys complete authority and impunity. Throughout the novel, any sally into the larger world by the characters is greeted by white racism and a hermetically segregated society, for example, the lynching of Celie's real father because his business prospered (p. 160). Sofia receives a sentence of twelve years for striking the mayor, and when Mary Agnes goes to see the white warden – he is her uncle – to intercede for Sofia, he rapes her (p. 95). No one can protest. There are scattered references to segregation, all recorded with helpless acceptance, as in the case of Nettie bound for New York by train: "The beds come down out of the walls, over the tops of the seats, and are called berths. Only white people can ride in the beds and use the restaurant. And they have different toilets from colored" (p. 126). Whereas Sofia's sons go to fight in World War II, to places that are only names to her – "He ast me do I know which part they be station in? France, Germany or the Pacific. I don't know where none of that is so I say, Naw" (p. 231) – Eleanor Janes's white husband says "he want to fight but got to stay home and run his daddy's cotton gin. Army got to wear clothes" (p. 231).

Jesusa also comes from a racist society where she knows Indian blood is undesirable, as she relates in the case of one of her spiritual masters: "There are no pictures of Tomás Ramírez. He was just a little Indian, so who would take his picture?" (p. 251). Although Jesusa insists on the relative lightness of her skin – "[My sister] Petra was much darker than me. My face is tan, but I'm not dark. She was really dark, her body and her face" (p. 31) – sometimes the shades seem to deepen: "Why the hell should I get married? . . . José is very short, very very short with fat pushed-out lips, and black as night; with him so black and me so dark, a fine pair of tadpoles we would of made" (p. 266). Obviously, this discrimination in Mexico parallels the prejudice of hue and cast that the black people in *The Color Purple* have against each other, a prejudice that always favors the lighter tone. The African Tashi refuses to marry Adam because "she had seen the magazines we receive from home [. . .] and it was very clear to her that black people did not truly admire blackskinned black people like herself, and especially did not admire blackskinned black women" (p. 243). Shug, who is "black as my shoe" (p. 28), knows that Mary Agnes will be a success as a singer because "yellow like she is, stringy hair and cloudy eyes, the men'll be crazy about her" (p. 111). But Mary Agnes feels uneasy with this distinction when she asks Harpo, "Do you really love me, or just my color?" (p. 95).

As we have observed here, racial segregation as recorded in *The Color Purple* and the alienation it spawns find no contemporary parallel in Latin America for many reasons. One of them is the general *mestizo* quality of the population; the ratio of colored to white people was always much higher than in North America. These matters deserve more investigation than space permits here, but Alice Walker's own impressions of revolutionary Cuban society and the sense of integration she finds in its black citizens are indicative of a patriotism and unity in that part of the world that do not conform to the black nationalism or separatism in the United States during the 1960s.[24] Obviously, what emerged in the United States was a reaction to enforced separation. Once again, although Jesusa is apparently a citizen of some country despite extreme class divisions, Celie moves outside her family boundaries only at great risk, and her folks play no public role in the geographic space they inhabit. With a light touch and through the voice of a politically unconscious spokeswoman, Alice Walker has implied here a weight of suffering by exclusion and oppression for blacks in the United States that has been lifted only in her lifetime.[25]

As we implied earlier, whereas Jesusa's political identity is more viable than Celie's, in the realm of personal relationships Celie enjoys all the advantages. Indeed, in the case of Jesusa, we see how damaging an unrelieved *machista* milieu is to the development of a positive female image, whereas the healing potential of women loving and supporting each other becomes the determining factor in Celie's life. If we can take Jesusa at her word, the image she projects of her intimate relations is one of cold, unfeeling harshness, without a hint of affection or tenderness. She describes – with a kind of pride in his business-like efficiency and their lack of contact – lovemaking only with her husband, though she may have had other and better lovers: "I never took my trousers off, I just rolled them down when he was using me. . . . Nowadays I see them necking and smooching in the doorways and to me it's strange, because my husband never went in for all that song and dance. He had what it takes and he used it. Period" (p. 86). "[W]e never spoke. That's why I don't know what love is; I never had it. I never felt a thing, and neither did he" (p. 108). We suspect it is for this sort of mechanical association that she tries to compensate throughout her life by adopting children – always boys – and through passing friendships with women, which always dissolve over Jesusa's protests that she does not care and prefers to be alone: "I was very fond of Iselda Gutiérrez, Prisca's mama, and if she says hello to me on the street, I say good morning or good night, but not with the respect we use to have" (p. 306); "I don't have any friends: I never did and never want to" (p. 182). It seems apparent that her cynicism owes much to this loneliness, which she often denies: "Sad? I'm very happy living by myself. I bite and scratch myself, fall down and pick myself again up all by my lonesome. I'm very happy. I never liked living in company" (p. 295).

Celie's story ends very differently, with the return of Shug, Nettie, and their children: "And us so happy. Matter of fact, I think this the youngest us ever felt" (p. 251) – and the most united and contented, she might have added, now that happiness no longer seems "just a trick" (p. 229). Celie's first inkling that such a thing as happiness exists comes with Shug Avery, and their lesbian relationship provides the only love Celie has ever known except that for her sister Nettie. Under the influence of that love, Celie blossoms: "My hair is short and kinky because I don't straighten it anymore. Once Shug say she love it no need to" (p. 229). Alice Walker gives Celie a multitude of lesbian inclinations, and, indeed, she seems to fall in love at first sight with Shug's photograph. Though Shug is bisexual, Celie has no use for men: "Take off they pants, I say, and men look like frogs to me. No matter how you kiss 'em, as far as I'm concern, frogs is what they stay" (p. 224). Whether biological, psychological, or mystically inspired, Celie's lesbianism can only have been fostered by her stepfather's raping her: "I cry and cry and cry. Seem like it all come back to me, laying there in Shug arms. How it hurt and how much I was surprise" (pp. 108–9). Nor was Mr. _____ a particularly solicitous lover, "He never ast me nothing bout myself. He clam on top of me and fuck and fuck, even when my head bandaged. Nobody ever love me" (p. 109).

Admittedly, Shug Avery cuts the most attractive figure in *The Color Purple,* and on her character Walker has lavished all the admiration and love she has expressed in her essays for black women singers of the past, those few souls free to express themselves and to be paid for their art.[26]

Shug emerges as a primary role model of a liberated woman, but other women of that circle, especially the brave and defiant Sofia, also touch Celie's life and help her to define herself through rebellion: "What you do when you git mad? she ast. I think. I can't remember the last time I felt mad, I say. [. . .] This life soon be over, I say. Heaven last all ways. You ought to bash Mr. _____ head open, she say. Think about heaven later" (p. 47). These are the female voices and presences that support Celie in her transition from drudge to person, a person who can even share a friendship with Albert. He has modified his earlier macho pose and starts to help Celie with her sewing while they talk about their love and admiration for Shug: "Shug act more manly than most men. I mean she upright, honest. Speak her mind and the devil take the hindmost, he say. You know Shug will fight, he say. Just like Sofia. She bound to live her life and be herself no matter what. Mr. _____ think all this stuff men do. [. . .] What Shug got is womanly it seem like to me. Specially since she and Sofia the ones got it. Sofia and Shug not like men, he say, but they not like women either. You mean they not like you or me" (p. 236). In this casual exchange Alice Walker sets aside stereotyped roles and rules for what individuals are to feel and be, and offers a final and revolutionary word on love, life, and the meaning of it all.

Jesusa's position on sex falls outside the pale of liberation and tends not only toward antifeminism but also toward machismo. Though she has women friends, as mentioned above, and is herself an apparently independent woman, on occasion she shocks us by her identification with men or a male point of view to the detriment of women. While working in a clinic for prostitutes – "they were all poor; poor cheap streetwalkers that give themselves for whatever they can get" – her sympathies suddenly turn to the men they might infect – "the truth is I feel sorry for men, poor things" (p. 200). Moreover, she forgives her husband's numerous infidelities because he is powerless against the women who pursue him: "Later I realized it wasn't really his fault; he was only doing his job as a man, because women chased after him on purpose" (p. 104). Several passages testify to her distrust of other women: "They had told my husband I was the paymaster's mistress. Naturally it was a woman who told him – what would you expect? They're all the same: when they're not wiggling their ass they're wagging their tongue and stirring up rumors just to see whose life they can ruin with their talk" (p. 100). Following ancient lines of antifeminist arguments, her friend Lola also defends men, particularly her son, against indecent women, who in this case take the blame for young men's experimentation with homosexuality because "women nowadays are such pigs that a young man doesn't know where to put it" (p. 186).

Meanwhile, macho behavior outrages her rebellious nature: "Men always take advantage, as if that had anything to do with being a man. That's the sickness of Mexican men: they think they're so macho just because they climb on top of us" (p. 178). In that light, it is understandable that Jesusa feels at ease in the company of Manuel el Robachicos, "who had that weakness for stealing boys" (p. 184), and the transvestite Don Lucho — "Here in the house he dressed like a woman. . . . In the evening he dolled himself up to receive his friends. He put on his earrings, his necklace and his stockings, and as a woman he was very handsome. No, he didn't mind if we saw it — why should he? He felt like a woman" (p. 186). "Pansies are a lot better than machos. It's almost as if their misfortune of being half man and half woman makes them better people" (p. 186). Nevertheless, Jesusa's liberality does not extend to lesbians — "las manfloras [. . .] jotas [. . .] chancleras y tortilleras" (p. 261). There she draws the line in an uncharacteristic puritanical stance: "If they're so eager, why don't they find a man? According to history down through the centuries, that's the way it's meant to be. If it's a sin between a man and a woman, imagine when a man goes with a man or a woman with a woman. It's disgraceful." It is somewhat remarkable, however, that sexual matters are so frankly discussed in this novel, as they are in *The Color Purple*, a fact that attests to the often cited greater tolerance for open sexual discussion characteristic of the poor, who perhaps have too many real problems to indulge in the rather conventional hypocrisy of the bourgeoisie.

We do not wish to dismiss Jesusa's dilemma. On the contrary, we suggest it is complex and that its roots are determined socially by a system in which everything male is revered, and all things female are somehow inferior. We do not hold that these phenomena are unique to the Hispanic world, since we observe in *The Color Purple* that feminist solidarity is still a rare commodity; for example, an unenlightened Celie encourages Harpo to beat Sofia to make her mind (p. 43). In Jesusa's world, however, we do not find female models like those of *The Color Purple* who live in anything like a liberated fashion, and therefore she must pattern her life after that of men. In order to participate in the war, and later also, she dresses as a man — "Hardly any women went to battle. Pedro took me along without orders from General Espinoza y Cordoba. That's why I dressed like a man, so no one would report me" (p. 109) — and often goes drinking, her most flamboyant vice, and carousing with men, ostensibly without any sexual interest. Without male companions, life can be a dull affair, and there is little future in being a woman: "But if it was up to me, I'd rather be a man instead of a woman. Of course, because they have more fun. You're a lot freer as a man and nobody makes fun of you" (p. 186). Nonetheless, Jesusa is a woman living in a profoundly *machista* society and must have suffered constant frustration while always concerning herself with the needs and nature of generically more fortunate men. Although she may be left alone, her father, like other men, "was a man, so he had to fall in love" (p. 67). Likewise, decisive attitudes on her part take on a male guise – "well, if I had balls" (p. 137) – and at her best she feels she can teach men to be manly: "I'll show him how to be a man" (p. 225). Conversely, there seems to have been no model and no opportunity for Jesusa to find joy or satisfaction in being a woman.

In conclusion, the testimonies of Jesusa and Celie indicate that there is a unity of vision and experience in the lives of poor women of color across geographic boundaries, and that in their cases it is often difficult to distinguish oppression by sex from oppression by class, race, and economic status. They overlap imperceptibly. Thus Jesusa and Celie speak, we believe, to the interests of Third World women, working women, and poor women and against the separation of economic and political issues, for example, from the so-called women's question as advocated in more conservative feminist circles or even in leftist con-claves.[27] If, indeed, "black women writers manifest common approaches to the act of creating literature as a direct result of the specific political, social and economic experience they have been obliged to share,"[28] it seems significant to show that millions of women of color representing an entire continent to the south, impoverished and brutalized for centuries, have shared that experience with them. Elena Poniatowska and Alice Walker, as allies and voices for poor women, have made that shared experience palpable and recognizable.

Nevertheless, as the women they write about establish inevitable contacts, the issues we have cited will emerge and must be dealt with. As North American blacks grow increasingly aware of their political power, their consciousness may extend more and more to peoples engaged in struggle outside their national boundaries who share with them a history of poverty and abuse, but are confronting specific economic and political problems aggravated by centuries of neglect. By the same token, progressive governments in Latin America must recognize and resist *machista* theory and practice while laying the groundwork for greater sexual freedom. In that regard, there is no doubt that women's active participation in the military aspects of national liberation movements and defense in Central America and the Caribbean has made inconceivable their relegation to traditional roles and tasks, and this liberating trend will continue to gather strength.

As a result of these and other developments, we feel that many natural alliances among the oppressed of the Americas will prosper. It has been our purpose here to show that profound ties do, in fact, exist among what we see as authentic literary creations, like Celie, Shug, Sofia, and Jesusa. Separated by language and perhaps by a certain cultural heritage, but separated mainly by centuries of lies and abuse from their so-called masters, when these women one day meet they nevertheless will know that they have embarked for some time on the same struggle.

NOTES

1 Alice Walker, *The Color Purple* (New York: Washington Square Press, Pocket Books, 1982), p. 175. All page references to the novel are to this edition.

2 This definition of black women's existence, experience, and culture as being beneath consideration, invisible, unknown to the "real world" of white and/or male consciousness is from Barbara Smith's pioneering essay, "Toward a Black Feminist Criticism" (Brooklyn, N.Y.: Out and Out Books), 1982; reprinted in *Conditions: Two* (October 1977), n.p.

3 See Alice Walker, "But Yet and Still the Cotton Gin Kept on Working . . . ," in *In Search of Our Mothers' Gardens* (New York: Harcourt Brace Jovanovich, 1983), pp. 22–32.

4 Alice Walker, "In Search of Our Mothers' Gardens," in *In Search of Our Mothers' Gardens,* p. 240. She continues in a vein that also conforms to the historical depiction of Celie and her world: "It is probably for this reason that so much of what I have written is about characters whose counterparts in real life are so much older than I am" (p. 240).

5 For what the civil rights movement meant in Alice Walker's own life and her reflections on those matters see her novel *Meridian* (New York: Washington Square Press, Pocket Books, 1976) and, among others, the essay "The Civil Rights Movement: What Good Was It?" in *In Search of Our Mothers' Gardens,* pp. 119–29.

6 See, for example, Barbara Christian, *Black Women Novelists* (Westport, Conn.: Greenwood Press, 1980); Roseann P. Bell, Bettye J. Parker, and Beverly Guy-Sheftall, eds., *Sturdy Black Bridges* (Garden City, N.Y.: Anchor/Doubleday, 1979); and *Black Women Writers (1950–1980),* ed. Mari Evans Evans (Garden City, N.Y.: Anchor/Doubleday, 1984).

7 The citations from *The Color Purple* will give some idea of the quality of the language, which represents Alice Walker's most sustained effort to write in the vernacular of southern black people. Of necessity, many authentic gems, like "teenouncy" (p. 83), "newmonya" (p. 27) – for "pneumonia" – and my favorite, "Columbus come here in boats call the Neater, the Peter, and the Santomareater" (p. 19), will be lost, whereas the southern predilection for biblical authority is recalled by "You know what the bible say, the fruit don't fall too far from the tree" (p. 240).

8 "I always called my godmother 'senora,' and she always called me 'María de

Jesús.' She never said a word to me all day long, but at night she gave me her orders for the morning." Elena Poniatowska, *Hasta no verte, Jesús mío* (Mexico City: Era, 1975), p. 45. All page references are to this edition. English versions are from Magda Bogin's translation in progress, to be published by Pantheon as *Here's Looking at You, Jesus.*

9   See p. 253 of *The Color Purple* and also Walker's essay, "Writing *The Color Purple*," in *In Search of Our Mother's Gardens,* pp. 355–60.

10 Juan Bruce-Novoa, "Elena Poniatowska: The Feminist Origins of Commitment," *Women's Studies International Forum* 6, no. 5 (1983): 509.

11 Cynthia Steele, "La creatividad y el deseo en *Querido Diego, te abraza Quiela,* de Elena Poniatowska," *Hispamérica* (October, 1985): 1. The translations of these phrases are mine. I thank Professor Steele, of Ohio State University, for allowing me access to her unpublished work. I also thank Professor Bell Chevigny, SUNY-Purchase, for sharing with me her paper "The Transformation of Privilege in the Work of Elena Poniatowska" and Professor Norma Klahn of Columbia University for the loan of many invaluable materials on Poniatowska that are difficult to find in this country. Professor Jean Franco of Columbia University has been, as ever, generous with her knowledge and time.

12 Her most famous book in this genre is *La noche de Tlatelolco* (*Massacre in Mexico*), trans. Helen R. Lane (New York: Viking Press, 1971), which records the testimonies of hundreds of witnesses to and victims of the killing of striking students and their supporters at the Plaza de las Tres Culturas by the Mexican army on October 2, 1968.

13 See, for example, the recent testimony of Omar Cabezas, a participant in the FSLN's compaigns against Somoza, *La montaña es algo más que una inmensa estepa verde* (Managua: Editorial Nueva Nicaragua, 1982). Especially in regard to the condition of women, there is the testimony of Domitila Barrios de Chungara, with Moema Viezzer, *Si me permiten hablar . . .* (*Let me Speak! Testimony of Domitila, A Woman of the Bolivian Mines*), trans. Victoria Ortiz (New York: Monthly Review Press, 1979); and a recent first-person narrative from Guatemala by Elizabeth Burgos Debray, *Me llamo Rigoberta Menchú* (Havana: Premio Casa de las Américas, 1983), which was translated by Ann Wright, *I, . . . Rigoberta Menchú: An Indian Woman in Guatemala* (New York: Verso Editions/Schocken Books, 1984).

14 Elena Poniatowska, "Jesusa Palancares," *Vuelta,* no. 24 (November 1978): 8. Also see Poniatowska's comments on Jesusa and the composition of *Hasta no verte Jesús mío* in *La sartén por el mango,* ed. Patricia Elena González and Eliana Ortega (Río Piedras, Puerto Rico: Ediciones Huracán, 1984), pp. 155–62.

15 See the author's prologue to Rigoberta's story for her detailed description of the way the interviews were planned and carried out, the material organized, and the final manuscript arrived at.

16 Poniatowska, "Jesusa Palancares" p. 11.

17 In "Jesusa Palancares," Poniatowska relates her initial difficulties with Jesusa's language, and particularly her profanity; some of the words she had

to look up in a dictionary of Mexicanisms, and others were current in the Spanish of several centuries ago (p. 9). Among Jesusa's many wonderful succinct and expressive phrases are "I'd rather do without than put up with a husband" (p. 173) and the classics "A tame horse turns out mean and a good man turns out a jerk" (p. 53); "It's my asshole, I can fly a kite with it if I want" (p. 267); "If you're born to be a tamale, heaven sends you the corn leaves" (p. 269).

18   One of Poniatowska's more recent works is a series of chronicles that deal with aspects of the Mexican national experience not often spoken of – the student movement of 1968 and some of its sequels, the occupation of land by the dispossessed of Morelos, and the creation of the Colonia Rubén Jaramillo under the leadership of peasant militants. She entitles this book, significantly, *Fuerte es el silencio* (Mexico City: Era, 1980). Another book, *Domingo 7* (Mexico City: Ediciones Océano, 1982), gives space to representatives of various opposition political parties in Mexico.

19   Poniatowska, "Jesusa Palancares," p. 7.

20   Poniatowska stated on one occasion before a European audience: "Latin American women writers come from very poor countries, very forsaken countries. You have no idea how poor our countries are, you can't even imagine it. . . . Latin American poverty is one of indifference. There is no one to go to, no one to tell: 'I haven't eaten, it's been days since I've eaten because no one cares, it doesn't matter' " (*Eco,* no. 257 [March 1983]: 462).

21   Nettie reminds Celie in one of her letters, "I remember one time you said your life made you feel so ashamed you couldn't even talk about it to God, you had to write it, bad as you thought your writing was" (p. 122).

22   See Joel Hancock, "Elena Poniatowska's *Hasta no verte Jesús mío:* The Remaking of the Image of Woman," *Hispania* 66, no. 3 (1983): 354, for a listing of Jesusa's occupations.

23   Oscar Lewis has observed in his introduction to *La Vida* (New York: Vintage Books, 1966) that in Mexico even the poorest slum dwellers have a rich sense of the past and a deep identification with Mexican tradition, including the names and careers of national figures (p. xvii).

24   See Alice Walker's essay "My Father's Country Is the Poor," in *In Search of Our Mothers' Gardens,* pp. 199–222.

25   A review by Leon F. Litwack in the *New York Times Book Review* (September 16, 1984) of Joel Williamson's *The Crucible of Race* (New York: Oxford University Press, 1984) reminds us of the world segregation built: "The optimism with which blacks greeted emancipation and Reconstruction ended in disillusionment and in a steady disengagement from the white world. Mr. Williamson describes how that disengagement became lasting alienation. If some blacks found comfort in their own institutions and families, still others abandoned farms and families, schools and churches, to live by their wits on the fringes of society" (p. 12).

26   In *In Search of Our Mothers' Gardens,* see references to Billie Holiday and Bessie Smith, among others, in the essays "Zora Neale Hurston: A Caution-

ary Tale and a Partisan View" (pp. 83–92) and "In Search of Our Mothers' Gardens" (pp. 231–43).

27 See, for example, Leslie W. Rabine, "Searching for the Connections: Marx-ist-Feminists and Women's Studies," *Humanities in Society* 6, nos. 2 and 3 (1983): 195–222, and June Howard, "Toward a Marxist–Feminist Cultural Analysis," *Minnesota Review* 20 (Spring 1983): 77–92, for theoretical grapplings with similar issues.

28 Smith, "Toward a Black Feminist Criticism."

12

The other face of the phallus

LUISA VALENZUELA

"Hic sunt leones" used to be written on ancient maps when cartographers did not know what could be found in unexplored territories. "Lions are here," meaning the frightening, the unknown.

"Hic sunt leones" seems now to be written the length and breadth of the woman's body, and all over the body of her literary work. Woman, and especially that mythical nonentity called womanhood, has practically always been mapped by men. Ever since the beginning of time we have been told by men what to do with our bodies, and chiefly with that portion of our bodies so full of menaces, so much like the other, hidden part: the mouth. Speech was controlled and censored; not a word should ever be out of place. Why? Because there are lions ready to jump at the very first instigation, in that precise moment when words are not controlled anymore and truths can be uttered by means of our bodies, without our even being aware of them.

Those truths, or those statements, may be shattering. I will try to analyze why, and how. The most important reason for writing this essay is to try to break this barrier of censorship by recognizing it, to make it disappear in some magical way by naming it.

The inner lions are our own lions. We have been talked into the idea of being part of Mother Earth: the woman as the promised land or, better, as the *terra incognita*. And there we chose to stay, as The Mystery – even to ourselves – so as not to wake the sleeping lions, not to face all of a sudden the possible horror of our passions and our desires. It is mainly that: desires, desires that cannot be confessed, that would deprive us of the support of men – as if we really needed it.

But we have been colonized to believe we do and are still unsure about looking at our own sex – our own genitals – as if that were not also a form of language. It is, and women writers know it even if they do not usually express that notion clearly. Writers are meant for that: to look and then tell what they have seen. But that look is usually more interior than exterior, goes more toward the invisible than the visible, so when women have looked between their legs not to find the phallus, they have really seen much farther away, farther in and farther back. That is not easy to acknowledge; one has to become very visceral to recognize it.

(These ideas are difficult to elaborate. It is like trying to walk into a swamp or in quicksand. This is the land that has to be explored, and I am just trying to find my way into it, not even exploring for the sake of my own language but trying to do it in English, involving thus a completely different approach and a completely different ethical proposition, as we shall see.)

In the border of this unknown land there is a milestone. Like the milestones in ancient times, this one has a cylindrical shape, quite bulky. You have guessed it: it is the phallus, the symbolic phallus, the great signifier, as Jacques Lacan would put it. Lacan, however, has something to add that very few men have been able to read correctly. In his structuralist interpretation of Freud, he points out that the phallus as a signifier is really the place of an absence, for both women and men. The baby attributes the phallus to the mother – she is the great protector, the ever-powerful benefactor – and as the baby grows older and wiser, he or she realizes that Mama does not have the organ, and Father has only its fleshy and not very reliable representation.

So all of humanity revolves around that lack, but each sex, I think, is on a different side of the phallus, and women, to reinforce their position, have to reinvent or restructure their language – reorganize their territory.

Again the phallic milestone and the marshes. Women are on the uncharted face of the phallus, that which has not yet been named. Men are on the safe side, the "civilized" face, where each thing and each sentiment and each behavior has its own name. Women are forced to use these names and so, finally, express men's ideologies. But names are irreplaceable, so what we must enforce is our own compound (and the chemical reaction might be different), impose our own chemistry, inject estrogens in our writing. That is far from being a mild thing to do. It should be done with force and subversion – with fury if necessary.

I have found a special form of language that expresses this idea in many Latin American women writers. I have not yet found it in any woman writer of the United States. I do not know what is to be blamed: puritanical tradition or the way I respond only to my own roots. This feminine language, if we can call it such, this obscure discourse coming from the depths of the guts, can be defined as a *fascination with the disgust-*

ing: in Spanish, "un regodeo en el asco." It has to do with mud and very visceral feelings and perhaps unnamed menstrual blood and love for warm viscosities.

Love? Maybe not, but rather a profound recognition of that form of life, of creation, that can be found in putrefaction: acceptance of the rejection spoken about by Georges Bataille, profound recognition of the engendering power of putrefaction. This is something that appears from time to time in subtle ways, in writers as different as Elvira Orphée and Luisa Mercedes Levinson.

The paradox is expressed with greater clarity in the exultant writing of Alicia Dujovne Ortiz. Like Clarice Lispector, to whom I return below, Dujovne Ortiz knows that one must overcome the barriers of repulsion, overcome them even in love, in order to commune with strangers, as occurs to Jacinta, the protagonist of the novel *El buzón de la esquina* (The Corner Mailbox).

> Jacinta finally saw them – thick, gray, rolling in the pleasure of coolness. Ten or twelve slugs, gathering every night around the sink out in the yard. Slimy trails down the walls, the floor a web of silvery threads, they were so cold and flabby that Jacinta was afraid of them.
>
> With the same fear that she had for sea creatures, for the iguana-bellied trees. But something stronger than fear forced her to stay near the sink, brooding on herself. And what about me? Am I any slimier? Is there any hardness in me, a shell? And after all, why did these slugs appear? Is someone trying to tell me something? Something after all happened at random. Everything in her life, for one or another reason, appeared as a proof . . . of love? Love, these slugs like cold turds?
>
> One night Jacinta finally bent down, terrified, all gooseflesh, and forced herself to kiss the slugs. And the slugs, just as terrified by the appalling touch of those warm lips, slithered away.
>
> So Jacinta, moved and fulfilled like a saint who has kissed the lepers' sores, felt her heart fill with glory and licked her lips still wet from the slugs, relishing the taste of smooth nothingness.[1]

The devouring female? It might be true – the woman all mouth, as Margo Glantz says, ready to incorporate everything, absorb all in order to give birth, the outside and the inside becoming one in the womb of a woman. But South American writers, apparently, are writing this in search of knowledge. The body has to know the disgust, absorb it meaningfully, in order to say all its words. There can be no censorship through the mouth of a woman, so words can finally come out with all their strength, that same strength that has been obliterated from feminine speech ever since the notion of "lady" was invented by men.

"Lady" – such is G. H., the protagonist of that tremendous, disconcerting, and tense interior journey represented in Clarice Lispector's *A paixão segundo G. H.* (The Passion According to G. H.). G. H. symbolizes, in the opening pages of the book, the woman as object, a luxury object that does not know itself as such. Her only preoccupations are cocktails and, as the plot begins, keeping the maid's room clean. She heads there only to ascertain that everything is in order. Order is subverted by a monstrous eruption: a gigantic cockroach that peers through the half-open door of the closet. Lacking any sense of self-identity, recognizing herself only in the virtual anonymity of her own monogram (like a brand on a cow), G. H. decides to recover predictability and closes the door on the insect, squashing it. The cockroach does not die immediately; it palpitates in the white mass that flowers from its black shell. G. H. then begins the irreversible voyage into herself, the recognition of a life that exceeds her and that she, in turn, must accept and perhaps even incorporate into her own life: "And I knew that as long as I felt disgust, the world would run away from me and I would run away from the world."[2]

This acceptance of the disgusting can be a form of atonement, a form of cosmic knowledge. But that is not easy at all, so Clarice Lispector tells us in her novel, and so *The Passion According to G. H.* can be read as a metaphor of this, let us call it a *female* access to knowledge which might – who knows? – generate in the womb. Although it *sounds* natural, it is not an easy knowledge – not at all. The experience is always a frightening one, and we are always alone.

G. H. finally overcomes her disgust, her horror, and says:

> I didn't want to think about it but I knew. I was afraid to feel in my mouth what I was feeling. I was afraid to touch my lips with my fingers and find remnants. I was afraid to look at the cockroach – which by now should have less white mass over its dark back. . . .
>
> I was ashamed of having become vertiginous and unconscious in order to do what I could never again know how I had done – for before having done it I had put aside my own involvement. I hadn't wanted to *know*. (p. 198)

There are so many forms of communion, and in such cases we should recognize not only the fear, but also the *shame*. Lispector speaks a great deal about that shame; not all women writers are always so aware of it, but it still is a mirror that has been put in front of our eyes for many centuries, because, returning to Bataille:

> The generative power of corruption is a naive belief responding to the mingled horror and fascination aroused in us by decay. This belief is behind a belief we once held about nature as something wicked and shameful: decay summed up the world we sprung from and return to, and horror and shame were attached both to our birth and to our death.[3]

Woman knows these truths and assumes the shame. She desacralizes them when she can, when they are not imposed on her from the outside as in the rites of purification that follow the first flow of menstrual blood of certain African and Amazonian tribes. It is no longer the shame of repugnance – shame is simply a form of fear of what is threatening – but the extraction of knowledge that can arise from repugnance, from the visceral.

Consequently, at times, many Latin American women writers can speak through Clarice Lispector: "The completion of a book is always something painful. An anguishing process. Once the suffering is over, or rather the birthing is done, I want the book to get out of here and take care of itself. I am like a very animal mother, the books are my cubs. I forget about them very quickly."[4]

This metaphor of the culmination of writing as a childbirth would horrify more than one North American woman writer. In her essay titled "Creativity vs. Generativity: The Unexamined Lie," Erica Jong discusses the possibility of the literary "birth" and exclaims, "How much more passive pregnancy is than creativity! Creativity demands conscious, active will; pregnancy only demands the absence of ill-will." She proposes that the metaphor of literary pregnancy is masculine, identifying, to be sure, with a false dichotomy enforced on women: "All my life I had mistrusted my body and overlooked my mind."[5]

The birth of her daughter changed her mind, gave her a more complete view of her body; but it was a body separated from her mind, distanced from all the viscosity and viscerality it engenders. This is why it is no longer a matter – and I believe that this is typical of literature written by women in the United States – of incorporating the repugnant as an act of love or accession to consciousness, but of investing what is consumed with repugnance. Is this the other side of the same coin?

In *Fear of Flying* Erica Jong finds her own voice and expresses with courage her inner contradiction. Her eating becomes, too, a rite of passage, a recognition of womanhood; but it is of a completely different nature, and Isadora, the protagonist, says about her adolescence:

Eustace Chesser, MD, was good on all the fascinating details ("How to Manage the Sex Act," penetration, foreplay, after-glow), but he didn't have much to say about *my* moral dilemmas: how "far" to go? inside the bra or outside? inside the pants or outside? inside the mouth or outside? when to swallow, if ever. It was all so complicated. And it seemed so much more complicated for *women*. Basically, I think I was furious with my mother for not teaching me how to be a woman, for not teaching me how to make peace between the raging hunger of my cunt and the hunger in my head.[6]

This dichotomy has no reason to exist where woman's language has not been censored, or where it has succeeded in eluding such censorship. As for proscribed food, gastronomic transgressions – which are so related to the word, which *are* the word inside out, traversing the orifice of the mouth and mobilizing the tongue – puritanism inherited or acquired has limited the exchange, barring accession to the world of miasmas, the world of the unconscious where the elements of decomposition become a rich fertilizer.

Only Maxine Hong Kingston, perhaps because her wisdom comes from the Orient, recognizes these almost alchemical possibilities of mutation. In her novel *The Woman Warrior* she avers, "Now I see that my mother won in ghost battle because she can eat anything – quick, pluck out the carp's eyes, one for Mother and one for Father. All heroes are bold towards food."[7]

Heroes and heroines must sometimes be very careful if they wish to avoid losing face. In this land of scales and prescriptions, Erica Jong in *Fear of Flying* reveals the unexpected dangers:

> I remembered a diet column in a medical journal of Bennett's. It seemed that Miss X had been on a strict diet of 600 calories a day for weeks and weeks and was still unable to lose weight. At first her puzzled doctor thought she was cheating, so he had her make careful lists of everything she ate. She didn't seem to be cheating. "Are you sure you have listed absolutely every mouthful you ate?" he asked. "Mouthful?" she asked. "Yes," the doctor said sternly. "I didn't realize that had calories," she said.
>
> Well, the upshot, of course (with pun intended) was that she was a prostitute swallowing at least ten to fifteen mouthfuls of ejaculate a day and the calories in just one good-sized spurt were enough to get her thrown out of Weight Watchers forever. What was the calorie count? I can't remember. But ten to fifteen

ejaculations turned out to be the equivalent of a seven-course meal at the Tour d'Argent, though, of course, they paid you to eat instead of you paying them. Poor people starving from lack of protein all over the world. If only they knew! The cure for starvation for India and the cure for the overpopulation – both in one big swallow! One swallow doesn't make a summer, but it makes a pretty damn good nightcap. (286–7)

Perhaps, after all, they are not conveying such different ideas, Latin American women writers and those of the United States. It must be the same swallow, after all, the same animal metaphor and the gulping, this incorporation of the semen – which is at the same time life in its different aspects. Viscosities, the unknown, but nourishing, in all senses.

It is not the raw product we will finally spit out but its digested symbol. Women's discourse, thanks to a digestion of all eatables, will avoid not only its own inner censorship but the outer one, which signaled women as disgusting and viscous. Through acceptance, recognition, and reelaboration, women's language will not be held anymore in the outer, swampy, and uncharted side of the symbolic phallus created by men's imagery. Women's language will earn a place in the phallus as a signifier, conquer its other face, which will then be spelled P-H-A-S-E. Perhaps then it will not be so phallic; it will become more related to the moon, symbolizing thus both men's and women's speech.

NOTES

1 Alicia Dujovne Ortiz, *El buzón de la esquina* (Buenos Aires: Calicanto, 1977), p. 63. This passage was translated especially by Alistair Reid.
2 Clarice Lispector, *La pasión según G. H.* (Caracas: Monte Avila, 1969), p. 195. All subsequent page references to this edition will appear in the text.
3 Georges Bataille, *Death and Sexuality,* trans. anonymous (New York: Ballantine, 1969), p. 50.
4 Interview by Santiago Kovadloff in *Brasil Cultura* (Buenos Aires: Publicacion de la Embajada), 1977, p. 27.
5 *New Republic,* January 13, 1979, p. 27.
6 Erica Jong, *Fear of Flying* (New York: New American Library, 1974), pp. 153–4. All subsequent references will appear in the text.
7 Maxine Hong Kingston, *The Woman Warrior* (New York: Vintage, 1977), p. 104.

13

Plotting women
Popular narratives for women in the United States and in Latin America

JEAN FRANCO

Mass culture has frequently been explained as a conspiracy to manipulate. The reason for this is not hard to understand. In the commercial development of radio, television, and popular literature in the United States and Latin America (which was distinct from their overtly propagandist use in Nazi Germany, for example), the claim was made that they were a response to what people wanted even though it was obvious that they were also creating new needs. Particularly in the case of radio and television this innocent appeal to the market was reinforced by the apparent neutrality of the technology, which was developed in advance of any particular content. As Raymond Williams has pointed out, radio and television "were systems primarily devised for transmission and reception as abstract processes, with little or no definition of preceding content."[1] In Third World countries, however, where new mass communications technologies brought in their wake a grotesquely maladjusted transnational culture, the possibility that mass culture was covert propaganda for consumer culture was more clearly appreciated. For example, Herbert Schiller's well-known study, *Mass Communications and American Empire,* detailed the way in which the U.S. technological superiority in the new media inevitably put into corporate hands the ability to disseminate values.[2] The term "cultural imperialism" was coined in the 1960s to describe this process, and studies began to appear that showed how even the most innocent forms of mass culture – Disney comics, women's magazines, and "Sesame Street" – covertly promoted individualism, capitalist enterprise, or simply alien traditions.[3] That the export of these values represented a corporate conspiracy was widely canvassed[4] and, indeed, gained credibility after the war of the media and the overthrow of Allende in Chile. Even so, conspiracy and manipulation theories of modern mass culture have tended to fall out of favor, first because of their elitist assumptions about reader or viewer reception and second because they failed to account for the appeal of the "alien" products and the fact that, in certain contexts, "alien" values could be used to resist or subvert authority. It is also increasingly clear that there is no such thing as a monolithic mass culture but, rather, widely varied forms of representation, discourse, and modes of address, which constitute quite distinct organizations of fantasy and experience within the dominant culture.

At the same time, the exportability of mass culture (and particularly U.S. mass culture) is a factor of major importance in contemporary Latin American societies. In the first place, it provides a common cultural repertoire that crosses national boundaries and thus tends, superficially at least, to blur the local idiosyncracies on which the idea of national character formerly depended. Second, most mass culture forms use formulas that can readily be adjusted to local circumstances. Third, as I shall point out in this comparison between women's popular romance in the United States and Mexico, mass culture has clearly a didactic function and operates as a socializing system that is now as powerful as schooling and religion, though its methods are vastly different from the methods of these institutions.

The use of formulas – that is, ready-made plots and ready-to-hand symbols – is both a major feature of mass culture and the target of most of the critical attacks from academics and high-culture critics. Theodore Adorno's analysis of jazz (by which he meant popular American music) was prototypical in this respect.[5] More recently, the attacks have tended to isolate the "closed narratives" that are characteristic of nineteenth-century "classical realism" as well as of modern mass literature, in which plotting toward a felicitous conclusion (and therefore a closure of meaning) is the major structural device, producing functional characters, situations, and descriptions. Although there are many subgenres of formula literature both in the United States and in Latin America, women's literature seems to have attracted the most attention because of its overwhelming popularity, on the one hand, and its repetitive poverty of form, on the other.[6] These critical speculations range from the denunciation of mass literature for women as degraded to claims that the audience "reads" in a way that is different from, though not necessarily inferior to, the reading of the "high-culture" audience.[7] In the following investigation, I shall be concerned primarily with what Peter Brooks calls "reading for the plot," and I shall deliberately play with all the ambiguities of the term "plotting" in English, some of which Brooks himself points out. Brooks, however, is concerned primarily with the narrative plotting of "great books," whereas my concern is also with plotting in the conspiratorial sense, for this is the crucial point where politics and fiction intersect.[8] It is no accident that Brooks devotes a whole chapter of his book to Freud and that much of the vocabulary is drawn from psychoanalysis. Especially in recent years, Freud has been of considerably more interest to literary critics, feminists, and those interested in the social constitution of gender differences than to psychologists. Feminists, in particular, have found in Freud and Lacan the outline of a course of human development that accounts for gender differences and, in particular, for the devaluation of women. Here we have another kind of plotting, one that maps out women's path in the human community and particularly in one of its major institutions – the family. The study of popular fiction in the United States and Mexico makes abundantly clear not only that the plotting of women into gender roles takes on new forms when they are considered both as consumers and as reproducers of the labor force but also that the international division of labor between privileged industrialized societies and Third World societies affects the way that corporate society regulates its fictions of the subject and of socialization.

I refer to corporate society because the mass culture with which I am dealing is primarily a corporate product and thus differs radically from individual or artisan production, which, however, corporations protect selectively through patronage. The propagandist arm of corporate society is advertising, the most ubiquitous and insistent of contemporary cultural forms and one that has, in crucial ways, formed new cultural paradigms. Advertising has constituted a totally new kind of imaginary repertoire, one that recycles all the imaginary repertoires of the past.[9] Advertising's anonymity, its use of images drawn from art, religion, patriotism, its exploitation of psychological needs, its evocation of the magic of the marketplace tend to obscure the close links (explicit in Spanish) between advertising and propaganda. As Judith Williamson has pointed out, advertising traps us in the illusion of choice. "Freedom" is, in fact, part of the most basic ideology, the very substructure of advertising. Outside the structure of advertisements themselves, it forms the fundamental argument always used to justify advertising: that it is part of the freedom of manufacturers to compete and part of our freedom to choose between the products of that competition.[10] The referent of the advertisement is the commodity sign, that is, the commodity as a sign of social distinction and discrimination and as a sign of cohesion between different groups of consumers. In similar fashion, comic strips, television shows, and radio programs carve out sectors of consumption, creating serialized communities of readers or viewers that sometimes depend on existing groupings along racial, sexual, or class lines but more often cut across them.[11]

The culture thus constituted no longer corresponds to the agrarian or industrial work cycles, to the biological span of human life, or to geographic communities. Nor does it rest on the legitimized authority of God or nation-state but rather on the apparently natural law of the marketplace. Thus, even though in the modern world people are still addressed as religious subjects (as Christians, Moslems, Jews) and as citizens (as Frenchmen or Romanians), the voice of advertising speaks to us primarily as "desiring machines," encouraging us to plug into whatever aesthetic or libidinal satisfaction is at hand. Advertising thus interpellates its subjects as no ideology has ever done before – as free subjects who appear to be unsubjected, who choose freely what they are to enjoy and to be without having to feel any special local loyalties or personal ties.[12] Perhaps the most innovative aspect of advertising, however, is its deployment of the imaginary repertoire of all previous cultures. In medieval Europe, people's cultural needs were satisfied by a single image in the local church, by sermons or histories of saints and feast days. In the nineteenth century, the intelligentsia read and reread the comparatively small number of great books (the Bible, *Paradise Lost, Don Quixote,* Greek and Latin classics), and they could appreciate the art of other countries only exceptionally by visiting museums or looking at engraved reproductions. In contrast, any individual today can dip into an immense archive of literature, religious beliefs, films, photographs, dance and can be transported rapidly to once exotic sites. Chinese art, Indonesian poetry, Brazilian music are readily available, giving the impression of an inexhaustible cornucopia. It is precisely this flexibility of modern culture that makes it impossible to speak of "a" dominant ideology or "a" message that it transmits. At the same time, the plurality of its deployment never adds up to "contradiction" and therefore does not produce new awareness or self-consciousness.

In fact, women's popular fiction in North and Latin America offers a guarded response to advertisement's appeal to perpetual indulgence. In contrast to advertising, its techniques and its barely disguised didacticism seem archaic. In North America, series such as Harlequin romances pave the road to wealth with all the snares and pitfalls of Christian's road to paradise in *The Pilgrim's Progress.* In the Mexican genres I have studied, the ethics are Victorian, and the novels plot women (and men) into lives of hard work and sacrifice. What has made mass literature of interest to critics (particularly feminists), however, is not its repetitive and anachronistic form but its popularity. Ann Barr Snitow, for instance, mentions the colossal sales figures of Harlequins and popular romances in the United States and justifies her study of books that are not art but "leisure activities that take the place of art," on the grounds that "it would be at best grossly incurious, and at worse sadly limited, for literary critics to ignore a genre that millions and millions of women read voraciously."[13] Janice Radway, in an important study of romance literature, illustrates how the corporate takeover of publishing encouraged the promotion of what she calls "category literature." Corporate publishers "believe it is easier to introduce a new author by fitting his or her work into a pre-viously formalized chain of communication than to establish its unique-ness by locating a special audience for it. The trend has proven so power-ful, in fact, that as of 1980, 40 to 50 percent of nearly every house's monthly releases were paperback originals."[14]

In their efforts to find reasons for these large sales, many feminist critics have turned to psychological explanations. Ann Barr Snitow, for instance, argues that these romances "feed certain regressive elements of female experience,"[15] but is reluctant to come down from the fence and either condemn or celebrate them: "To observe that they express prima-ry structures of our social relations is not to claim either a cathartic usefulness for them or a dangerous power to keep women in their place." Rosalind Coward, writing on romance as an expression of women's desire, believes that such fiction "restores the childhood world of sexual relations and suppresses criticism of the inadequacy of men, the suffoca-tion of the family, or the damage inflicted by patriarchal power. Yet it simultaneously manages to avoid the guilt and fear which might come from that childhood world. Sexuality is defined firmly as the father's responsibility and fear of suffocation is overcome because women achieve a sort of power in the romantic fiction."[16] Thus, for Coward, women pay a high price for fictional power and enjoyment – a price that involves evading the pain of self-assertion by remaining perpetual chil-dren. Furthermore, any power that the heroine or reader is likely to attain, according to Coward's interpretation, has little effect on the larger structures of authority that determine the heroine's path to the paradise of consumption. In fact, most feminist critics want to have their cake and eat it, want to show that the formula is restrictive, yet want to find that it offers space for resistance. For instance, in an illuminating analysis that owes much to Freudian criticism, Tania Modleski suggests that the very tightness of the plot indicates the scope of women's resentment, which can be controlled only by making the heroine perform a "disappearing act."[17] The reader, for her part, is forced into a kind of schizoid reaction, being the surveyer of the heroine while also being invited to identify with her and hence to be the surveyed. Modleski argues that, far from

achieving undiluted escape, the reader experiences a compulsion to repeat the reading because there is no real-life resolution of these contradictory feelings.[18] Though Janice Radway criticizes such literary readings of
romance in her book *Reading the Romance* and tries to correct them by
showing how the romances are read and evaluated by real readers, her
conclusions bear out some of Modleski's assertions. Radway's readers
invariably stressed enjoyment of repeated readings, their need for escape
from family and daily routine, and their preference for the kind of romance in which satisfactory characters and resolutions remove the anxieties and enigmas posed by the plot. In short, what we discover in recent
criticism in the United States is the tendency not to blame the reader and
to stress women's active participation in reading. Yet, in a way, rescuing
the reader is not the point. Mass culture offers a map for integration into
the system but does not imply social integration, that is, necessary com-
pliance with corporate ideologies.[19] This is a point to which I shall return
later.

Any analysis of popular fiction for women must focus on the formulas
and particulary on the plotting, which, as Peter Brooks notes, is inevitably bound up with questions of time-boundedness, with plot as "the
internal logic of the discourse of mortality."[20] Because, however, popular literature depends on repeated schemata, it would seem to be very
different from the sophisticated plotting discussed by Brooks and to have
more in common with archaic oral storytelling, which depended on
repetition and other mnemonic devices. The classic study of the fairy tale
is Vladimir Propp's discussion of the morphology of the Russian fairy
tale in which he showed how a comparatively small number of narrative
functions could result in a large variety of surface realizations.[21] However-
er, it is important to stress that the fairy tales on which Propp drew
emerged within an orally transmitted culture and were related within the
context of community rituals and practices. Modern romance formulas,
in contrast, have been devised on the basis of market studies that are
targeted to particular sectors of the population and meet well-tested
needs. Moreover, they are addressed to a serialized community, which
means that they are generally read in isolation by women who thus seek
to make a private space in the midst of the demands of the family and
everyday life. The formulas, in both cases, provide a temporal framework that encourages a reading for the plot even though the outcome can
easily be anticipated. Yet as investigations of the Harlequin romances
have shown (and this is probably also true of orally transmitted tales),
readers or listeners identify with particular characters and are not concerned with underlying similarities to other novels.

As Borges demonstrates in his short story "Death and the Compass," formula plots are more interesting than might at first be supposed, both because they play on never-satisfied desires for solution (and death) and because they link reading and writing to plotting, treachery, and conspiracy.[22] In Borges's story, the reader's plot is worked out by Lonnrot, who reads a series of clues according to his own prejudices and comes up with a neat solution, which, unfortunately, turns out to be a trap devised by his enemy, Red Scharlach. Scharlach's plot is more ingenious because it depends on knowledge of Lonnrot's prejudices and also on the use of accidental and random elements. This story is an interesting contrast to the split mind of women's popular fiction (particularly Harlequin romances) since it suggests both the naive anxiety for a felicitous solution and the hidden resentment that powers the vengeful "author," Red Scharlach, in his bid to thwart this solution. What makes Borges's story pertinent to the study of Harlequins and other formula literature is that it suggests that the reader's plot and the author's plot do not necessarily coincide and that the latter has a distinct advantage in what is an unequal power relationship. Comparison between Borges's fiction and women's popular fiction may seem strange; yet it reveals two contrasting aspects of double plotting designed to lift the reader out of everyday life.

"Death and the Compass" is a microdemonstration of the exercise of knowledge and power: There is the reader's knowledge that structures the first plot out of the expectation of repetition, and there is the "second" plot, which can be anticipated neither by knowledge drawn from experience nor from knowledge drawn from other plots because it uses the random and the fortuitous. This is the modern plot par excellence.

On a less sophisticated level, both Harlequins and Mexican *libros semanales* (i.e., weekly comic-strip books) also present a manifest reader's plot and an authorial plot. The first can be described as a plot that incorporates elements from everyday experience, such as resentment and violence; the authorial plot resolves these tensions in a publicly acceptable form, so that plot resolution is not intended to thwart the reader's expectations but rather to suggest forms of system incorporation that not only allow women a social role but also promise social recognition. The brevity of this essay obliges me to select a single example of the Harlequins for discussion even though this appears to privilege one instance of a repetitive plot structure. Fortunately, other critics (e.g., Janice Radway) have read exhaustively in order to isolate the invariable elements. I shall therefore concentrate on one popular Harlequin, *Moonwitch* by Ann Mather. I choose this example because it explicitly plots women into corporate society.

Sara, the heroine of *Moonwitch,* has a humble background. She is an orphan, brought up by a grandfather who, on his deathbed, bequeaths her to the Kyle Textile Corporation, believing this to be controlled by his old friend J. K. In fact, the corporation has been taken over by J. K.'s son Jarrod, and the father is living in retirement in the Kyle manor house. Despite his misgivings, Jarrod accepts Sara as his ward but turns her over to J. K., who becomes her companion and guides her through the unfamiliar social world she has now entered. It is no accident that this social world is represented by the manorial space of the Kyle house, for this is the anachronistic space of patriarchy that is based on a feudal master-slave relationship. Sara's training is essentially a programming into corporate society. At the same time, she faces the typical double binds of the Harlequin heroine – that is, she is seductive and yet cannot afford to give in when Jarrod attempts to seduce her.

It should be stressed that, although the sexual encounters in such books as the Candlelight Ecstasy romances are often more titillating and "modern," the archaic formula of postponement of pleasure used by the Harlequin is still a powerful attraction to women readers all over the world. Thus, though prevented from responding sexually before marriage, Sara appears in seductive situations (half-naked on a beach in Jamaica), and it is always she, rather than the male, who must exercise self-control in order to reach the final goal of marriage. Furthermore, though she will attain upward mobility through marriage, she is not allowed to be ambitious for money. Indeed, Jarrod treats her badly as long as he believes her to be seducing him for his wealth. This double bind is transcended only when the patriarch J. K. dies, leaving Sara his valuable porcelain collection. Overcome by grief, she spurns the collection, thus proving that she is not simply after money. Disinterestedness is the shortest road to wealth for the Harlequin heroine.

The function of the Harlequin plot is twofold. In the first place, it reproduces anxiety situations that are insoluble, but this insoluble plot is then overcoded by a second plot – that is, the plot we read in the light of the successful outcome. The two plots center mainly on the hero's character, which in the first plot is enigmatic and hostile, just as adult society is enigmatic and hostile to most women, who are forced to learn how to behave by trial and error. This hostility is likely to cause resentment. The second plot ensures that we read the story in order to correct any misunderstanding as to the hero's character. The corporate hero is, in reality, benign and considerate and when successfully "read" will lift the heroine up to her proper place as reproducer of consumer society. This clearly suggests that anxiety is an essential element in consumer society and shows how women are taught to use the tactics of the weak – seduction – in order to negotiate a modest place in a society whose rules they have not made and from which they are initially estranged.

As Tania Modleski points out, the first plot is presented as an incorrect reading, that is, the misunderstanding of the hero's true character.[23] Thanks to the ending and the marriage contract, this misunderstanding can be corrected. Thus the marriage contract is itself of dual significance since it recognizes that the heroine is worthy to take her "true" place in society, while showing that this acceptance must come from outside, from the patriarchal order itself. Misreading marks women's accession to the symbolic order; that is to say, misrecognition is a basic part of their training. Men are repressive, cruel, and powerful, and the only way to get by is to learn what society says women "truly" want. What is unpleasant and even unnatural can be tamed by the right tactics. Thus the second plot maps the paths that allow the first plot to be controlled. The powerful male figure has to be "reread" not as an oppressive tyrant but as a master of social rules that the heroine must learn, just as the hero has to learn to soften his will to power. At the same time, Harlequins exploit the preconstructed expectations that stem from the reader's experience of unequal gender relations in order to negotiate a more satisfactory contract with corporate consumerism. However, it is a contract that one can negotiate only by falling back on the tactics of the weak – that is, on seduction rather than outright confrontation.

If women's popular fiction offers an oddly hedged response to self-indulgence in the United States, this hedging is even more apparent in literature produced in societies of scarcity. Mexico is particularly interesting as a vantage point from which to monitor this literature, both because it is a major producer of "photonovels" and other types of popular fiction and because the productions of corporate Mexico conflict in significant ways with an older nationalist ideology.

The *libro semanal* draws on material from the sensational press and thus implicitly acknowledges the prevalence of violence in everyday life, a violence that cannot be avoided by devising romantic plot structures. This does not mean, however, that the novels confront violence directly; rather they use it to attract the reader and then overlay an explicit moral that prompts the correct reading of such events. In this respect, the *libro semanal* is akin to the religious story in which the random persecutions and events of a holy person's life are reinterpreted by the voice of God. When this kind of utterance is deployed in a secular discourse, it produces a narrative problem, for there is no universal system of belief that will give unquestioned authority to the moral. This moral voice strives to achieve the status of an aphorism or *doxa* but lacks the power of religion. Nor does it necessarily conform to state ideology, for this overt message not only is frequently out of line with the events of the story but introduces values that have little in common with the nationalist ideology that has, for so long, dominated the discourses of postrevolutionary Mexico.

It is perhaps hardly necessary to recall the fact that in Mexico the revolution had constituted the semantic axis around which social meanings were transmitted and understood and in relation to which sexual, racial, and class categories had been defined. The power of the state to monopolize the production of meaning has now been severely challenged, however, not only by the criticism of the intelligentsia seeking to widen the democratic basis of society but also by the alternative meanings that were increasingly available in mass culture productions. As early as the 1940s, U.S. advertising firms and U.S. paperback books and magazines such as *Selecciones de Reader's Digest* had begun to attract the interest of certain sectors of the public. Though the government was able to control films (even censoring government-subsidized films like *Las abandonadas* when sectors such as the military were offended) and to place indirect pressure on publishers, there was plainly a growing gulf between the ideal image of Mexico and people's everyday life culture and practices. This became painfully apparent in the 1960s, both in the use of force in the 1968 massacre of students at Tlatelolco and in the *Children of Sánchez* scandal. Though the methods and conclusion of Oscar Lewis, the compiler of *The Children of Sánchez,* are open to criticism, the government's attempted censorship of the Spanish version was an index of the wide difference that had opened up between the government's image of the Mexican and everyday reality. Lewis presents a family many members of which aspire vainly to individual realization and who are not at all spurred on by revolutionary collectivism.[24] They are torn by jealousy and rivalry and dominated by a father who withholds affection but not punishment, leaving his children with an unsatisfied craving for paternal recognition. This was the Mexico into which television was introduced in 1950.

The trend away from the reformist state (*el estado de compromiso*) to a deregulated society that made scarcity the major incentive of the work force has generally been presented under the euphemistic label "modernization." Because women were now a major factor in the development of new industries, women, too, had to be modernized. Magazines and popular literature all over Latin America played a major role by showing the desirability of "modernity," as Michèle Mattelart pointed out in a study of women's magazines sold in Chile during the early 1970s.[25] In a study of "photonovels" (i.e., novels that use photographic stills and a brief text to tell the story), Cornelia Butler Flora and Jan Flora likewise argued that this literature was an instrument for integrating the population into the labor force as well as into a consumer culture. The authors divide photonovels into three categories: (1) disintegrative/integrative, that is, as to the way they break down old patterns and integrate readers into new ways of thinking; (2) pure escape; and (3) consumer-oriented. Obviously, these are not narrative categories and, as content categories, they are not clearly distinguishable. Nevertheless, the Floras' conclusion is persuasive, for it gives this literature a performative role. "Seen as an evolutionary process, these stories separate a woman from her actual environment and prepare her to accept the necessity of marginal participation as consumption is added to her function of reproduction of household labor."[26]

In contrast to photonovels, *libros semanales,* or comic-strip novels, have attracted little critical attention,[27] despite the somewhat idiosyncratic manner in which the modernization plot is written. There are two major publishers of these comic-strip novels. The novels I shall discuss here are published by Novedades Editores, a subsidiary of Mex-Ameris, which is controlled by the powerful O'Farrill interests. This conglomerate also publishes such magazines as *Claudia* and *Bienestar,* two photonovels – *Rutas de pasión* and *La novela musical* – as well as fashion and sports magazines and crime literature. Romulo O'Farrill Sr. is the partner of Emilio Azcárraga in the television company Televisa.[28] The novels are produced under the general editorship of Ms. Ibáñez Parkman and include various genres – *vaqueros* (cowboy magazines), crime novels (directed to the male public), and sentimental novels, which are intended mainly for women.[29] Each series sold around 800,000 copies per week before the recent economic crisis, which caused a dip in sales that affected novels for women more than novels for men.[30]

The comic strips are crudely drawn and often use the shorthand indices of emotion conventionalized in U.S. comics, which are left untranslated in Spanish. For instance, "Snif, Snif" indicates weeping. The color of the comics is a monotonous sepia, and the covers are often unattractive. They have neither the glossy appeal of the photonovel nor the escapist fantasy provided by the romance fiction produced under the name of Corín Tellado.[31] Precisely because the *libros semanales* are so unglamorous and are so clearly intended for women who are integrated or about to be integrated into the work place, they require a different kind of modernization plot, one that cannot simply hold out the carrot of consumption.

The distinctive feature of the *novela semanal* is its explicit moral, a moral that often strikingly conflicts with the apparent plot. In *Los nuevos ricos* (The Nouveaux Riches, vol. 32, no. 1541, March 9, 1984), the plot appears to focus on adultery. The wife of Luis Felipe, who has married him only for his money, seduces his brother Luciano. The novel begins at the dramatic moment when Luciano, shocked at his own conduct, commits suicide. The family and Luis Felipe, who know nothing of the affair, are baffled by this tragedy, but before they discover its cause, there is an unexpected and apparently disconnected flashback to Luis Felipe's father, whose origins are now explained in some detail.

Luis Felipe's father is a *nuevo rico* who began life as a peasant. One day as he returns from work in the fields accompanied by an aunt, he finds the family home destroyed and his parents dead. A Mexican reader might immediately connect this destruction to the revolution or the Cristero War, but the novel avoids such historical specificity and turns it into an accidental tragedy. Soldiers, in search of a fugitive, had mistakenly caused the deaths. The novel thus manages at once to allude to the violence of the past without indicating that this violence brought about social change and to suggest that violence comes from the forces of the state. The "accident" drives the father and his aunt from the village and into the city, where they make a fortune selling fruit. They become the "new rich" of the title; in due time, the father marries and has two sons, Luciano and Luis Felipe, whose upbringing he neglects because of his concern with money. At the end of this flashback, we return to the adultress, who is now haunted by the dead Luciano and who dies in remorse. This second "accident" will have the same result as the first. Luis Felipe decides that he can no longer live with his parents and must make his own way in life, starting from scratch.

Now the best that can be said about this plot is that it is incoherent. Certainly, if the reader were to draw a moral lesson, it might concern the evils of adultery. Yet the adultery turns out to be a side issue. The explicit moral printed at the end of the story is "Money and social position kill even the sincerest feeling. Luiciano and Luis Felipe's parents forgot that they owed their children love and instead amassed a large fortune which, as the novel shows, was of no use to them." What seems to be the plot of the story, a plot that arouses anger at the conduct of an unscrupulous temptress, turns out to be a secondary matter that is punished by supernatural means. The "sin" of the older generation – their egoism – has to be dealt with on the level of everyday life. Egoism and moral blindness prevent them from being suitable guides for their children, who have to seek their satisfaction outside the traditional family.

This seems a strange conclusion for a country like Mexico in which the family has, at least in theory, always provided a network of support. It also contrasts in startling fashion with the Victorian treatment of sexually aberrant behavior, which was often exposed and punished, the better to cement the ties between generations. *La Traviata* is a classic example of a father–son relationship cemented by the sacrifice of the courtesan, whose death allows the family to triumph over sexuality. In the Mexican *novela semanal*, the family is an obstacle to individual progress, and adultery is one of the consequences of members of the same family inhabiting the same house. Unlike Freudianism, which makes "separation" from the mother and the oedipal conflict a crucial stage in childhood development, this novel stresses separation as an *adult* process that frees the individual from the weight of the past represented by the older generation. Though never officially stated, the official ideology of postrevolutionary Mexico, which was, at least in theory, based on the desirability of state-directed (paternalistic) reform with each generation building on the contribution of the prior generation, is here undermined by an individualistic self-help philosophy.

Though I cannot claim to have read more than a small number of these novels, I have read a sufficient number to make it clear that the attack on the older generation in *Los nuevos ricos* is not an isolated example. Again and again, such stories exploit violence, rape, and sensation only to place the blame in the end squarely on the shoulders of the older generation. In one of the novels, *Las abandonadas* (The Abandoned Girls, vol. 32, no. 1537, February 10, 1984), the children of a "fallen" mother and a cruel father eventually escape from the father's house and find work in the city. The moral states: "Parents must never betray their children's trust. Children are soft wax which can be molded. Unhappy children become unhappy adults but happy children will form homes that are filled with peace and love."

Clearly this moral does not follow from the logic of the conclusion, since "the abandoned girls" should be as evil as their parents. Once again the conclusion we might naturally draw from the life story is thwarted, this time because the moral of the story suggests a culture of poverty thesis according to which the older generation passes on its defects to the next. If children are "soft wax," how can they escape from evil parenting? In this case, we can only conclude that children can break the cycle by making a break with the family and going to work in the city.

In both the examples I have discussed, the focus is not so much on women as on the family as an institution. Mexican postrevolutionary policy had encouraged the secularization of public life while leaving the traditional patriarchal family untouched and absorbing machismo into its national image. The Mexican family is thus an extremely complex institution, not only a source of considerable tensions, especially among the poor, but a source of support and daily communication that the state and its institutions cannot replace. It is interesting, therefore, that many of the *novelas semanales* place less emphasis on romance than on working or on marriage as a working partnership. In *Lo que no quiso recordar* (What She Did Not Want to Remember, vol. 22, no. 1557, June 29, 1984), the heroine Chelo marries a friendly architect after some misadventures with an unscrupulous brother-in-law, who had tried to blackmail her into a relationship. The moral declares that "true love means faith and trust in one's partner and the knowledge that, despite hardship, trouble and economic difficulty, their mutual love will make them confident that all will turn out right in the end."

Though, in this case, the reader might have reached this conclusion without prompting, the suggestion that marriages face economic hardship is not reflected in the plot. Yet it is not a totally gratuitous observation, for it serves as a warning that the romantic element should not blind the reader to the fact that marriage is a working relationship. It underlines the fact that in this Mexican popular literature, unlike the Harlequin, romance is not the issue and readers are expected to use real-life experience to evaluate the story.

One explanation of the disjunction between plot and explicit moral message may be rooted in the origin of the stories – that is, everyday life as told in readers' letters or in the popular press. The latter provides a diet of violence and sensationalism that has few parallels in the rest of Latin America. Why violence should be so popular among Mexicans is not altogether clear, unless it has to do with the desire to dramatize lives that may otherwise seem pointless. At the same time, since the violence is attributed in the novels mainly to a regressive mentality, it clearly belongs to the past that the novel condemns and not to the modern life toward which the readers are supposed to aspire. In the modernization tale, it is the ingrained habits of the "typical" Mexican – violence, machismo, and drunkenness – that have to be repudiated, and since men of the older generation do not seem likely to reform themselves, women must simply break away from the traditional family and embrace the work ethic.

This is underscored by the fact that even the advertisements generally downplay the cornucopia of consumerism in order to emphasize self-help courses, utilitarian items like sheets, and door-to-door sales jobs. Women are thus addressed not primarily as consumers but as potential workers whose fulfillment will be within the work force (the plots often emphasize this) rather than in romantic marriage. In presenting this message, advertisements offer a critique of the old macho type personified by Pancho Villa, whose posthumous role in the building of nationalist ideology exceeded his achievements in the revolutionary struggle. Octavio Paz's *El laberinto de la soledad* and Carlos Fuentes's novel *La muerte de Artemio Cruz*, to mention two well-known examples, deal with the profound interpenetration of nationalism and machismo and the destructive effect on politics and everyday life.

In Mexico, the overlapping of old and new discursive formations, old and new plots, old and new proverbial wisdom gave rise to many contradictions that surface in popular narrative. Loyalty to the neighborhood network, to one's place of origin (Viva Jalisco), or to the extended family had been key themes in popular songs, mythology, and film. Though much nationalist and regional sentiment, especially feelings associated with place of origin and the family, is still conveyed on film and television and in popular literature, there is also a systematic parody of "tradition" in the media [32] and a devaluing of the residues of more archaic ways of life – machismo, superstition, veneration of the older generation (though these may also resurface in new organizations like that of the *concheros,* or drug cults). In order to persuade people of the need to separate themselves from the past, the comic-strip novel imitates exemplary literature in showing the evils of machismo and portraying the hard-drinking male who assesses his virility through violence, especially violence against women, like a barbarian. The ideal male in the comic-strip novel is the young professional or young worker who can be trusted to form a nuclear family in which the wife will also go out to work. I shall return to the apparently emancipatory aspects of this literature later. But it should again be stressed here that the organization of plot material in the *novela semanal* is different from that in the Harlequin novel. The *novela semanal* is not written exclusively from the female point of view and does not incorporate itself into the social norm. Rather, women are invited to see themselves as victims of a plot, the plot of the old Mexico that has passed on the tradition of machismo and thus harmed them. If, instead of reading themselves into the plot as helpless victims, they turn their resentment against the older generation of men and separate themselves from this influence, they can expect to succeed. The solution suggests the need for struggle rather than escapism. The determinism of one generation transmitting its defects to the next can be transcended, and women can start life anew as members of the work force.

It is therefore not surprising to find an explicitly feminist ideology in some of the *libros semanales.* In *Una mujer insatisfecha* (An Unsatisfied Woman, vol. 32, no. 1580, December 7, 1984) the heroine is married to a boring and impotent businessman who believes in patriarchy and the traditional values of family life. Luisa is repelled by his puritanical attitude to marital relations and quarrels with her Italian mother-in-law, whose ideas on marriage are strictly traditional. She sets up her own consultancy as a designer and meets another man but refuses to enter into a relationship that promises to be as oppressive as the one with her husband. Back in her mother's home, she hangs up the telephone when her new lover calls, feeling "free, happy and without ties." More surprising is the plot of *Desprestigiada* (The Disgraced Woman, vol. 32, no. 1572, October 12, 1984), in which the heroine, a flirt who likes to pick up male visitors to the Pyramids, is raped by a "foreigner" (probably a Central American) who works in the post office. When she discovers that she is pregnant, she has an abortion thanks to the help of a traditional *curandera* and a woman doctor. But the foreigner rapes her a second time, because he wants a child he can adopt and take back to his own country. The rape (which is a somewhat unusual adoption procedure) is, however, less germane to the conclusion than the birth of the illegitimate child. The foreigner's plan to seize the baby is thwarted when he is picked up as an illegal immigrant, and it is Luisa who brings the baby up until the child is weaned. The reader might expect this to be the ending, but this is not a story about a girl's redemption through motherhood. Rather, as soon as the child is old enough to be left with another person, she is handed over to Luisa's mother and Luisa goes back to her old life, picking up men at the Pyramids. The only moral lesson is that in the future she must be more careful.

There is considerable irony in this attack on machismo in the guise of liberation. It plays on the sentiments of 1968, plays on the difference between the modernity of the young and the blind conformity of the old. It does so thanks to the anachronistic melodramatic plot, in which random acts of violence can be justified only on the grounds of the heroine's final social integration. Even so, the moral and the ending are often so arbitrary in relation to the sequence of events that they highlight the arbitrary nature of all narratives, including the master narrative of nationalism with its appeal to rootedness, to place, and to community.

In older forms of social narrative, the "story" tended to be woven out of lived experience. This term, now rightly treated with suspicion because of its empirical bias, must nevertheless be introduced because the process of human life ("the logic of mortality") cannot help but be the most powerful of paradigms. We fell in love and married and had children, and all this seemed to happen naturally. Of course, we were still woven into a social plot in which marriage and the family not only satisfied our needs for affection and recognition but also contributed to social reproduction. Nevertheless, this plot was built on events – childhood, adolescence, maturation – that appeared to be natural. The modernization plot works against this formerly "natural" state of affairs, showing that life stories are not what they seem. In Harlequins, romance is a prize available only to those who learn the conditions under which female power can be exercised. In the *libros semanales,* the family is not seen as the inevitable source of satisfaction for women.

It is intriguing that there are photonovels being produced in California that use real-life material to persuade Mexican men to stay in Mexico. The series, *Los mojados* (The Wetbacks), is based on the tragedies of Mexicans who emigrated to the United States in search of the "accursed dollar" and who found only disaster and death.[33] Thus real-life stories persuade one sector of the population – women – that the family and the province are not their only destiny, whereas *Los mojados* persuades men to stay at home and not swell the immigrant population of the United States. Mass culture narrative thus deals with problems that go far beyond entertainment. By addressing itself to serialized readers, it can appeal to private feelings and private lives. Yet this literature commutes private sentiments into stories that map out (plot) the way different sectors of the population can be incorporated into the international division of labor. Whereas the Harlequin romances use the powerful parallel between the stages of socialization and a ritual of passage from adolescence to womanhood, the *libros semanales* often depict a violent break between women as workers and women as family members. The plots of both, however, seem to depend on the fact that women experience considerable anxiety and uncertainty as to where they stand in relation to society. The *libros semanales* reveal that there is not a single model for the sex–gender system under capitalism, but rather multiple options. Furthermore, when these options contradict women's everyday practices or beliefs, they have to be plotted as a simulation of real life in order to persuade the readership to change its attitudes. The *libro semanal* thus bears some resemblance to the CIA guerrilla manual, which, since it could not appeal to the real-life situations of Nicaraguans, resorted to simulating events (e.g., an execution) in order to provide such experience.[34]

Far from being peculiarly postmodern, this kind of plotting belongs to the hallowed tradition of the church with its staging of miracles and marvels. The "literary resources" printed at the end of the "contra" manual could quite well have come from a Jesuit manual. But the church, whatever its capacity for manipulation, had both its transcendental signified and its moral code, which went hand in hand with belief in an afterlife. In contrast, the *libro semanal* offers travail without utopia, and self-reliance without any moral standpoint to help one deal with human relations other than that offered by the disembodied corporate voice.

Women, then, are plotted in different ways according to their position in the international division of labor. Curiously, it is women in the most affluent sectors (or those who can aspire to that affluence) who are invited most vigorously to give up their cultural capital (that which would permit them to "think like a man") and find security in their own narcissistic image. In the lower strata of the international division of labor, work or individual emancipation takes the place of romance. These novels suggest that "love" is a luxury, a fantasy not for all women but for middle- and upper-class women seeking the complementary man who will heal the split in their personality. What women want is provided by the Harlequin romance in a very efficient way, but it disguises the fact that this is the only way of being truly "incorporated." If the *libro semanal* is more problematic, it is because it does not address what women want, but rather disguises economic oppression as emancipation from the violence and oppression of working-class men. Significantly missing from mass literature is any form of female solidarity; it reinforces the serialization of women, which is the very factor that makes their exploitation both as reproducers of the labor force and as cheap labor so viable even in corporate society.

Plotting is a social as well as a literary device, and clearly, although it is important to recognize that reading the plot does not mean being committed to the social system it maps out, it is also important to understand the perplexing disjunction that is now taking place at the level of morality. "The area of belief which concerned religion, sexual and personal morality, and the sanctity and social significance of the family, has collapsed in modern bourgeois culture," according to one group of critics.[35] Harlequins map out the conditions for consumerism and *libros semanales* for incorporation into the work force, but whereas the former retain traditional morality in almost nostalgic fashion within the ethical vacuum of consumerism, the latter insist on emancipation from the restraints of a family that is now a hindrance to capitalist development in Mexico.

Both kinds of mass literature I have examined seem to indicate that women find a great deal of satisfaction in stories that promise an illusory form of social recognition and provide a parenthesis to everyday life in which that recognition is withheld. Thus, even though this literature plots women's lives with regard to system integration, it also points to personal needs that arise from the ethical vacuum of late capitalism, which offers little more than raw competition, the fetishism of the commodity, or in Mexico, the exploitation of the runaway shop.

NOTES

1   Raymond Williams, *Television: Technology and Cultural Form* (London: Penguin Books, 1974), p. 25.
2   Herbert Schiller, *Mass Communications and American Empire* (Boston: Beacon Press, 1971); see also Schiller, *Communication and Cultural Domination* (New York: International Arts and Sciences Press, 1976).

3   A. Dorfman and A. Mattelart, *Para leer al pato Donald,* 2nd ed. (Mexico City: Siglo xxi, 1972); Ariel Dorfman, *Reader's Nuestro que estas en la tierra, Ensayos sobre el imperialismo cultural* (Mexico City: Nueva Imagen, 1980).

4   See, for instance, Evelina Dagnino, "Cultural and Ideological Dependence: Building a Theoretical Framework," in Frank Bonilla and Robert Girling (eds.), *Structures of Dependency* (Stanford, Calif.: Stanford University, 1973, mimeographed), pp. 129–48. Discussions of cultural imperialism were particularly widespread in the early 1970s. Some of these discussions are still reflected in Vol. 1 of Armand Mattelart and Seth Siegelaub (eds.), *Communication and Class Struggle* (New York: International General, 1979), and in publications such as *Comunicacion y Cultura,* published by Galerna in Buenos Aires in the early 1970s. Seth Siegelaub also published several volumes of a bibliography of marxism and the mass media; see *Marxism and the Mass Media; Towards a Basic Bibliography* (New York: International General). The most recent issue I have consulted is number 3 (1974).

5   Theodor Adorno, "On popular music," *Studies in Philosophy and Social Science* (New York) 9 (1941): 17–28.

6   There is scarcely a deconstructionist critic these days who does not have harsh words for the classical realist text. The criticism originated with Roland Barthes; see especially *S/Z,* trans. Richard Miller (New York: Hill & Wang, 1974). For more recent discussions, see Catherine Belsey, *Critical Practice* (New York: Methuen, 1980), and Kaja Silverman, *The Subject of Semiotics* (New York: Oxford University Press, 1983).

7   See, for instance, Stuart M. Hall, "Encoding and Decoding the Media Discourse," Stenciled paper no. 7 (Birmingham University, Center for Contemporary Cultural Studies, 1979).

8   Peter Brooks, *Reading for the Plot* (New York: Knopf, 1984).

9   Judith Williamson, *Decoding Advertisements: Ideology and Meaning in Advertising* (London: Marion Boyars, 1978).

10   Ibid., p. 42.

11   The term "serialized" is used by Jean Paul Sartre in his *Critique of Dialectical Reason,* trans. Alan Sheridan-Smith (London: New Left Books, 1976), to refer to groups of people like those in lines at bus stops who are together for a common purpose but are not otherwise bonded. He also describes radio audiences as serialized communities.

12   The notion of interpellation comes from Louis Althusser's definition in "Ideology and Ideological State Apparatuses: Notes towards an Investigation," in *Lenin and Philosophy and Other Essays* (New York: Monthly Review Press, 1971), pp. 127–86. Interpellation describes the process whereby people are constituted as subjects by such cultural agents as schooling, religion, and the media and the way they recognize themselves (are "hailed") as subjects.

13   Ann Barr Snitow, "Mass Market Romance: Pornography for Women Is Different," in Ann Snitow, Christine Stansell, and Sharon Thompson (eds.), *Powers of Desire: The Politics of Sexuality* (New York: Monthly Review Press, 1983), p. 246.

14 Janice A. Radway, *Reading The Romance: Women, Patriarchy and Popular Literature* (Chapel Hill: University of North Carolina Press, 1984), p. 36.
15 Snitow, "Mass Market Romance," p. 247.
16 Rosalind Coward, *Female Desire: Women's Sexuality Today* (New York: Paladin, 1984), p. 196.
17 Tania Modleski, *Loving with a Vengeance: Mass Produced Fantasies for Women* (Hamden, Conn.: Archon Books, 1982), p. 37.
18 Ibid., p. 57.
19 Radway, *Reading the Romance*, p. 176.
20 Brooks, *Reading for the Plot*, p. 22.
21 Vladimir Propp, *Morphology of the Folktale* (Bloomington: Indiana Research Center in Anthropology, 1958).
22 See Jean Franco, "The Utopia of a Tired Man: Jorge Luis Borges," *Social Text* 4 (Fall 1981):52–78.
23 Modleski, *Loving*, pp. 41–2.
24 Oscar Lewis, *The Children of Sánchez,* (New York: Random House, 1963). On the transformation of everyday life under the impact of the new media, see Raul Cremona, "El poder de la cultural de la televisión," in Moises Ladrón de Guevara (ed.), *Política cultural del Estado Mexicano* (Mexico City: Secretaría del la Educación Pública, 1983), pp. 201–26.
25 Michèle Mattelart, "Notes on 'Modernity': A Way of Reading Women's Magazines," in Mattelart and Siegelaub (eds.), *Communication*, pp. 158–70.
26 Cornelia Butler Flora and Jan Flora, "The Fotonovela as a Tool for Class and Cultural Domination," *Latin American Perspectives,* issue 16, vol. 5, no. 1 (Winter 1978):134–50.
27 Except for Charles Tatum and Harold E. Hinds, "Mexican and American Comic Books in a Comparative Perspective," in Juanita Luna Lawhn, Juan Bruce-Novoa, Guillermo Campos, and Ramón Saldívar (eds.), *Mexico and the United States: Intercultural Relations in the Humanities* (Texas: San Antonio College Press 1984), pp. 67–83.
28 Carola García Calderón, *Revistas femeninas: La mujer como objeto de consumo* (Mexico City: El Caballito, 1984).
29 The interview was conducted by Tununa Mercado in September 1984 in Mexico City. There are several series of novels, some of which, like Vaqueros (Cowboys), are addressed to a male public.
30 This information was given by Ms. Ibáñez in the interview mentioned in note 29.
31 For a brief discussion of the Corín Tellado novels, see Calderon, *Revistas femeninas.*
32 For instance, in the use of the *charro* (Mexican cowboy) who improvises poetic commentaries on the Televisa news program *24 Horas.*
33 The publishers, who are not named, give a box number address in San Isidro, California.
34 *Psychological Operations in Guerrilla Warfare,* with essays by Joanne Omang and Aryeh Neier (New York: Vintage Books, 1985).
35 Nicolas Abercrombie, Stephen Hill, and Bryan S. Turner, *The Dominant Ideology Thesis* (London: Allen & Unwin, 1980), p. 138.

III

Perspectives on literary criticism

14

Introduction

GARI LAGUARDIA

In the process of evaluating and interpreting texts, criticism contributes, implicitly and explicitly, to the definition of a literary tradition. The critic's object is a group of texts, which are meaningfully related to one another insofar as they share a code of reference. The critic's discourse itself contributes significantly to the identification of the elements and relations that eventually constitute such a shared code. For U.S. and Spanish American critics the question of a shared code of reference is problematic given the relative brevity of their nations' histories, compounded by the fact that their literatures are written in the languages of nations with a longer history.

For the European critic the shared code of reference, given the long history and dense network of literary conventions in any of the major European languages, is a given to be periodically reinterpreted and redefined. For the American critic, however, such codes have had to be in a sense "invented" out of very diverse materials.

The earliest American critics both in Spanish America and in the United States were keenly aware of the need to develop some instrument, thematic or formal, that would identify and privilege their national literatures at the same time that it was being "invented." Awareness, however, did not always guarantee successful execution. In fact, the project was impossible if one insisted on an American literature that suddenly came into being at a particular time.

Many of the earliest critics of American literatures stressed the need to break with the models provided by Europe – but how was this to be done? For some of them it was simply a matter of imitating American forms. The privileged American form was nature, particularly when at the early stages of national formation American society seemed to lack the requisite majesty. Thus writers like Andrés Bello and Henry Wads-

271

worth Longfellow would insist that the American writer, insofar as he or she was "American," imitate nature, which would in turn provide the necessary ingredient for underwriting the Americanness of their discourse.[1] It may be, and was, adduced that this solution was far too simple. Nonetheless, there was another thrust to the projects of Bello and Longfellow. Both represent an American tendency to appropriate European discourse and become the master of it.

Bello has often been criticized for not succeeding in breaking with standard neoclassical forms even as he populated his poetry with a profusion of "American" nature. Where Bello did succeed, however, was in establishing a privileged position for American Spanish. Recognizing that language is essential to an identity that requires a distinguishing characteristic, he produced a grammar based on "American principles" that succeeded not only in identifying a particular "American" Spanish but in canonizing it. The importance of this gesture, apart from whether it was, in fact, directly responsible for future linguistic developments, was that at the end of the nineteenth century it was Spanish American literary language that provided the basis for a renewal of Spanish literary expression.

Longfellow, too, appears not to have succeeded in achieving the identity with "American" nature that would have rendered his discourse "American" and "original." Poe testily said of him, "The simple truth is, that what ever may be the talents of Professor Longfellow, he is the Great Mogul of the Imitators." For Poe he was an imitator not of nature, which itself would have merited opprobrium by his lights, but of European writers: "As he pored over the pages of the Spanish, and then the great Northern writers, his imitation took a new direction. Soon to save labor, he began to filch a little here and a little there . . . he stole with more confidence, until stealing became habit, and so second nature."[2] Poe's remarks, justified or not, imply a conception of literature in which originality is crucial to its value. Yet for Poe as for Emerson, originality is not a function of a particular extrinsic natural or social circumstance but a function of a particular mind. Unlike Emerson, however, Poe considers the mind to be underwritten, not by any posited "American" quality such as democratic individualism or by any immanent sense of a transcendent "American" nature, but rather by the apprehension and realization of certain formal operations. This made Poe useful to later French writers and, through them, to the modernists.

Nonetheless, what Poe ignores, or is simply unconcerned with, is the fact that Longfellow, as George Ticknor's heir at Harvard, was himself engaging in a critical project that would naturalize "America's universality," without which originality would have a limited and isolated value. That is, he was exemplary of the U.S. tendency to become master reader and interpreter of the cultures of others. Ticknor, we may remember, was a very early American prototype of the graduate scholar, one of the first practitioners of what became a massively institutionalized endeavor. In 1843 Ticknor published a history of Spanish literature that surpassed anything produced by the Spaniards themselves and remained for at least forty years the preeminent manual in the field. The growth of the U.S. university witnessed a multiplicity of projects like these in all fields of the humanities. By the twentieth century this type of activity was second nature, and the number of U.S. critics who could be considered authorities in foreign literatures was so numerous that it would be easy to imagine, within the perspective of the academy, that U.S. literary discourse was a natural and perhaps preeminent partner in Western discourse. It is worth noting that the first literary history of Spanish America was written, in 1916, by a U.S. scholar named Alfred Coester. Coester himself was trained by J. D. M. Ford, the holder of the same Smith Chair of Romance Languages occupied earlier by Ticknor, Longfellow, and James Russell Lowell.

Bello's appropriative thrust did not yield a similar bounty for many reasons. For one, Spanish America's "Europeanness" was more problematic because of the large-scale survival or presence of non–European cultures. Equally important was the region's fragmentation and its consequent inability to create stable and powerful institutions from which critics could "naturalize" and "institutionalize" a presumably universal discourse that could equalize native literary production within the broad matrix of "universal" discourse. Finally, there was nothing like the inexorably expanding projection of political and economic power that accompanied the growth of the United States as a nation and inevitably made its literature appear central and universal.

Thus, it is in the thirty years that begin with World War I, when the U.S. projects itself on the world stage in a massive way, that U.S. criticism crystallizes a project long in preparation. It is during this period that U.S. criticism reaches back and re-creates its points of origin in the New England Renaissance (Van Wyck Brooks and, after him, F. O. Matthiesen) or in the realism of the Gilded Age (Vernon Parrington and Alfred Kazin). These retrospective points of origin will then serve as a focus of debate and will expand backward to the Puritans and forward to the modernists. It is early during the same period (1914–50) that American literature becomes so established that it can be rejected by writers who are nonetheless inextricably part of it. This rejection, however, has its own agenda. Eliot and the New Critics (Ransom, Tate, Brooks, and Warren), besides being poets themselves and contributing to the first native sally of U.S. writers into critical theory as such, establish a canon of their own. Significantly, this canon virtually eliminates the nineteenth century, the century of origin for U.S. literature. Instead it goes back to the British seventeenth century and from there to the modernist twentieth century. Among other things this canon allows these critics simply to posit U.S. modernism (themselves) as a seamless and natural part of the British and European canon.

The period that begins with World War I also sees the emergence in Spanish America of a number of critics concerned with defining a Spanish American canon and with developing a methodology capable of doing it justice. The fact that Spanish American literature – above all because it is composed of multiple national literatures – does not have the same historical cogency that U.S. literature does, prevents these critical discourses from achieving the varied and complex but coherent dialectic that was sketched above for U.S. criticism. Nonetheless, some comparable tendencies can be discerned. In the period that immediately follows World War I, two critics – Alfonso Reyes (Mexico) and Pedro Henríquez Ureña (Dominican Republic) – are exemplary. Although their work was both geographically and thematically diffuse, both of them contributed to and exemplified an identifiable set of approaches. Both were nourished by the literary accomplishments of *modernismo,* and both were influenced by the idealist morals and aesthetics of Arielismo derived from Rodo's influential essay. In addition both addressed – Henríquez Ureña more systematically than Reyes – the question of a canon. Henríquez Ureña made important contributions to the coalescence of the Spanish American canon. Centered on *modernismo,* this canon points behind it to the faltering start of Spanish American romanticism and forward to the twenties and the subsequent new directions of Spanish American literature. It was, in fact, one of Henríquez Ureña's pupils, Enrique Anderson-Imbert, who wrote the most comprehensive history of Spanish American literature. For his part, Reyes, who like Eliot and the New Critics was also a great poet, illuminated a possibly defining tradition for Spanish American literature with his studies of seventeenth-century Spanish baroque literature. Later writers, such as José Lezama Lima and Severo Sarduy, develop the idea that Spanish American literature springs in essence from the baroque style. This turn to the seventeenth century provides an opportunity to privilege Spanish American literature by rooting it within a complex verbal tradition whose heir it became even as Spain entered into a historical decline. Reyes also wrote *El deslinde: Prolegómeno a la teoría literaria* (1944), which was the most ambitious essay in literary theory yet written by a Spanish American. That work, intended merely as a prelude to a more extensive investigation, was never finished.

Roberto Fernández Retamar, the Cuban poet and critic, includes *El deslinde* in a list of aborted attempts to produce comprehensive literary theory by Spanish Americans. He contends that since wide-ranging theory depends on "universals" and since Spanish America has not even produced a comprehensively coherent theory of its own literary production, it is hardly likely that any putatively general theory of literature by a Spanish American will be successfully written until it can account for Spanish American particularities as well as literature in general. Attempts by Spanish Americans to formulate a general literary theory at the present juncture would in the end be inapplicable to Spanish American literature. So it is, in Fernández Retamar's view, with Félix Martínez-Bonatti's phenomenological essay *Fictive Discourse and the Structures of Literature* (1960, trans. 1981), which the Cuban critic sees otherwise as the only complete and self-contained theoretical statement on literature by a Spanish American.[3]

Be that as it may, the above discussion hints at a problem concerning literary theory in Spanish America. Namely, does American literature articulate its own refractory particularities, or can it be described entirely within putatively universal theories rooted in the Western tradition? This may also be asked of U.S. literature. The New Criticism, as noted, dealt with that problem by avoiding it through a flanking operation that derived the language and norms of U.S. criticism from a reading of the British and European traditions even as U.S. literature itself was being canonically formulated by U.S. literary historians.

By the 1950s the New Criticism was dead as an official movement in the United States. Nonetheless, it left behind an important legacy. It naturalized and institutionalized a body of techniques for practical and theoretical criticism that became capable of acquiring a life of its own, thus underwriting an increasingly autonomous discipline of literary theory and criticism in the United States. In contrast, Spanish America has not yet succeeded in developing a body of criticism that itself is the source of critical comment relatively independent of literary texts. Books written in the United States in the forties and fifties, such as Edgar Stanley Hyman's *The Armed Vision* (1948), René Wellek and Austin Warren's *Theory of Literature* (1949), and W. K. Wimsatt and Cleanth Brooks's *Literary Criticism: A Short History* (1957), in which U.S. critics are a major or important part of the discussion, have no parallel in Spanish America even today.

As late as 1968, in one of the very few surveys of critical theories undertaken by a Spanish American, *Métodos de crítica literaria,* Enrique Anderson-Imbert declared, "Let us admit that the subject is unrewarding . . . the criticism of criticism." More to the point, although generous allusion is made to French, German, British, and U.S. critics, scarcely anything is said about Spanish American critics. In a bibliography of more than a hundred items there are only three Spanish Americans: Henríquez Ureña, Reyes, and Martínez-Bonatti. These, moreover, receive next to no mention in the text itself.

A glance at recent developments in the practice of literary criticism in the Americas may be misleading. It appears that since 1970 both Spanish American and U.S. criticism have been functioning on similar wavelengths. Structuralism, poststructuralism, reception theory, Barthes, Foucault, Lacan, Jauss, and Iser – to mention only a few representative movements and theorists – permeate criticism in both Americas. Nonetheless, the similarity is spurious. For Spanish Americans these theories have provided tools, as Jean Franco has suggested, for an increasingly sophisticated sociocriticism. In the United States, however, critics conditioned by the immanentist textualism of the New Criticism and the autonomous literary system of Northrop Frye – although challenged by critics like Gerald Graff, Edward Said, and Frank Lentricchia – have adopted these theories for the production of very sophisticated exercises that make literature ever more self-referential and solipsistic.

If we find that the United States today betrays a well-established tradition of self-conscious, self-referential, and confident literary theory, whereas in Spanish America, literary theory not only "appears late and is little practiced"[4] but is also tied – obsessively – to the definition of its literature's particularity and consequent role in society and the world, what grounds are there for a comparative exploration?

The essays in this section, none of which pretends to make a major theoretical statement, indicate some directions this exploration may take by taking issue, directly or indirectly, with the presumed universality of literary theory. Gene Bell-Villada points out that the "universalist" assumptions of much U.S. high theory reflect historical and social conditions underwritten by U.S. power. Centering his discussion on Northrop Frye, he shows how that critic's presumably disinterested theorizing reflects certain attitudes sparked by the cold war and indicates how Spanish American criticism provides alternatives. Gari Laguardia focuses on the pitfalls and incoherencies that threaten able Spanish American critics who, uncritically desiring incorporation into the presumed plenitude of Western discourse, are sucked up by powerful discourses that have their own ideological agendas. Edmundo Desnoes, the Cuban novelist, shows how his desire to bridge cultures, arising in part from his experiences in Cuba and the United States, was thwarted by the fact that readers of his *Memories of Underdevelopment* as well as viewers of the film version in the two countries experienced it in entirely different ways. Michael Wood's essay examines Wallace Stevens and Octavio Paz – two poets whose work has inspired much critical theory – and shows how both try, perhaps futilely, to create a critical space in their poems that defines and articulates their American experience.

NOTES

1 See Longfellow: "We wish our native poets would give a more national character to their writings. In order to effect this, they have only to write more naturally. . . . This is particularly true in descriptions of natural scenery. . . . When [our poets] sing under an American sky and describe a native landscape, let the description be graphic as if it had been seen and not imagined" (Richard Ruland, ed., *The Native Muse: Theories of American Literature from Bradford to Whitman* [New York: Dutton, 1976], p. 257).
2 Edgar Allan Poe, *Essays and Stories* (New York: Library of America, 1984), pp. 771, 777.
3 Roberto Fernández Retamar, *Apuntes para una teoría literaria hispanoamericana* (Mexico City: Nuestro Tiempo, 1975), p. 75.
4 Ibid., p. 53.

15

Northrop Frye, modern fantasy, centrist liberalism, antimarxism, passing time, and other limits of American academic criticism

GENE H. BELL-VILLADA

I

Despite renewed competition from New Haven, Northrop Frye remains the most influential and by far the best-known North American literary critic. His imposing but lucid system still helps us find order in the literature of the past, and his influence is now being felt in the Latin American academic literary field as well. I believe that Frye's system, however, comes under strain when applied to current writing from the two Americas. His formal categories do not jibe with the shared features of many contemporary works, and his philosophical assumptions, not-withstanding Frye's transhistorical and universalist claims, are actually symptomatic of his times, and hence increasingly confining as the years go by. It is most ironic that, however monumental Frye's attempt to free literary study from New Critical parochialism and from Arnoldian or marxian or any other such sociocultural concerns and biases, in the end Frye too shows himself to be advocating certain presupposed social and aesthetic values, to be propagating the norms and attitudes of a particular cultural institution and of a moment in history.

When I refer to Frye, of course, I mean first of all his ambitious and encyclopedic *summa critica,* the *Anatomy of Criticism* (1957), as well as his popularizations, *The Well-Tempered Critic* (1962) and *The Educated Imagination* (1964). In my view, the period of the 1950s and early 1960s had a great deal to do with the kind of general theory Frye develops in these works, and I shall begin by investigating that temporal (and temporary) context, after which I shall take a look at the outer literary limits of Frye's scheme. With *The Critical Path* (1971) we find a much changed Frye, a thinker less confident, less secure, a man whose dearest assumptions are being severely tested, even challenged, by the student upheavals of the 1960s. In examining Frye's *Critical Path,* it is my intention to address the broad issue of antimarxism and suggest that antimarxism poses major obstacles to a genuine understanding of Latin American literature.

Frye's objective was to build "a theory of criticism whose principles apply to the whole of literature."[1] With great erudition, boldness, and sweep (and with memorably fine prose) he demonstrated the creative role of convention, traced six phases of literary form in descending movement from mythic to ironic, and showed that many works, even idiosyncratic ones, can be fitted within those broad patterns. Still, Frye's grand system is the product of a particular time and place, and it inevitably bears the marks of that time and place. Two temporal contexts of Frye's theory are (1) the global politics of the 1950s and early 1960s, and (2) the absorption of literary life by the then-expanding university.

The *Anatomy* and its sequels appeared during those decades when North American centrist liberalism emerged triumphant on the world scene. Fascism, with its neofeudal cults of heroism and its desperate bid for European supremacy, had been morally discredited, defeated in battle, and pacified by cold war political economy. Soviet influence had been contained; the Soviet Union had even withdrawn from Austria, Finland, and Yugoslavia, limiting its harsh rule to five countries on a Soviet buffer zone. Western Europe, weakened by war, and in a quasi-colonial relationship with the United States, was reconstructing under Marshall Plan auspices and American anti-Left guidelines. Latin America, with the exception of Perón's Argentina, was firmly under U.S. control. Hovering above this was a North America enriched by war, economically far ahead of its capitalist or communist rivals, blessed with mature and relatively benign institutions, and wealthy enough to cushion or at least conceal radical social divisions. In this unique set of circumstances the organic totality known as "the American Way of Life" leaped into global prominence, became not just a local arrangement but a universalist principle. Because of the accident of American world domination, American theory and practice became a model for world emulation.

Remote though it seems now, the broad U.S. consensus was that this state of affairs was permanent. Henry Luce's phrase "the American Century" expressed not only wishful thinking at Time-Life but popular folklore. These notions also took hold among the intellectuals, who eternalized the present and assumed its stable perpetuation into the future. The North American system was celebrated as a norm for all times and the goal toward which all societies were striving. Moreover, because the political philosophy of John Locke has enjoyed a long and mostly unchallenged hegemony on these shores, the tendency was to perceive all other forms of thought as "ideological." Books like Daniel Bell's *The End of Ideology* (1962) and especially Walt Rostow's *The Stages of Economic Growth* (1960) are steeped in American universalism. Rostow explicitly presents his theory as a countermodel to marxism (then narrowly equated with Sovietism) and subtitles his book *A Non-Communist Manifesto*. Frye's ideas, let it be said, are the product of a major thinker, one whose system shows far greater depth and staying power than do the ideological projects of a Rostow or a Daniel Bell. Nevertheless, these three theorists belong to the larger intellectual family of their times. They presuppose an ongoing, suprahistorical order, a social order free of ideological conflict, an endlessly growing economic order of mass consumption and, in literature, with its ever-repeating conventions and archetypes, an eternal and unchanging "order of words."[2]

The cultural context of Frye's general theory is that moment when criticism had completed its move from free-wheeling Bohemia, general magazine, aesthetic sect, and partisan struggle of whatever political stripe to a universalist institution – the liberal North American university, with its ideal of standing above all conflicts and preferences and studying all phenomena with equally disinterested objectivity. Frye states this ideal early in the *Anatomy*, where he says that just as "there are no definite positions to be taken in chemistry," there are none to be taken in criticism.[3] The critic is under no obligation to defend any set of values. As he puts it elsewhere, "Criticism has no business to react against things, but should show a steady advance toward undiscriminating catholicity."[4]

This is not the place to consider the merits and demerits of the academic literary locus, though no doubt most critics and novelists prefer drawing a steady salary to living hand-to-mouth (even on Bleecker Street). What interests me is the functioning and the limits of Frye's "undiscriminating catholicity." Obviously no one gives equal time to all works or authors. We assign *Hamlet,* not *Titus Andronicus; Light in August,* not *Mosquitoes.* These are received valuations, which are time-tested and accepted. There are others originating in aesthetic or social fashion – hence Dreiser is gently scorned by Frye, Eliot accepted without question. For works coming out here and now, the task of judging is performed by book reviewers, other writers, and the informal oral network of the general public. These combined processes result in a "canon" of texts deemed worthy of academic attention. But evaluation gets done, even in division-of-labor fashion, and it determines what works will be studied, even in encyclopedic systems like those of Frye. The index to the *Anat-*

omy shows generous entries for the high modernists Eliot and Joyce, whereas completely absent are divergent figures like Brecht or William Carlos Williams, certainly major artists in their spheres. Also absent is Dos Passos, a writer whose legacy was to persist and grow in Mailer and Doctorow, as well as in the Spanish novelist Cela and among numerous Latin Americans. In a sense this choice was made not by Frye but by preexisting university judgments, which were passed not by condemning or despising authors who abide by other rules but – the common North American procedure – by ignoring such authors.

Once in the academic arena, criticism speaks less to the tastes and commitments of the general reader than to the unformed student or the advanced specialist. Accordingly, Frye's references to life and institutions outside of literature are mostly to the teaching of "the humanities" and to "liberal education." The result is a conscious emphasis not on the production or promotion of new works but on the consumption of established ones. Frye says in *The Educated Imagination,* "I'm speaking to you as consumers, not producers, of literature."[5] In the *Anatomy* he writes:

> It is the consumer, not the producer, who benefits by culture, the consumer who becomes humanized and liberally educated. . . . The contemporary development of the technical ability to study the arts, represented by reproductions of painting, the recording of music, and modern libraries, forms part of a cultural revolution.[6]

One need not scant the value of these technical advances to note that Frye's "cultural revolution" sounds much like the cultural department of the consumer society. In this regard he shows more than a slight resemblance to Rostow, who saw the mass-consumption stage as the ultimate social utopia. What is distinctly absent in Frye, conversely, is the sense of literature as process, as change, as a system being ever modified by the efforts of new authors, movements, and centers of production.

The *Anatomy* usefully and brilliantly demonstrates the existence of received conventions, shows the importance of repetition in poetic history. This usefulness reaches its limit when the time comes to account for what is new and distinctive in any work, author, or genre. For Frye, of course, what makes a work original is that it is more conventional, "more profoundly imitative."[7] This argument, besides begging the question, presents a neoclassical criterion for aesthetic judgment. As with any academic neoclassicism, Frye's theory recognizes continuity rather than change, accepted rather than emergent phenomena. To take our own analogy from chemistry, since Frye has his: Just as water, though made up of elements already present in the order of nature, is still a newer substance in the history of the order of nature, similarly, realist narrative may have biblical or Sumerian forebears, but the bourgeois novel becomes a dominant presence only in bourgeois society. Pablo Neruda's long poem about the Spanish Civil War, entitled "España en el corazón" ("Spain in the Heart"), is very clearly organized around epical conventions and classical formulas. At the same time, however, it modifies those conventions along marxist lines, depicting not an individual but a collective hero (the Spanish people) and pointedly inverting the *ubi sunt?* motif by responding to the question not with an elegiacal lament for the dead, but with a celebration of class struggle.

A key development in both Americas in recent years has been the rise of fantasy as a vital method of literary representation. In Spanish America, to mention the obvious names, there are Borges, Rulfo in *Pedro Páramo,* Cortázar's short stories, and some of the major work of Donoso, Fuentes, and García Márquez. In North America we have Barthelme, Pynchon, Coover, Ishmael Reed, and Malamud to some extent. These authors, as is known, skillfully combine realist description and plausible narrative with completely unreal and impossible sorts of actions.

The fantastic is absent in Frye's system, except for stray comments about its use in satire and in ghost stories. The reason is simple. Before Borges, fantasy as we now know it had led a marginal existence on the sidelines of realism and romance. Until its recent flowering, fantasy was the distinctive mode of prophetic eccentrics like Kafka or of minor authors like Poe and Chesterton. Balzac, Flaubert, and James did have their metaphysical sides and wrote some fine fantasies of their own, but their realist texts remain their chief contribution. Frye's theory of mode and genre thus proves to be built on past canons of evaluation and as such is yet another grand episode in the history of taste. The *Anatomy* organizes the literary status quo and describes it superbly, but it is also bound to that status quo. It is worth noting that Todorov's theory of the fantastic begins with an attack on the *Anatomy of Criticism,* and Eric Rabkin's study does not even make mention of Frye, the implication being that Rabkin does not need him.[8]

In the wake of Frye's influence, some U.S. critics now claim that what García Márquez, Cortázar, and all the rest have been writing are not novels, but romance and satire.[9] The archetype for this sort of argument is the ancient myth of Procrustes, who used to seize innocent travelers and then stretch their bodies or cut off their legs, in order to make them fit onto his bed. It is the literary equivalent of those discussions of Peronism or Venezuelan politics or *latifundio* through European categories of fascism, constitutionalism, or feudalism. (Latin American literati have voiced their own complaints about the indiscriminate application of metropolitan models to Latin American writings, as we shall see later.) Critic and political writer both become so trapped by a system that they ignore the specifics of their subject. For instance, Frye rightly says that romance depicts not "real people" but "stylized figures" and "psychological archetypes."[10] Bearing this in mind, one notes in *Hopscotch* or *One Hundred Years of Solitude* the subtle and complex portrayal of characters like La Maga and Ursula and the detailed picture of their relations with others. Or one notes, in stories like "End of the Game" or "Artificial Roses," an almost Jamesian feel for the fine web of interpersonal relations. And one realizes that Cortázar and García Márquez seem less attracted by abstract categories than by concrete experience. That is, they operate, not in the mental domain of romance and satire, but in mimesis, representation (which is not necessarily bourgeois realism).

The sense of the past is strong in García Márquez, Rulfo, and Fuentes. The history of the Plate region and of Europe are a commanding presence in much of Borges. Indeed an important subgenre in both Americas today is the "fantastical history," in which actions take place within a historical setting, and fictional characters mingle with real-life ones. Some of the most outstanding instances of this genre are *One Hundred Years of Solitude,* Fuentes's *Terra Nostra,* Alejo Carpentier's *Concierto barroco,* Pynchon's *Gravity's Rainbow* and *The Crying of Lot 49,* Doctorow's *Ragtime,* Coover's *The Public Burning,* and Ishmael Reed's *Mumbo Jumbo* and *Flight to Canada.* Though fantastical, some of these works have proved to have real cognitive value. *One Hundred Years of Solitude,* for example, is required in many Latin American history and politics courses in this country. This fact alone identifies the book as a reliable guide to the Latin American past; it suggests that the story of Macondo is both beautiful *and* useful (*dulce et utile,* as the Roman poet said). A statement by Frye aptly describes this drift in Latin American and recent U.S. fiction: "The novel tends to expand into a fictional approach to history."[11]

Prose fiction in Latin America has taken up the role and function once held by the classic novel in bourgeois Europe – the job of dealing intelligently and imaginatively with social life and cultural values. If it has satirical aspects, so do such long-acknowledged European novels as *Don Quixote* and *Joseph Andrews.* Its fantastical workings stand outside Frye's categories. Fantastical history conveys more than the awesome powers of myth or romance, covers a wider range than does the cerebralism and intellectualism of satire, and evokes emotions more positive than does demonism or irony. Fantastical history is both objective mimesis and its inspired negation – perhaps the source of Todorov's "hesitation" effect, whereby the reader responds to a text both as reportage and as allegory, as realism and as romance.[12] The *Anatomy,* as it turns out, is not a universal map but a retrospective taxonomy, an account of the literary phases of the Eurometropolitan past, and an attempt to freeze that past into a presupposed future. When I first encountered Walt Rostow and his five stages of economic growth, I asked: What comes after the fifth stage? Rostow thought that the fifth stage was forever; in just two decades his grand projections are slowly going bust.[13] In the same way, as literary forms change and new ways of writing come into being, Frye's scheme will inevitably recede into the past, and the *Anatomy* will become another grand theory, to be regarded someday much as Italian Renaissance theories, or French neoclassical ones like Boileau's, are now regarded by us.

II

Frye's earlier work has a sunny optimism, in keeping with its prosperous and stable times. *The Critical Path* (1971) gives us an altered Frye. Its dark melancholy also reflects its moment, those years when the academic order was being defied and occasionally disrupted. There is a corresponding break in method. Whereas the *Anatomy* proposed a stability model of endless repetition, *The Critical Path* formulates a conflict model, sees an age-old clash between what Frye calls "myths of concern" (which hold societies together) and "myths of freedom" (which promote tolerance and inquiry). We have no time to examine these categories other than to note their old-fashioned and schematic idealism, their treating social conflict in terms of myths rather than forces, and above all their abstracted distance from political events. At one particularly disturbing moment, Frye witnesses the People's Park incident in Berkeley, California – a nasty incident that involved a confrontation between street people and the police and in which a demonstrator was accidentally killed by a stray tear-gas canister. As Frye watches the mayhem and mass arrests, he sees neither broken heads nor civil disorder – but demonic symbolism, the pastoral mode, the myth of expulsion from Eden, and the murder of Abel archetype.[14]

Frye traces his clash of myths from earliest antiquity. When he reaches modern times, however, we realize that *The Critical Path* has been leading up to a defense of the academy before 1960s radicalism, for *The Critical Path* is an instance of a genre that flourished in that decade – the antiradical tract. Frye is a gentle and urbane man, and he avoids the shrill alarmism of a Norman Podhoretz or Nathan Glazer, but his book exhibits the same familiar stock of convention – the outrage at student "violence" ("the shouting and smashing and looting and burning of our times"),[15] the lofty indifference to words like "capitalism"[16] (then deemed superannuated and irrelevant by official liberalism), the likening of campus radicals to Nazis,[17] the appeal to psychologistic explanations for student activism (not Bruno Bettelheim's mechanical Freudism, but a mythic Jungianism), the treatment of marxism as a religion, and silence on Vietnam. *The Critical Path* is Frye's own "noncommunist manifesto," an attempt to exorcise the specter of marxism – never by confronting its actual arguments (which Rostow at least did) but by putting it beyond the pale and consigning it to the oblivion of theology.

This Frye stands in the larger tradition of antimarxism, which throughout this century has been a primary impulse in American life, intellectual life included. Intellectual antimarxism works less by repression (though this, too, occurs) than by the construction of social, political, and cultural models aimed at refuting, discrediting, or relativizing Marx. The pattern can be traced in criticism. The Agrarians who became the New Critics were neofeudal conservatives. Their manifesto in favor of the Old South, *I'll Take My Stand,* had as its originally projected title *A Tract Against Communism.* Their literary doctrine emerged not only in reaction to historicism (itself the social doctrine of bourgeois progressivism) but against what they saw as the "sociologism" of the 1930s Left. The triumph of New Criticism during the cold war was due in some degree to the purge of the Left and its ideas from the academy. At this point Frye builds a literary system standing apart from social change and external history. Change returns in the 1960s, and a troubled Frye writes his own personal "tract against Communism." Also around this time Harold Bloom, bringing a kind of social Darwinism to poetic history, locates aesthetic changes in individual competitiveness and triumphs, rather than in group affinities, ideological conflicts, and socially induced needs. Some brands of structuralism, like that of Foucault, are now used as a way of analyzing shifts and substitutions without seeing movement or struggle, of studying discourse and "author-ity" without seeing class, property, or brute force, and of being up on prestigious fashion without seeing the socioeconomic roots of fashion systems.[18] Roland Barthes has also entered American criticism – not, however, Barthes the marxist journalist of *Mythologies* or *Writing Degree Zero,* but Barthes the narcissistic hedonist of *Pleasure of the Text* and Barthes the technocratic scheme builder and lemon squeezer of *S/Z.* The impact of Louis Althusser's structuralist marxism and of his European disciples (Macherey, Eagleton) has been minimal here, outside of the tiny circle of academic-graduate-literary-leftist theorists. All this comes as no surprise, given that the United States, where Lockean liberalism exists not just as an idea but as a way of life, is also the world leader of antimarxism.

Latin America presents a different picture. There, as in much of Europe, marxism enjoys a great deal of intellectual respectability. Many Latin American writers either are clearly defined marxists or make use of marxist concepts in their work, as does Fuentes, for example. Indeed, it is a fact both significant and striking that the three greatest Latin American poets of the early part of this century – Neruda, Vallejo, and Nicolás Guillén – were also marxist activists. Besides living for their causes, two of them were to perish as a result of their militancy – Vallejo from overwork for the Spanish Left, Neruda from complications following harassment at the hands of Pinochet's troops. This fact becomes especially dramatic when one recalls how many leading North American poets of the same period – Eliot, Pound, Frost, the Agrarians – were ultraconservative and occasionally fascist in their political views.

To a great extent, marxist categories serve as the "ground," the conditions for a great deal of thinking in Latin America. The leftish tone and outlook of educated Latin Americans is often remarked by foreign observers, and it is not idle to speculate that a substantial majority of Latin American novelists, poets, journalists, editors, teachers, and social researchers accept the marxist world view as a mode of analysis and as a tool for the imagination. Even explicitly anticommunist Latin American writers – and there are relatively few – present themselves as democratic socialists equally opposed both to centralized dictatorship and to capitalist exploitation and U.S. meddling; and they unabashedly employ the marxian concept of class and phrases like "American imperialism" as agreed-upon terms of objective description. Marxist language and intuitions are by now so respectable in Latin America as to have become commonplace in such unlikely spots as the official rhetoric of the Mexican government or in the Catholic church ranks, with its "Liberation Theologians" and activist priests.[19]

One need not seek far for the origins of these ideas: The twenty-five percent unemployment and mass poverty, the vast slums and unrelieved starvation, the greedy and corrupt ruling classes, and the domination by U.S. economic and political interests all add up to a reality too obvious to be ignored by the enlightened and compassionate. The bleak, brutal Manchester of Marx and Engels was a hopeful and civilized place by comparison to the Guatemalas of today. The dismal Latin American panorama, moreover, cannot be elucidated through the liberal schemes and projections of American social science; for the continued existence of those inhuman conditions even in countries such as Venezuela and Colombia, with their constitutional forms, regular elections, and relatively moderate governments, casts doubt on the viability of Latin America's liberal-capitalist presence and future. Of course, the bloodthirsty military dictatorships, be they intermittent or chronic, provide further proof for the unworkability of the liberal social model to Latin American leftists.

All of this explains Latin American intellectuals' readiness to accept the marxist view. For an illuminating parallel, it may help to recall Depression-era literary culture in the United States. Daniel Aaron, in his account of the American 1930s, *Writers on the Left,* shows genuine understanding for the many novelists, poets, and critics who at the time "expressed . . . their feeling of outrage at what they saw with their own eyes."[20] It was not darkest Moscow but, paraphrasing Aaron, the glaring facts of mass joblessness and misery, coupled with dictatorship in Europe, that were to shape consciousness and give rise to literary leftism in that era. Latin America's "depression," however, predates the 1930s, was never terminated through reforms or world war, and has gotten generally worse, with no relief in sight. Under such circumstances one can only expect marxist thought to survive and come into its own, to become not just a passing fashion of a decade but, among those who choose to write about significant experience, a permanent and shared way of thinking and imagining, even of living and dying.

This simple marxist presence has been noted by the great Mexican poet Octavio Paz:

> Marxism has penetrated so profoundly into history that, in some way or other, at times without realizing it, we are all Marxists. Our moral judgments and categories, our idea of the future, our opinions about the present or about justice, peace, and war, everything – even and including our negations of Marxism – is impregnated with Marxism. It is now part of our intellectual lifeblood and our moral sensibility.[21]

In context Paz's words have a universalist intent and are profoundly accurate, but the quotation applies more to Latin America than to the north, where liberal individualism is all but thought of as "human nature" to the same degree that marxism is resisted as "ideology." (Virtually every American liberal theory since 1945, from developmental economics to McLuhanism and sociobiology, has been an attempt to reconstruct social reality without Marx.) The fact that Octavio Paz is a fairly conservative individual, who in many ways is antimarxist, makes his observations all the more striking.

Certain misjudgments and misreadings arise out of this intellectual split between Latin American marxism and American-style liberalism. It is not uncommon for centrist critics to reject Neruda's political verse, judging it inferior to his bleak hermetic poetry of personal anguish and usually dismissing it as leftist nonsense. Rather than consider its artistic strengths and weaknesses, they dismiss this body of writing solely because of its choice of subjects – the battle of Stalingrad, workers' struggles, the United Fruit Company – much as French neoclassical critics were wont to deride Shakespeare because he portrayed low-life figures and ignored courtly rules. In an aside that names no names but evokes Neruda and brings in a few stereotypes, Karl Shapiro attributes the decline of poetry in U.S. universities to the lamentable influence of "South American Marxists who supply . . . large doses of angst, warmed-over surrealism, anti-American hatred, and latino blood, sweat, and tears."[22]

Shapiro's antimarxist assumptions are spelled out frankly and unembarrassedly, even naively; but there are also more sophisticated strategies in which antimarxist evaluations are conveyed via arguments alleging flaws in structure, such as the occasional essay in which the banana company chapters in *One Hundred Years of Solitude* are pronounced the weakest in García Márquez's novel. Constrained by the governing academic doctrine that what counts in art is not content or subject matter but style and form, the method of these critics is to stand on apparently neutral formalist ground and sublimate antimarxism into a negative assessment of García Márquez's literary craft. Alexander Coleman, for instance, believes that the episode of the workers' strike and the massacre in the plaza presents "a catastrophic conflict in tone" with the rest of the book. As Coleman says, "It is as if a chapter from *The Grapes of Wrath* were intercalated into the *Amadís of Gaul*."[23] The clear implication here is that a serious and sympathetic portrayal of workers' struggles has no place in a fantastical text. The deeper suggestion is that U.S. business imperialism is an unsuitable subject for art; nor does *The Grapes of Wrath* seem to rate too highly in Dr. Coleman's canon.

Still, for all their complex strategies, it is the ideology imbedded in García Márquez's book that irks his critics. This came through in a recent piece by Anthony Burgess for *The New Republic,* where he remarked that *One Hundred Years of Solitude* "impressed me rather less than it seems to have impressed others." He grants that the book "has undoubted power, but its power is nothing compared to the genuinely literary explorations of men like Borges and Nabokov." Actually, the widespread but highly debatable "imputation of greatness" to García Márquez's novel, Burgess asserts, "has more to do with content – especially when it is social or political – than with aesthetic values."[24] In a word, people laud *One Hundred Years* because it is leftist, and not because of its art. Burgess's suggestion is not intrinsically invalid; history has seen its share of novels and poems inordinately acclaimed because of their ideological message. Burgess's reasoning seems a trifle ingenuous, however, when one recalls that his own most successful novel, *A Clockwork Orange,* depicts an unhealthy socialist England of the future, where Soviet operatives secretly influence Laborite officials, where roving thugs babble in an Anglo-Russian billingsgate, and where the state intrudes so broadly in private life that even hoodlums come off sympathetic by comparison.

Literary judgment in such cases is clearly hampered by political prejudice. Misperceptions also arise in the area of practical analysis. I shall demonstrate the workings of this epistemological blind spot in critical treatments of a short story by Alejo Carpentier entitled "Like the Night." The political biography of this Cuban author shows a familiar Latin American pattern. In 1927 his leftist involvements earned him several months in a Havana jail cell. Years later, from 1959 until his death in 1980, he held a number of official posts within the Cuban revolutionary government, meanwhile producing some fine sociopolitical novels. In a letter written to me in 1972, Carpentier frankly admitted that "I am a Marxist in my attitudes, activities, and in the duties I perform in my daily life."

Carpentier's story "Like the Night," in a series of self-contained episodes from four different epochs, presents four young foot soldiers on the eve of war: a Greek youth about to set sail for Troy, a young Spaniard ready to help conquer the Indies, a seventeenth-century French boy headed for the Louisiana Territory, and an American G.I. about to set out for the European World War. All these youths believe in their wars; they accept the official rhetoric and reasons for them. All of them swagger some, and a couple of them allude to civilians with disdain. Then, in the final episode, we are aboard ship and back again with the Greek boy. He gets the word from a seasoned, middle-aged professional warrior: All that business about Helen being kept prisoner, he says, is pure propaganda. On the contrary, sweet Helen has been squealing with joy in her bedroom romps with Paris. The real aims of this war, says the old pro, are "to sell more pottery, more cloth, more vases . . . and to open ways of access to Asia and put an end to Trojan competition."[25] The Greek novice, shaken by these words, stares out at the wine-dark sea and weeps.

Anyone who is aware of marxist issues will immediately recognize that Carpentier's final scene gives us the economic interpretation of history, specifically dramatizes the marxian view of war as a drive for markets and raw materials; and yet, of the many published examinations of the story I have read, only one article refers to the doctrinal content of the ending.[26] This is a serious omission, a bit like summarizing a crime movie without mentioning the eventual capture of the criminals (or repeating someone's joke without the punch line). For example, Roberto

González Echevarría (a Yale professor whose book on Carpentier is certainly the most thorough such study now available) says of "Like the Night" that "it represents nothing more than Spenglerian doctrine taken to its ultimate consequences."[27] This seems very wrong, and not only because of its categorical quality, for González simply ignores the *marxian* doctrine that Carpentier inserts as an explanation of war's *causes*. To depict in synchronic fashion (as Carpentier does) the common cultural features of war is in no way a denial of the socioeconomic history of war.

Moreover, with their insistence on theories of cyclical repetition and on *miles gloriosus* motifs, interpreters like González Echevarría disregard the many social and historical changes brought into play by Carpentier's narrative. It is virtually never mentioned that "Like the Night" outlines a subtle but unmistakably evolving relationship to war, a slowly modifying attitude that, for want of a less stale word, might be termed "progress." In the first episode, the Greek youth wishes to fight only for narrow reasons of personal courage and uncritical national pride. The Iberian section already hints at some skepticism when the soldier's father, a humble artisan, muses that the war is being organized "for the benefit of the few."[28] In addition, the stated justification for overseas conquest is not narrow tribalism and bellicosity for its own sake, but rather the converting of the conquered to a universalist doctrine – Christianity. Socially, this signifies that the aims of the war are no longer pure plunder or enslavement, but overseas settlement by Spaniards and the winning of spiritual loyalty from a conquered labor force. The next episode presents notable differences. The French soldier shows none of the anticivilian swagger exhibited by the Greek and the Spaniard. Christian religiosity also comes off less than positive – mention is made of the tarnished public image of the Crusades. Most important of all, the religious justifications are placed in serious doubt by the soldier's sweetheart. She happens to be under the influence of Michel de Montaigne, whose clear intellect and open mind here symbolize the rational, critical spirit of the European Renaissance. Appropriately, the young lady cites Montaigne's condemnation of Spanish overseas actions and also invokes his very modern point that Indians have no need of Christian doctrine, since their own religious beliefs suit them fine. In the mental realm, at least, we have come a long way from enthusiastic militarism and gullibility.

With the American G.I.'s episode, we find a completely different set of values and attitudes. This scene gives us a soldier who is quite saddened about leaving for war and whose girlfriend even ridicules his heroic self-image. Heroism and war by now have lost their ancient luster. Moreover, the infantryman sees this war not as intrinsically laudable but as a necessary evil, a war to end war, a struggle for principle, for an era "when man would be reconciled with man."[29] It is worth noting that, for his fourth soldier, Carpentier does not choose a U.S. marine about to land in, say, Nicaragua or a blond-haired Aryan about to push into Poland. In pointed contrast to his former soldiers of fortune, Carpentier now singles out a draftee embarked on a war of liberation. So, although throughout history wars are fought, one finds distinctive changes in attitude, progress in rationalizations and aims, gradual evolution from sheer vengefulness to abstract principles. We move from militarist bluster to high-minded religiosity, from rational skepticism about that religiosity to a secular ideal of ending war itself. These changes in the meaning of warfare sketch out an unmistakable progression toward hope, an *apertura* toward peace – and not the wistful pessimism of recurrent cycles. When Carpentier's critics emphasize recurrence and repetition (be it through Spengler, Frye, or any other such static thinker) at the expense of historical change, they are blinding themselves to the essential marxist experience of "Like the Night." For, unlike marxism, which is evolutionary and progressive in its outlook, cyclical theories of history are inherently conservative; they are, as E. H. Carr once put it, "the characteristic ideology of a society in decline."[30]

Mario Benedetti, the Uruguayan novelist and essayist currently exiled in Cuba, once remarked that "European literary criticism continues to assess Latin American artists through European models."[31] As we have seen, much the same could be said, mutatis mutandi, about North American literary criticism that deals with Latin America. In this regard Benedetti poses a series of polemical questions:

> Should Latin American Literature, at the moment of its greatest flowering, be made meekly subject to the canons of a [European] literature that is formidable in its traditions but is now going through a period of crisis and fatigue? Should a novel like *One Hundred Years of Solitude* be assessed according to the rules of the *nouveau roman . . .* ? Should structuralist criticism be thought of as the inevitable yardstick with which to measure our letters? Or, on the contrary, together with our poets and novelists, shouldn't we also be creating our own critical focus, our own methods of investigation, our own evaluative guidelines, produced by our very own conditions, interests, and needs?[32]

Benedetti's last question elicits an obvious reply, and in the past few decades exactly that sort of critical project has been taking gradual shape in Latin America. On the one hand, there are the nonfictional labors of such literary practitioners as Borges, Paz, Vargas Llosa, and Lezama Lima, their essays and longer studies treating a wide variety of European as well as Latin American subjects. In their search for a usable past and present, they write with equal ease on Whitman, Flaubert, or Sartre as on the Mexican colonial nun Sor Juana or on Buñuel or García Márquez, thereby redefining and "naturalizing" the high points of world culture for themselves and their Hispanic readers.[33]

On the other hand, there is the work of full-time critics based either in the universities or in journalism and often in both. Particularly worthy of note is the late Angel Rama, a learned Uruguayan critic and editor whose occasional writing for the general press treats not only Latin American matters but also metropolitan authors like Ruskin and Styron. Of Rama's numerous examples of in-depth scholarship, his 300-page study *Transculturación narrativa en América Latina* stands out as one of the most impressive works of "total" criticism ever produced in any language.[34] As the title suggests, Rama demonstrates the ways in which narrative fiction becomes acculturated and transformed in the Latin American environment. Rather than accept existing literary modes, myths, symbols, and genres as autonomous essences and universals emerging self-sufficiently out of one another, Rama instead brings to bear an ample but clearly profiled theoretical apparatus that conjoins Amerindian ethnography, urban sociology, structural anthropology, physical geography, economic history, and a nonsectarian marxist outlook together with stylistics, semiotics, theory of fiction, and traditional literary scholarship – all serving to capture the enormously complex process of historical *development* of narrative in Latin America since independence.

Particularly illuminating for our purposes is Rama's showing how literary works grow out of constant shifts in regional imbalance, class power, and the successive literary forms imported through imperialism: that entire political, social, and cultural arena of domination and resistance. Rama caps his performance with a superb biographical examination of José María Argüedas, noting the Peruvian author's novitiate with the *indigenistas* of the 1930s (a movement Rama considers to have been produced by the upwardly mobile *mestizo* class) and then proceeding to a thorough analysis (narrative, linguistic, historical, mythical, and even musical) of Argüedas's legendary novel of cultural conflict, *Deep Rivers*. By reconstructing the world-historical picture as well as fully apprehending an individual text, Rama's *Transculturación* provides an exhilarating instance of what literary criticism can do when it combines the global perspectives of marxism with the specific insights of a broad array of academic subdisciplines. The book came out shortly before Rama's death in an airplane crash in 1983, and one can only wonder what greater work may have issued from his pen had he not first been deported from the United States and then killed so senselessly.

In another admirable critical venture, Françoise Pérus, a Frenchwoman who lives in Mexico, locates *modernismo* (the Latin American art-for-art's-sake movement) within such larger social contexts as the rise of dependent capitalism around 1880, the problematic ties between lyric poetry and mass journalism, and the broad range of political stances adopted by actual *modernistas* – from Martí's uncompromising revolutionism, to Darío's wavering aristocratism and nationalism, to the protofascism of Lugones and Chocano. At the same time Pérus is extremely generous, authoritative, and wise in her judgments about the aesthetic value of the poems she analyzes from different stages of these poets' careers. In all, hers is a pioneering effort in the sociology of *l'art pour l'art,* one that avoids facile evaluations built on nonpoetical or sectarian criteria and that, moreover, gets firmly beyond such tired, all-purpose clichés about "alienation, formalism," and "decadence."[35]

Latin American literary critics are always extremely sensitive to the problem of cultural imperialism – the hegemonic influence that European and North American magazines, books, and movies can exert on Third World audiences. A first-rate exploration of this sociocultural fact is (and the title tells all) *The Empire's Old Clothes: What the Lone Ranger, Babar, and Other Innocent Heroes Do to Our Minds,* by the exiled Chilean novelist and journalist Ariel Dorfman.[36] In his examinations of Donald Duck and other ubiquitous, industrially produced fictions, Dorfman duly takes into account the "nonpolitical" elements of folktale and narrativity, alluding to such psychological classics as Otto Rank's *The Myth of the Birth of the Hero* and Bruno Bettelheim's *The Uses of Enchantment.* At the same time, however, Dorfman shows that those seemingly guileless Disney stories contain powerful ideological messages that preach economic individualism and disseminate colonialist attitudes – and concretely demonstrates, moreover, that such products have consequences in a Latin American setting. Rather than approach Mickey Mouse through the false "neutrality" of Jungian archetypes, Dorfman observes how mass culture is socially produced, conveys social ideologies, and helps reinforce and bring about certain social results.

Whatever one may think of marxism and its pertinence to the ghosts of time past and the nightmares of the present, if literary works like Carpentier's story are to be taken seriously, if thinkers like Rama and Pérus and Dorfman are to reach a receptive North American audience, and if the cultural and political ferment to the south of Texas is to be properly understood, then literary critics working north of the Río Grande must be prepared to deal with this totality in its own terms – in this case the terms raised by a marxism that, in Latin America, is simply a part of social and intellectual experience. When Frye dismissed marxism as a theology rather than accept its contribution to social thought and knowledge, he revealed the limits of his catholicity of taste. In dealing with Latin American literature, North American critics have a job to do if they are to help overcome the intellectual barriers of antimarxism. Just as one cannot fully understand Dante without having the rudiments of medieval theology, or Milton without an awareness of Puritan preoccupations, or Dostoyevsky without some idea of the impact of Western rationalism on Russian traditions, or T. S. Eliot without an inkling of the attractions of conservative humanism and European neo-Catholicism, similarly a full grasp of the work of modern Latin American poets and novelists is not possible without some experience of marxist theory, some acquaintance with its history in the real world.

A word about the ethical context of Northrop Frye's literary doctrine is in order. Frye's theory is now catching on in the study of children's literature, and in his foreword to a book on literary education in the schools, Frye exhorts the following:

> Ultimately, everyone exposed to literary education has to try to become a Prospero, otherwise he becomes a Caliban. From the stuttering Dick-and-Jane readers to the foul-mouthed blather of the Watergate transcripts, we realize how many Calibans there are who are quite right in saying: "You taught me language; and my profit on't / Is, I know how to curse."[37]

Frye's reading of the Prospero–Caliban dichotomy is the orthodox Western one: Prospero is civilization; Caliban (who is likened to the Watergate rogues) is barbarism. Thanks to Fernández Retamar and other Third World authors, we now know that this view mythologizes the global status quo and empties the Prospero–Caliban relationship of its history.[38] After all, Caliban was there before Prospero, who used his magical European powers to conquer the island and subjugate the natives. As Caliban himself says in act I, scene ii,

> This island's mine, by Sycorax my mother,
> Which thou tak'st from me. When thou camest first,
> Thou strok'st me, and made much of me, wouldst give me
> Water with berries in't. And teach me how
> To name the bigger light, and how the less,
> That burn by day and night. And then I loved thee . . . .
> Curs'd be I that did so! All the charms
> Of Sycorax, toads, beetles, bats, light on you!
> For I am all the subjects that you have,

Which first was mine own king. And here you sty me
In this hard rock whiles you do keep from me
The rest o'th'island.

If Caliban curses Prospero with European words, it is because the European idiom was imposed by Prospero. Today's Calibans are also employing Prospero's language, less to curse him than to know his wiles and resist them. North American critics of Latin American culture need not transform themselves into Caliban, but they now have the task of paying heed to him, even sympathizing with him if they can.

NOTES

1   Northrop Frye, *Anatomy of Criticism: Four Essays* (New York: Atheneum, 1965), p. 14.
2   I am aware that there must be nuances of attitude and feeling that, in Frye's writings, would certainly be Canadian rather than United States in character. Unfortunately I lack the acquaintance with Canadian life that would enable me to perceive such differences. I feel perfectly justified, however, in discussing the United States and Canada as a single unit. Despite their differing origins as nation states, both countries share the language, culture, and political traditions of England. In addition there is the background of British settlement, a 3,000-mile border, and an integrated economy in which fifty percent of Canadian manufacturing is U.S.-owned. The two nations have a great deal more in common than, say, France does with Belgium or Switzerland. If countries as different as Mexico and Argentina can in good conscience be dealt with as "Latin America," there is nothing illogical about thinking of Canada and the United States as "North America."
  In this regard, a Canadian journalist has noted that "there are probably no two major nations in the world with more in common than Canada and the United States" (Gary Vineberg, Letter to the Editor, *New York Times Magazine,* June 19, 1983, p. 89).
3   Frye, *Anatomy,* p. 19.
4   Ibid., p. 25.
5   Northrop Frye, *The Educated Imagination* (Bloomington: Indiana University Press, 1964), p. 134.
6   Frye, *Anatomy,* p. 355. Had Frye written this passage some eight years later, the allusion would surely have been not to modern libraries but to paperbound books.
7   Ibid., p. 97.
8   Tzvetan Todorov, *Introduction à la littérature fantastique* (Paris: Editions du Seuil, 1967), pp. 13–24; Eric Rabkin, *The Fantastic in Literature* (Princeton, N.J.: Princeton University Press, 1976). Frye's entry for Franz Kafka in the *Anatomy* lists obviously "allegorical" works like *The Trial* and "The Penal

Colony" but omits a more problematic work of modern fantasy like "The Metamorphosis," this in spite of its much greater reputation.

9   For example, Alfred J. MacAdam, *Latin American Narratives: The Dreams of Reason* (University of Chicago Press, 1977). See also my review of this book in *Review* 23 (1979):79–91.

10   Frye, *Anatomy*, p. 304.

11   Ibid., p. 306. In this connection one might recall Flaubert's *Sentimental Education*, which is commonly considered one of the most useful accounts of the revolution of 1848 and its aftermath.

12   Todorov, *Littérature fantastique*, p. 36.

13   W. W. Rostow, *The Stages of Economic Growth: A Non-Communist Manifesto* (Cambridge University Press, 1960), pp. 166–7. In Rostow's words, "Billions of human beings must live in the world, if we preserve it, over the century or so until the age of high mass-consumption becomes universal."

14   Northrop Frye, *The Critical Path: An Essay on the Social Context of Literary Criticism* (Bloomington: Indiana University Press, 1973), p. 146.

15   Ibid., p. 148.

16   Ibid., p. 137. "American society is usually called a 'capitalist' society, especially in the Communist countries. . . . In general, it is perhaps true to say that in the countries technically called capitalist, capitalism is not a belief that is desperately defended as a myth of concern." In the light of the new-found intellectual respectability of Milton Friedman and the rise of a religiously procapitalist New Right in the United States, Frye's observation is now considerably dated.

17   Ibid., p. 155. "A certain amount of contemporary agitation seems to be beating the track of the 'think with your blood' exhortations of the Nazis a generation ago, for whom 'relevance' . . . was a constant watchword."

18   See, for example, Lucille Kerr, "The Paradox of Power and Mystery: Carlos Fuentes's *Terra Nostra*," *PMLA* 95 (1980):91–100. Though Fuentes's novel is about a vast historical conflict, he even quoting Marx's *Eighteenth Brumaire* at one crucial point toward the end, Dr. Kerr's only references to a writer or theorist of history are three brief footnotes citing Foucault. Moreover, she misapplies Foucault's theory of the politics of the body to Fuentes's novel, which has to do with struggles between various religious and political groups. For an interesting reading of Fuentes's marxist conceptualization of history, see Becky Boling, "A Literary Vision of History: Marxism and Positivism in *Terra nostra* by Fuentes," *Latin American Research Review* 19, no. 1 (1984):125–41.

19   For elaboration see my "Two Americas, Two World Views, and a Widening Gap," *Monthly Review,* 34 (October 1982):37–43. The Venezuelan journalist Carlos Rangel, though himself antimarxist, has noted that marxism in Latin America enjoys the status of a "folklore." See Carlos Rangel, *Del buén salvaje al buén revolucionario* (Barcelona: Monte Ávila, 1976), p. 36.

20   Daniel Aaron, *Writers on the Left* (New York: Avon Books, 1965), p. 168.

21   Octavio Paz, *El arco y la lira,* 2nd ed. (Mexico City: Fondo de Cultura Económica, 1967), p. 258; translation mine.

22 Karl Shapiro, "The Critic Outside," *The American Scholar* 50 (Spring 1981):210.
23 Alexander Coleman, "Beyond *One Hundred Years of Solitude,*" *New Boston Review* (January 1977):22.
24 Anthony Burgess, review of *Chronicle of a Death Foretold, The New Republic,* May 2, 1983, p. 36.
25 Alejo Carpentier, "Like the Night," in *War of Time,* trans. Frances Partridge (New York: Knopf, 1970), pp. 154–5.
26 M. Roberto Assardo, "'Semejante a la noche' o la contemporaneidad del hombre," in Helmy Giacoman, ed., *Homenaje a Alejo Carpentier* (New York: Las Américas, 1970), p. 224.
27 Roberto González Echevarría, *Alejo Carpentier: The Pilgrim at Home* (Ithaca, N.Y.: Cornell University Press, 1977), p. 224.
28 Carpentier, "Like the Night," p. 140.
29 Ibid., p. 150.
30 E. H. Carr, *What Is History?* (London: Penguin Books, 1964), p. 43.
31 Mario Benedetti, "Temas y problemas," in César Fernández Moreno, ed., *América Latina en su literatura* (Mexico City: Siglo Veintiuno Editores, 1972), p. 367; translation mine.
32 Ibid., pp. 367–8.
33 In this connection, see my "Lit.Crit. in Latin America, or the Advantages of Underdevelopment," *American Book Review* 5, no. 6 (September–October 1983):4–5.
34 Angel Rama, *Transculturación narrativa en América Latina* (Mexico City: Siglo Veintiuno Editores, 1982).
35 Françoise Pérus, *Literatura y sociedad en América Latina: el modernismo* (Mexico City: Siglo Veintiuno Editores, 1976).
36 Ariel Dorfman, *The Empire's Old Clothes: What the Lone Ranger, Babar, and Other Innocent Heroes Do to Our Minds* (New York: Pantheon Books, 1983).
37 Northrop Frye, Foreword to Glenna Davis Sloan, *The Child as Critic* (New York: Teachers College Press of Columbia University, 1975), pp. xiv–xv.
38 Roberto Fernández Retamar, *Caliban: Notes Toward a Discussion of Culture in Our America,* trans. Lynn Garafola, David Arthur McMurray, and Robert Márquez, in special issue of *Massachusetts Review* 15, nos. 1–2 (Winter–Spring 1974):7–72. As Fernández Retamar explicitly says on p. 24, "Our symbol then is not Ariel . . . but rather Caliban."

16

Marvelous realism/ marvelous criticism

GARI LAGUARDIA

Ever since the rise of the New Criticism more than fifty years ago the proposition that literary texts are autonomous and self-sufficient has been one of the most persistent critical notions in the United States. Even now, long past the heyday of New Criticism proper, its fundamental proposition lives on in the work of one wing of American deconstruction. These critics have largely abandoned the values the New Critics "discovered" and canonized, but have preserved their privileging of the text as a complex self-sustaining network of rhetorical operations beyond which it is unnecessary and improper to go.

Whereas the "founder" of deconstruction, Jacques Derrida, does not delimit the textual field to the literary text and its canon, extending instead this field to the world viewed as discourse, critics like the late Paul DeMan and J. Hillis Miller stop short of extending textuality beyond the boundaries of literary texts. DeMan's position basically was that literary texts had already done a critical operation on themselves and that the critic's task was to identify how a given text accomplished this. What every text has to "say" is in essence that whatever it advances as "true" is, in fact, not "true," and moreover the text is aware of its own dissembling, which it proceeds to "deconstruct." The critical act itself, then, is a repetition of the text's own reflections about itself. These critics' meticulously close readings of texts thus abolish the distinction between practical and theoretical criticism.

Here I do not propose to address the theoretical aspects of deconstruction. Rather I want to show how these notions of textual autonomy become problematic when a critic desires to hold onto them and at the same time discuss a particular body of texts such as "American literature." As a corollary, I shall demonstrate how under these circumstances any privileging of "literary autonomy" is not, in fact, believed by

the discourse that advances the notion, which itself is motivated or underwritten by "extratextual" concerns. Then I shall argue that, as a clear
instance of this, critical discourse on "Latin American literature" tra-
duces the notion of "autonomy" whenever it tries to advance it. How
this happens in the Latin American critical texts discussed here provides,
finally, an example of a problematic aspect of literary relations between
the Americas.

Avowals of literature's autonomy or fundamental antirealism become
problematic when a critic proposes to tie a discussion of a text to the
cultural aggregate from which it arises. What can be said in such a
theoretical context about the literature of the United States or Latin
America (or any other literature) if one is to grant the cultural aggregate a
substantive position – a signification of difference – in the phenomenon
so labeled? To put it simply: How can American literature exist?

In these terms a deconstructor who wishes to preserve the term might
contend, as does Joseph Riddel, for example, that "American literature"
is an oxymoron.[1] In relation to "literature" the term "American" is
simply a reflection of the basic contradictions exemplified by the former.
That is, literature itself, as writing, suffers from the basic contradiction
of being original and secondary at the same time. Granting this basic
deconstructionist proposition it can then be averred that "American"
reflects the same contradictions, since while positing itself as "new" it
also enters an established tradition belatedly. Thus "American literature"
is a doublet expression of what is at root an "original secondariness" and
therefore a redundant oxymoron. Viewed somewhat differently, however, the same logic can be used to discover a tautology, America[n] =
literature, implicit in the terms of the argument advanced to define the
oxymoron. That is, if America is an original secondariness and literature
is likewise an original secondariness, America = literature. In a significant way the gap opened up by Riddel's formulation of an oxymoron is
brought to closure by the tautology that underwrites it, which his discourse does not explicitly acknowledge but nonetheless advances. If we
pursue Riddel's argument further, this paradoxical turn may disclose the
different conditions that inform criticism in the United States and Latin
America.

Riddel locates his oxymoron at a Derridean "abyss," the point where
"American poetry" recognizes the irreconcilability of its presumed identity with a stable point of origin. There, paradoxically, it realizes itself
through the recognition that "the fiction of Being can be entertained, not
as that which has been lost and can be recuperated, but as that which has
been invented as a pure fiction so that it can be destroyed, or deconstruct-
ed, in 'the beginning again.' "[2] Consequently, Riddel proposes a "non-

tradition" of American Adamic poets, each of whom discretely in series repeats this project. Charles Olsen, the latest of that line constituted by Riddel, is represented as contending that the poem "must be a 'glyph,' a mark in nature, a mark signifying the intercourse of man and nature, the place of man, his placement toward nature, the meeting point of an irreducible dance . . . it is a threshold like the 'skin' where man and nature interact, the place of the dance or play. . . . The skin . . . is not a thing or a place at all. . . . No history can begin from this non-origin."[3]

This stream of images exhibits the euphoric air that befits its articulation of a deconstructor's paradise. That paradise – or utopia – is dominated by play (fun, erotics) and purity ("irreducible difference"), which erase the anxiety that usually arises when the concepts of history and "origins," with the difficult and often messy particulars that sustain them, are brought to the fore. This imagery implies that by getting to the bottom of things ("nature") we enter a realm where fiction ("no history," "nonorigin") is eternally and repetitively present. This fiction, explicitly nonempirical, nonetheless implies a goal, the poem, the achievement of which ineluctably suggests the reentry of history and origins into the process of signification. However, this second-order history and origin, having been absorbed by fiction, are therefore purified by that negation and rendered into a sign capable of sustaining without regret desires that are not only paradisiacal but imperial.

Riddel represents Olsen's "projective verse" as going "back behind Homer in order to come forward beyond Melville and romanticism."[4] This is a marvelously ambitious flanking operation that appropriates the entire tradition of Western discourse by "decentering" it to America (the United States). This almost military application of imaginative force to theory cannot be so insouciantly expressed by any Latin American theorist. In fact, the option for a paradise of "American poetics" as articulated by Joseph Riddel is not available to Latin American critics and writers.

The fact is that the empirical givens that plausibly certify the preeminence of the United States in Western culture are not substantially threatened by rhetorical gestures that either bracket it out of literary discourse or put into question the images of "America" generated by its literature and criticism. On the contrary, the empirical stability of U.S. cultural institutions not only informs and certifies the ambitious projection of Olsen's image (however figurative) but also underwrites the presumably "radical" activity of many "deconstructors," rewarding their insights with recognition, comment, and promotion. Critics can put the entire concept of an American literature into question while at the same time their own identity as critics and in turn the value of their textual objects are continuously validated by the solidity and power of the institutional network they inhabit. It is thus emblematic that in articulating contradictions inherent in positing an "American poetry" Joseph Riddel's own discourse installs a tautology that negates the denial of authority implied by his "oxymoron."

This "safety net" is not available to a Latin American critic or writer who wishes to deconstruct the culture into which he or she is inserted. Not propped up by a dense, empirical network of institutions and the power with which they underwrite discourse, they run the risk of disarticulating themselves into nothing or simply becoming supplements of cultures that do possess institutional power. When Martí declared that there would not be a Latin American literature until there was Latin America, he was being neither provincial nor obtuse. He was, rather, registering an awareness of the essential contingencies that had to come together before a particular culture could project itself as "universal."

Thus the Latin American critic who desires incorporation into the mainstream of Western critical discourse (the operative model for "universal") and who is simultaneously confronted with the temptation of a full-blown antirealist position becomes subject to conflicting demands. On the one hand, he is repelled because, unable to take Latin America's Westernness or non-Westernness for granted, he is obliged to constitute his subject historically; yet an antirealist position makes this impossible. On the other hand, an antirealist position is attractive because it allows the critic to ignore as irrelevant historical and social data that traduce his or her desire for the presumed plenitude of universal discourse. Faced with such a situation, a significant and influential segment of Latin American high criticism has attempted to create a critical space where these contradictions (and similar ones) can be overcome by the selective incorporation of enough elements of a presumed reality to provide a reasonable ground for the exercise of willed subjectivity.

A good example of this is Octavio Paz's seminal essay "A Literature of Foundation." There he states: "To invent reality or to rescue it? Both. Reality recognizes itself in the imaginings of poets – and poets recognize their imaginings in reality. Our dreams are waiting for us around the corner. Spanish American literature, which is rootless and cosmopolitan, is both a return and a search for tradition. In searching for it, it invents it. But invention and discovery are not terms that best describe its purest creations. A desire for incarnation, a literature of foundations."[5] This essay was written in Paris in 1961. Around that time, building on the work produced during the 1940s and 1950s by individual writers such as Borges, Carpentier, Asturias, and Rulfo, a younger generation of writers began producing work that self-conciously acknowledged that it was part of a collective literary movement and proposed to engineer a broad renewal of Latin American literary language.

To the degree that the writers and critics who were identified with the movement took it upon themselves to demystify the older traditions of Latin American narrative and, beyond that, the "language" of Latin America itself, their project was deconstructive. Carlos Fuentes, for example, declared that "given the corruption of Latin American language any true act of language is a revolutionary act."[6] He contended that the avowals advanced over the centuries by Latin American discourse masked other projects: "The Renaissance language of the conquest hides the medieval core of the colonial enterprise . . . the Enlightenment language of Independence hides the survival of the feudal order, and the positivist language of nineteenth century liberalism masks the surrender to financial imperialism."[7]

At the same time the "Boom" proposed a reconstructive project that among other things implied a "new" beginning for Spanish American literature, the creation of the proper ground for its definition and the constitution of itself, through its texts, as the arbiter and signifier of this new reality. In fact, the novels produced during the sixties succeeded in inserting themselves as a central point of reference in the history of the Latin American novel, succeeded like no other movement since fin-de-siècle *modernismo* in disseminating Latin American literature internally and abroad and succeeded in provoking a wider series of political aesthetic and moral discourses.

It is interesting that, because of its self-consciously avant-garde posture, the "new narrative" stimulated Latin American critics to search for and incorporate new methods of interpreting these works, but it did not meet equal success in ensuring that such criticism would accomplish for critical discourse what it had so well accomplished for fiction. The heady success of this fiction encouraged a tendency – supported by emerging critical theories in the world at large – to privilege the text by alternately considering it "autonomous" or, in a reversal of traditional procedures, textualizing the world outside of it (or better, considering the "world" part of the textual field). This turn is implicit in the cited Paz essay. However, the triumph of fictionality did not always produce the intended liberation from historical determinisms. The play of signs that constitutes such a world is not always as free as might be imagined. Sometimes a refusal of "history" or the "world" only disarms critical discourse, leaving it prey to discursive forces that do function within "history" and "reality" and that will surreptitiously determine its signification and dissemination in ways that traduce the stated aims of such criticism. I shall now examine Latin American writing that exemplifies this problem.

Emir Rodríguez Monegal has been one of the most influential critics and promoters of the "Boom." Besides being one of the most active and influential disseminators of Latin American literature in the United States, he is the author of important books on Bello, Neruda, and Borges, editor of the collected works of José E. Rodó, and author of scores of critical essays. He has never been a theoretically systematic critic. A hugely well read man, in possession of a virtually unrivaled bibliographical command of modern Latin American literature, his criticism can be characterized largely as a combination of traditional scholarship (i.e., scrupulous attention to textual history: editions, sources, etc.), a bent – unusual in Latin America – for psychoanalysis as an interpretative tool, and a nuanced, New Critical sensitivity to textual pattern and detail.

To these components of his "technique" of interpretation can be added a set of concerns and attitudes that crystallize explicitly during the 1960s in tandem with his extensive work on and with the writers of the "Boom." Like Octavio Paz he laments the lack of what the former calls a "critical space" in Latin America and desires at the same time that Latin American writers be considered integral participants in "universal" discourse. Although he has not proposed any systematic program for achieving these ends, he has repeatedly alluded to Latin American critical attitudes and practices that presumably impede their realization. Chief among these in his view are provincialism, ideological straitjackets, and lack of familiarity with up-to-date critical techniques. To counter these shortcomings he has consistently advocated that Latin American critics adopt a cosmopolitan interest in all current theory by reading extensively European and U.S. literature and criticism. Moreover, as a way out of ideological straitjackets Rodríguez Monegal implies that respect for the primacy of the text and its autonomy provides a healthy corrective. This specifically involves a distancing from "politics."

Now, "politics" is by nature an ambiguous term. It can refer to a narrow range of activity, say supporting one candidate as opposed to another, or imply a much broader range of material involving most aspects of social and personal interaction. Just what "politics" means to Rodríguez Monegal is never made quite clear, except that it is most often connoted negatively whenever it touches on literature. In these cases it is virtually always left wing. In fact, "politics" and "ideology" are frequently indistinguishable from representations of left-wing activity in Rodríguez Monegal's discourse. To these he opposes ideas of openness, variety, freedom, and general antidogmatism, which crystallize into textual values of complexity, ambiguity, and novelty. For Rodríguez Monegal, as with the New Critics in the United States, these are the privileged determinants of the positive worth of literary activity.

For example, Rodríguez Monegal criticizes the Argentine author David Viñas for allowing the "world vision" of his novels to be limited by "ideological schemata which are anterior to the contemplation of reality."[8] These schemata are derived from "Sartrean existentialism" and to a degree from "Lucien Goldmann" (N327). In contrast, he praises Carlos Fuentes, Vargas Llosa, and such U.S. writers as James Jones and Norman Mailer for dealing with similar themes but without the presumed "chromatic monotony" derived from taking an a priori position (N326). Vargas Llosa, for example, "creates a very differentiated and non-stereotypical series of military types" in *La ciudad y los perros*, whereas in *Los hombres de a caballo* "Viñas succeeds in portraying only two or three conventional types" (N326). Fuentes, for his part, demonstrates a more accomplished understanding of the soical, economic, and political ambience in which Latin Americans are inserted (N327) than does Viñas. In Funtes's novels "there is a world," whereas in Viñas's *Dar la cara* there is only a "monotonous procession of characters" (N327).

Rodríguez Monegal frames his criticism of Viñas by inscribing him within the generation of Argentine critics and writers to which he belongs. This generation was one that set out to do more than "the mere exercise of literary criticism" (N315). They are "more interested in disciplines such as sociology and philosophy than in stylistics or literary history" (N315). They are "not critics who have studied the foundational work of the Russian formalists, the truly revolutionary labor of the Cambridge school or that of the north American New Criticism" (N315). For these writers "the reality from which the work arises is more important than the reality that the work creates" (N315).

Whether Rodríguez Monegal has accurately characterized Viñas and his generation is not at issue here. What is are the contradictory criteria that underlie Rodríguez Monegal's portrayals and evaluations. On the one hand, "reality" is not denied. Fuentes is superior to Viñas, in part because of his more inclusive portrayal of it in his novels. On the other hand, Viñas, in Rodríguez Monegal's view, implicitly suffers from the limitations of his generation, one of which is the supervaluation of the "reality" of the world as opposed to the "reality" of the text. Rodríguez Monegal could have avoided these contradictions by simply basing his arguments on formal criteria: He could have performed a "Russian formalist" or a "North American New Critical" analysis of Viñas and let it go at that. Conversely, he could have attacked Viñas's left-wing "realism" by arguing that it is an impoverished "realism." The problem is that the first strategy would have deprived him of the opportunity to critique a particular ideology, whereas the second might have suggested too directly that his own critical discourse was also ideological.

Not wanting to give up "reality" to the Left and at the same time wanting to transcend it, Rodríguez Monegal's tendency is to constitute reality in the text, where it is more feasibly manipulated by his own liberal values. Comparing a novel by Manuel Puig *(La traición de Rita Hayworth)* with the work of David Viñas, he grants that Puig "reflects and documents . . . a zone of Argentina brought to light by Perón" (N376). In particular, one section of this novel "demonstrates . . . the political background and gives some keys to understanding the mediocrity, the resentment, the frustration of the entire social body" (N376). Yet unlike Viñas, Puig does not approach the issue tendentiously but on a level Viñas "had never explored and that is, paradoxically, the only one that permits a total access: the level of language" (N376). Although this statement might elicit nods of assent from some literary critics and theorists, it remains to be asked, What is this "level of language"? How is it, moreover, that this "level" is the "only one that permits total access"? Why is it paradoxical?

Structuralism, semiotics, and deconstruction provide familiar answers to these questions, but these are not the ones Rodríguez Monegal adduces. He does not, in fact, adduce any. Rather his readers are obliged to decipher what that "level" is by the more concrete terms and categories that Rogríguez Monegal uses in contrast to it. Discussing some novels of José Donoso, Rodríguez Monegal marks the point at which his "full maturity" as a novelist emerges. This maturity is achieved when he transcends the limitations of an expansive "realist" novel of customs and focuses repeatedly on a few obsessive themes that allow for symbolic variety and complexity (N239).

What are these themes? "It is always a world that is based, on the one hand, on a woman, a mother or grandmother . . . and on the other on the frankly incestuous relations of this woman with a male in her family or with a younger man" (N239). The repeated construction of similar relationships allows for the "presence of a deeper reality in these novels . . . a reality that completes the world of the surface" (N246). It is interesting that Rodríguez Monegal's analysis of David Viñas also uncovers an underlying sexual nucleus. In that case it is the ambivalent relationship between men who live by the code of machismo. "The double theme of friendship and betrayal frequently intersects with the theme of the attraction and repulsion of homosexuality" (N329).

Yet whereas for Donoso the repeated return to obsessively particular sexual relations is what allows access to a presumably deeper and richer narrative practice, for Viñas it does not. Though presumably a leavening for his tendentious politics, Viñas's sexual symbolism betrays a "primitive conception of true virility" – a conception that is suited to "children and more or less disturbed adolescents" and appropriate only to one of Viñas's novels, the theme of which is "the terrors of childhood" (N329). The issue here is not the superior literary virtue of one neurosis as opposed to another. The point is that Rodríguez Monegal presents the reader with two similar situations: realist novels underwritten by sexual symbolism. In one case the sexual symbolism rescues the realism and marks its "maturity"; in the other it merely leavens the realism and marks its immaturity.

There may well be many reasons to rate Donoso a better novelist than Viñas, but Rodríguez Monegal's analysis provides only one (implicit at that): Viñas offers an avowedly left-wing critique of the Argentine military caste, whereas Donoso's portrayal of the Chilean bourgeoisie is presumably not politically tendentious. The question that must now be repeated is this: If texts are in fact autonomous, how is it that similar symbolical articulations lead to opposing evaluations: narrative maturity for one, immaturity for the other? If we discard the unlikely notion that Rodríguez Monegal considers one "neurosis" more mature than the other, we can only conclude that the ideological network that frames each text is what determines its value.

Similar problems arise in more comprehensive contexts when Rodríguez Monegal considers the contemporary novel as a whole. I shall now examine three articles in which Rodríguez Monegal attempts to provide a general overview of the "Boom" and its significance in the development of Latin American literature. The first of these has had a varied life. It appeared originally in Life en Español in 1965, then in the same year in English in an expanded version as "The New Novelties" in Encounter, and finally in Rodríguez Monegal's book Narradores de esta América. In this article Rodríguez Monegal declares that one of the most significant accomplishments of the "New Novel" in regard to the older Latin American narratives was a great advance in character protrayal. In his view this development was sufficiently momentous as to incarnate a "new" Latin American man. "The New Novels," Rodríguez Monegal stated there, "fix their gaze on the new man the Latin American continent is now producing. They project towards the future their vision of these lands and peoples . . . they are both mirrors and anticipations" (N9). All of this is in marked contrast to older realist narratives, in which the individual according to Rodríguez Monegal is reduced to a "cipher."

In 1971, in an article entitled "Una escritura revolucionaria," Rodríguez Monegal returned to this point when he declared that in older Latin American narratives "the representation of human conflicts became generalized: passions aquired the anonymous color of the mass. Economic and social forces of nature in the abstract . . . were opposed to the disinherited and oppressed . . . geography was all, man nothing" (N33). In contrast, the "New Novels" present the reader with "complete and ambiguous characters that 'appear' as complete human beings" (N34). The qualities of these "complete human beings" insofar as they were *explicitly* articulated were related to a shift in the placement of characters from the country to the city and more cosmopolitan settings. In these settings the individual characters were presumably allowed a greater option of moral choice and more autonomy in their fictional development.

Two things should be noted here. First is the clustering of such qualities as the fullness of the individual person, cosmopolitanism, modernity, and free will. These are opposed to masses, determinism, and oppression. Then there is the generally euphoric tone that accompanies these avowals explicit in the evocations of various actualizations of the "new." The values evinced by the above are not in themselves devoid of an ideological component. Neither "marxist" nor conservative, the advancement of individualism, novelty, and freedom can be viewed as a "liberal" discourse evocative of the ideology that informed the Alliance for Progress.

Be that as it may, in the United States in 1969 none of the above would have seemed particularly novel to critics at what was then the cutting edge of literary criticism: structuralism, semiotics, and deconstruction. Therefore, when writing directly for such an audience on the contribution of the new Latin American novel, Rodríguez Monegal introduces a new element, language, as the salient object of innovative activity. There Rodríguez Monegal asserts that Lezama Lima writes a "summa" of form, "a metaphorical play of language, the mirror of both the visible and invisible world." Cortázar's *Rayuela* is a novel in which form "becomes what used to be its content." *Cien años de soledad* "only achieves complete coherence in the deep reality of its language." *Tres tristes tigres* "sets up right in its core the negation of its truth . . . and . . . ends up by demolishing the carefully built edifice of its own fiction" (shades of Derrida and DeMan). For Puig, Sánchez, Sainz, and Sarduy (basically very different writers) "the thing is the language . . . Marshall Macluhan's popularized formula 'the medium is the message.'" Their novels use "the word not to say something in particular about the world which is outside literature, but to transform the linguistic reality of the narrative itself . . . the novel is *the* reality and not a creation parallel to reality itself."[9]

How do we account for the "play of language" with its implied negation of "complete human beings" being sandwiched chronologically between the two pieces that opt for "man"? In the usual practice of literary criticism a concept such as the play of language is not compatible with concepts of character portrayal and projections of a new society. Methodological purists may prefer that critical approaches be deployed discretely with philosophical consistency. Rodríguez Monegal appears capable, however, of holding to two contradictory conceptualizations concurrently: "New men" and "complete human beings" are stressed in 1965, 1966, and 1971, whereas the "play of language" is highlighted in 1969.

Yet there is, in fact, a consistency in Rodríguez Monegal that is not strictly one of methodology but rather has to do with ideological preferences and values. Both the "play of language" and "complete human beings" are terms that stand in opposition to formulas implicitly or explicitly related to "deterministic" or "collective" forces. The concepts of free choice and pluralism can thus mediate the marriage between the apparently contradictory terms "play of language" and "complete human beings." Viewed in such a manner, Rodríguez Monegal's criticism is political in a broad sense. More precisely it draws a stage where the literary text can be represented as producing images that are identified with cultural forms that are esteemed as powerful.

In this regard Rodríguez Monegal's biography of Borges is exemplary.[10] In this book, one of his most accomplished, he reads Borges's life in light of his texts and vice versa. Given the book's genre as biography, there is no question here of insisting on pure textual autonomy or severing the ties between text and "reality." Nonetheless, some aspects of history and "reality" are distinctly privileged as "readers" of Borges's texts. A consideration of those privileged aspects produces some insight into the meaning of "complete human beings."

Rodríguez Monegal tells us that Borges read English before Spanish and that he has always found English culture and literature superior to the Spanish. This anomaly with its implied tensions is attributed to an "unconscious conflict." The unconscious conflict arises because "he was taught Spanish by his mother and English by his paternal grandmother" (B22). This gives rise to an oedipal conflict between father's "code" (English) and the mother's "code" (Spanish), which is initially resolved in favor of the father. However, "at the unconscious level . . . he never accepts it. And only in mother's discarded and despised code – Spanish –

will he succeed in symbolizing all that archaic repressed material: the stuff bodies (and poetry) are made of" (B26).

This is fine, but is what is repressed and then expressed only the mother's code? Is there not a social dimension to this tension also?

Rodríguez Monegal tells us that Borges himself in his early "nativist" period rejected "the usual Argentine view of progress (an attempt to be 'almost' North American or European: that is to be somebody else)" (B207). Yet when those critics Rodríguez Monegal calls "literary nationalists" criticize Borges in the same spirit, he castigates them. Responding to one such attack, he defends Borges's poetic treatment of *truco,* an Argentine card game: "Instead of using the symbols of Argentina to emphasize what is unique (and thus parochial) in them, Borges uses them to show what is universal about them. In his poem about *truco* what Borges wants to show is not the quaint peculiarities of the popular card game but the fact that any game makes us unreal: in following the rules we repeat the games other men have played before us and for a while we are those men" (B423). Continuing his attack on the literary nationalists, he paraphrases Borges and accuses them of insisting "that a writer demonstrate he is Argentine or Zulu" (B424). Now, perhaps Borges's "nationalist" critics were making banal and stupid points; but that is an issue best resolved elsewhere. At issue here, rather, is the manner in which Rodríguez Monegal characterizes Borges's attackers and the way in which he defends Borges, identifying with those cultural values he perceives in him. On the one hand are "quaint peculiarities," "parochial" and "nationalist"; on the other are "universal" and "other men." It is interesting and revealing that the positive factors are mediated by "makes us unreal," a characterization that constitutes a veiled admission that reality is unbearable.

What the "reality" insisted upon by the "literary nationalists" means to Rodríguez Monegal is betrayed by the arbitrary juxtaposition of "Argentine" and "Zulu." To position this identification he follows Borges by counterposing the examples of Shakespeare and Racine, to whom literary nationalism would have been allegedly unintelligible. It would seem that, in fact, the Shakespeare who in *Richard II* wrote "This sceptered isle, this England" understood literary nationalism well enough. However, it is more useful to point out that what is being thrashed out here is a Southern Cone version of the conflict between "Palefaces and Redskins." As is often the case, Sarmiento's century-old polemic puts all of this in clearer perspective. Annoyed at Martí's critiques of the United States and of the "exotic creoles" who pandered to Europe, Sarmiento replied: "[Martí] . . . needs to regenerate himself, educate himself receiving inspiration from the country he lives in [the United States]. . . . I should like Martí to give us less Martí, less Spaniard and less South American and more Yankee, the new type of modern man."[11] For Sarmiento "South American" was frequently a distasteful appellation that connoted, in his words, a "semi-indian, semi-Spaniard."[12] We can now see more clearly that the imaginative trajectory Rodríguez Monegal's discourse draws for Borges signals a series of displacements and repressions that are complementary to what the critic had analyzed in another context as the conflict between the codes of the grandmother and the mother. Yet this movement from a rejection of wanting "to be somebody else" to becoming "other men," "unreal," and finally "universal" neither is explicitly tied by the critic to the formerly analyzed linguofamilial anomaly, nor receives the sophisticated analysis devoted to the first. Rodríguez Monegal's quasi-Lacanian formulations, however illuminating, do not provide an explanation as full as what his own discourse suggests. Indeed it is odd that in the second instance cited here, Rodríguez Monegal's "analysis" becomes simply an occasion to attack "literary nationalists" who also happen to be marxists.

All of this suggests that, notwithstanding Rodríguez Monegal's statement that "politics should be left to politicians and writing to writers," his own critical activity does not quite conform to the clear distinction he himself prescribes. The fact is that one of the underlying aims of Rodríguez Monegal's critical activity, quite explicit in his general overviews of the "Boom," is to establish the evidence for a viable literary "modernity" in Latin America. Although he makes an effort to build a case for this modernity in terms of an expanded human consciousness and in terms of mastery of "advanced" techniques, he fails to register clearly the fact that both of these elements are contingent on concrete historical contexts and depend on values particular to given forms of social organization and development. It is this failure to register and contextualize the full import of his own position that disarms Rodríguez Monegal's criticism on its own terms and makes it no less a political statement than that of the various "nationalists" and "marxists" he so vigorously attacks.

Fundamentally the "politics" of Rodríguez Monegal's criticism do not depend on elaborate theorizing, nor do they draw their validity from a specific and measured consideration of concrete historical and social data. Rather they establish themselves through homeopathy with the cultural norms and values of societies like that of the United States where these have been powerfully constituted. One striking example of this occurs in Rodríguez Monegal's extended treatment of two incidents in 1971 during one of Borges's many tours of the United States. One scene takes place at Columbia, the other at Yale. They are here juxtaposed to convey a particular effect.

At Columbia University Borges is accosted by a "representative of a group of Puerto Rican students" (B453). Rodríguez Monegal reports that "the student insulted Borges, making a remark about his mother's supposed profession and concluding that Borges had nothing to say about Latin America because he was already dead" (B453). Borges became enraged and challenged the student to "settle matters outside." Commenting on the incident Rodríguez Monegal strikes a pose of liberal, if condescending tolerance. He reports that he assured Borges that the attack arose out of a "political situation" that was part of a "larger state of unrest." Borges, in short, was only a proxy victim. Rodríguez Monegal does not have to register any offense directly, since the civil reader is presumably repelled by the coarseness of the Puerto Rican's attack and moved by the elderly Borges's "chivalrous invitation" to duel proffered while "holding his cane in trembling hands" (B453).

Rodríguez Monegal might have made the point that the student may have been responding – inappropriately only because of the formality of the occasion – to certain aspects of Borges's own public discourse. Borges, after all, has made many political statements, some intemperate, during his career. He described the now ousted military junta of Argentina as "gentlemen," he praised Pinochet, he signed a manifesto supporting the Bay of Pigs invasion of Cuba, he inscribed a copy of his translation of Whitman to Richard Nixon, and he once said that because Mexicans "like to play at being Red Indians . . . they have nothing at all."[13] Recognition of the fact that the student was only responding in kind to a long history of similar statements by Borges, however, would only have detracted from the symbolic value of the confrontation: a restaging of Sarmiento's conflict between barbarism and civilization.

Nonetheless, Rodríguez Monegal is not entirely in control of his symbolic projection. The substance of the Puerto Rican representative's attack oddly parallels statements by Rodríguez Monegal himself. The crude statement that Borges "was already dead" echoes Rodríguez Monegal's statement, itself an echo of Borges, that "by becoming 'Borges,' Borges had finally ceased to matter . . . the other Borges (that is, Borges) slowly receded into nothingness" (B440). The perhaps cruder comment about Borges's mother is also echoed in Rodríguez Monegal's text. Reconstructing Borges's childhood from a psychoanalytic perspective, Rodríguez Monegal avers that "Mother was like the beautiful concubine in some of the tales of the *One Thousand and One Nights* that Father (and later Georgie) loved to read in Richard Burton's unexpurgated translation" (B23). Ironically the student's statement itself was only tangentially directed at Borges's mother. By translating the student's expletive (the Spanish equivalent of SOB) into the baroque "his mother's supposed profession," Rodírguez Monegal's language calls attention to his own interest throughout the book, consistent with his tendency to use psychoanalytic insights, in the intense but strange relationship between Borges and his mother. In this light, the portrayal of the Puerto Rican student's verbal assault on Borges becomes something more than another occasion for insinuating that politics brutalize culture. The "play" of Rodríguez Monegal's own discourse has eluded him and inserted within his intended rhetorical demonstration another scene, a "return of the repressed." That is, it has fleetingly materialized the anxiety-ridden reflection that both the critic and his antagonist are, so to speak, cut from the same cloth: an "other" in *cosmopolis.*

This "return of the repressed" is rapidly canceled by another visit recounted immediately thereafter. From Columbia with its angry Puerto Rican the reader is transported to Yale, Rodríguez Monegal's home institution, where "I was . . . chairman of [the] Spanish and Portuguese Department and of the Council on Latin American Studies" (B453). There, instead of protestors, Borges encounters an audience of "writers and critics" and hundreds of devotees. There is only one brief, untoward scene. When the crowd overflows the originally scheduled auditorium Rodríguez Monegal finds another, larger one but "the janitor . . . began to complain loudly that he had not been warned" (B454). This Caliban is soon quieted down and "the planned intimate conversation on literary matters took place" (B454). From Columbia to Yale, from vulgarity to civility, from the lumpen to the intellectual, from the political to the literary, Borges and his Ariel finally find their proper place: "Borges began by answering, with his subtlest irony, questions politely put forth by writers and critics. That won them completely. He is one of us, they felt" (B454).

Becoming "one of us," Rodríguez Monegal and Borges accede to what Paz in his seminal article had already declared twelve years before to be the case with Latin Americans: "We are now the contemporaries of all men."[14] Yet for Rodríguez Monegal "all men," like "complete human beings," are identified paradoxically with a particular group of "men," which in turn is not like some others. That is, one is a "complete human being" when a particular group certifies it. At the end of his life, Sarmiento, cranky and irritable, retained the virtue of direct candor that this discourse lacks; annoyed at the criticisms leveled at the United States by Latin American intellectuals, he took the bull by the horns and said, "Let's *be* the United States!"[15]

Rodríguez Monegal's most ambitious and influential effort on behalf of the "Boom" in particular and Latin American literature in general – his role as founding editor of the journal *Mundo Nuevo* – illustrates, to a greater degree than the apotheosis at Yale, the problem entailed by Sarmiento's dream. The Chilean novelist José Donoso, himself a luminary of the "Boom," tells us that in 1966 the editor of *Encounter* recruited Rodríguez Monegal to edit a new literary journal in Paris to be called *Mundo Nuevo,* which would be devoted to the dissemination of the best Latin American writing and criticism.[16]

It is germane here to recall the history of the famous British journal. That journal was founded in 1953 under the auspices of the Congress for Cultural Freedom and "with Irving Kristol, Stephen Spender and later [Melvin J.] Lasky at its head, was the official answer to the 'anti-Americanism' . . . which disfigured the English cultural scene." Years later Thomas Braden, who had been supervisor of cultural activities at the CIA, reported that the agency "placed one agent in a Europe-based organization of intellectuals called the Congress for Cultural Freedom."[17] This agent was, in fact, the cofounder (with Melvin Lasky) of the organization, Michael Josselson. Braden also said, "Another agent became an editor of *Encounter.*" Braden remarked that these "agents" and those placed in a number of other organizations (e.g., the National Student Association) "could not only propose anti-communist programs to the official leaders of these organizations but they could suggest ways and means to solve the inevitable budgetary problems. Why not see if the needed money could be obtained from 'American foundations'?"[18] At the time that Rodríguez Monegal was recruited as editor of *Mundo Nuevo* the editors were Melvin J. Lasky, Stephen Spender, and Frank Kermode. Which one of the three recruited Rodríguez Monegal is not mentioned by Donoso. Of the three, only Lasky was aware of the CIA connection.

Regardless, *Mundo Nuevo* functioned for three fruitful years under Rodríguez Monegal's editorship. In Donoso's view it "exercised a decisive role in defining a generation. . . . *Mundo Nuevo* was the voice of the Latin American literature of its time . . . the history of the Boom, at the moment in which it was most united, is written in the pages of *Mundo Nuevo.*"[19] True enough, much distinguished writing appeared in that journal's pages. Nonetheless, the entire enterprise became tainted when a wave of revelations in the late 1960s about the CIA's infiltration of cultural organizations eventually exposed *Mundo Nuevo's* sponsoring organization, the Congress for Cultural Freedom, as a CIA conduit. Rodríguez Monegal resigned, claiming that he had always thought that *Mundo Nuevo* was financed by the Ford Foundation. There is no reason to disbelieve him. It should be noted, however, that writers like Julio Cortázar for some reason or other refused from the beginning to collaborate with the journal.[20]

The point, of course, is not that Rodríguez Monegal was a CIA collaborator. He was hardly the only critic or writer to have been used in that manner without foreknowledge.[21] The real point is that, in a trenchant way, an organization not known for its naïveté saw the political value of the professional skills of a critic who would eventually make explicit his desire to be considered "one of us" by U.S. critics and writers, all the while insisting on the autonomy of literature in relation to politics.

If we view the founding of *Mundo Nuevo* and its "decisive role in defining a generation" intertextually through the prism of the "play of language," the point emerges more trenchantly still. For a moment let us disregard the strictly "political" aspects of the CIA's role in this affair and concentrate instead on the images produced by the encounter of "discourses" in Paris. We might remember that in Paris Octavio Paz projected a "literature of foundations" and predicted that "our dreams are waiting for us around the corner." If not around the corner, the Congress for Cultural Freedom, a partner of the CIA in the foundation of *Mundo Nuevo,* was also in Paris. Now let us consider the words "to found" and "fund(s)" and their connotations of generative power. This leads directly to a representation wherein the incarnation of a desire, *Mundo Nuevo* (The New World), the scene of writing for a new Latin American literature, is produced through insemination by the CIA. Abstracted from specific historical circumstances, the verbal image of a central intelligence in congress with freedom and criticism giving birth to a "New World" appears as an articulation of utopia. Absolved from interpretation, it can be appreciated as the "erotics of fiction" called for by Susan Sontag in her famous article "Against Interpretation." To give this paradise a more appropriately Borgesian conceit we can compare it to Babylon of the Babylon lottery, where a mysterious company (Spanish abbreviation: cia) controls the lives of its citizens through play, all the while remaining inaccessible and unreachable. Or, perhaps, the CIA is the personification of the Hegelian "cunning of reason," which directs and determines the transformative dialectics of history – the same forceful agent, perhaps, that underwrites Charles Olsen's imperial poetic gesture, flanking not only Homer and the European tradition but Latin America as well.

The above is heavily freighted with irony; but irony or no, it makes a point that must be made. The point is that, apart from the "rightness" or "wrongness" of the ideology that absorbs Rodríguez Monegal's discourse, ideology permeates his discourse and determines its meaning. It is doubly ironic, then, that ideology asserts itself even as its instrument attempts to constitute "ideology" as an undesirable element in criticism and indeed, is the motive for such a gesture.

We have seen that Rodríguez Monegal attempts to expunge ideology from criticism by means of a never well developed argument that is based on literature's presumed autonomy. Problems arise, however, when Rodríguez Monegal is unable to articulate clear distinctions between literature and the reality from which it is supposedly autonomous. When ideology is brought to the fore as part of the argument, incoherencies inevitably arise. Thus David Viñas, we recall, is criticized both for his idealism (imposing "ideological schemata which are anterior to . . . reality") and an overvaluation of reality (for him "the reality from which the work arises is more important than the reality that the work creates").

Since the 1960s and 1970s Rodríguez Monegal has, on occasion, hinted at the possibility of an impasse. One instance is his recent preface to an important book by the Brazilian critic Irlemar Chiampi.[22] Advancing Chiampi's book as a model path out of the critical impasses of the previous two decades – now characterized as a "veritable dark ages of criticism"[23] – he generously includes some of his own previous work in the ranks of misconstructions. Nonetheless, the principal exemplars of critical failure remain the familiar leftists and followers of "Sartre, Luckacs, and Goldman."[24] In his view, however, a new generation of Latin American critics has arisen that has superseded the useless debates of the old. They have been motivated by "the massive diffusion in Spanish America of the theories of the Russian formalists, the North American 'New Criticism' and French structuralism and semiotics." Rodríguez Monegal goes on to recite an honor roll of critical theories that have finally been assimilated by Spanish Americans: "The pioneering work of Schlovski, Tyanov, Eichenbaum, – the new insights of Bakhtin . . . Kayser . . . Warren . . . Wayne Booth . . . Northrop Frye . . . the work of Barthes and Genette, of Todorov and Julia Kristeva, of Ph. Hamon, Bremond and Greimas . . . the anthropology of Lévi-Strauss, Lacan's Psychoanalysis, the philosophy of Foucault, Derrida and Deleuze became effective tools for overcoming the ideological tendencies of the formulas heretofore in use . . . New Marxist approaches . . . Jauss . . . Lotman . . . allow the reading of the new narrative with a rigor that seemed impossible."[25]

The heterogeneous nature of the list and euphoric tone of its declamation suggests the familiar criticism that it is one more example of dependence on foreign models; but this is to miss the subtlety of Rodríguez Monegal's implicit justification for their use. In Rodríguez Monegal's view the value of these methods has been proved by their successful application to "the texts of our continent." Like many early U.S. and Latin American writers and critics, Rodríguez Monegal suggests that discourse can become "American" by referring to American things.

Since the various critical discourses find fruitful applicability to American fictional discourses, it can be sustained that this demonstrates that the method in question was prefigured by the text. The other virtue of Rodríguez Monegal's heterogeneous list is that it permits the evocation of an even-handed pluralism that even admits some marxism (Jauss, Lotman).[26] Thus Rodríguez Monegal's argument tries to authorize the "Americanness" of almost every prominent contemporary methodology and in the same breath invests that "Americanness" with the overarching value of "pluralism" and universalism.

The full import of Rodríguez Monegal's preface, however, is inseparable from the book to which it is appended. Chiampi's book is an attempt to establish a conceptual base and a methodology for the interpretation of Latin American literature. To do so she centers on the concept of "marvelous realism" as the distinctive mode of Latin American narrative. She shows how it can describe most of the discourses that over the course of literary history have addressed themselves to the problematic issues of American identity, difference, and self-articulation. Moreover, that mode finds its fullest expression in modern and contemporary Latin American narratives. Thus Chiampi's theories have profound implications for canon formation. The canon that Chiampi's work derives from and sustains is virtually identical to the one that Rodríguez Monegal and the writers of the "Boom" did so much to advance. In this light Chiampi's great achievement is that she provides a way of talking about these works that absorbs their manifold social and historical contexts and allusions into a reasonably value free formalist discourse.

By implicitly enshrining the works long publicized and advocated by Rodríguez Monegal and at the same time creating a specialized discourse whose formalist gesture defuses their potentially conflictive "content," Chiampi's work advances the possibility of sustaining a level of circumscribed autonomy for these texts. She has thus accomplished what Rodríguez Monegal himself has been unable to do.

It remains, however, that Chiampi's work potentially cuts both ways. In light of this contingency Rodríguez Monegal's preface – which introduces Chiampi's work as the culmination of attitudes, approaches, and preferences that he has long held – can be read as an appropriative gesture that hopes to ensure that Chiampi's work will not be read in a way that goes against that grain.

In fact, Chiampi's discourse can be turned back on its preface. At one point, explaining that marvelous realism is a suitable vehicle for the expression of certain constant incongruities of Latin American self-conceptions, Chiampi remarks, supplementing the Mexican philosopher Leopoldo Zea, that "our incongruity . . . resides in constituting ourselves, in regard to the colonizer's model, as a false copy, a simulacrum, a thing which is and is not, that affirms and denies the model."[27] She adds that "the discourse of marvelous realism, articulated on the denial of contradiction, poetically enunciates that logical and ontological impossibility." Clearly, Chiampi's formulation can be taken as a description, not only of a prominent mode of fictional discourse and its genesis in a particular type of historically determined consciousness but also of criticism, like Rodríguez Monegal's, which operates in tandem with that fiction.

Is not marvelous realism, as an articulation that denies contradiction while poetically emulating it, an apt description of Rodríguez Monegal's avowals of literature's autonomy on the one hand and its participation in the world on the other? Does it not describe Rodríguez Monegal's positivistic avowals of correct methodologies on the one hand and his evocation of the neoidealism of free textual play on the other? More concretely, if as Chiampi contends marvelous realism arises from a "false copy" of the self, is not Rodríguez Monegal's complex dramatization of Borges's visits to Columbia and Yale a stunning example of its procedures? Finally, is it not exemplified in the bizarre figurative possibilities evoked by *Mundo Nuevo*'s relation to the CIA?

NOTES

1 Joseph Riddel, "Decentering the Image: The 'Project' of 'American' Poetics?" in Josué V. Harrari, ed., *Textual Strategies: Perspectives in Post-Structuralist Literature* (Ithaca, N.Y.: Cornell University Press, 1979), p. 322.

2 Ibid., p. 358.

3 Ibid.

4 Ibid., p. 327.

5 Octavio Paz, "A Literature of Foundation," trans. Lysander Kemp, in José Donoso and William Henkin, eds., *The Triquarterly Anthology of Latin American Literature* (New York: Dutton, 1969), p. 8.

6 Carlos Fuentes, *La nueva novela hispanoamericana* (Mexico City: Joaquín Mortiz, 1969), p. 94.

7 Ibid., p. 93.

8 Rodríguez Monegal, *Narradores de esta America II* (Buenos Aires: Alfa, 1974), p. 327; cited in the text hereinafter as N followed by page number.

9 Rodríguez Monegal, "The New Latin American Narratives," in Donoso and Henkin, eds., *Anthology*, pp. 21–5.

10 Rodríguez Monegal, *Jorge Luis Borges: A Literary Biography* (New York: Dutton, 1978); cited hereinafter in the text as B followed by page number.

11 Quoted by Roberto Fernández Retamar in *Calibán: Apuntes para la cultura de nuestra América* (Mexico City: Diogenes, 1979), p. 54.

12 Ibid., p. 54.

13   Conversation with Paul Theroux in *The Old Patagonian Express* (New York: Pocket Books, 1980), p. 432.

14   Paz, "Literature of Foundation," p. 8.

15   Quoted by Retamar, *Calibán,* p. 52.

16   José Donoso, *The Boom in Spanish American Literature: A Personal History,* trans. G. Kolovakos (New York: Columbia University Press, 1971), p. 104.

17   Christopher Lasch, "The Cultural Cold War," in Barton J. Bernstein, ed., *Towards a New Past: Dissenting Essays in American History* (New York: Pantheon, 1968), p. 329.

18   Quoted in ibid., p. 349.

19   Donoso, *Boom,* p. 104.

20   Ibid., p. 103.

21   In his article Lasch tells of how Frank Kermode, innocent of *Encounter*'s connection with the CIA, threatened Conor Cruise O'Brien with a libel suit if he persisted with his allegations to that effect. In the end it was Conor Cruise O'Brien who obtained a judgment against *Encounter,* which had in the meantime slandered him in a column. When the CIA's connection with *Encounter* was, in fact, publicly verified, Frank Kermode resigned. More recently a less innocent reader of this article for another press slyly questioned the above with "Is this libel?" For a contemporary account of the CIA's connection with the Congress for Cultural Freedom, see *Newsweek,* March 6, 1967, pp. 28–30. For Rodríguez Monegal's reply to questions on the subject from *Agence France Press,* see *Mundo Nuevo* 25 (July 1968):1.

22   Irlemar Chiampi, *El realismo maravilloso: Forma e ideología en la novela hispanoamericana* (Caracas: Monte Avila, 1983), pp. 1–13.

23   Ibid., p. 10.

24   Ibid., p. 11.

25   Ibid., p. 12.

26   To be sure, Jauss is hardly a marxist critic, and Lotman, although Soviet, is a formalist.

27   Chiampi, *El realismo,* p. 199.

17

Bridge over troubled waters

EDMUNDO DESNOES

L. A. is L. A. (Latin America, not Los Angeles) and USA is USA (it could not be anything else), and never the twain shall meet. I have met, as a Cuban writer, with audiences throughout the United States, from New York, Boston, and Philadelphia to Tucson, Austin, San Francisco, and Eugene. Sometimes I had the impression at these meetings of being a creature from another planet, dealing in cultural and political science fiction. When we discussed either my novel, *Memories of Underdevelopment*, or its film version, we were physically in the same place at the same time – but we were making completely different assumptions, assumptions that changed the nature of the cultural object and the flow of the discourse. Any "meeting" requires at least a nutshell knowledge of the context in which one is attempting to communicate. Difficulties are rooted in assumptions we take for granted and that produce a cross-eyed contact. The connotation of "L.A. is not L. A." depends on the context.

One of these premises, obvious as it may seem to educated readers and audiences, is that art is a universal language. As Sartre asked, what does the Parthenon mean to a black African? Recently I showed a student from Jamaica the famous (for Western art students) winged lion so prominent in the piazza of St. Mark's in Venice, and he immediately thought of the Rastafari movement – of the King of Kings, the Lion of Judea – which had such an uplifting effect on the blacks of the New World: the sense of dignity that a black king brought to the descendants of slaves (independent of the deleterious effect of Haile Selassie's rule in Ethiopia). Things are what they are in a given context – but also what they say to the particular receiver is a context itself.

This brings me to the other main assumption of literary and cultural analysis. The meaning and value of any and all works of art are estab-

319

lished by experts, establishment art critics, academics – and there is very little research on the way people react to, or decode, any given novel or film. Intellectuals, of course, including myself, are not what I call people. So little has been done for the "implicit reader," an "implicit reader" now bugging most structural, semiotic, or even ideological analysis. We are unable to pin him or her down and give flesh and blood to that skeleton – flesh and blood indispensable for producing a respectable model of the reading process.

My ambition, doomed to failure, is to bring to the foreground the issue of the reader, the decoder within our continent, America (another one of those words we all struggle with, some of us resenting its appropriation by the United States), by dealing with different reactions to my novel and its film version in Our America, as Jose Martí referred to Latin America, and Your America, with all its hegemonic implications. This essay was originally miswritten in English for an English-speaking audience, with most of the cultural hang-ups of both you and me.

Now for the concrete examples and experiences, which are really abstractions if we accept that the concrete, as Hegel and Marx viewed it, is the totality and not the detail. The concrete is society and not a book; the concrete is capitalism and not an isolated commodity.

How can we bridge the context, the concrete reality of the systems and subsystems (economic, social, historical, and psychological) that separate, to simplify, north from "south of the border, down Mexico way" as that song first put it in my adolescence? (The word "down" was crucial from whatever side we may look at it.) I have tried to bridge the gap, which is both a need and a naïve endeavor, in my fiction and my cultural essays. Here I pretend to be writing mainly as a novelist; but I had to start out by dealing, even if superficially, with the context of this amorphous universe referred to as Latin America – a living myth, although Bolívar and Martí, the founder and the consolidator of such an arduous project, worked on it so deeply, in theory and in practice, that today it is taken for granted in spite of the enormous differences, say, from Brazil, Mexico, Argentina, or Venezuela to Paraguay, Nicaragua, or Haiti. This is to say nothing of how much Cuba tears apart and yet brings together Latin America. Not so long ago Che Guevara started a war based on this project – and died for it in the jungles of Bolivia or, to be more precise and ironic, in a Bolivian schoolhouse.

As a writer I have to start from a philosophical abstraction, the individual and his or her relation to society: the individual and personal history. I was born in Cuba of a Spanish-speaking father, Cuban, and an English-speaking mother, Jamaican. I was educated both in Cuba and in the United States. I spent a third of my life in the United States and the rest in Cuba. I lived in Cuba during my adolescence, under a neocolonial republic, culturally influenced and economically manipulated by the United States, and during the most radical revolution ever to have taken place in this old New World.

So I start with a dichotomy, a torn, if not split, personality, a psychological and spiritual need to bridge the gap between both hemispheres, and a deep humanistic assumption: Peoples with different backgrounds can understand each other (regardless of whether they are above or below geographically, individually, or socially). I am strongly against an almost irrational and frequently voiced conviction: that north is north and south is south and never the twain shall meet. I cannot accept, or rather believe (since I cannot prove it is a fact or will ever become one), that understanding between Latin America and Anglo-America is impossible, that blacks have an experience of exploitation that is incommunicable, that men will never be able to understand the humiliation forced on women, that gender, class, race, history separate us sadly, that these differences cannot be redeemed. It might be a fantasy but it is part of the ground I walk on. If it were not there, I would not get out of bed in the morning.

Memories of Underdevelopment was written from these humanistic, universal, desperate assumptions. I have never been interested in Latin America as a world in itself, or pleasure in itself. To live instead of vegetate there must always be something larger than ourselves. To begin with, economic ties, which I accept as the bottom line, prove isolation to be absurd and impossible. More than a hundred years ago Marx wrote:

> The bourgeoisie has through its exploitation of the world market given a cosmopolitan character to production and consumption in every country. In place of old wants, satisfied by the productions of the country, we find new wants, requiring for their satisfaction the products of distant lands and climes. In place of the old local and national seclusion and self-sufficiency, we have intercourse in every direction, universal interdependence of nations. And as in material, so also in intellectual production. The intellectual creations of individual nations become common property. National one-sidedness and narrow-mindedness become more and more impossible, and from the numerous national and local literatures there arises a world literature.[1]

This was written in 1847, and since the Communist Manifesto rivers of blood, raw materials, and industrial products have flowed, strengthening the "interdependence of nations." But at the same time, tragically and in spite of Marx's predictions, class exploitation, unequal economic and cultural exchange between countries have increased. The proletariat has not become unified, breaking down class and national barriers. Nowhere has alienation come to an end; nowhere has the individual assumed the center of his or her world and begun to develop all human possibilities. Marx's economic and social analysis has proved much more accurate than his utopian vision of the future; yet the struggle – economic, social, and cultural – has not ceased; especially in Latin America.

There is a moral element in Latin American political thinking, a moral obsession (although the individual is still the wolf of other individuals in Our America) that I consider the main contribution of Latin America to modern radical thought and action. I believe this tradition – a morality that includes all humankind – has been kept alive from Bolívar to Che Guevara. It was José Martí who wrote, when advocating Cuba's independence from Spain: "It is a world we are holding in balance, not only a couple of islands we are about to free. . . . A mistake in Cuba is a mistake in America, a mistake in present-day humanity."[2] Nationalism never had for Bolívar, Martí, or Che the danger of chauvinism; nationalism was a form of internationalism, of joining and contributing to world freedom and justice.

I have never been interested in what was closed, secret, local in Latin America, but in what could be understood and felt as a contribution to the rest of the world. "What we all know together," as Antonio Machado wrote, "is what no one knows by himself."

In *Memories* the revolution, the early creative and precarious period of the revolution that led to the missile crisis, is seen through the eyes of a middle-class narrator. This was not only because it was easier for me to talk through the voice of a character with a background similar to my own, to exorcise my liberal background, but also because I thought it was the best way to reach a broad audience – national and international.

The bourgeoisie, regardless of what Marx thought, is today the only universal class – because of what it has and does not want to lose (fear and self-interest move us all, as Napoleon said), because of its economic, cultural and political outlook. There is more in common among members of the French, Brazilian, U.S., Peruvian, British, Indian, Pakistani, or Swedish middle class than among the members of the proletariat of those countries.

The first translation of *Memories* was published in the United States in 1967. In Cuba it was seen as a portrait of the limitations of a middle-class pseudointellectual unable to cope with a revolution that demanded participation and action, rather than of the intellectual understanding that Sergio displayed while remaining within the margin of security given to middle-class existence. He could try to understand the social changes but could not participate. Therefore, he began feeling above it all and ended, during the missile crisis, aware of his isolation, recognizing that objectively he had been below it all when he had assumed a haughty superiority. Yet the *New York Times* reviewed the novel on the traditional assumption, in the context of the inevitable struggle of the individual against society. " 'The artist, the true artist,' the protagonist writes in his diary, 'will always be the enemy of the State.' It is the only positive statement in this profoundly, despairingly antipolitical book," wrote Eliot Fremont-Smith. He concluded: "This painfully, ironically honest novel, or testament, shows that place where the anguished private and political selves intersect, the solitary place of exile. Not unfamiliar territory, but it has rarely been portrayed with such cruel, compelling intensity, or with such dedication of mind, heart and art."[3] It becomes "unfamiliar" territory when the context changes. Existential anguish is quite different from political isolation in a tightly knit and demanding revolution. It is not that "private and political selves intersect"; they are forced to integrate, strike a balance.

I have quoted "dedication of mind, heart and art" not just out of vanity (which by the way is a vital creative incentive; Swift priced his wit above a title of nobility and a carriage driven by six horses) but because "art" is another Western myth – stronger in the United States than in Latin America, especially Cuba – a belief that the artist is the conscience of society, a superior being who can fathom the depths of the human heart. An artist can see deeper than a philosopher, a plumber, or a political leader. This belief, absolutely naïve and idealistic, would create chaos – worse than the present ominous chaos – if the ideas of our "immortal artist" were the accepted norm of conduct in society, any society.

The film, which was shown in the United States in 1973, was also received as an example of individual courage faced with a hostile state. Although the film included footage from the actual Bay of Pigs invasion and other visual documents to place plot and characters in context, the revolutionary statement eluded viewers and reviewers. Here again we can say that the change of medium did not touch the premises and assumptions used in decoding and judging the meaning and value of the film.

There is a sacred text dealing with mechanical reproduction, photos, and especially film, a seminal study by Walter Benjamin. In the thirties he saw mechanical reproduction as a powerful instrument for destroying the "aura" created by original works of art, unique and isolated, as well as a process (film and photography) that would give a more accurate, detailed, realistic description of the world around us – a new means of destroying the mystery of art and revealing to large audiences the true nature of the material world.[4] Benjamin failed to see that things become more symbolic than descriptive in a photo or a film. It is not a slice of reality but an interpretation of reality in disguise. The aura of films is even more powerful, pervasive, than the aura surrounding a painting by Giotto or Picasso, more so if it is a prestigious entertainment commodity signed by Eisenstein, Hitchcock, Godard, or even Woody Allen – which takes us back to context reading.

Memories, like most cultural objects, is ambiguous, is reinterpreted by each reader and viewer, and by time, which also changes the context, if it survives. I have tried to write with a complex transparency, but failed to get my meaning across, because things are opaque unless one considers the system and the individual receiver of the cultural object.

The writer is not the only creator, nor the critic the only intelligent reader.

NOTES

1   "Manifesto of the Communist Party," *The Marx–Engels Reader,* ed. Robert C. Tucker (New York: Norton, 1978), pp. 476–7.

2   José Martí, "The Third Year of the Cuban Revolutionary Party: The Spirit of the Revolution and Cuba's Duty to America," in Philip S. Foner, ed., *Our America* (New York: Monthly Review Press, 1977), pp. 360–1.

3   *New York Times,* June 12, 1967, p. 43.

4   Walter Benjamin, "The Work of Art in the Age of Mechanical Reproduction," in Hannah Arendt, ed., *Illuminations* (New York: Schocken, 1969), pp. 217–52.

18

The poet as critic
Wallace Stevens and Octavio Paz

MICHAEL WOOD

> It would be prodigious if a critic became a poet and it is impossible that
> a poet should not have a critic within him.
>
> – Baudelaire

I should like to make two general remarks by way of introduction. First, the space I describe in what follows, the space Stevens and Paz
seek to create, in their prose, for their poems, is not a political space. It is
not even a secretly political space, one of those false fronts conservatism
so often throws up when it says something is not political. This space
does not prejudge the politics that go on immediately outside it. Brecht
needed the space in East Berlin just as much as Stevens needed it in
Hartford, Connecticut.

Second, I have tried to blur a little the line between poetry and criticism – not because I do not think there is any difference, but because I
do not think there is a *single* difference, and the traffic on the border is
worth watching. A working principle, if the blur is too much for us and
we hanker for a firm distinction after all, might be that if a poem looks
like a work of criticism – as "The Waste Land" does, for example – it
probably is. It will not stop being a poem for that reason. If a critic starts
claiming that his criticism is poetry, however, we should no doubt reach
for the largest pinch of salt we can find.

In the opinion of Pierre Menard, a French writer apparently invented
by Jorge Luis Borges – it is wise not to be dogmatic in these affairs –
"thinking, analyzing, inventing" are not abnormal mental acts but the
ordinary life of the intelligence.[1] I construe this remark to mean, among
other things, that criticism too is a normal act, as normal as reading, and
indeed inseparable from all intelligent reading – not a gratuitous activity
that odd, sectarian fraternities indulge in. I agree that the appearances at
the moment are not in Menard's favor. Matthew Arnold, who was not,

as far as I know, invented by Borges, defined criticism as an exercise of curiosity; and T. S. Eliot, a rather stuffy English critic invented by the American poet T. S. Eliot, went even farther and saw criticism as "an instinctive activity of the civilized mind."[2]

I roll out these familiar phrases in order to arrive at a first question. What would it mean for a culture to lack criticism, as Octavio Paz has frequently suggested Latin America does? Would this mean simply a lack of curiosity, and what, then, would *that* mean? If we compare the criticism of two cultures, are we comparing curiosities? The ordinary, local life of the intelligence? Particular activities of the civilized mind?

I prefer Arnold's curiosity to Paz's view of criticism as constructing a "system of relations" between literary works.[3] The best criticism is less orderly than that, less abstract too. But Paz also speaks of "intellectual space,"[4] and this seems to me an extremely valuable notion. Criticism can create space around poems and plays and novels, a world of echoes and answers; and if critics will not do it, poets and other writers have to do it for themselves. This, indeed, is a major task of the poet as critic. Curiosity, we may say, cannot do it all; it needs a little help from its friends. A poet as critic is, as Eliot said, usually "implicitly defending the sort of poetry that [the poet and his or her] friends" write.[5] The space to be created is the space of readership. But Paz and Stevens have this in common that they write not only about poems but about poetry, and it may be interesting to compare the spaces they seek to create, not only for a certain kind of poetry, but for poetry as distinct from other human activities.

There are a number of similarities between Paz and Stevens that are relevant here. First, both are critics *in their poems;* many of their poems are criticism. I shall give some examples later. Both are, occasionally, *only* critics in their poems, since both have written poems that do not manage to animate or quicken their intricate arguments and so remain closer to an outline or program than to a poem that speaks its own language. Second, both Paz and Stevens believe firmly in history, at a time when many people do not. "The pressure of reality," Stevens says, "is, I think, the determining factor in the artistic character of an era, and, as well, the determining factor in the artistic character of an individual."[6] And Paz: "To examine the possibilities of poetry is to ask a question not about poems but about history."[7] Furthermore, and this is the corollary of their at first sight rather submissive views of poetry in the world, both poets see poetry as a form that is in trouble, embarrassed, lacking confidence. Nobility is no longer a plausible notion, Stevens suggests, and so poetry itself is not as plausible a practice as it was. "After *Une Saison en*

Enfer," Paz says, "one cannot write a poem without overcoming a feeling of shame."[8]

Implausible, hounded by history, poetry becomes a form of *opposition.* For Paz it is a permanent evocation of otherness, the other life *in* our life; Stevens is more formal: "We define poetry as an unofficial view of being."[9] Finally – this last, striking similarity summarizes and rests on the others, perhaps – both Stevens and Paz consider poetry to be public in a particular way. It becomes common property without ceasing to be a private utterance. "La poesía no dice: yo soy tú; dice: mi yo eres tú."[10] I do not think I can translate this aphorism of Paz's. Stevens's version of precisely the same thought is that it is the poet's task to become his own readers; "his function is to make his imagination theirs."[11] This is a way of making *their* imagination theirs, for as Stevens eloquently puts it, "the poem comes to possess the reader and . . . naturalizes him in his own imagination and liberates him there."[12]

Where Paz and Stevens differ, and where my argument begins, is in their perceptions of the reality that is putting such pressure on the writer and his writing. I hesitate to say that we have here an "American" reality and a "Mexican" reality, and I hesitate for a number of reasons. Both Paz and Stevens are too idiosyncratic to be simply representative, and in any case the reality in question here is a picture, a rendered reality, not an unassorted deck of facts and events. Nevertheless, the reality described by Paz and Stevens is specific enough and familiar enough to take us beyond their individual cases, and a brief account of these descriptions will, I hope, make this clear.

For Stevens reality is oppressive because of its *weight.* We live, he says, "in a leaden time and in a world that does not move for the weight of its heaviness."[13] But it is also oppressive because we are its accomplices. There are moments in history, Stevens believes, when the balance between reality and the imagination tilts toward one of its ends. Indeed, he seems to believe, although he is not explicit on this score, that the balance always tilts one way or the other. Our age, he feels, is an age favorable to reality, which makes things hard for the imagination. Our reality does not leave us room to think, and *that* is the space Stevens seeks to create in his criticism: "By the pressure of reality, I mean the pressure of an external event or events on the consciousness to the exclusion of any power of contemplation."[14] What Stevens asks is not that we *choose* between the imagination and reality, but that we meet reality's oppression with the resistance of the imagination, "the imagination pressing back against the pressure of reality."[15] A phrase like "the pressure of reality," even colored by the metaphor of heaviness, sounds vague enough, but Stevens had something quite specific in mind. The year is 1942, Stevens is speaking at Princeton:

> This much ought to be said to make it a little clearer that in speaking of the pressure of reality, I am thinking of life in a state of violence, not physically violent, as yet, for us in America, but physically violent for millions of our friends and for still more millions of our enemies and spiritually violent, it may be said, for everyone alive.
>
> A possible poet must be a poet capable of resisting or evading the pressure of the reality of this last degree, with the knowledge that the degree of today may become a deadlier degree tomorrow.[16]

Escapism loses its pejorative sense and includes what Stevens calls an adherence to reality. It is an answer to reality, not a flight from it, an "imagination of life"[17] – of the life, precisely, that reality often denies. The poet "must create his unreal out of what is real,"[18] and a subtle and funny poem, "Mrs. Alfred Uruguay," written a year or two before Stevens's talk at Princeton, shows what an intricate process this can be. The lady looking for reality ends up on an abstract mountain, whereas the poet, down in the villages, finds the imagination's home:

> So what said the others and the sun went down
> And, in the brown blues of evening, the lady said,
> In the donkey's ear, "I fear that elegance
> Must struggle like the rest." She climbed until
> The moonlight in her lap, mewing her velvet,
> And her dress were one and she said, "I have said no
> To everything, in order to get at myself.
> I have wiped away moonlight like mud. Your innocent ear
> And I, if I rode naked, are what remain."
>
> The moonlight crumbled to degenerate forms,
> While she approached the real, upon her mountain,
> With lofty darkness. The donkey was there to ride,
> To hold by the ear, even though it wished for a bell,
> Wished faithfully for a falsifying bell.
> Neither the moonlight could change it. And for her,
> To be, regardless of velvet, could never be more
> Than to be, she could never differently be,
> Her no and no made yes impossible.

Who was it passed her there on a horse all will,
What figure of capable imagination?
Whose horse clattered on the road on which she rose,
As it descended, blind to her velvet and
The moonlight? Was it a rider intent on the sun,
A youth, a lover with phosphorescent hair,
Dressed poorly, arrogant of his streaming forces,
Lost in an integration of the martyrs' bones,
Rushing from what was real; and capable?

The villages slept as the capable man went down,
Time swished on the village clocks and dreams were alive,
The enormous gongs gave edges to their sounds,
As the rider, no chevalere and poorly dressed,
Impatient of the bells and midnight forms,
Rode over the picket rocks, rode down the road,
And, capable, created in his mind,
Eventual victor, out of the martyrs' bones,
The ultimate elegance: the imagined land.[19]

Poetic truth, Stevens says, is "an agreement with reality, brought about by the imagination."[29] But an agreement is the reverse of submission.

The world for Paz is not heavy, but faceless; not a world at all, only reality: "world without image, reality without world and infinitely real."[21] It is oppressive not because of its weight or because it lacks meaning – technology loads the world with all too many constricting, short-sighted meanings – but because it lacks direction, because it is going nowhere, "a space swollen with objects, but bereft of future."[22] The space the poem needs, the space this criticism seeks to create, is a space of waiting, a delay that functions as a promise. A poem, Paz says, is "an empty space fraught with imminence."[23] "Poetry: a quest for a here and now."[24] Mallarmé's legacy, Paz insists, is not a poetic idiom but the space made possible by that idiom; and in this ghostly place, neither present nor future nor past, a genuine *apparition,* an irrecusable image, is an enormous gain. A brief gain of just this kind, the emergence of a face in the faceless universe, is celebrated in Paz's poem "Objects and Apparitions." I quote, in full, Elizabeth Bishop's translation:

Hexahedrons of wood and glass,
scarcely bigger than a shoebox,
with room in them for night and all its lights.

Monuments to every moment,
refuse of every moment, used:
cages for infinity.

Marbles, buttons, thimbles, dice,
pins, stamps, and glass beads:
tales of the time.

Memory weaves, unweaves the echoes:
in the four corners of the box
shadowless ladies play at hide-and-seek.

Fire buried in the mirror,
water sleeping in the agate;
Solos of Jenny Colonne and Jenny Lind.

"One has to commit a painting," said Degas,
"the way one commits a crime." But you constructed
boxes where things hurry away from their names.

Slot machine of visions,
condensation flask for conversations,
hotel of crickets and constellations.

Minimal, incoherent fragments:
the opposite of History, creator of ruins,
out of your ruins you have made creations.

Theatre of the spirits:
objects putting the laws
of identity through hoops.

"Grand Hotel de la Couronne": in a vial,
the three of clubs and, very surprised,
Thumbelina in gardens of reflection.

A comb is a harp strummed by the glance
of a little girl
born dumb.

The reflector of the inner eye
scatters the spectacle:
God all alone above and extinct world.

The apparitions are manifest,
their bodies weigh less than light,
lasting as long as this phrase lasts.

Joseph Cornell: inside your boxes
my words became visible for a moment.[25]

Weighty or faceless, reality is a challenge for the poet, a threat to poetry; not to be taken lying down. Returning to my earlier questions we can say that, if a culture lacked criticism, it would lack not only curiosity but substantial resistance to the suasions of the real. Poetry would be left to its own devices. In this respect Paz and Stevens share a vision of a world endangered by efficiencies, by our own complicity with an order of things that hems the imagination in. As I hope my discussion of Stevens made clear, it is not a question of reasserting some vague romantic right to dream. It is a question of finding room for curiosity, for the mind's freedom from immediate circumstantial need, the violence that narrows our life to a series of strategies for survival.

But weightiness and facelessness are hardly the same; and I do see a representative quality in the anxieties expressed by Stevens and Paz. Stevens's reality *is* an American reality; it is the reality of power and politics and unshakeable material fact, acutely described by Lionel Trilling, who was thinking not of Stevens but of Dreiser: "Reality, as conceived by us, is whatever is external and hard, gross, unpleasant. Involved in its meaning is the idea of power conceived in a particular way. . . . Power is assumed to be always 'brute' power, crude, ugly and undiscriminating, the way an elephant appears to be."[26] That sounds fierce enough, and we can see why a poet would want to resist such a reality; but it is also a consoling reality, because in its disagreeable fashion it is *there,* and that is just what Paz's Mexican reality is not:

My steps along this street
Resound
     In another street
In which
     I hear my steps
Passing along this street
In which
Only the mist is real.[27]   (Trans. by Charles Tomlinson)

Americans picture themselves as beleaguered by reality, whereas Mexicans picture themselves disappearing – a haunting unreality *is* their reality. The confrontation is too stark and simple no doubt, but, more important, these pictures are only pictures. Reality is real enough everywhere, and we are not bound to be as fastidious about it as Stevens or Paz. Still, a picture of ghosts is quite different from a picture of elephants, and it is a virtue of comparisons of this kind that they characteristically lead to a double question. Can we be more precise about the difference between these two pictures? And since the pictures are plainly selective to the point of being mythological – both Mexican and American realities are a good deal more *various* than these images allow – what is the use of these pictures, what help or escape or truth are people pursuing when they see themselves in this way, beset by blunt American power or lost in a Mexican mist?

NOTES

1 J. L. Borges, *Ficciones* (Buenos Aires: Emecé, 1956), p. 56.
2 T. S. Eliot, *To Criticize the Critic* (New York: Farrar, Straus & Giroux, 1965), p. 19.
3 Octavio Paz, *Corriente alterna* (Mexico City: Siglo xxi, 1967), p. 40.
4 Ibid., p. 39.
5 Eliot, *To Criticize the Critic*, p. 16.
6 Wallace Stevens, *The Necessary Angel* (New York: Vintage, 1965), pp. 22–3.
7 Octavio Paz, *El arco y la lira* (Mexico City: Fondo de Cultura Economica, 1956), p. 253.
8 Ibid., p. 257.
9 Stevens, *The Necessary Angel*, p. 40.
10 Paz, *El arco y la lira*, p. 261.
11 Stevens, *The Necessary Angel*, p. 29.
12 Ibid., p. 50.
13 Ibid., p. 63.
14 Ibid., p. 20.
15 Ibid., p. 36.
16 Ibid., pp. 26–7.
17 Ibid., pp. 65, 67.
18 Ibid., p. 58.
19 Wallace Stevens, *The Collected Poems*, S. F. Morse, ed. (New York: Vintage, 1982), pp. 248–50.
20 Stevens, *The Necessary Angel*, p. 54.
21 Paz, *El arco y la lira*, p. 275.
22 Ibid., p. 257.
23 Ibid., p. 264.
24 Ibid., p. 265.
25 Octavio Paz, *A Draft of Shadows* (New York: New Directions, 1979), pp. 83, 85.
26 Lionel Trilling, *The Liberal Imagination* (New York: Doubleday, 1953), p. 209.
27 Octavio Paz, *Selected Poems* (Harmondsworth, England: Penguin, 1979), p. 59.

Index

333